SolidWorks® 2011
Assemblies Bible

SolidWorks® 2011 Assemblies Bible

Matt Lombard

Wiley Publishing, Inc.

SolidWorks® 2011 Assemblies Bible

Published by
Wiley Publishing, Inc.
10475 Crosspoint Boulevard
Indianapolis, IN 46256
www.wiley.com

Published by Wiley Publishing, Inc., Indianapolis, Indiana

Published simultaneously in Canada

ISBN: 978-1-118-00276-6

Manufactured in the United States of America

10 9 8 7 6 5 4 3 2 1

For general information on our other products and services or to obtain technical support, please contact our Customer Care Department within the U.S. at (877) 762-2974, outside the U.S. at (317) 572-3993 or fax (317) 572-4002.

Library of Congress Control Number: 2011932103

Trademarks: Wiley and related trade dress are registered trademarks of Wiley Publishing, Inc., in the United States and other countries, and may not be used without written permission. SolidWorks is a registered trademark of Dassault Systèmes SolidWorks Corporation. All other trademarks are the property of their respective owners. Wiley Publishing, Inc., is not associated with any product or vendor mentioned in this book.

Wiley also publishes its books in a variety of electronic formats. Some content that appears in print may not be available in electronic books.

About the Author

Matt Lombard is an independent engineering consultant specializing in plastic parts and complex shapes. He also writes a blog on SolidWorks, which you can find at `www.dezign stuff.com/blog`. Matt lives in the picturesque Shenandoah Valley of Virginia, where he enjoys reading the classics and fishing.

Credits

Senior Acquisitions Editor
Stephanie McComb

Project Editor
Jade L. Williams

Technical Editor
Charles Culp

Copy Editor
Marylouise Wiack

Editorial Director
Robyn Siesky

Business Manager
Amy Knies

Senior Marketing Manager
Sandy Smith

Vice President and Executive Group Publisher
Richard Swadley

Vice President and Executive Publisher
Barry Pruett

Senior Project Coordinator
Kristie Rees

Graphics and Production Specialists
Ana Carillo
Jill A. Proll

Quality Control Technician
Laura Albert

Proofreading
Christine Sabooni

Indexing
BIM Indexing & Proofreading Services

Media Development Project Manager
Laura Moss

Media Development Assistant Project Manager
Jenny Swisher

Media Development Associate Producer
Marilyn Hummel

Contents

Contents

Contents

Contents

Contents

Contents

Contents

Part V: Using Specialized or Advanced Techniques   423

Chapter 18: Using DriveWorks Xpress 425

Contents

Contents

Contents

Acknowledgments

I would like to acknowledge the efforts of the staff at Wiley for their dedication in editing the text of these books. It can be a difficult job making sure that a technical subject is treated properly. I'd also like to thank Charles Culp, the technical editor, for taking the time out of his schedule to make sure the material is accurate. Thanks also to Kim and Zoey, who help with the details in life allowing me to do this kind of work.

Introduction

SolidWorks is a huge, sprawling topic. There is a lot for you, the reader, to know, and for me to write about. As a result, with the 2011 edition, I have taken this book from a single volume of an immense scope to two individual volumes, each still fairly large, one covering parts and part drawings, and the other covering assemblies and assembly drawings. There is some overlap between these topics, but I have tried to divide the material evenly and in a way, that makes the most sense for the reader. Depending on your needs, you will probably find both volumes to be very useful references.

This book is primarily meant as an encyclopedic desk reference for SolidWorks Standard users who want a more thorough understanding of the software and process than can be found in other available documentation. As such, it is not necessarily intended to be a guide for beginners, although it has elements that beginners would find useful. Nor is it necessarily intended as a classroom guide, but I have seen people use it for that as well.

Beginners will find the step-by-step tutorials useful. However, because you are only a beginner for a short period of time, the book is intended to be most useful when you reach an intermediate level, as it takes a more conceptual approach to explaining functionality. I try to help you make the decisions about how to apply the tools to your tasks rather than demonstrating simple tasks that you will never need to do again. You will not learn to model a teapot in this book, because in your work, knowing how to model a teapot will probably not help you. However, you will learn how to make decisions that should enable you to model just about anything you want, including teapots.

To keep the size of the book manageable, I have tried to avoid topics found only in SolidWorks Professional or Premium, although I do talk about these topics when they are relevant.

While the book does point out limitations, bugs, and conceptual errors in the software, and from time to time ventures into the realm of opinion, in every case this is meant to give you a more thorough understanding of the software, and how it is applied in the context of everyday design or engineering practice.

The overall goal of this book is not to fill your head with facts, but to help you think like the software, so that you can use the tool as an intuitive extension of your own process. As your modeling projects become more complex, you will need to have more troubleshooting and work-around skills available to you. Along with best practice recommendations, these are the most compelling reasons to use this book.

Thank you for your interest.

About This Book

You will find enough information here that this book will grow with your SolidWorks needs. I have written tutorials for most of the chapters with newer users in mind, because for them, it is most helpful to see how things are done in SolidWorks step by step. The longer narrative examples give more in-depth information about features and functions, as well as the results of various settings and options.

This book includes many details that come from practical usage and is focused on the needs of professional users, not on student learners. My approach is to teach concepts rather than how to push buttons.

How This Book Is Organized

This book is divided into six parts.

Part I: Introducing Assembly Basics

This part explores basic concepts and terminology used in SolidWorks. You need to read this section if you are a new SolidWorks user, especially if you are new to 3D modeling or parametric history-based design.

Part II: Working with Assemblies

This part takes a deeper look at creating parametric relations to automate changes.

Part III: Creating and Using Libraries

This part examines the functionality within the 2D drawing side of the software. Whether you are creating views, making tables, or customizing annotations, you will find these chapters useful.

Part IV: Creating Assembly Drawings

This part examines several types of advanced techniques, such as surface modeling and multi-body modeling. This is information you won't find in other SolidWorks books, and is explained here by someone who uses the functionality daily.

Part V: Using Specialized or Advanced Techniques

Specialized functionality, such as sheet metal and plastics, requires detailed information. This part includes the topics that are key to unlocking all the power available in SolidWorks.

Part VI: Appendixes

The Appendixes in this book contain additional information, such as the contents of the DVD and other sources of help.

Icons Used in This Book

This book uses a set of icons to point out certain details in the text. While they are relatively self-explanatory, here is what each of these icons indicates:

Caution

The Caution icon warns you of potential problems before you make a mistake.

Cross-Reference

The Cross-Reference icon points out where you can find additional information about a topic elsewhere in the book.

New Feature

The New Feature icon highlights features and functions that are new to SolidWorks 2011.

Note

The Note icon highlights useful information that you should take into consideration, or an important point that requires special attention.

On the DVD

This icon points you toward related material on the book's DVD.

Tip

Each Tip provides you with additional advice that makes the software quicker or easier to use.

The *SolidWorks 2011 Assemblies Bible* is unique in its use of the following two icons:

Best Practice

The Best Practice icon points out recommended settings or techniques that are safe in most situations.

Performance

Each Performance icon elaborates on how certain settings, features, or techniques affect rebuild speed or file size.

These icons point out and describe techniques and settings that are either recommended or not recommended for specific reasons. Best practice is usually considered very conservative usage, where the stability of the parametrics and performance (another way of saying *rebuild speed*) are the ultimate goals. These two aspects of SolidWorks models are usually weighed against modeling speed (how long it takes you to create the model).

You should take Best Practice and Performance recommendations seriously, but as guidelines rather than as rules. When it comes right down to it, the only hard and fast rule about SolidWorks is that there are no hard and fast rules. In fact, I believe that the only reason to have rules in the first place is so that you know when you can break them. Parametric stability and modeling speed are not always the ultimate goals and are often overridden when work-around techniques are used simply to accomplish a geometric goal.

Because not everyone models with the same goals in mind, a single set of rules can never apply for everyone. You must take the best practice suggestions and apply them to your situation using your own judgment.

Because I actually use the software in my work, I viewed it from a practical standpoint while writing this book. I approached the software objectively as a tool, recognizing that complex tools are good at some things and not so good at others. Knowing the strengths and limitations of the software is helpful to you. Pointing out negatives in this context should not be construed as criticizing the SolidWorks software, but rather as preparing you for real-world use of the software. Any tool this complex is going to have imperfections. I hope that some of my enthusiasm for the software also shows through and is to some extent contagious.

Terminology

An important concept referred to frequently in SolidWorks is *design intent*. As a practical matter, I use the phrase *design for change* to further distinguish design intent from other design goals.

You will need to be familiar with some special terminology before continuing. In many cases, I use a SolidWorks vernacular or slang when the official terminology is either not descriptive enough or has multiple meanings. For example, the word *shortcut* can mean several things in the SolidWorks interface; it is used to describe right mouse button (RMB) menus as well as hotkeys. As a result, I have chosen not to use the word *shortcut* and instead substitute the words *RMB* and *hotkey*.

I frequently use RMB to refer to right mouse button menus, or other data that you access by clicking the right mouse button on an item. The word *tree* refers to the list of features in the FeatureManager.

Differences are frequently found between the names of features on toolbars and the names in the tool tips, menus, or PropertyManager titles. In these cases, the differences are usually minor, and either name may be used.

Most functions in SolidWorks can work with either the object-action or the action-object scenarios. These are also called *pre-select* and *select*, respectively. The Fillet feature shows no difference between using pre-selection and selection, although for some fillet options such as face fillet, pre-select is not enabled. Most features allow pre-selection, and some functions, such as inserting a design table, require pre-selection. Although you cannot identify a single rule that covers all situations, *most* functions accept both.

Frequently in this book, I have suggested enhancement requests that the reader may want to make. This is because SolidWorks development is driven to a large extent by customer requests, and if a large number of users converge on a few issues, then those issues are more likely to be fixed or changed. Again, the enhancement request suggestions are not made to criticize the software, but to make it better. I hope that you will join me in submitting enhancement requests.

SolidWorks is an extremely powerful modeling tool, very likely with the best combination of power and accessibility on the MCAD market today. This book is meant to help you take advantage of its power in your work and even hobbyist applications. If I could impart only a single thought to you, it would be that with a little curiosity and some imagination, you could begin to access the power of SolidWorks for geometry creation and virtual product prototyping. You should start with the assumption that there is a way to do what you are imagining, and that you should be open to using different techniques.

Because I wrote this book to help you look beyond simply asking what different buttons do, I hope that it will help you develop an intuition for thinking like the software. Jeff Ray, CEO of the SolidWorks Corporation, has said that the goal is to make the software as "intuitive as a light switch." While most people will agree that they have some work left to achieve that particular goal, I believe that approaching the interface intuitively, rather than attempting to remember it all by rote, is the best method. Good luck to you.

Contacting the Author

If you want to contact me, to ask a question about the book's content or to make a suggestion for improving future editions, the best ways to do this are through e-mail (matt@dezign stuff.com) or my blog (http://dezignstuff.com/blog). On the blog, you can leave comments and read other things I have written about the SolidWorks software, CAD, and engineering or computer topics in general. If you want to contact me for commercial help with a modeling project, my e-mail address is the best place to start that type of conversation. I always look forward to hearing what real users think about the material.

Thank you very much for buying and reading this book. I hope the ideas and information within its pages help you accomplish your professional goals.

Part I

Introducing Assembly Basics

Understanding Assemblies

This chapter serves as an overview of some of the different tools and techniques that are available to SolidWorks users in assemblies. Most importantly, this chapter discusses the various purposes that you might have for creating assemblies. The second emphasis of this chapter is to help you understand various methods for using external references. More than anything, this chapter prepares you for important decisions that you will need to make relating to your modeling methods in SolidWorks found throughout this book.

If you take the SolidWorks training class from a SolidWorks reseller, all assemblies seem to take the same form and have the same function. You may then take this way of working back to your office and start applying it there. However, if you do this, you could be missing out on many other ways of using assemblies. While SolidWorks definitely seems to have a certain orthodoxy in mind for the assemblies functionality, there are actually an array of techniques that you can use to achieve a wide range of goals.

This chapter helps you identify some of the ways in which you can apply SolidWorks assemblies functionality to accommodate your goals and your workflow style. You are encouraged to experiment and evaluate some of these methods to find out what suits your needs best. You don't have to accept the established techniques. In fact, as you will see in this chapter, the established techniques tend to be less efficient, and especially less robust, than some alternative methods when you start making changes to your assemblies.

A lot of these alternative methods have been developed by many different users of other CAD packages over the years and have become universal to some extent. They have been adapted to SolidWorks use in different forms.

Understanding the Purpose of Assemblies

In the physical world, assemblies exist for several reasons:

- Separating materials
- Allowing relative motion
- Reducing material
- Allowing for different manufacturing techniques
- Allowing for disassembly or repair

In a CAD model, you need to follow these physical-world reasons for making individual parts and putting them together in assemblies, but CAD models can also have additional requirements. Independent of the reasons stemming from physical-world requirements, CAD assemblies might have some unique reasons for existing:

- Depicting an assembly process such as order of operations
- Specifying dimensional assembly relationships and tolerances
- Establishing clearances and limits of motion
- Visualizing motion and spatial relationships between parts
- Designing parts in-context
- Creating a parts list for assembly (Bill of Materials, or BOM)
- Creating a parts list for purchasing
- Automating data entry through PDM (product data management)
- Staging renderings
- Creating data for downstream applications such as animation or motion analysis

You can probably come up with a number of additional reasons for making CAD assemblies. In fact, almost as many reasons exist for making assemblies as there are people making those assemblies.

If you are trying to drive product development with a single top-level assembly, you might run into situations where the various functions of the assembly start conflicting with one another. For example, you might have an assembly where a part flexes. It is difficult or impossible to make flexible parts work effectively in SolidWorks with dynamic assembly motion. Another situation might be in-context relations where the parent and child components move relative to one another. Or maybe you need an assembly for a rendering and the assembly has to have multiple instances of in-context components, which can be tricky to manage. You get the picture. You can't always do everything with a single assembly.

It is certainly possible to have multiple assembly files for a single product. In fact, in some cases, it may be necessary. Rendering is probably one of the most common reasons for you to create a new assembly. Conflicts between external references and motion are another common reason to create a new assembly document.

Identifying types of assemblies

The average SolidWorks user thinks an assembly is a collection of parts put together with mates that position parts and may also allow motion. In this kind of assembly, you might use patterns, configurations, in-context techniques, and so on. The goal of the assembly is probably to simulate reality in the way it looks and moves.

Driving an assembly with base part and mates

This is considered "orthodox" SolidWorks assembly usage, and is the way the SolidWorks training materials describe creating assemblies. Insert a part or subassembly at the origin, which becomes fixed in place automatically, then start mating parts and subassemblies to the base component and add on from there.

This is the most frequently used assembly type in SolidWorks, but this type is also the most prone to failure, and the least likely to allow for relationships to exist between the parts. If you have been doing this kind of work already, and have made changes to the parts and watched the assembly update, you know that there are all sorts of things that can go wrong with this arrangement. Mates coming into conflict, flipping direction, or losing references are the most common errors that you might see when mating parts directly to one another in an assembly.

It is hard to imagine an assembly in real life where the parts don't depend to some extent on one another for their size or shape. So having a SolidWorks assembly where each part is modeled independently doesn't reflect real-world design intent very well, nor does it really use the advantages of parametrics and associativity that are touted so much in SolidWorks.

It is difficult to criticize an assembly modeling method that has been used for so long by so many people, but the high failure rate of mates attached to edges and faces speaks for itself. This is a problem that SolidWorks has tried to solve for many releases of the software, but the failure rate hasn't changed much, if at all. You may find that the software even tries to hide certain types of mate errors to make them easier to ignore.

The difficulty arises from the underlying methods built into the software. All of the faces and edges of parts are created using a history-based modeling system. Each feature is created in order, in a recipe for creating the final piece. The assembly, however, is generally not history-based. So mates attach to faces. If the faces change in such a way that the mate can't attach anymore, the mate fails. If the faces change in such a way that the way the mate works changes, parts can move in a way you don't expect. If you add fillets, or draft, or split a face to add color, or do any of a number of things that change the way the software internally identifies the faces or edges, then the mates you have applied will either fail or change the way it locates or allows parts to move.

The bottom line for the method of mating to base parts is that it is unreliable through changes. Of the methods that are presented in this book, this is the most common yet least reliable method. This is not the fault of the software, but of the method. The reason this faulty method is the most popular is because it is the easiest, and requires the least planning.

When SolidWorks first appeared on the market in the mid-1990s, it became very popular not only because it was inexpensive but also because it was much easier to use compared to products such as Pro/ENGINEER. Pro/ENGINEER taught methods for putting parts and assemblies together that were tedious but worked better through changes.

As an example of where you might use this kind of assembly, think of a robotic arm. Figure 1.1 shows an assembly that was created with bottom-up techniques and was assembled with face-to-face mates.

FIGURE 1.1

Mechanical parts using mates to locate and enable motion

But if you were to create, say, a scale model of a car, as shown in Figure 1.2, the method of independently designing each component, especially something like body panels, and then mating them together wouldn't make much sense. Other methods in the other types of assemblies shown later in this chapter will help with this type of design.

FIGURE 1.2

FIGURE 1.2

Considering how you would design the parts of a scale model car

It would be difficult or impossible to design the body panels of the car such that they fit together well and looked smooth next to one another using the bottom-up with mates method.

Driving an assembly with sketches and planes

One way to avoid the potential pitfalls of mating to a base part is to replace the changeable faces and edges with items that are more stable. The stability hierarchy listing items from the most to the least stable looks like this:

- Assembly or part origin
- Assembly or part standard planes
- Reference geometry (plane, axis, point)
- Reference geometry from inserted parts (from using the Insert ⇨ Part command)
- Sketch lines and midpoints
- Sketch endpoints
- Surface model faces
- Solid model faces
- Edges and vertex points
- In-context items
  - Reference geometry
  - Faces
  - Edges

An easier way to remember this without memorizing the list is that the more parents something has, the less reliable it is as a reference. This becomes more applicable if external references are involved, such as inserted parts or an in-context situation. Edges created by fillets or chamfers are lower on the list of stable references than other edges.

There is no clear answer to the question, "Is this reference stable enough?" It is entirely possible for you to be completely successful using in-context edges for all your model references. In order for that to happen, you would have to plan your model very well and avoid any big topological changes (changes to the number or function of faces) to the model.

Cross-Reference

Chapter 10 covers in-context modeling in more depth, and Chapter 19 covers inserted parts. ■

When you are building a part, selecting references from near the top of the previous list can be challenging, especially when faces and edges are so easy to use. You need to evaluate how much editing and rework you think you will generate when changes that you haven't necessarily planned on have to be made. Much of this ties into the design intent discussion from the *SolidWorks 2011 Parts Bible*.

Now consider the two examples mentioned in the last assembly modeling method — the robot arm and the model car. You could design the robot easily with the sketch layout, but simulating the motion in 3D would be difficult if you did it in conjunction with the sketch. The model car would still be difficult to assemble, and if you were just using sketches as the references between parts, it would be difficult to design the body panels such that they fit together smoothly.

Modeling parts in place

In-context design is discussed in more detail in Chapter 10, but here you will get some idea of what to look forward to, and why this book isn't just about in-context design by itself. Modeling parts in the context of an assembly that contains other parts enables you to make relationships between the parts. Those relationships are managed by the assembly. The parts have to be arranged spatially with respect to one another, and the references to the files must also be managed.

When you see a sales demonstration, the technique of using edges of other parts from the assembly to make a new part looks very compelling, especially when you make a change to the other part and the new part updates as well. It's hard to argue with that kind of functionality. But the price you pay for that sort of associativity is that you have to manage the relationship between three files: the parent part, the child part, and the assembly. And further, within the assembly, the relationships are made between specific instances of the parts, so if you have multiple instances of each, you have to do something to remember which pair of parts is the driving pair.

Also, model history with parts does not work the same with assemblies. The relationship between the parts does not have any memory, so if you started the in-context relationships before the parent part was complete, and then put fillets over the edges that you had referenced, your in-context references would fail.

Take another look at the robot arm and the model car examples. Using in-context methods, you could certainly design the robot arm, but again you might run into some problems with getting it to move correctly while maintaining the references. However, with the model car, getting the parts in the right place wouldn't be any problem because you would be modeling the parts in-place. On the other hand, you might be able to get the shape to flow smoothly, but it is still doubtful. In-context modeling can copy 3D surfaces between parts, but for an improved workflow for this type of work, you will have to read further into this chapter.

An example of a part where modeling in-context works well is a table with legs, as well as a fixture that sits on the table, as shown in Figure 1.3. The in-context work lines the holes up between the parts. There is no relative movement between the parts, and the individual parts are not likely to be used in other assemblies.

FIGURE 1.3

Using the in-context method to its best advantage

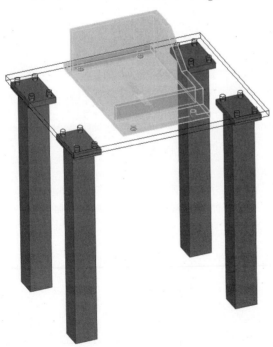

The ideal situation to use in-context techniques is when two parts are assembled face-on-face, the shape of the contact faces are the same or offset, and there is a set of holes used for fasteners. Complex shapes are generally not a good candidate for in-context methods. The main point is that there is no relative motion between the two parts.

Modeling parts as multi-bodies

Another method you can use to model parts is to start the models in a multi-body part. It is not recommended to use this method for creating finished parts as multi-bodies, but getting some of the major parts on an assembly started as a single part and then breaking them out into individual parts for details can be a very effective method.

Say you are modeling a riding lawn mower, and you need to create the plastic cowling on the front of the mower. The cowling is made up of multiple pieces because some of them are different colors, and some are transparent. The complex shapes of the cowling encompass multiple parts. If you were to model one part, and then try to model another part independently that shared some of the same shape, it would be very difficult or impossible to get the shapes to match acceptably.

One answer to this problem is to create the shape in a single part, then break the single part into individual bodies, and then save the bodies external to the original part. When you put these parts back together into the assembly, each part can be placed so that its origin matches with the assembly origin. Because the parts all started from the same part, they will all share the same origin. This makes putting the parts back together much simpler. It makes assembly for motion more difficult, but parts that have a shape in common are more likely to be fixed with respect to one another.

Multi-body modeling has advantages over in-context modeling in that it reduces external references (although saving bodies out as parts creates an external reference), but it also has some drawbacks. If you were to take all the features of individual parts and stack them into a single feature tree in a single part, you would probably be unhappy with the result. By making all of the features for all parts within a single part file, you make troubleshooting much more difficult, and rebuild times are dramatically increased. Add to this the inability to reuse parts, do individual revision management, or perform simple assembly operations such as dynamic motion, exploded views, or BOMs, and following the multi-body method through to finished parts becomes very unattractive.

The best option for using multi-bodies to create parts for an assembly is to start the parts in multi-body mode, and then as soon as the inter-body references are no longer needed, transition the bodies to separate parts.

Multi-body modeling may not do so well when parts are repeated, or where purchased components represent a large percentage of the total parts. While you do have mate-like functionality for placing bodies within a multi-body part, it is probably not the best use of this method. Figure 1.4 shows a product that is designed as a multi-body part but involves many difficulties because of reused parts and hardware.

FIGURE 1.4

Reusing parts is not a strength of multi-body methods.

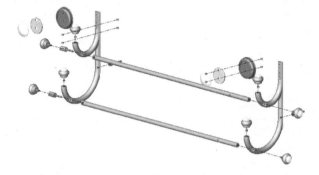

Revisiting the test for each method, you would find that the robot arm is well suited to being designed as a multi-body part and then reassembled with mates in an assembly. In fact, the multi-body method is probably the best method for this type of work, maintaining references between parts, and then assembling the parts into an assembly mechanism with motion.

The model car, with its shape that flows between parts, would still be awkward, although it could be done as individual parts. You will now look at the last method to see if this helps with the car model.

Inserting a master model

You will learn about the master model technique in Chapter 19. In a nutshell, a master model is a single part where you place sketches, reference geometry, surfaces, and maybe some solids, and then insert that part into other parts to use a reference to build each individual part. Using this technique makes in-context work unnecessary, and eliminates some of the dangers of creating too many features in a multi-body part.

You assemble parts in this manner the same as with the multi-body part method. Take each part, and drop it into the FeatureManager of the assembly. This aligns the part origin with the assembly origin, and because each part was built from the same master model, all parts share the same origin.

Take another look at the robot arm and model car examples. The robot arm may be a little awkward using this method, but it works. The multi-body method is probably best for this type of design.

On the other hand, the master model method brings real power to projects such as the model car. You can design the entire outside of the car as if it were a single part, and then break it up into individual parts. In Figure 1.5, notice how some parts that will be manufactured as a single part can be easily pulled off of the master model. Sketches within the master model can help define breaks between parts and even if there is relative motion — for example, with the doors.

FIGURE 1.5

Pulling parts off of the master model

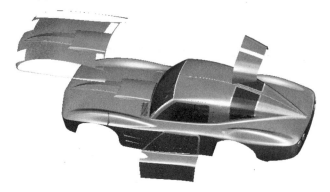

Excluding some parts

Methods such as those mentioned previously are great for any part that is unique to an assembly, but should not be used for library type parts. If you have a part that will be used in more than one assembly, it should not have any external references. To be clear, all of these methods create external references except bottom-up assembly (where parts are modeled individually, and then assembled to one another or to a skeleton).

Any library parts that you have, or standard hardware such as nuts, bolts, washers, and so on, should not be modeled with references, nor should you use them in multi-body parts.

Without sounding against multi-body modeling, several SolidWorks users think eliminating the distinction between assemblies and parts would be a good thing. That point of view works for only the simplest small assemblies with simple parts. It's easy to come up with situations in which the tree management tools required to maintain models built using that philosophy through changes do not even exist in the software.

Creating an alternative to multiple assemblies

It may seem very inefficient to re-create or copy assemblies for different uses. In Chapter 8, you will learn about another way: using assembly configurations. If you are already familiar with part configurations, assembly configurations work on a similar principle. Assembly configurations are a great tool with a lot of theoretical benefits and practical limitations. As with most other functions in SolidWorks, when you need to create assemblies for multiple purposes, you may find that assembly configurations meet your needs. Or you may find it easier to just save out a copy of the assembly, knowing that changes for the sake of rendering do not diminish the usefulness of the data for something like exploded views, or managing external in-context references.

Creating Assembly Templates

When you have assemblies with different purposes, you may also need multiple assembly templates. One example of using assembly templates to help reuse work is saving an animation in a template. If you save an assembly template that contains a default turntable animation, then you can put other assemblies right into the turntable template and you've got an instant display animation. (Animation is covered in detail in Chapter 23.)

Another example of a useful assembly template would be a rendering setup with environment, background, and lighting. Putting a part or assembly into the template before doing a stock rendering can help you standardize renderings and work through them more quickly.

The steps to create an assembly template are similar to those for setting up a part template:

1. Specify a custom location for all your templates. You can do this at Tools ➪ Options ➪ File Locations ➪ Document Templates. You should save it in a location such as D:/ Library/Templates/. For a group of users, you may want to use a network location so you can share the templates.

2. Start with an assembly that has most of the settings you intend to use.

3. Add whatever animation, scene, or light settings you want. You may have to add a dummy assembly to get the settings right, and then delete it before saving it as a template.

4. Set the options in Tools ➪ Options ➪ Document Properties the way you want them. Pay special attention to the Drafting Standard, Units, Model Display, and Image Quality settings.

5. Rename the standard planes as appropriate. If your assembly template is bound to be used for injection mold tooling, you may name planes to establish the Parting Plane. If you are creating architectural assemblies, you may have planes called Plan View, Side Elevation, and North Elevation.

6. Make sure the custom properties (found at File ➪ Properties ➪ Custom) for the assembly template are set the way you want them. Remember that you can use Tags in some ways like custom properties. In fact, custom property settings might be a reason for making separate assembly templates. You might have a different set of custom properties for a tooling assembly used in manufacturing as opposed to a

product assembly that is shipped to customers. You may also choose to change the default settings for showing annotations such as cosmetic threads and shaded cosmetic threads (click the right mouse button (RMB) on the Annotations folder in the Feature Manager and select Details for these options)

7. When you have all of the document-specific settings the way you want them, save the assembly file as a template. Choose File ⇨ Save As, and SolidWorks directs you to the folder where you have specified that your templates will go.

Figure 1.6 shows the Tools ⇨ Options ⇨ File Locations interface where you should set your templates' locations.

FIGURE 1.6

Establishing the location of your templates

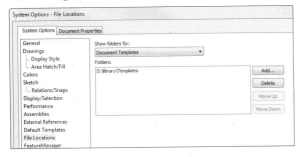

Using assembly templates is easier than creating them. To choose from a number of assembly templates, you have to use the Advanced interface on the New Document dialog box. If you use the Novice interface, you can only choose the default templates.

If you want to use only a single assembly template, and set that one as the default, first save the template to a location as described previously, and then set the default assembly template at Tools ⇨ Options ⇨ Default Templates.

If you would like to devote an entire tab of the New Document dialog box to just assemblies, then in Windows Explorer, in the folder specified in your template locations, create a new folder named Assemblies or something relevant. This folder name will show up as a tab in the Advanced interface for the New Document dialog box.

Note

The Novice interface displays a button that says Advanced, and the Advanced interface displays a button that says Novice. ∎

Figure 1.7 shows the Novice and Advanced interfaces.

FIGURE 1.7

Starting a new assembly from the Novice and Advanced interfaces of the New Document dialog box

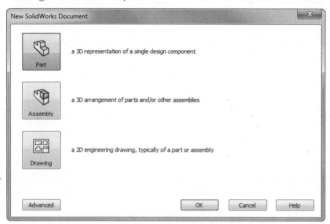

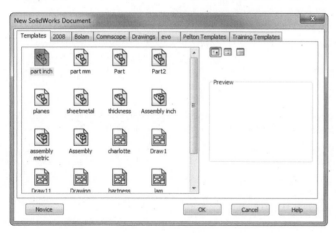

Putting Parts into Assemblies

When you are building an assembly, several ways exist to put parts into assemblies:

- Choose Insert ⇨ Component
- Drag and drop from Windows Explorer
- Drag and drop from other SolidWorks windows
- Drag and drop from the Design Library window
- Ctrl+drag to add a second instance of a part that is already in an assembly
- Create an assembly from a part
- Create a part in-context

The first part that you put into an assembly is always fixed (meaning locked into position). When parts are fixed automatically, the origin of the part is always located at the origin of the assembly, but parts may be manually fixed at any location in the assembly.

After the first part, any additional parts you put into the assembly will either fall where you drop them if you drop them in the graphics window or be positioned at the assembly origin if you drop them into the FeatureManager.

One of the most valuable methods is to use SmartMates and Mate References. SmartMates enable you to Alt+drag a part by specific geometry on the part and drop it onto specific geometry on another part; a mate is then automatically created between the parts. SmartMates do take some practice, but they help you save a lot of time and frustration when putting an assembly together from parts. Mate References are similar, except that you have to set them up beforehand (and so they work best on library type parts), and they enable a part to snap into place when you drag it into an assembly.

Understanding External References

External references are one of the most time-consuming aspects of assemblies, and all assemblies and assembly replacement techniques have them. An external reference is any reference to a file outside of the current file. So in its simplest form, part files in an assembly create external references, because the assembly references the parts.

You can easily recognize external references of all kinds by the -> symbol following a feature in the FeatureManager. Figure 1.8 shows a portion of an assembly FeatureManager that contains the symbol. You can also find this symbol on externally referenced features within a part.

FIGURE 1.8

The external reference symbol on a sketch and a feature

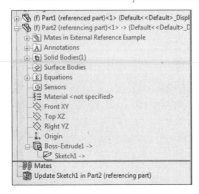

Referencing external files in-context

In-context techniques are all about external references. External in-context references in an assembly occur when one part in the assembly has some sort of geometrical reference to another, such as offsetting an edge of a part, using a vertex of a part with a coincident sketch relation, or using a face of another part as a sketch plane. All of these references are saved in Update Holders that reside in the assembly FeatureManager, but SolidWorks hides them by default. Figure 1.9 shows a simple assembly FeatureManager with a single Update Holder. You can show the Update Holders in an assembly by right-clicking the top level name of the assembly in the FeatureManager and selecting Show Update Holders.

FIGURE 1.9

Displaying an Update Holder that keeps external reference information

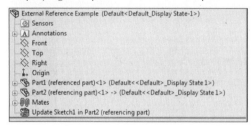

To view the contents of the Update Holder, right-click the Holder or any part or feature that contains external references, and select List External References from the menu. The information stored in the Update Holder shown in Figure 1.9 is shown in Figure 1.10.

FIGURE 1.10

Showing the contents of the Update Holder

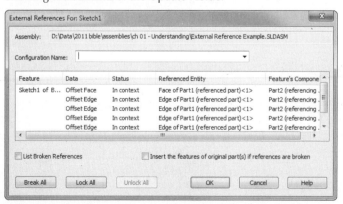

In the example shown in Figure 1.9, four edges of Part1 are offset into Part2. Also, the Part2 sketch into which the edges are offset uses a face of Part1 as the sketch plane.

Note

The Insert the features of the original part(s) if references are broken option in the External References For dialog box does not apply to assembly in-context situations. It only applies to inserted parts (what the Help system calls "derived parts"). Inserted parts are also external references where references can be broken. You will find more information on this topic in the next section. ■

Each Update Holder holds the external reference information for a single feature. If a sketch and a feature have different external references (for example, the sketch might reference face edges, while the feature might reference a vertex in the other model for an Up To Vertex end condition), there will be a different Update Holder for each. The external reference information has several components:

- The name of the assembly where references are made
- The configuration of the assembly where references are made
- The feature where the reference was created
- The type of entity that was referenced, and which part it is in
- The part from which the reference was created

Referencing external files from a part

Chapter 19 is all about referencing external files from a part. As a preview of what you will see in that chapter, you can insert one part into another part to use in a number of ways, such as the following:

- A starting point, for example, adding secondary operations to a cast part
- A tool, for example, using the Indent feature to create a clearance for an interfering part
- A Boolean operator, for example, to subtract one part from another
- A set of reference geometry, for example, inserting the surface of a car door to create the outer skin of the door

To create these external references, SolidWorks provides four different features or functions:

- Insert Part
- Insert Into New Part
- Split
- Save Bodies

External references within parts can be broken in the same way that in-context relations can be broken. External references in parts have just one fewer component compared to assemblies — parts obviously do not list an assembly where the reference was created.

For parts, two different kinds of external references exist: inserted parts (on the left in Figure 1.11) and stock parts (on the right in Figure 1.11). Figure 1.11 shows these two types of references inserted at the top of different part FeatureManagers. Notice that they both have the in-context external reference symbol (->) after the first feature.

FIGURE 1.11

Two kinds of external references in SolidWorks parts

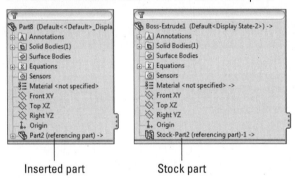

Inserted part   Stock part

The inserted part allows you to bring across planes, sketches, features, and even the entire part if you want, but on the down side, it forces you to bring all bodies to the new part (you can select solid or surface, but you can't select which bodies). The stock feature enables you to select which bodies you bring to the new part, but it only allows you to bring solid bodies (not surfaces) and does not allow you to bring reference geometry, sketches, or features.

Summary

If you have taken the SolidWorks training classes, even the advanced training classes, you may not have seen the entire range of what you can do with SolidWorks assemblies. Keep an open mind about being able to accomplish more by using assemblies that are built for different purposes.

External references in assemblies tend to intimidate a lot of users, but if you know where to find the necessary information, and how to handle the data, you can have complete control over your assembly models, and you don't have to be afraid of techniques such as in-context or master model.

Navigating the Assembly Interface

The SolidWorks interface for working with assemblies offers a wide range of tools. You will often find more than one way to do almost everything. Most of the tools are the same as those found in the general parts interface, but this chapter will show you special techniques for using these tools to make your job easier with assemblies.

Once you have mastered the various interface elements and customized your SolidWorks installation, working with assemblies becomes much more efficient and satisfying. Your command of the interface will come with practice and experience. Many existing users may discover features in this book of which they were not aware, even though they have used the software for years.

Each interface element identified in Figure 2.1 is explained in detail within this chapter. You won't see all of the elements shown in Figure 2.1 at the same time; the figure was assembled to show as many interface elements as possible.

IN THIS CHAPTER

Discovering elements of the SolidWorks interface

Exploring the interface

FIGURE 2.1

Elements of the SolidWorks assembly interface

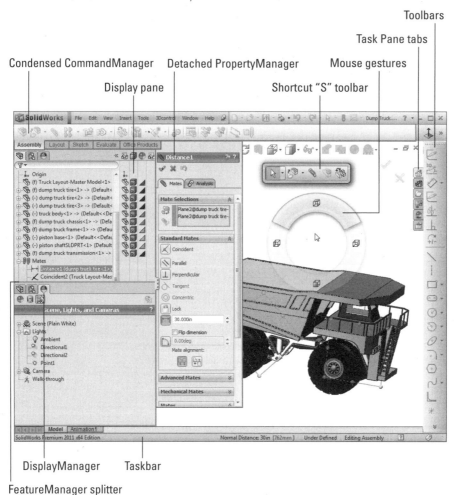

Identifying Elements of the SolidWorks Assembly Interface

Most of the elements of the assembly interface are the same as the part interface. (You can find a complete description in the *SolidWorks 2011 Parts Bible*.) This chapter describes the elements of the SolidWorks interface that are either unique to assemblies or vital to the assemblies' functionality.

Using the CommandManager and toolbars

Remember that the CommandManager saves settings for parts, assemblies, and drawings. This means that it may have different tabs when you are in each of these document types, and you can set each type to have the features and functions that you need.

The CommandManager is less useful in assemblies than it is in parts. Of course, everything depends on what you plan to do in assemblies, but most users generally use fewer tools in assemblies than they do in part documents. In parts, it is common to use the Features tab as well as Sheet Metal, Weldments, possibly Surfaces, and some other CommandManager tabs. In assemblies, the Assembly and Evaluate tabs are the most relevant.

When you edit a part in the context of the assembly, the assembly CommandManager turns into the part CommandManager with some additional tools. Figure 2.2 shows the CommandManager in an assembly when editing a part (with large icons and text removed).

FIGURE 2.2

The CommandManager when editing a part in the context of an assembly

One of the most common mistakes when editing parts in an assembly is to forget which mode you are in — Edit Part or Edit Assembly. Notice the ghosted Edit Part icon where the sketch Confirmation Corner goes (upper-right corner). Also notice that the Edit Part icon in the Assembly toolbar appears depressed. If you have room in your interface, the name of the assembly or the part shows on the title bar. Figure 2.2 shows the interface at a low resolution (1024 x 768), and only part of the height. At this resolution and with the menus pinned along with the title bar toolbar, there is little room for the filename.

Notice that the first five icons on the left side of the CommandManager in Figure 2.2 are assembly tools. They are, respectively,

 Edit Component

 No External References

Hide/Show Components

 Change Transparency

 Assembly Transparency

Notice that the Hide/Show Components and Change Transparency icons are nearly indistinguishable. On the interface, the transparency icon is ghosted somewhat. Remember that tool tips can be a very effective way to remember what various icons in the interface signify until you have learned them thoroughly.

Introducing the assembly tools

The tools on the Assembly toolbar are not all available by default, and if you are new to SolidWorks, or are experienced with the software but only use assemblies superficially, you may not be familiar with all of the available tools. The names of the tools are listed in Table 2.1, as displayed in Tools ⇨ Customize for the Assembly toolbar.

TABLE 2.1

Assembly Toolbar

Tool	Description	Tool	Description
	Insert Components		New Part
	New Assembly		Copy with Mates
	Linear Component Pattern		Circular Component Pattern
	Feature-Driven Component Pattern		Mirror Components
	Large Assembly Mode		Show Hidden Components
	Hide/Show Components		Change Transparency
	Change Suppression State		Edit Component
	No External References		Smart Fasteners
	Make Smart Component		Mate

Tool	Description	Tool	Description
	Move Component		Rotate Component
	Replace Components		Replace Mate Entities
	Exploded View		Explode Line Sketch
	Interference Detection		Clearance Verification
	Hole Alignment		Assembly Xpert
	Assembly Transparency		Belt/Chain
	New Motion Study		

Notice that the small New Part icon is different from the large icon; the small version looks very much like the Smart Fasteners icon. All of these tools are covered in depth throughout this book. You can use the index to find where each topic is covered in detail. Chapter 7 is devoted exclusively to using the Assembly tools.

Using the Heads-Up View toolbar

The Heads-Up View toolbar appears along the middle of the top edge of the graphics window. Figure 2.3 shows the default arrangement of the Heads-Up View toolbar, and it is shown in relation to the rest of the interface in Figure 2.1. This toolbar is not configurable for each document type. It is either on or off, and the icons on it remain the same for parts, assemblies, and drawings.

FIGURE 2.3

The Heads-Up View toolbar

You can customize the Heads-Up View toolbar by using the Toolbars dialog box (Tools ➪ Customize ➪ Toolbars). Customization includes turning the Heads-Up View toolbar on or off and adding or removing buttons. If you have multiple document windows or multiple viewports showing, the Heads-Up View toolbar only appears in the active window or viewport. This toolbar often overlaps with other interface elements when several windows are tiled or if the active window is not maximized. If it is pulled out of the FeatureManager, it can run into the PropertyManager, as well as the Confirmation Corner or the Task Pane.

Using the Shortcut "S" toolbar

The Shortcut toolbar is also known as the "S" toolbar because by default, you access it by pressing the S key. You can customize this toolbar for each document type and another toolbar for sketches, so it can have different content for sketches, parts, assemblies, and drawings. To customize the "S" toolbar, right-click it when it is active and click Customize from the right mouse button (RMB) menu, as shown in Figure 2.4.

FIGURE 2.4

Right-click the Shortcut "S" toolbar to customize it

Many people claim to have customized the "S" toolbar to such an extent that they have been able to remove the CommandManager and all other toolbars from their interface. This may be true if you use a limited number of sketch entities, sketch relations, and feature types, or if you make extensive use of flyouts on the "S" toolbar. However, if you work with a wide range of tools (say, surfacing, sheet metal, and plastic parts), you may need some additional toolbar space. It is completely possible to have access to most of the software's functions with the "S" toolbar and either the Menu Bar toolbar or the CommandManager. The CommandManager gives you the most flexibility, but it also requires the most space.

Working in the assembly FeatureManager

The FeatureManager in assemblies has some special working modes (see Figure 2.5). It does many of the same things that the part FeatureManager does, but because it manages parts rather than features, you can expect some differences.

You will also encounter some special icons in the assembly FeatureManager. Here is a list of some of these icons; they will all be explained in more detail throughout this book.

FIGURE 2.5

The FeatureManager for a simple model

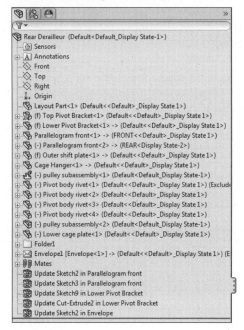

- **Lightweight and Hidden Lightweight.** Lightweight components have data loaded from the assembly only. Hidden Lightweight have the data loaded but are not visible.

- **Out-of-Date Lightweight and Hidden Out-of-Date Lightweight.** Out-of-date lightweight parts exist when changes have been made to the original part, but it hasn't been reloaded yet into the assembly. The symbol notifies you that what you see in the assembly may not represent the current state of the part.

- **SpeedPak.** SpeedPaks are derived configurations that use only body or face geometry (no parametrics) to display parts and subassemblies within upper-level assemblies. You will learn more about all of these techniques later in this book.

- **Envelope.** An Envelope is a part in an assembly that is not counted toward the Bill of Materials (BOM) or mass properties. Its primary function is to designate an area for selection. It could designate the range of motion of an operator or piece of machinery, or an area where noise may be above a certain decibel level. Envelopes are intended to be used as part of the Advanced Component Selection that you can access through the menus at Tools ➪ Component Selection ➪ Advanced Select.

- **Update Holders.** Update Holders contain the information about external references in assemblies where in-context references have been made. They are hidden by default, but you can show them by right-clicking the name of the assembly and selecting Show Update Holders.

- **Flexible Subassembly.** SolidWorks solves assembly mates within the assembly document by default. This means that any mates (and motion) associated with a subassembly will not be solved in the upper-level assembly. If a joint is in a subassembly and you want it to move while displayed in the upper-level assembly, you must make the subassembly a flexible subassembly, using the Component Properties dialog box.

- **Display Pane.** You can open the Display Pane flyout from the FeatureManager by clicking the double arrows at the top-right corner of the FeatureManager. The Display Pane helps you to visualize where appearances, display styles, or hidden bodies have been applied in a part document and where appearances have been applied at various levels (overrides) in an assembly document. The Display Pane is helpful when you're looking for colors that are applied to the model at some level other than the part level.

- **Rollback Bar.** The Rollback bar at the bottom of the FeatureManager enables you to see the part in various states of history. You can add features while the Rollback bar is at any location. You can also save the model while it is rolled back.

- **FeatureManager Filter.** One of the most useful elements of the FeatureManager is the FeatureManager filter. The filter resides at the top of the FeatureManager. If you type text in the filter, SolidWorks searches part names, descriptions, tags, comments, document properties, mates, and configuration names for matching text, and only shows matching components in the window. The filter is very useful for quickly finding parts, features, mates, or anything else that shows up in the part or assembly FeatureManager.

Working with multiple document windows

You may sometimes have the luxury of working on a single part at a time, but more often you will have several documents open at once. Fortunately, SolidWorks has several methods for dealing with "information overload," to help you sort through it all.

Managing open windows

Like most Windows applications, SolidWorks can arrange the open document windows in one of several ways that are available through the Window menu (see Figure 2.6):

- **Cascade.** This is most useful for accessing documents that are to be edited one by one.
- **Tile Horizontally.** This is most useful for wide and short parts.
- **Tile Vertically.** This is most useful for tall, narrow parts, or documents where you want to compare items in the FeatureManager.
- **Arrange Icons.** When windows are minimized to icons, this menu selection arranges the icons neatly, starting in the lower-left corner of the window.

FIGURE 2.6

The Window menu

The images in Figure 2.7 are meant to show the arrangement of the windows, not the content of the windows. Also, remember that you can use the F9 key to close the FeatureManager; the F10 key to remove the toolbars to create extra interface space when arranging several windows in the graphics window; and the F11 key to remove portions of the interface and enable you to work full screen.

Part I: Introducing Assembly Basics

Window arrangements: Cascade, Tile Horizontally, and Tile Vertically

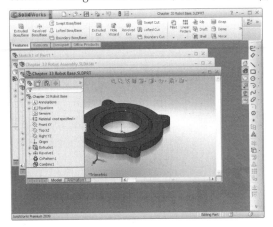

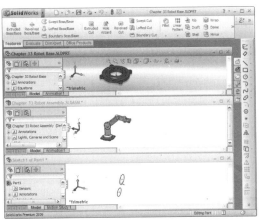

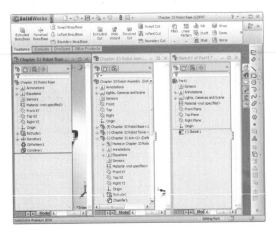

30

Understanding the Interface for Moving and Mating

Moving and Mating operations are exclusive to assembly documents and so have some unique interface elements. For the easiest type of moving parts that are set up for dynamic assembly motion, there is no interface at all. You just select the part and drag the cursor. This type of moving is not always as precise as you might need, so SolidWorks enables other types of moving with different interfaces.

You can prevent the motion of components while dragging by turning off the option found at Tools ➪ Options ➪ Assemblies ➪ Move components by dragging. This option is turned on by default.

While moving a part with the default (select) cursor, you can choose some options from the RMB menu to help you move the component. Figure 2.8 shows a portion of this RMB menu.

FIGURE 2.8

Selecting other options for moving parts in an assembly

The Move option simply opens the Move Component PropertyManager, where you can access the options and controls shown later in this section.

The Move With Triad option brings up a triad with wings and concentric rings, shown in Figure 2.9. This may seem confusing at first, but its function becomes clearer as you use it.

FIGURE 2.9

Using the triad to move components

The arrows enable you to move parts along that direction only. The rings enable you to rotate the part around that direction only. The flat "wings" between the arrows enable you to move the part in a plane parallel to the flat wing. To use these wings correctly, you must sometimes reposition the view so you can see the wing properly in order to select it.

The small, blue ball at the center of the triad enables you to move the triad to a more convenient location. It does not snap to any geometry. Moving it only gives you a better view or makes it easier to select parts of the triad without selecting something in the background.

Using the Move Component interface

The Move Component tool enables you to move parts in an assembly using various methods. Figure 2.10 shows the interface for this tool.

SolidWorks allows you to move parts in assemblies using the following methods:

- Free Drag
- Along Assembly XYZ
- Along Entity
- By Delta XYZ
- To XYZ Position

All of the following movement options are available for both translation and rotation.

FIGURE 2.10

Available options in the Move Component interface

Free Drag

Using the Free Drag option is the same as just dragging parts with the cursor without using the Move Component tool at all. When you drag a part with open degrees of freedom in the assembly graphics window, you might notice that the Move Component icon in the assembly toolbar momentarily depresses.

Free Drag exists as an option in the Move Component PropertyManager because several options can be used in conjunction with Free Drag that give you a wider range of capabilities, such as collision, clearance, and physical dynamics.

Free Drag enables the part to move according to whatever open degrees of freedom have been allowed by the mates. This concept is dealt with in more detail in later chapters.

Along Assembly XYZ

The Along Assembly XYZ option displays a small triad on the screen, shown in Figure 2.11.

This interface only allows you to move the part along one axis at a time. You can try to free-drag the part, and you will most likely move the part in the direction you want if you bring the view into an orientation such that the direction you want to move is parallel to the screen.

To ensure that you are moving in a particular direction, you can click the cursor near one of the X, Y, or Z legs of the triad. There is no cursor snap, nor does one leg change color, so you can't really be sure that you are going to move a part in a specific direction until you see the part actually moving. This is not as reliable as the Move With Triad option.

FIGURE 2.11

Using the triad with Along Assembly XYZ

Along Entity

If you want to move a part in a particular direction that is not aligned with the coordinate system of the assembly, you can use the Along Entity option. This requires you to have an edge, axis, or sketch line that goes in the direction you want to move the part.

By Delta XYZ

You can use the By Delta XYZ option to move a component when you know the specific distance and direction you want to move the selected parts. Figure 2.12 shows this PropertyManager along with the same triad from the Along Assembly XYZ option.

FIGURE 2.12

Moving a component using the By Delta XYZ option

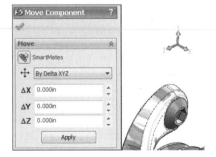

To XYZ Position

This PropertyManager, like the other Move Component PropertyManagers, doesn't have a selection box to show you what is selected. If you use this option to move a component, then the component's origin is moved to the specified XYZ point unless you have a point on the model selected, in which case that point is moved to the specified XYZ point. Figure 2.13 shows the To XYZ Position PropertyManager.

FIGURE 2.13

Using the To XYZ Position option to move a part

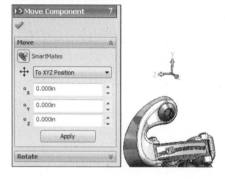

Selecting Move Component options

Not all of the options in this panel of the Move Component PropertyManager apply to all movement methods. The three options are

- Standard Drag
- Collision Detection
- Physical Dynamics

The Standard Drag option simply refers to dragging parts visually on the screen.

Collision Detection allows parts to move until they interfere with another part. When the parts touch, SolidWorks makes a sound. The performance of this type of movement is highly dependent on the complexity of shapes in the assembly and your hardware specifications. Figure 2.14 shows the PropertyManager options for Collision Detection.

Physical Dynamics is like Collision Detection except that when parts touch, instead of stopping, they push the other parts. You can use this type of motion if you have an assembly where the parts are not highly constrained. You need to remember that it does not take into account factors such as momentum, material properties, or anything other than contact and mates.

FIGURE 2.14

Using options for Collision Detection

Dynamic Clearance

Dynamic Clearance is an option in the Move Component PropertyManager that you can use while moving parts by dragging. It works by placing the minimum clearance dimension between parts when one of them is being dragged. You can use Dynamic Clearance in conjunction with other options in the Move Component PropertyManager. Figure 2.15 shows the Dynamic Clearance panel of the Move Component PropertyManager.

In the Advanced Options panel, the Highlight Faces option highlights the faces that would collide or are being measured between for minimum clearance. The Ignore Complex Surfaces option tells SolidWorks not to calculate complex faces; this speeds up calculations in situations where speed is a problem.

Using the Mate interface

The SolidWorks Mate interface works slightly differently from some of the other functional interfaces. Normally, you get into a rhythm with the button pushes and keyboard strokes, but the Mate interface slightly breaks up this rhythm. The SolidWorks developers set up the interface based on the assumption that you are going to make multiple mates every time you use the Mate PropertyManager.

Considering workflow

The normal workflow for tools is that you use the tool, and when you click the green check mark icon, the interface closes, unless it is a feature that has the pushpin in the

PropertyManager, and you have the pushpin pushed. In this case, it keeps the interface open so you can do multiple iterations. For example, the Offset Entities PropertyManager, shown in Figure 2.16, has a pushpin.

Using the Dynamic Clearance option with Move Component

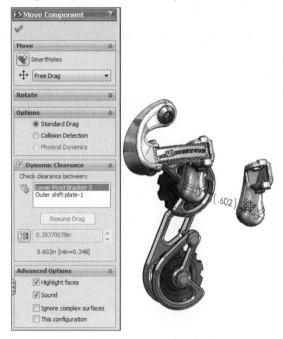

Comparing the Offset Entities interface to the Mate interface

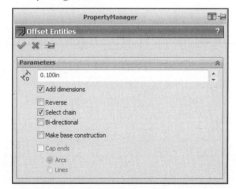

Here is the workflow for the Offset Entities PropertyManager without using the Push Pin feature:

1. Within a sketch, preselect an edge (you can also select the edge after Step 2).
2. Click the Offset Entities toolbar button.
3. Set the options.
4. Click the green check mark icon.

When you click the green check mark icon, the PropertyManager closes.

Now here is the workflow for the Offset Entities PropertyManager using the Push Pin feature, which allows you to perform multiple offset operations:

1. Within a sketch, preselect an edge (you can also select the edge after Step 2).
2. Click the Offset Entities toolbar button.
3. Click the pushpin.
4. Set the options.
5. Click the green check mark icon.
6. Make another selection set.
7. Change the options.
8. Click the green check mark icon.
9. Repeat Steps 6, 7, and 8 until you are done.
10. Click the green check mark icon again.

The Mate interface, shown in Figure 2.17, has a pushpin for the PropertyManager, but not for the Mate function; to close the Mate function, you need to click the green check mark icon twice (and make the second click when there is nothing selected in the interface), or click the red X. So the Mate feature works like Offset Entities if the Offset Entities pushpin were always pushed in. This is why the Mate workflow is not standard — because it assumes that you want to use the pushpin, without giving you the option.

Looking at the rest of the Mate interface

In all fairness, there is more to the story about the Mate interface than just a little interface inconsistency. Some tools exist that help you get through the mates quickly.

RMB OK

 Possibly the single biggest time-saver in the Mate interface is the RMB OK feature, which allows you to simply click the RMB to apply the mate and move on to the next selection. It's fast, and once you get used to it, you will wish the rest of the interface had this little gem. Some other features have it and some don't.

Multiple Mate mode

 The icon for Multiple Mate mode is in the Mate Selections panel, shown in Figure 2.18. With Multiple Mate mode, you select one entity that you want to mate several parts to, such as a center plane that all the parts in an assembly use to line themselves up.

FIGURE 2.17

The Mate function does not have its own pushpin — it behaves as if the pushpin is always pushed in.

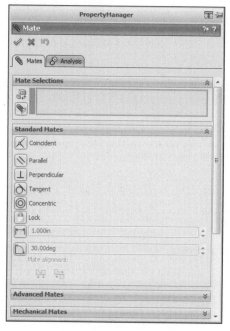

The workflow for this tool is as follows:

1. Initiate the Multiple Mate tool.

2. Click the Multiple Mate Mode icon.

3. Click the common entity that you want to mate other parts to.

4. Click each entity that you want to mate to the common entity.

5. Use the RMB OK feature to continue, or click the green check mark icon twice to exit the feature.

Using Multiple Mate mode

Mate shortcut bar

The Mate shortcut bar, shown in Figure 2.19, brings most of the options from the Mate PropertyManager out to where your cursor is. This shortcut bar makes it easy to change mate types, enter a distance or angle value for a mate, or flip the direction of the mate.

Selecting options with the Mate shortcut bar

Summary

SolidWorks assemblies have a lot of functionality and settings that are not found in other document types. The interface remembers settings for different document types, which saves you time when switching between parts and assemblies. The features mentioned in this chapter are described in more detail throughout this book.

Visualizing Assemblies

With assemblies, even more than with parts, the ability to visualize the geometry is highly important to the success of a modeling project. Between manipulating the view and manipulating the model, you have to be able to see all sides of geometry. Add to that section views, transparency, and mixed-mode display with shading and wireframes, and you have some extreme visualization power at your fingertips.

Manipulating the View

Whether you are working in parts or assemblies, manipulating the view is one of the most important and frequent things that you will do in SolidWorks. You can customize and disable the Heads-Up View toolbar, shown in Figure 3.1, by using the same method that you use for all other toolbars, through the Tools ⇨ Customize dialog box.

Tip
Some mouse drivers change the middle-button or scroll-wheel settings to do other things. Often, you can disable the special settings for a particular application if you want SolidWorks to work correctly and still use the other functionality. For example, the most common problem with mouse drivers is that when the model gets close to the sides of the graphics window and the scroll bars engage, the middle mouse button (MMB) suddenly changes its function. If this happens to you, you should change the function of the MMB to Middle Mouse Button from its present setting. ■

FIGURE 3.1

Use the Heads-Up View toolbar to easily access most visualization tools.

Using arrow keys

You can use the arrow keys on the keyboard to manipulate the view in predictable and controllable ways. You can use the Shift, Ctrl, and Alt keys to customize this behavior.

The arrow keys enable you to rotate to the following views:

- **Arrow.** Rotate 15 degrees. To customize this setting, choose Tools ➪ Options ➪ View.
- **Shift+arrow.** Rotate 90 degrees.
- **Alt+arrow.** Rotate in a plane flat to the screen.
- **Ctrl+arrow.** Pan.

Using the middle mouse button

Most, if not all, mice sold today have middle mouse buttons (MMB), usually in the form of a clickable scroll wheel.

The MMB or scroll wheel has several uses in view manipulation:

- **MMB alone.** Rotate.
- **Click or hover on edge, face, or vertex with MMB, and then drag MMB.** Rotate around selected entity.
- **Ctrl+MMB.** Pan.
- **Shift+MMB.** Zoom.
- **Double-click MMB.** Zoom to fit.
- **Scroll with wheel.** Zoom in or out. To reverse direction of the zoom setting, choose Tools ➪ Options ➪ View.
- **Alt+MMB.** Rotate in a plane flat to the screen.

Clicking the triad

The triad in the lower-left corner of the graphics window gives you another great way to manipulate the view. You can click any leg of the triad, and the view rotates such that the leg you clicked points straight out of the screen. Shift+clicking an axis rotates the view 90 degrees about that axis. Alt+clicking an axis rotates the view 15 degrees about that axis. Using Ctrl in combination with either Shift or Alt reverses the direction of the rotation.

When you move the cursor right over the axis you want to click, the axis appears highlighted in yellow. Figure 3.2 shows the triad in action.

FIGURE 3.2

Using the triad to rotate the view

To summarize this method:

- **Click axis.** Axis points out of screen.
- **Double-click axis.** Axis points into screen.
- **Shift+click axis.** View rotates 90 degrees around axis.
- **Ctrl+Shift+click axis.** View rotates 90 degrees in the opposite direction.
- **Alt+click axis.** View rotates 15 degrees around axis.
- **Ctrl+Alt+click axis.** View rotates 15 degrees in the opposite direction.

Using mouse gestures

Mouse gestures are an interface method that you can customize to do anything a SolidWorks toolbar button can do, but by default, this method controls view orientation. Figure 3.3 shows the default configuration of the mouse gesture donut.

FIGURE 3.3

Click+drag the right mouse button (RMB) to access the commands on the donut.

It may take a little time for you to get used to the interface. It works best when you understand what the commands are before you use them, so that you can invoke the Top View command in a single motion. It does not work well if you have to initiate the interface with a very short RMB drag, and then drag again to select the command. For this reason, it might be better to limit the donut to four commands rather than eight, and set it up intuitively such that the top view is an RMB stroke up, a right view is an RMB stroke to the right, and so on.

You can customize the mouse gesture donut by selecting Tools ⇨ Customize ⇨ Mouse Gestures. This works like the Keyboard (hotkey) customization, where you can turn gestures on or off, set the mouse gesture donut to four or eight sections, and change the icons on the donut.

While the icons you put on the donut are not limited to view manipulation commands, this particular interface appears to work best when you use it for view manipulation.

Using the Magnifying Glass

You can invoke the Magnifying Glass by pressing the G key, and dismiss it when you select something or when you press Esc. To change the hotkey it is associated with, choose Tools ⇨ Customize ⇨ Keyboard. Magnifying Glass is listed in the Other category. The Magnifying Glass allows you to magnify a small area of the view so that you can make a more precise selection.

The magnified area follows your cursor as it moves, and you can zoom in and out by scrolling the MMB. Ctrl+MMB-dragging keeps the Magnifying Glass centered on the cursor. Pressing Alt and scrolling the mouse wheel creates a section view parallel to the view. Figure 3.4 shows the Magnifying Glass in operation, cutting a section view through an assembly.

FIGURE 3.4

Using the Magnifying Glass with the section view

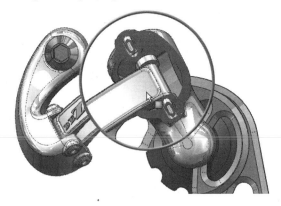

The Magnifying Glass shows up automatically for certain sketch repair operations. It does not have a permanent home in the menus or on the toolbars. You can only access it through the G shortcut key, so the only place you will see it listed is in Tools ⇨ Customize ⇨ Keyboard ⇨ Other.

Note

The intended purpose of the Magnifying Glass is to select small items. You may use it to magnify parts of your drawing, but remember that it will disappear as soon as you select something. ■

Investing in a 3D mouse device

There is no better way to manipulate the view of a 3D part than using a 3D mouse device such as those sold by 3Dconnexion. Other manufacturers offer similar devices such as the SpaceController and Asteroid. These devices allow you to manipulate the model on the screen as if it were in your hand. They are also very appropriate to use with assemblies, as you can use them to manipulate underdefined parts in the assembly.

Some 3D mouse devices also have a good number of programmable buttons that you can use for fast access to functionality such as section view, the "S" toolbar, or the Magnifying Glass.

Controlling Appearances

Appearances in SolidWorks have undergone a huge transformation since the 2007 release. Previous to that, color controls had been difficult to access; at one point, they were buried four levels deep in RMB menus. After a decade of development, SolidWorks 2007 finally consolidated the color interface. But then SolidWorks 2008 completely changed how you control the visual properties of parts. Figure 3.5 shows the Appearance PropertyManager (note that the default appearance is labeled Color).

The Advanced configuration of the Appearance PropertyManager (activated by clicking the Advanced toggle button at the top of the window) has three additional tabs, named Mapping, Illumination, and Surface Finish. These parts of the Appearance PropertyManager are shown in Figure 3.6. These options offer you a wide range of flexibility for altering the appearance of the part.

FIGURE 3.5

The Appearance PropertyManager

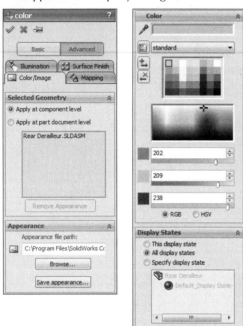

When part appearances are applied in an assembly, you have to consider the override order. *Override order* is the hierarchical order in which one appearance overrides another. For example, an appearance applied to the assembly overrides all other appearances that might be applied. An appearance applied to the part in its own window will be overridden by any other applied appearance. The hierarchy of overrides looks like this (from weakest to strongest):

- Default appearance
- Part
- Body
- Feature
- Face
- Component
- Assembly

When you apply an appearance to a part in the assembly, the popup toolbar that allows you to define the override level at which you would like to place the appearance looks like Figure 3.7.

FIGURE 3.6

The Appearance PropertyManager has several tabs for other properties.

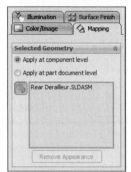  

FIGURE 3.7

You can use these override options when applying an appearance to a part within an assembly.

The icons on the toolbar from left to right are Face, Feature, Body, Part, and Component. The component is just a part or subassembly within an upper-level assembly. You cannot apply an appearance as a subassembly component; it is either the part or the entire subassembly.

Removing appearances and overrides

Just as important as the ability to apply appearances is the ability to remove appearances. Figure 3.8 shows the front face of the truck cab selected and accessing the Appearances drop-down list. From the drop-down list, you can see that the feature called Split Line1 has a black color (appearance override) applied, while the part has an orange color. The red X symbol to the right of each appearance icon enables you to remove that particular appearance.

Another method to remove appearances is to use the Appearance PropertyManager, shown in Figure 3.5. Notice that below the selection box is a grayed-out button that says Remove Appearance. If your selection has an available appearance that can be removed, this button becomes activated.

If you remove an appearance, SolidWorks will use the next applied appearance on the previously mentioned hierarchy list. So removing an appearance applied to a feature causes the appearance applied to the body to be displayed; in this case, no appearance was applied to the body, so it goes next to the part. Because the part color is orange, removing the black cab color causes the faces of the cab to change from orange to black.

FIGURE 3.8

You can remove appearances and overrides.

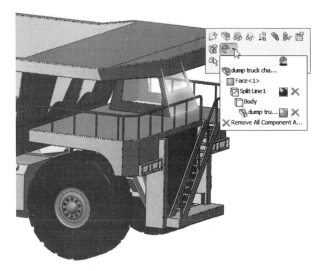

If you remove all appearances from the part, SolidWorks reverts to the default appearance. You can change the default appearance by right-clicking an appearance in the Task Pane and selecting Set as Default Appearance, as shown in Figure 3.9.

The option at the bottom of the drop-down list in Figure 3.8, Remove All Component Appearances, removes any appearances applied at the component level. In the drop-down list shown in Figure 3.8, you can't see any component-level overrides; you can only see the appearance applied to the dump truck chassis at the part level (in the part's own window).

If, however, you look at the assembly colors using the Display Pane, you can see this additional level of information.

Using the Display Pane

The Display Pane flies out from the right side of the FeatureManager via a set of double arrows at the upper-right corner. It displays a quick list of which entities have appearances, transparency, or other visual properties assigned. It also shows hidden parts or bodies for assemblies and multi-body parts. The Display Pane is shown in Figure 3.10.

FIGURE 3.9

Setting a default appearance

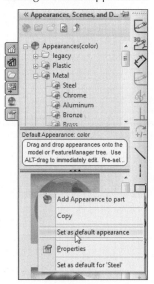

FIGURE 3.10

Use the Display Pane to sort out appearances problems.

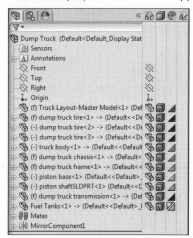

Notice that in the second column from the right, in the last row (the Fuel Tanks component), the Display Pane shows two triangles. The upper-left triangle indicates an appearance override. The part color is gray, while the component override is yellow.

The Display Pane also shows that the Truck Layout Master Model part is hidden, and that the Truck Body part is displayed in wireframe.

The Display Pane is not just a billboard that shows the state of visual properties of parts in the FeatureManager; you can also use it to change the settings. If you click any of the icons following part names in the FeatureManager, you can change the Hide/Show state and the display mode (such as shaded or wireframe), as well as add or remove overrides and even transparency. For visualization, the Display Pane is one of the most useful interface developments added to SolidWorks.

However, the Display Pane doesn't show you everything you need to know. For even more visual and display information, you need to use the DisplayManager.

Using the DisplayManager

You can access the DisplayManager through a tab at the top of the FeatureManager area, next to the ConfigurationManager tab. Figure 3.11 shows an example of what you will see when you open the DisplayManager.

FIGURE 3.11

Opening the DisplayManager

The DisplayManager contains information on three types of visual data in SolidWorks: Appearances; Decals; and Scene, Lights, and Camera. Some of this information is redundant, as it is shown in both the Display Pane and the Appearances callouts in the graphics window. But it is also presented in a unique way.

Controlling Appearances with the DisplayManager

Appearances can be displayed in three different ways in the DisplayManager: by history, alphabetical order, and hierarchy. You can control this option by using the Sort Order drop-down list at the top of the panel window. Figure 3.12 shows how the History option assigns appearances to parts and features. This enables you to edit the appearance for an entire selection of geometry at once. You can also add to the selection set using the RMB menu option Attach To Selection.

FIGURE 3.12

Sorting the appearance assignments by history

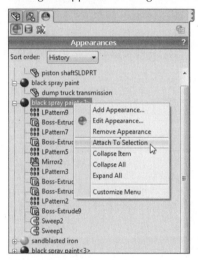

The "history" means that the appearance assignments are sorted in chronological order based on when the materials were assigned to the various parts. There is no reordering as in the history-based feature tree in parts. You might use this feature to keep track of which appearances were edited or added most recently to help you access them.

The Alphabetical listing just lists the appearances alphabetically. This is a great way to group similar appearances together, even from various parts in an assembly.

The final sorting option is Hierarchy. This is the most useful of the three (with the History sorting being second). You can see how it lays out the information in Figure 3.13. Hierarchical sorting organizes the appearance assignments by the override list given earlier in this chapter, namely Components, Face, Features, Body, and Part.

FIGURE 3.13

Sorting appearances by hierarchy

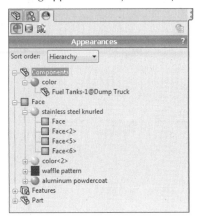

Applying decals

The second item that the DisplayManager manages is decals. You can apply decals to parts or components at the assembly level. Each decal is listed separately, and indented underneath the decal is the geometry to which it is applied. In the example in Figure 3.14, two decals are applied to the truck, one at the assembly level and one at the part level. This is reflected in the way the decals are listed in the DisplayManager.

FIGURE 3.14

Using the DisplayManager to manage decals

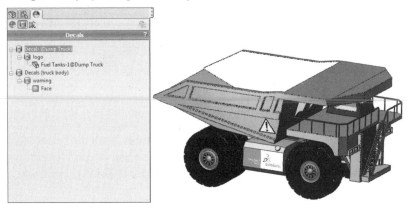

You can get a preview of the decal if you hover the mouse over the name of the decal in the DisplayManager panel, as shown in Figure 3.15. Decals can be hidden or deleted from the RMB menu. You can also hide decals from the View menu.

FIGURE 3.15

Displaying previews of decals and RMB options for decals

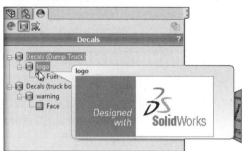

The examples in these images use sample decals that install with the SolidWorks software. The samples are stored by default at `C:\Program Files\SolidWorks Corp\SolidWorks\data\graphics\Decals`. If you want to make your own decal, you should first create a custom location, not in a SolidWorks installation path, where you store all your custom decals; in fact, any decal (even a sample decal) that you use on your models should be stored here.

To establish a location for custom decals, go to Tools ➪ Options ➪ File Locations, and select Custom – Decals from the drop-down list, as shown in Figure 3.16.

FIGURE 3.16

Establishing a library location for custom decals

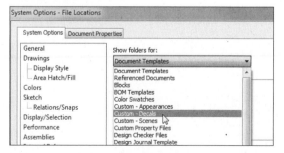

With this item selected, browse to your established library folder for other custom items, and add a new folder for decals. You can add multiple locations if you need to do that. These locations show up in the Decals section of the Appearances tab on the Task Pane.

Note

All of the sample decals use a `*.p2d` **extension, which stands for PhotoWorks2 Decal. PhotoWorks2 is now a defunct product, and it is no longer required to apply decals. If you try to drop common image types into the Task Pane directly by dragging from Windows Explorer, SolidWorks gives you an error. Once you get the images converted to *.p2d, you cannot easily convert them back to a common image type.** ■

A Word on Decal Masks

Many sources of information assume that you know what a mask is and what it does, but SolidWorks users are typically mechanical designers and engineers, not graphic designers. Following is an explanation of the mask technique.

Images are saved in files as rectangular-shaped data. All image files cover the geometry of a rectangle of some size or shape. But you don't always want to apply an image as a decal that is purely rectangular. Look at the warning decal from the earlier dump truck example. The sign is triangular, but you are still working with a rectangular image. The figure below shows two different applications of the warning decal, one with a mask that blocks out the unneeded area and one without a mask.

Warning decal with mask

Warning decal without mask

A mask is essentially a black-and-white image that removes or blocks out the background of another image. The mask is black where you don't want the image to appear, and white where you want the image to show. This figure shows how the mask on the warning decal works:

Warning decal mask detail

You can create masks with many photo-editing software packages, such as IrfanView (`www.irfanview.com`). Change the image to a black-and-white picture (Image ⇨ Decrease color depth ⇨ 2 colors), and then invert the colors to get the mask (Image ⇨ Negative). You need to save the mask file to the same directory as the decal. The following progression of images demonstrates this process.

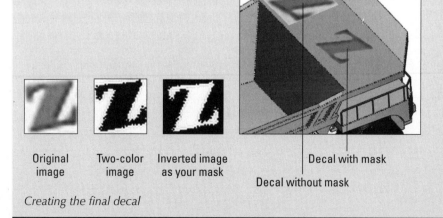

Original
image

Two-color
image

Inverted image
as your mask

Decal with mask

Decal without mask

Creating the final decal

To create a new decal, right-click in the Decal area of the DisplayManager and select Add Decal. Click the Browse button to browse to the image file you want to use as a decal. SolidWorks accepts the following image types to create decals:

- bmp
- hdr
- jpg
- jpeg
- png
- psd
- rgb
- tga
- targa
- tif
- tiff

The application of decals in the assembly seems to have several quirks. Sizing the decal may move it unpredictably, and it seems to project onto all faces rather than just a single face. When the decals are applied on the part level, results are much better.

Controlling Scene, Lights, and Cameras

The Scene, Lights, and Cameras feature has been covered in the *SolidWorks 2011 Parts Bible* in sufficient detail that it isn't covered in this book. The only thing that needs repeating is that the scene is now a document property, and overrides scene or background settings from previous versions. If you prefer a plain background to one of the standard SolidWorks scenes, use the setting at Tools ⇨ Options ⇨ Colors, and make sure the Plain option is selected.

Creating a walk-through

 A walk-through is an animation that simulates what a person would see as they walk through a large-scale design. It was developed primarily for the new architectural tools that are being added to SolidWorks, but it may also be appropriate for certain types of equipment, facility, or site design. Like much of the new functionality that SolidWorks has introduced, some seemingly crucial tools you might need to be successful with the Walk-through feature remain to be developed and implemented. The 2011 release is the first one that offers the Walk-through feature, so you should see a more complete offering in the next release.

This chapter looks at the very large dump truck, which is a good example of equipment design where a walk-through can be useful. To access Walk-through, go to View ⇨ Lights and Cameras ⇨ Add Walk-through. Figure 3.17 shows the walk-through area of the DisplayManager along with the model used for this example. You can do walk-throughs using an interface to direct an avatar, or you can drive the camera along a sketched path. The sketched path method has some overlap with MotionManager animation, which is covered in Chapter 23. Walkthrough is also part of the Large Scale Design, which is covered in Chapter 18.

FIGURE 3.17

Using the DisplayManager to create a walk-through

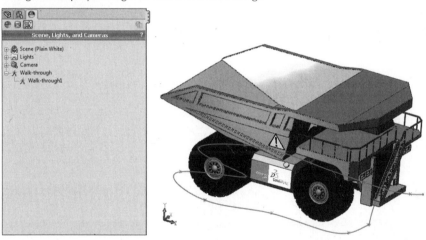

The interface for the walk-through consists of two elements — the PropertyManager and the horizontal toolbar; the initial setup is controlled by the Walk-through PropertyManager, shown in Figure 3.18.

In the PropertyManager, you select a base plane that acts as a floor, and then establish a camera height to simulate the height of your eyes off the floor. If you intend to drive the walk-through using a sketch, you can select the sketch elements in the Motion Constraints selection box. For the most fluid motion, you can use splines. You can also use 2D or 3D sketches.

FIGURE 3.18

Using the Walk-through PropertyManager for the initial setup

Capturing the walk-through requires an interface that is significantly different from other SolidWorks tools, as shown in Figure 3.19. While the interface and documentation refer to an "avatar," you will not see any sort of virtual manikin walking through the model, except in SolidWorks sales demonstrations.

FIGURE 3.19

Using the special walk-through interface

Once you are in this mode, the scroll wheel on your mouse works backwards from standard SolidWorks functionality for zooming.

On the DVD

The dump truck files used for this example are on the DVD. This is a good model for practicing. ■

Here are the steps to create a walk-through:

1. Select a suitable model, preferably one with an interior that you want to virtually wander around inside. This feature works best with models on the scale of buildings.

2. Click the DisplayManager tab in the FeatureManager area.

3. Click the Scene, Lights, and Cameras button.

4. Right-click the Walk-through entry in the list, and select Add Walk-through.

5. Establish a floor or vertical direction using a plane, planar face, edge, or axis, and indicate which end is up. Also, establish the height of your eyes above the floor with a sketch plane for the path.

6. If you are using a sketch path, select the sketch segments in the Motion Constraints selection box.

7. Click the Capture Walk-through button. If you are using sketches to drive the motion, just click the Forward button on the interface, and the camera "walks" along the path. If you are not using sketches, use the arrows on the interface to make the camera (called an avatar in this interface) move.

8. Generate and save the video using the controls on the toolbar.

Using Display States

One of the most commonly used and powerful visualization aids available in SolidWorks is the display states functionality (see Figure 3.20). Display states is simply the ability to save different arrangements showing parts shaded, shaded with edges, in wireframe, with hidden lines removed (HLR), with hidden lines in gray (HLG), or to change colors or hide parts entirely.

FIGURE 3.20

Display states in an assembly

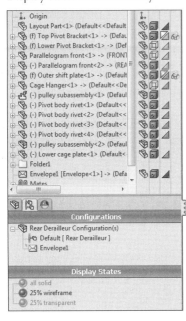

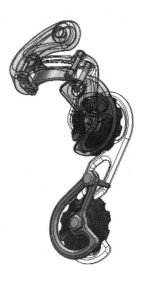

Display states are a great alternative to configurations when it comes to efficiency and speed. Configurations and display states are covered in more detail in Chapter 8, but to summarize the difference, configurations require more processing power (rebuild time) and data storage (file size) than display states. If you are in the habit of making configurations for assemblies just to change the visual characteristics (including Hide/Show), you should consider using display states for that instead.

In addition to being able to use display states to differentiate parts in an assembly, you can use display states for bodies within parts. These capabilities are discussed in this chapter because display states are an extremely valuable tool for visualization in both parts and assemblies.

You can find display states in the lower half of the ConfigurationManager. Notice in Figure 3.20 that the settings you change in display states are also recorded in the Display Pane. To add a display state, right-click in the Display States section of the ConfigurationManager. To activate a different display state, just double-click a grayed-out state.

Using Edge and Wireframe Settings

Using edge and wireframe settings for displaying assemblies can be a very effective way to make interior assembly parts more visible without some of the visual confusion that transparent parts sometimes create. In hand-drawn illustrations, artists often use line drawings to simplify the display of parts, and to some extent you can borrow from that technique within SolidWorks.

For example, the bicycle derailleur assembly shown in Figure 3.20 makes use of wireframe and transparency, as shown in Figure 3.21 in a different view. While a transparent part shows what is behind it, it is still more distracting than a wireframe part. Moreover, wireframe parts can be shown with hidden edges removed or hidden edges visible. As a result, wireframe display offers more options.

FIGURE 3.21

Combining display modes can be very effective in visualizing an assembly.

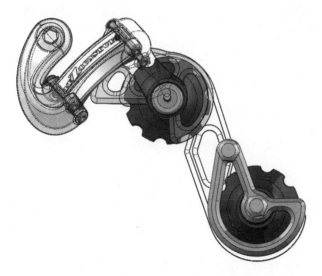

Making the case for shaded with edge display

Years ago, using shaded display with edges slowed computer performance noticeably, but with the development of modern hardware (and to some extent software), adding edges to the shaded display does not slow down performance to the same degree. It makes the display clearer and helps you interact with the parts better. With edge display turned on, you can see where the faces are broken up without any highlighting.

You can use the setting that displays the wireframe and edges, choosing a similar shade as the actual shaded part. There are several reasons for using this setting. The first is that when you change between shaded and wireframe modes, the part doesn't change color, and not all of the parts in the assembly turn black. The default setting for SolidWorks parts is that the wireframe is black, and the edges displayed in Shaded with Edges mode are also black. Having the edges and wireframe colors follow the shaded color just makes a lot of sense.

The setting that makes wireframe and shaded modes the same color is found at Tools ⇨ Options ⇨ Document Properties ⇨ Model Display ⇨ Apply same color to wireframe, HLR and shaded. This setting is shown in Figure 3.22.

Making the wireframe and displayed edges the same color as the shaded model

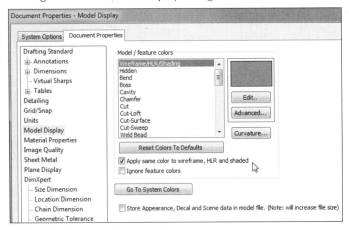

This is a document property, but you can override it by using a system option, found at Tools ⇨ Options ⇨ Colors ⇨ Use specified color for Shaded With Edges mode, shown in Figure 3.23.

This option is turned on by default. If you want the edges to be the same color as the shaded part, you have to turn it off, in addition to selecting the Apply same color to wireframe, HLR and shaded setting (from Figure 3.22) for each individual part (which means it should be set up in the templates that you use to make the parts).

For example, if you have a red shaded model, and use Shaded With Edges mode, the edges of the model vary between pink and dark red, depending on the shade of red you use. The edges always contrast slightly with the shaded color, but the contrast is less than if the edges are always black.

FIGURE 3.23

Overriding the edge color settings

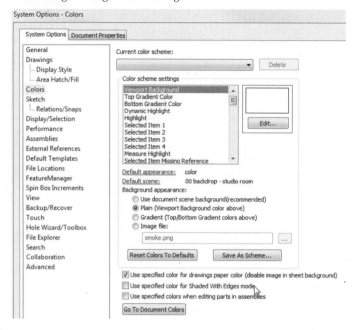

Using tangent edge display

Taking the control of the display of edges one step further, you can also use the tangent edge settings. These settings are found in the View ⇨ Display menu, and are as follows:

- **Tangent Edges Visible.** Displays tangent edges as solid lines, just like all other edges.

- **Tangent Edges as Phantom.** Displays tangent edges in a phantom line font.

- **Tangent Edges Removed.** Displays only non-tangent edges.

The Tangent Edges Removed setting leaves parts looking like a silhouette. You may prefer the phantom setting because you can easily distinguish between edges that actually look like edges on the part and edges that only serve to break up faces on the model. The Tangent Edges Visible setting conveys no additional information, and is the default setting. Figure 3.24 shows a sample part with all three settings.

Samples of the tangent edge settings

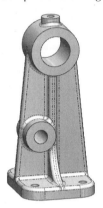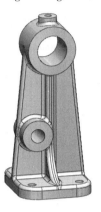

Tangent edges with font   Tangent edges visible   Shaded with edges with tangent edges removed   Shaded without edges with tangent edges removed

Using Assembly Visualization

 Assembly Visualization is a feature that enables you to sort or display parts and subassemblies in an assembly in various ways, including by filename, quantity, mass, or a custom property value. When you click column headers to sort the names of components in the assembly, you can move the sliders on the left side of the FeatureManager to change the display colors of the parts.

You can expand or collapse subassemblies by clicking the assembly symbol at the top of the tree, or you can disable the color display by clicking the color gradient scale. Value bars can also be displayed to show the relative value of each assembly component.

Figure 3.25 shows a model of a bicycle sorting subassemblies by mass. The gray value bars are superimposed on the text in the FeatureManager area. You can open an assembly on your computer and try this for yourself to see the color display.

You can access the Assembly Visualization feature on the Evaluate tab of the CommandManager when an assembly is active, or through the Tools menu. The toolbar icon is with the Tools icons, and you can find it by choosing Tools ⇨ Customize or through the Tools menu in an assembly.

By right-clicking below the FeatureManager Filter when Assembly Visualization is active, you can also save the resulting sorted list to a file in a number of formats, including, xls, xlsx, txt, csv, and pdf.

FIGURE 3.25

Assembly Visualization offers several ways to sort and display the components in an assembly.

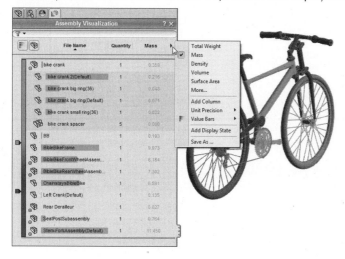

Tutorial: Using Assembly Visualization

This tutorial walks you through the steps necessary to use the Assembly Visualization tool in SolidWorks.

1. **Close other open documents by choosing Window ⇨ Close All.** If you have any documents open from the DVD, you can save them using the Save As command.

2. **Open the assembly file** `BibleBikeAssembly ch3.sldasm` **from the DVD.**

 3. **Select the Assembly Visualization tool from the Tools menu.** You can also select it on the Evaluate tab of the CommandManager or from a custom location by choosing Tools ⇨ Customize ⇨ Commands ⇨ Tools and dragging Assembly Visualization to the toolbar of your choice.

 4. **Toggle the Flat/Nested view icon to see its effect on the tree display.**

5. **Click each available heading to see the tree sorted, based on your selection.**

6. **Turn off the assembly coloration by single-clicking the red to blue fade.**

7. **Sort the tree based on mass.**

8. **Show the tree in flat rather than nested display.**

9. **Click and drag the red and blue sliders up and down to focus on a range of weights.**

 10. **Click to toggle the Value Bars to show the relative weights of parts.**

Summary

Visualization is a key function of the SolidWorks software. It can be either an end to itself if you are showing a design to a vendor or client or a means to an end if you are using visualization techniques to analyze or evaluate the model. In both cases, SolidWorks presents you with a list of tools to accomplish the task. The tools range from the analytical to the cosmetic, and some of the tools have multiple uses.

Part II

Working with Assemblies

Building Efficient Assemblies

C hapter 1 provides a brief introduction to the basics of assemblies, the basics of mating, and so on. The process for putting assemblies together remains the same for assemblies of any size, but once the assembly passes a certain point — and this point is likely different for each user or application — the assembly will benefit from some sort of organization or management techniques. This chapter introduces you to the tools and techniques that are available to help you manage performance issues as well as general-use issues, efficiency, browse-worthiness, and searchability.

Identifying the Elements of an Assembly

From Chapter 1, you know that an assembly can contain parts and mates, and real-world assemblies can become very complex. As the number of parts and design requirements for an assembly grows, you may need to add some of the following types of assembly elements:

- Assembly equations
- Assembly layout feature
- Assembly layout technique
- Assembly reference geometry (plane, axis, point, coordinate system)
- Parts
- Subassemblies
- Folders for parts
- Folders for mates
- Mates
- Assembly features (cuts that are made once the parts are assembled)
- Component patterns
- Mirror components
- In-context reference placeholders
- Smart Fasteners
- Smart Components
- Virtual components
- Envelopes
- Assembly configurations
- SpeedPaks
- Display states
- Assembly Design Table
- Assembly Bill of Materials (BOM)
- Hidden/Suppressed/Lightweight/SpeedPak performance techniques
- Sensors
- Hole Series

You may already be familiar with some of these elements from having worked with part documents. Shown in Figure 4.1, these elements are described in detail throughout this book.

Understanding standard reference geometry items

The three standard planes and the Origin in the assembly FeatureManager design tree should all be familiar to you, as should the other standard items, such as the Annotations, Design Binder, Sensors, and Lights and Cameras folders. These items offer the same standard functionality as their part document counterparts.

FIGURE 4.1

Elements of an assembly

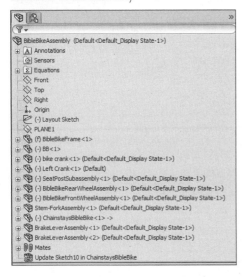

Note

Remember that you can choose Tools ⇨ Options ⇨ FeatureManager page and permanently select or deselect various folders under the FeatureManager header. Also be aware that when some folders are set to Automatic, they do not automatically turn on when they should. In this case, you can manually set them to Show. ■

Working with assembly equations

Assembly equations work like part equations, but with some additional complications and considerations. For example, one of the additional features of assembly equations is the ability to drive the dimensions of one part from another part. The syntax is slightly different for assemblies, as shown in Figure 4.2. Overall, issues with equation order and using driven dimensions on the right side of the equation are the same between parts and assemblies. New in SolidWorks 2011 is the ability to save equations out as a file with a *.txt extension and share the equations between documents.

Cross-Reference

Equations are discussed in detail in Chapter 12. ■

FIGURE 4.2

An assembly equation driving one part from another

Solving external references

Notice the "->" symbol after the Equations folder in the assembly FeatureManager. This means that there is an external or in-context reference. An *external reference* means that aspect of the part is dependent upon something outside of the part. This has file management implications because you must maintain the names of the files so that they always recognize the other file involved in the external relation. *In-context* means that one part has a relation to another part in positions determined by an assembly. So in this case, the in-context external reference can only be solved if the original part, the referenced part, and the assembly where the relationship was created are all open at the same time.

Cross-Reference

In-context references are discussed in depth in Chapter 10. ■

When one part drives another part in this way, the assembly must also be open to drive the relationship. If just the two parts are open individually, then changing the driving part does not update the driven part; because the relationship was created in the context of the assembly, the assembly must also be open to facilitate the change.

Understanding link values and global variables

Link values and global variables also work in assemblies, but they do not work between parts. Local assembly sketches can use these functions, and the parts can use them when edited in the context of the assembly, but they cannot cross any document barriers (links must remain within a single document).

Renaming

Equations update with new part names regardless of how you rename the parts. Names of subassemblies also update when you rename assembly files. This includes renaming a document using the Save As command, using SolidWorks Explorer, or using Windows Explorer. It also includes redirecting the assembly to the new part name, as well as renaming the assembly using each of these techniques. If the assembly can find the part and recognizes the part as the one that it is looking for, then the equation will work.

Some of the methods named previously for renaming parts are not recommended. SolidWorks Explorer and the Save As methods can be effective when used properly.

References between files are a different issue altogether from an equation's references to local filenames.

Recommendations

While assembly equations are certainly a valid way to control part sizes, you should use assembly or part configurations, possibly with design tables, to accomplish something similar. Equations and configurations do not mix well because the two methods conflict over which one controls the dimensions. Configurations with design tables are recommended over equations.

Cross-Reference

Assembly configurations and design tables are discussed in Chapter 8. ■

Caution

You may have unexpected results if a single dimension is controlled from more than one location. For example, if you have a part-level equation and an assembly-level equation, then one of the equations will be automatically set to Read Only and will not be used. ■

Using an assembly layout sketch

 SolidWorks has an assembly feature called Layout that uses a 3D sketch to lay out the major functions of an assembly, and even details of parts. The word *layout* also refers to a technique using 2D sketches in an assembly to do exactly the same thing. The distinction between the technique and the formal assembly feature is bound to be confusing. The Layout feature only works in assemblies, but layout techniques have been used in parts as well as assemblies for many years. This chapter describes the technique, and the Layout feature is discussed in Chapter 6.

When you look at the two functionalities, the feature is definitely intended to be used as an in-context tool, while you can more easily use the technique as a reference for controlling part position (through mating) rather than as a way to directly control the sizes and shapes of the parts. So when you see a reference to a *Layout* (capital), this refers to the formal feature. When you see a reference to a *layout* or *layout sketch* (lowercase), this refers to a technique where a sketch is used at the assembly level to control the assembly in some way.

Cross-Reference

The Layout feature is described in more detail in Chapter 6, while the technique using assembly sketches to lay out an assembly is described in this chapter. The material in this chapter is written as if the Layout feature does not exist, mainly to give you a straightforward view of how the technique works without worrying about two different functions at the same time. ■

The layout sketch is a very useful tool for laying out a mechanism in an assembly or even details on parts within the assembly. Sketches in the assembly have the same characteristics as they do in the part environment. In Figure 4.3, the assembly layout sketch is indicated with a heavy, dashed line for emphasis.

FIGURE 4.3

An assembly layout sketch controls the geometry of the frame and the overall bicycle assembly.

When combined with in-context techniques, assembly layout sketches can help to determine the shape of parts, or the location, size, or shape of features within the parts. You can also use layout sketches to mate assembly components to far more robust and dependable mates, rather than mating part to part. The sketch shown in Figure 4.3 is used for both of these techniques. The shape of the frame and the major pivot points are established in the 2D sketch. The wheels are also mated to the sketch.

When you use an assembly layout sketch for either the in-context part building or simply part positioning, the main advantage that it offers is to give you a single driving sketch that enables you to change the size, shape, and position of the parts. You can use as many layout sketches as you want, and you can make them on different sketch planes. This enables you to control parts in all directions.

Caution

When using layout sketches, it is assumed that the relationships are created such that the sketch drives everything else. However, there is nothing preventing you from using other elements in the assembly to drive the sketch. You should avoid this type of conflict, called a circular reference. It can create sketches that change with every rebuild and can seriously impact rebuild times. When using any type of in-context relations (relations between items in an assembly), you need to be careful to establish one or more driving entities, which are not in turn driven by other entities.

To take this a step further, it is best to avoid daisy chaining, where A drives B, B drives C, and so on. It is a better practice to make A drive both B and C directly. This saves on rebuild times and troubleshooting and reduces future problems with lost references. ■

One of the drawbacks of this technique is that you give up dynamic assembly motion. To move the parts, you have to move the sketch and rebuild. The part does not move until the sketch is updated. If you need to combine layout functionality with dynamic assembly motion, refer to the Layout feature in Chapter 6.

Working with virtual components

Virtual components are parts that are saved so they are internal to the assembly. You can save them out so that they are external to the assembly and can be reused in other assemblies. You can also convert external components to virtual components. Virtual components, as the name suggests, can be either parts or subassemblies.

You may consider using virtual components for certain types of parts that need to be in the assembly but might not require drawings, such as glue, paint, oil, and so on. You may even use virtual components to model purchased subassemblies that flex; for example, you could use a hinge, and use the hinge assembly as a part in a library. However you choose to use virtual components, make sure that they will not cause you any difficulties downstream in file management, data sharing, or other requirements.

Best Practice

Virtual components are useful for concept work in assemblies, but using them is not considered a best practice. Their main limitation is in the form of data management and reuse. You should limit your use of virtual components because the technique promotes what many users and administrators consider to be sloppy practice. Of course your specific situation will dictate best practice for your company.■

Creating assembly reference geometry

Planes and axes are frequently created within assemblies to drive symmetry or placement of parts. You can use assembly layout sketches to create the reference geometry entities. When you create reference geometry within the assembly in this way, be aware that the normal history-based parent/child relationships are still followed. The familiar icons for reference geometry entities are also used in the assembly tree.

Comparing history-based and non-history-based portions of the assembly tree

Because features such as sketches and reference geometry are history based and found in the assembly tree, at least a portion of the assembly FeatureManager is history based. However, not all of it is. For example, the list of parts and subassemblies is not history based.

Sketches and reference geometry may appear before or after the list of parts, subassemblies, and mates. All the remaining entity types that can be found in the assembly FeatureManager are also history-based features, and you can reorder them in the tree. However, several situations can disrupt the process. Under normal circumstances, sketches and reference geometry at the top of the assembly FeatureManager are solved, then the parts are rebuilt if required, and then the mates. This ensures that the sketches and reference geometry are in the correct locations so that if parts are mated to them, all the components end up being the correct size and in the right position.

Assembly-level reference geometry can be created that references component geometry instead of layout sketches. This creates a dependency that changes the usual order. For example, the planes are usually solved before the part locations, but when the plane is *dependent* on the part location, the plane has to be solved *after* the part. If a part is then mated to the plane, you are beginning to create a dependency loop, such that the plane is solved, followed by the part, then the plane again because the part has moved; and then the mate that goes to the plane has to resolve the part.

Best Practice

If you are a bit confused by all of this, don't worry. You can simply follow this rule: do not mate to anything that comes after the mates in the assembly FeatureManager tree. This includes assembly planes or sketches that are dependent on part geometry, as well as assembly features such as cuts, in-context features, component pattern instances, Hole Series, or Smart Fasteners.

This is probably a lot of information if you are a new user, but if you remember this rule, you can avoid creating models with circular references, where A is dependent on B, which is dependent on A — a never-ending loop that causes major problems for large assembly rebuild times. ■

Understanding parts and subassemblies

Parts and subassemblies are shown with their familiar icons in the design tree. You can reorder and group them in folders (which is covered in the next section), and also edit the hierarchy of parts and subassemblies within an upper-level assembly.

The primary task of parts and assemblies is to help you organize your data. Information that relates to the geometry of a single manufacturable item is put into a part. Information that relates to the relationships between the parts is put into an assembly.

You may hear some people argue that there is no real need for parts and assemblies to have different file types — that a part file should be able to handle both the geometric data and the relations between items. You can find CAD programs that work like this, but they tend to be either older or less powerful.

Organizing the data into different file types is actually necessary because it helps your computer know when to calculate which data. For example, if your computer had to rebuild all the features in every part as well as all the mates, rebuild times would suffer greatly.

In addition, parts in an assembly are different from bodies within a part. If you have bodies within a part, all of your features are in one big list, rather than segmented into individual lists for each part. This is important for three reasons: rebuild times, troubleshooting errors, and reusing data. Part features that are in a big list with other part features cannot be organized or separated easily for other purposes.

The advantages of trying to build an assembly as a single part are unclear, other than simplifying file management. It would be highly impractical for any assembly with more than a few simple parts.

Parts are sometimes shown with a feather icon, which indicates a lightweight part, and assemblies can have an icon that indicates a flexible subassembly. Special icons also exist for hidden and suppressed components.

 Indicates a lightweight part

 Indicates a flexible subassembly

 Indicates a hidden component

 Indicates a suppressed component

Creating folders

 You can create folders to organize and group both parts and mates. (This technique is discussed in detail later in this chapter.) Folders help you organize the items in an assembly FeatureManager to make the tree easier to navigate. For example, if you have a large number of fasteners, you should put them in a folder so you can see the overall structure of the assembly rather than a huge list of one item. In this way, folders can help you organize data that is not appropriate for a subassembly to organize for you.

Organizing mates

 The Mates area remains a constant, single folder, but you can organize it by reordering the mates and grouping them into folders. Each mate is shown with a symbol corresponding to the type of mate it is, but the mate folder is shown as a pair of paper clips.

Applying assembly features

In manufacturing, once parts are assembled, secondary machining operations are sometimes applied to them to ensure that holes line up properly, or for other purposes. For example, assembly features can be cut extrudes, cut revolves, or hole features. These features appear only in the assembly, not in the individual parts.

You should not confuse assembly features with in-context features. In-context features are created when you are editing a part in the assembly with a reference between parts, but the sketch and feature definition are in the actual part.

Some new assembly features have been added to SolidWorks 2011 that don't necessarily fit the secondary operations description, such as the ability to make fillets and chamfers as assembly features.

Using component patterns and mirror components

 Component patterns can pattern either parts or assemblies by creating either a pattern defined in the assembly or a pattern that follows a pattern feature created in a part. The pattern is listed as a feature in the assembly FeatureManager, and all the instance parts appear indented from the pattern feature in the design tree. You can hide or suppress each instance, change its configuration, and in most ways control it as if it were a regular part in the design tree.

Because the options for locally defined patterns are comparatively limited, users generally like to use part feature patterns to drive the component patterns when possible.

Component patterns are listed at the bottom of the assembly FeatureManager with a set of components under a LocalPattern icon. The component instances under the LocalPattern can be controlled in several ways, including through assigned configurations, colors, and display states. The pattern can even be dissolved, leaving the components but removing the intelligent pattern that places them.

 Mirror components are listed under a special MirrorComponent icon after the mates.

Performance

To improve performance, it is best to pattern subassemblies if possible. If it is not possible, then patterning a group of parts is the next best option. Making multiple patterns, one for each part, is an inefficient way to accomplish the same thing. ■

Looking at in-context reference Update Holders

 It is difficult to get a good picture of assemblies in general without including a discussion about in-context references, but to treat the subject properly, it also requires its own section, and in fact, this book gives in-context modeling its own chapter (see Chapter 10). When you create a reference between parts in an assembly, the assembly needs to remember which parts are involved in the reference and what assembly creates the spatial relationship between them.

When you create the relation, a placeholder has to remain in the assembly to hold this information. This placeholder is called an *Update Holder*. The Update Holders do not display by default. To see them, you must right-click the top level in the FeatureManager and select Show Update Holders. They only exist when in-context references exist in the assembly, and there is one Update Holder for each in-context sketch or feature. You cannot do very much with the Update Holders, other than query them for parent/child relations and to list the external relations, but they serve as a reminder that you have in-context references to maintain. For more information on this feature, see Chapter 10.

Popular perceptions of in-context techniques aside, in-context modeling is a powerful extension of parametric design techniques. If you follow the best practice suggestions outlined in Chapter 10, you will soon gain confidence and master this technique rather than being intimidated by it. The functionality works, and if you do not abuse it, it will serve you well.

Using Smart Fasteners

 Smart Fasteners are assembly features that automatically select Toolbox parts for use in standard-sized holes, and you can use them in many different ways. The Smart Fastener feature in the assembly FeatureManager is used to edit the definition of the Smart Fastener, which can include adding items such as nuts and washers. You can also use Smart Fasteners in conjunction with the Hole Wizard to place appropriate holes and matched fasteners, all in a single step.

Cross-Reference

Smart Fasteners, the Toolbox, and the Hole Wizard are discussed in detail in Chapter 14. This is the only functionality beyond what is found in SolidWorks Standard edition that is dealt with in this book. ■

Applying the Hole Series

The Hole Series is a Hole Wizard–type feature that you apply in an assembly. This wizard leaves the feature icon in the assembly but also adds features directly to the individual parts. It also adds in-context Update Holders to the assembly FeatureManager, as shown in Figure 4.4. The Hole Series is designed to go through a series of parts, placing the appropriate hole type in each part: counterbore, through, threaded, and so on.

FIGURE 4.4

Adding in-context Update Holders

Using SpeedPaks

 A SpeedPak is a derived configuration of an assembly that keeps only selected solid bodies and faces but can represent the rest of the assembly with non-selectable display data. You can use a SpeedPak to replace an entire subassembly within an upper-level assembly. SpeedPaks are intended to increase performance with very large assemblies and drawings.

Figure 4.5 shows the SpeedPak PropertyManager on the left, which you access by right-clicking an active configuration and selecting Add SpeedPak. Each configuration can have only one SpeedPak.

The center image in Figure 4.5 shows the configuration list with the SpeedPak indented under the Default config, and the entire assembly. The right image shows the SpeedPak inserted into an assembly document, consisting of a single face and two solid bodies. Notice the special icon associated with SpeedPaks. You can change a part in an assembly from or to a SpeedPak in the same way that you would change a configuration using Component Properties.

Remember that this is a tool for increasing assembly speed, and to increase speed there is always something that you have to give up. A SpeedPak is similar to Lightweight assemblies and components in that it is display-only data. If your expectations of the tool match its actual functionality, you will be very satisfied with what the SpeedPak offers. For this reason, it is important to understand the abilities and limitations of SpeedPaks.

Using ghosts

You can use any faces or bodies that you select in the Include lists either manually or through the Quick Include sliders (which automatically select bodies and faces based on size) in assemblies to mate to or in drawings to dimension to. Any geometry that is not selected is included as a ghost — it displays, but you cannot select it. When you move the cursor near ghost geometry, the ghost fades away, revealing only selectable geometry. Notice at the bottom of the SpeedPak PropertyManager that you can also choose to remove the ghost data and further increase the memory savings.

Sharing self-contained data

The SpeedPak is self-contained. All the selected face and body geometry is saved inside the assembly. If you want to send someone a visual representation of an assembly, you can make a SpeedPak configuration and send only the assembly file — no parts are required. This is the equivalent of being able to put an eDrawing file into an assembly.

Using SpeedPaks with drawings

You can even use SpeedPaks with drawings. Just remember that only edges created by the faces or bodies in the Include lists can be dimensioned to. Some functionality exists for the ghost data, such as BOM inclusion and numbered balloons. Ghost data displays as gray on the drawing, while geometry in the Include list is black.

FIGURE 4.5

Managing SpeedPaks

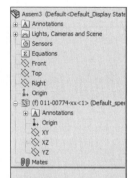

Model of Garmin assembly from the SolidWorks demo sets

Using Subassemblies

The primary tool for organizing assemblies is the subassembly. A subassembly is just a regular assembly that is used as a component in another assembly.

Best Practice

You are not limited to a specific number of levels of subassemblies, although for different sizes and types of assemblies you should establish a best practice for your company. For example, you might establish a guideline that suggests that assemblies of 100 parts or fewer go no deeper than three levels. ■

You can use several criteria to determine how subassemblies are assigned:

- Performance
- BOM
- Relative motion
- Pre-fabricated, off-the-shelf considerations
- According to assembly steps for a process drawing
- To simplify patterning

The underlying question here is based on the multiple functions of your SolidWorks assembly model. Is the assembly intended primarily for design? For visualization? For documentation? For process documentation? When used primarily for design, the assembly is used to determine fits, tolerances, mechanisms, and many other things. As a visualization tool, it simply has to look good and possibly move properly if that is part of the design. As a documentation tool, how the model relates to the BOM is important, and so is the order in which subassemblies are added. As a process tool, you need to be able to show the assembly in various intermediate states of being assembled, likely with configurations.

Companies create multiple assembly models for different purposes. Sometimes the requirements between the different methods are contradictory and cannot all be met at the same time with a single set of data. Again, depending on what information you need to be able to extract from your SolidWorks models, you may want to approach assembly modeling and organization differently, and you may need to create multiple assembly models to accomplish everything.

Creating subassemblies from existing parts

You can create subassemblies from parts that already exist in an assembly. To do this, select the parts that you want to add to the subassembly by holding the Shift or Ctrl key, or using box select techniques, and then select Form New Subassembly Here from the right mouse button (RMB) menu. You are then prompted to assign a name or possibly select a template for the new subassembly.

Caution

When creating a new subassembly from existing parts or when moving parts into or out of a subassembly from the upper-level assembly, some things may be lost. For example, mates are moved from the upper level to the subassembly. If you have in-context relationships, they may be removed. You cannot easily undo operations that create subassemblies. ■

Once you have created the subassembly, you can add or remove components using the drag-and-drop method. For example, Figure 4.6 shows the cursor that indicates that the part named Left Crank is being moved into the subassembly named bike crank. To move a part out of a subassembly, you can simply drag the part into the upper-level assembly.

FIGURE 4.6

Moving parts into a subassembly

Note

When you are dragging a part out of an assembly and into another one, you may again see the cursor symbol that appears in Figure 4.6. If you do not want this to happen, hold down the Alt key while dragging. The cursor symbol changes to the Reorder cursor (a reversed, L-shaped arrow), and the part is placed after the subassembly rather than within it. ■

Inserting a new subassembly

Along with the RMB menu option Form New Subassembly Here, which takes existing parts and puts them into a newly created subassembly, you can use another option called Insert New Subassembly. The names of these functions do not adequately describe the difference in what they do. Insert New Subassembly inserts a blank subassembly at the point in the design tree that you indicate by right-clicking it. You can place components into the subassembly by dragging and dropping them from the main assembly, or you can open the assembly in its own window and insert parts by using the usual methods, such as drag and drop, or the Insert ⇨ Component tool.

Dissolving subassemblies

If you would like to get rid of a subassembly but want to keep its parts, then you can use the Dissolve Subassembly option through the RMB menu. This option has some of the same consequences of the Form New Subassembly Here option in that mates are moved from the subassembly to the upper-level assembly, and you may lose in-context relations and assembly features.

Organizing for performance

In SolidWorks, performance refers to speed. Subassemblies can contribute to speed-saving modeling techniques by segmenting the work that the software needs to do at any one time.

Solving mates

The mates that contribute to putting the pieces of an assembly together are solved at the top assembly level. Under normal circumstances, subassemblies are treated as static selections of parts that are welded together, and their mates are not solved at the same time that the top-level assemblies' mates are solved. This segmenting of the mates leads to improved performance by only solving one set of mates at a time.

Mates are usually solved as a single group unless there is a special situation, such as mates to in-context features, component pattern instances, or an assembly feature, all of which have already been described in this chapter. When one of these situations occurs, the mates have to be divided into separate groups or solved multiple times. This is done behind the scenes so that the user does not have to worry about it. Multiple rebuilds affect the user only in terms of rebuild times.

Using flexible subassemblies

 When you put a subassembly into an upper-level assembly, the mates for the parts of the subassembly are not solved in the upper-level assembly. This means that if a subassembly is a mechanism, the mechanism does not allow Dynamic Assembly Motion in the upper-level assembly, and it is considered rigid. For example, in Figure 4.7, the front fork is a linkage mechanism, but it is also a subassembly. Without reassembling the parts of the fork in the upper-level assembly, you can allow the mates from the fork subassembly to be solved in the upper-level assembly by using the Solve As option in the Component Properties dialog box, shown in Figure 4.7. When you select the Flexible option, you enable the mates of this subassembly to be solved in the upper-level assembly, which allows the parts of the subassembly to move in the upper-level assembly. To access the Component Properties dialog box, right-click the subassembly and select Component Properties from the menu.

Flexible subassemblies have become more reliable and easier to use over the last several releases of SolidWorks. You should work with them or do some experimentation to see if they assist your modeling process. If you find they cause trouble in some situations, they are easy enough to deactivate.

Working with legacy data

If you have assemblies that were built in older versions of SolidWorks (such as SolidWorks 2001 and later), you should know that mates used to be split up into multiple *mate groups*, which represented the groupings that mates were solved in. This was forced by mating to the history-based features in the assembly FeatureManager. SolidWorks no longer displays mate groups, but the groups are still used in the background to solve mates. This is another change that SolidWorks has made to the software that simplifies the user's interaction with it, but it also makes it obvious that things are now happening behind the scenes that you can't control.

FIGURE 4.7

Creating a flexible subassembly

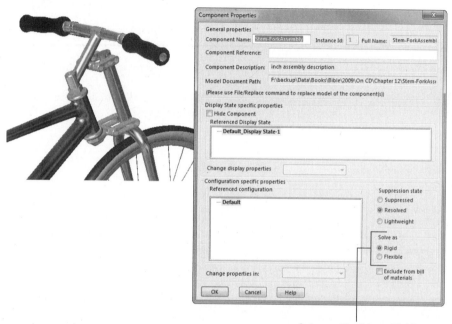

Solve as Flexible or Rigid

Organizing for the Bill of Materials

The Bill of Materials, or BOM, is a table that is placed either into a drawing of an assembly or in an actual assembly. This table shows the parts used in the assembly and includes other information, such as part numbers, quantities, descriptions, and custom property data.

Cross-Reference

SolidWorks BOM functionality is discussed in depth in Chapter 17. ■

Businesses often represent assemblies and subassemblies in various ways by using Manufacturing Resource Planning (MRP) or Enterprise Resource Planning (ERP) software. The methods that accountants and manufacturers use to organize assemblies are not always the same as those that engineers or designers might choose, but some companies require the BOM on the drawing to match the MRP or ERP Bill of Materials.

Best Practice

When you are forced into modeling something in an unnatural way to satisfy an outside demand such as special BOM requirements, it might be best to detach the unnatural part and model normally. In the situation mentioned here — where MRP is forcing how the assembly is put together by requiring the BOM to match MRP — you should separate the BOM from the assembly structure rather than building an assembly that makes other SolidWorks functions difficult. This ensures that the BOM becomes a manually maintained document. Alternatives to this approach would be to make configurations or entirely new assembly documents to drive the BOM. ■

Grouping subassemblies by relative motion

A more natural way to group subassemblies is by considering relative motion. In the bicycle example, each wheel is a separate subassembly because it moves as a unit relative to the rest of the assembly. Figure 4.8 illustrates where relative motion might be on the bicycle.

FIGURE 4.8

Grouping subassemblies by relative motion

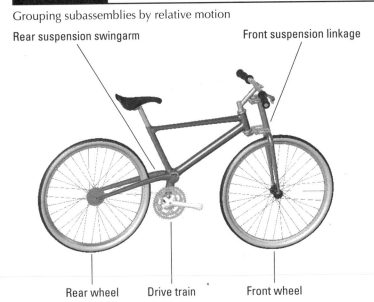

Rear suspension swingarm

Front suspension linkage

Rear wheel   Drive train   Front wheel

Grouping subassemblies by relative motion is great for assembly modeling, but it does not usually reflect product reality very well. Using this method, you often end up with parts in the subassembly that will have to be disassembled in order to actually put the physical parts together. However, if your only consideration is ease of modeling, then you should probably use this method.

Organizing groups of purchased components

If you are modeling a product that is created from a shopping list of purchased components, then it may make the most sense to organize your subassemblies into groups of parts that are purchased together. In fact, purchased subassemblies are often modeled as single parts, except when relative motion is required in the purchased assembly.

For example, in the bicycle assembly, the sprockets on the rear wheel are purchased as a separate unit, and yet the part that mounts onto the wheel moves relative to the sprockets that are driven by the chain. This is an example of a purchased part that would be modeled as a subassembly to show relative motion. The bicycle chain, another purchased subassembly, has not yet been added to this assembly, and is a more complex model. The desire to show all of the individual links moving through the path may override both the complexity of assembling it and the performance considerations of exercising all of the mates.

Although the BOM method of organizing assemblies sometimes leads to unnatural solutions, you should not discard it altogether. If you can devise concessions in order to make the BOM work automatically, then you should do this.

Depicting an assembly process

Manufacturing and assembly processes need to be documented as well as individual part design. You often need to create exploded-view assembly instructions for manufacturing or service documentation at each step of a multistep assembly process. Figure 4.9 shows an example of this type of process documentation.

This is certainly a task that is different from the initial design or modeling of the assembly, and it may require an entirely separate assembly model. Generally, you can perform the different steps by using a separate configuration for each process step, with exploded views for each configuration.

Influencing item numbering

Balloons number the parts according to the item number that is used in the BOM, but, of course, you do not know the item numbers until the BOM is created. You can influence the item numbers by reordering the parts in the assembly (which is discussed later in this chapter), by manually editing item numbers, or by manually numbering the balloons.

Separating steps

Each step corresponds to an assembly configuration (discussed in Chapter 8), and you can place them on a separate sheet of the drawing (discussed in Chapter 16). Each configuration can have multiple exploded views, if necessary, to show all the steps.

FIGURE 4.9

Assembly process documentation

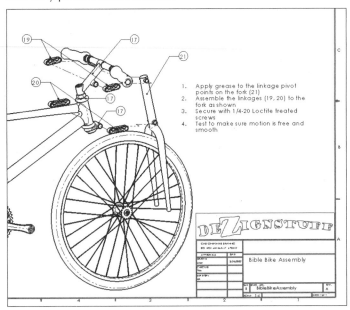

Patterning considerations

The most efficient way to pattern large numbers of components in an assembly is to pattern a single subassembly with all the components to be patterned in it. While this may not be easily combined with some of the other considerations that were mentioned previously, it is another option that you can use to organize assemblies.

Using Folders

Folders are primarily used in the assembly FeatureManager for grouping parts and mates into either special classifications for easy browsing, or groups that you can easily hide and show, or suppress and unsuppress, as appropriate. Figure 4.10 shows some examples of these folders.

Folders that are used to organize components and mates

Creating folders in the FeatureManager

You can add folders to the assembly FeatureManager in one of two ways:

- By adding existing components to a new folder
- By creating an empty new folder

Using Add To New Folder

To use the Add To New Folder tool, right-click a component or mate (or selection of components or mates) and select Add To New Folder from the menu. This moves the component or mate into the folder. Folders do not affect the assembly in any functional way; they are simply for organization, to speed browsing and selection.

Using Create New Folder

To simply create a new folder without putting anything into it right away, right-click either the Mates area or the components list and select Create New Folder from the menu.

Adding items to existing folders

To move an item into an existing folder, just drag the item (component or mate) onto the folder. If the folder is expanded, showing its contents, then you can also drag the item as if you were reordering a feature in the FeatureManager of a part, and drop it in the list of items where you would like it.

If you are dragging a part or assembly and trying to put it immediately after an assembly, a cursor like the one shown in the center image in Figure 4.11 may appear. This cursor means that the part is going to become part of the assembly. If this is not what you are trying to do, then hold down the Alt key while dragging; the part is placed into the folder immediately after the assembly, instead of being made a part of the assembly. The third image in Figure 4.11 shows the cursor with the Alt key pressed.

Reordering items in the tree

There are times when you may want to reorder items in the assembly tree. For example, you may want to place items close to one another in the tree, or you may be preparing to put items that are next to one another into a single folder. You may also want to reorganize components for the BOM display.

You can reorder mates simply by dragging them. Mates display in the order in which they are created, but the order is not significant. You can reorder them however you like.

Components also display in the order in which they are added to the assembly, and you can reorder them in any way you like.

FIGURE 4.11

Moving items into folders

Best Practice

It is often useful to have an ordering strategy that helps you work with the model. For example, you should try to keep the biggest parts, the parts that everything else is mated to, or the part that is treated as "ground," as the first part(s) in the assembly. Then put the fasteners and other cosmetic or BOM-driving parts at the end of the tree, usually in a descriptive folder. ■

Working with Tree Display Options

Display options for items in the FeatureManager are often overlooked but can be useful for displaying data about parts, subassemblies, mates, and features. Figure 4.12 shows the RMB options. You must right-click the top-level assembly name in the FeatureManager to access this menu.

Note

All these options are available for parts and drawings as well, except for the View Features option and the View Mates and Dependencies option, which are related to assemblies. ■

Showing feature names and descriptions

If you are so thorough that you have added descriptions to your features, then you are doing well. The center image in Figure 4.12 shows a section of the FeatureManager for the bicycle frame part; some of the features have had descriptions added with both of the options for feature names and feature descriptions turned on. The image to the right in Figure 4.12 shows the result of turning off the feature name, with only the feature description option turned on. If no feature description has been created, then the feature name displays. Feature descriptions always appear in double quotes.

FIGURE 4.12

Tree display options in assemblies

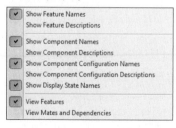  

Showing component and config names and descriptions

The image on the left in Figure 4.13 shows the default arrangement of displaying component and configuration names in the assembly FeatureManager. This example uses the rear wheel assembly from the bicycle assembly. In assemblies, you cannot turn off the component names and the component descriptions. SolidWorks issues this statement when you try to turn off both the name and the description: "You cannot hide both the component name and the file name. At least one must be visible in the tree."

FIGURE 4.13

Component name options

Using names other than the part filename in the assembly FeatureManager

The message in the previous paragraph distinguishes between the *filename* and the *component name* that is listed for individual parts or subassemblies in the assembly FeatureManager. You can specify the component name in the Component Properties dialog box by right-clicking the component in the assembly FeatureManager and selecting Component Properties.

However, you can assign a name for a component that is different from the filename only if a special setting is turned off. (The setting defaults to on.) You can access this setting by choosing Tools ➪ Options ➪ External References ➪ Update Component Names When Documents Are Replaced. These are the steps that you have to go through if you want to change how the part and subassembly names display in the assembly FeatureManager.

After going through the steps in the preceding paragraph, you still receive the warning message about the filename and the component name. This is apparently an "unintended feature," or bug, and should say that you cannot turn off both the component name and the component description at the same time.

There may be a situation where you want to show a name other than the filename in the FeatureManager. For example, your company may be using sequential part numbers for the filenames that are difficult to read, and you want something descriptive in the design tree so that you do not need a cross-reference sheet next to your computer that equates filenames to meaningful descriptions.

If you prefer, you can avoid a lot of problems by just using the part description instead of the filename or the component name. The choice is up to you.

One of the problems with using the component description is shown in Figure 4.14, where the user did not enter proper descriptions for the parts, and SolidWorks used the default description in the templates. The tire and spokes use configurations, which display in the figure.

FIGURE 4.14

An example of what can occur when you do not enter proper descriptions for parts

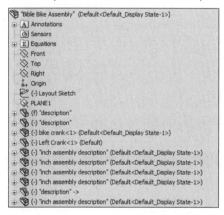

Using Component Reference per Instance

SolidWorks 2010 added Component Reference capabilities. In the Component Properties dialog box, shown earlier in Figure 4.7, the second row from the top enables you to enter Component Reference information. This is typically used in electrical diagrams for similar components with different values, such as power ratings, capacitance, or resistance. Instances of the same component in a SolidWorks assembly that have the same Component Reference can be listed together on a BOM. Instances with different Component References are listed separately on the BOM. Figure 4.15 shows parts listed in a pattern that have Component References listed for each instance.

In order for Component References to be used in balloons on an assembly drawing, the drawing must have a BOM with a Component Reference column. BOMs are handled in detail in Chapter 17, where the topic of Component References will be revisited.

FIGURE 4.15

Listing parts in an assembly containing Component Reference information

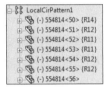

Viewing features, mates, and dependencies

The last set of options shown in Figure 4.12 determines whether you see the part features or the assembly mates after the name of each component in the assembly tree. The default setting is for the part's features or the subassembly's components to display, just as if the part or subassembly were open in its own window.

The View Mates and Dependencies option can also show the features, but they are placed into a separate folder. This option makes it very easy to see the mates that are assigned to an individual component. For example, in Figure 4.16, the image to the right shows the mates directly under the BibleBikeFrame part. This often makes troubleshooting much easier because it isolates the mates for a single part. Notice also that the first folder under the part name in the image to the left in Figure 4.16 is the Mates folder. This indicates that, regardless of whether you choose to display mates or features, you always have easy access to the other type.

FIGURE 4.16

You can view features, as well as mates and dependencies.

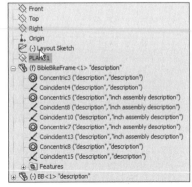

The View Mates tool is extremely valuable for looking at how an assembly is held together with mates. When you right-click a component in the assembly and choose View Mates from the RMB menu, SolidWorks highlights the component you clicked, and makes all parts that mate to that component transparent. Any parts that are not related are hidden. SolidWorks also displays a small dialog box with the list of mates touching the component you clicked.

Figure 4.17 shows this arrangement using the Bible Bike assembly. If you are a SolidWorks veteran, this works very differently from the way View Mates worked in the past, but you will probably agree that this is a big help in mate visualization.

If you Ctrl-select multiple components before starting the View Mates tool, SolidWorks no longer displays the common mates in bold format; it just lists them at the top of the dialog box.

Showing mates in the PropertyManager pane

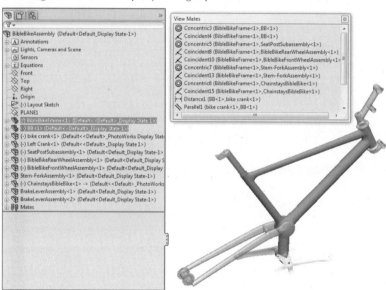

Working with Assembly Tools

SolidWorks is incredibly complex software and contains a variety of tools that allow you to do many small tasks. This is particularly true with assemblies. Users expect so much of the software in various areas, and everyone needs something different. Many tools exist to help you put together, maintain, and evaluate efficient assemblies. This section describes important tools that don't fit into the other categories.

Using Sensors

 Sensors provide an alert if a monitored value goes outside of a specified range. Sensors can be used in parts or in assemblies. The types of values that you can monitor with sensors are dimensional values, mass, volume or surface area, interference detection between selected components, and Simulation data (stress analysis values).

To create a sensor in an assembly, right-click the Sensors folder in the assembly FeatureManager. If the Sensors folder is not there, choose Tools ➪ Options ➪ FeatureManager page and turn it on. Figure 4.18 shows the Sensor setup interface.

FIGURE 4.18

Setting up a sensor in an assembly

Using the AssemblyXpert

 You can find the AssemblyXpert on the Tools menu, or choose Tools ➪ Customize from the menu to place it on the Assembly toolbar. AssemblyXpert gives suggestions about things you can do to improve the performance of an assembly, such as updating files to the new version and looking at Large Assembly Mode, and existing errors in the assembly mates, in-context, and supposedly circular references.

The AssemblyXpert does not identify circular references. A circular reference is a list of parts referencing other parts where the references form a loop, with one part as the start and end point. AssemblyXpert could not find this kind of reference loop.

Figure 4.19 shows the results in the AssemblyXpert dialog box. Notice that the results include the information formerly included with the Assembly Statistics: part and subassembly count, along with mates, unique parts, and so on.

AssemblyXpert results

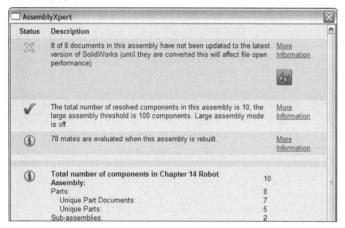

The information in the AssemblyXpert is certainly useful, particularly for newer users who may not know to look for things like this already. You can use it as both a diagnostic and a learning tool.

Tutorial: Arranging Assemblies

In this tutorial, you take an assembly that is already put together, group its components into subassemblies, and then convert one subassembly into a flexible subassembly. Note that some of the commands and RMB options you are asked to select may not be shown on the truncated RMB menus. To remedy this, click the double-arrow at the bottom of the RMB menu or choose Tools ➪ Customize ➪ Options from the menu, and click the Show All button for both shortcuts and menu customization.

Follow these steps to learn how to effectively arrange items in an assembly:

1. **Start by opening the** `Robot Assembly .sldasm` **file from the DVD.**

    Notice that the names for the files are long and somewhat difficult to read. This would also apply for files that use sequential numbers for the filename instead of a descriptive name.

2. **To display a more readable name, right-click the name of the assembly at the top of the FeatureManager, select Tree Display from the menu, and then turn on Show Component Descriptions.** Repeat these steps, and this time turn off Show Component Names.

   Figure 4.20 shows the display of the FeatureManager after the change. Even the top-level assembly uses its description rather than its filename.

FIGURE 4.20

Simplifying the FeatureManager display to include descriptions

Notice that two components still use their clumsy filenames rather than easy-to-read descriptions. This is because descriptions were never entered for those two components.

3. **Open the Large Cylinder Piston part by left-clicking the part in the FeatureManager and then clicking the Open icon.** Choose File ⇨ Properties from the menu and make sure the Custom tab is active. Create a new property called **description**, assign a type of text, and then enter **large cylinder piston** for the value. Save the part (Ctrl+S is a fast way to do that) and then flip back to the assembly (the fastest way to do that is to hold down Ctrl and press Tab).

   If the display has not yet updated, press Ctrl+Q to force the tree to rebuild.

4. **Open the Large Cylinder Body part.** In this part, choose File ⇨ Save As from the menu. Leave the name as is, but where it says Description, enter **large cylinder body**, as shown in Figure 4.21. Click Yes when asked if you want to replace the document of the same name. Flip back to the assembly when you are done. You may have to rebuild to see the change update.

FIGURE 4.21

Adding a description in the Save As dialog box

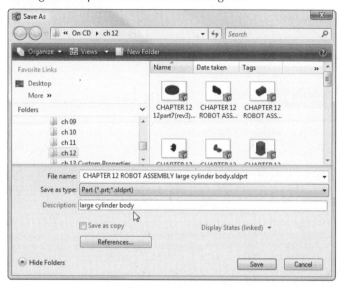

5. **Press and hold Ctrl and select the large cylinder piston and the large cylinder body parts from the FeatureManager.** Then right-click and select Form New Assembly Here from the menu. If your assembly template has a description, it appears in the FeatureManager. If not, the filename appears.

   You have just created an assembly as a virtual component while the parts are external documents. If you switch the tree display to show filenames, you see what is shown in Figure 4.22; the name of the assembly is `Assem1^Robot Assembly`. So the virtual component gets a default name (Assem1) followed by the name of the parent assembly (Robot Assembly) to ensure that it has a unique name, if there are other virtual components in other assemblies.

6. **Press and hold Ctrl and select the Base Motor, the Main Arm Motor, and the Cradle, and make another new subassembly.** After you create this subassembly, right-click it and select Save Assembly (In External File) from the menu. Change the name of the assembly from Assem2 to Cradle. Save it in the same path as the rest of the parts.

   Once a virtual component is saved externally, you cannot use the Undo command to reverse it, but you can right-click the external file in the FeatureManager and select Make Virtual from the menu.

FIGURE 4.22

The newly created virtual component subassembly and its external parts

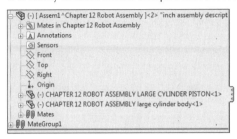

In Figure 4.23, notice that several of the mates came along into the new subassembly. These are the mates between the motors and the cradle. The mates that locate the cradle to the other parts in the assembly have remained in the upper-level assembly.

FIGURE 4.23

The cradle assembly brings along internal mates

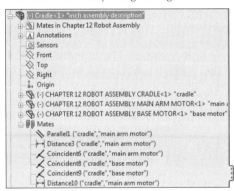

Note that you cannot undo the subassembly operations. If you need to remove the assembly but keep the parts, right-click the assembly and select Dissolve Subassembly from the menu.

If you try to move the parts in the assembly, you should notice that all parts work as they should, except that the Main Arm does not move up and down. This is because you turned the cylinder and piston into a subassembly, and the subassembly mates are not solved in the top level, which means the subassembly cannot move within itself.

To get around this, you need to make the subassembly into a flexible subassembly, which will solve the subassembly's mates in the top-level assembly.

7. **Right-click the cylinder subassembly in the FeatureManager, and select Component Properties from the menu.** In the lower-right corner of the dialog box, there is an option to Solve as Rigid or Flexible. Change this setting to Flexible.

After you click OK and return to the assembly, the main arm moves as it did originally, and the piston moves in and out of the cylinder. Notice that the symbol for the assembly changes when it is changed to a flexible subassembly.

Tutorial: Managing the FeatureManager

This tutorial uses the `BibleBikeAssembly.sldasm` file located in the Chapter 4 folder on the DVD. Open the file and follow these steps to learn about managing the FeatureManager:

1. **Create a new subassembly within the existing assembly using the parts BibleBikeFrame and ChainstayBibleBike.** Name this new assembly `FrameAssembly.SLDASM`.

2. **Reorder the new FrameAssembly to the top of the design tree.**

3. **Reorder the other parts and assemblies so that the bigger assemblies appear higher on the list, and the parts appear at the bottom.** (Remember that Alt+dragging a component prevents it from being placed into a subassembly.)

4. **Drag the part called BB (for Bottom Bracket) into the Frame Assembly (drag without using the Alt key).** The assembly FeatureManager at this point is shown in Figure 4.24.

FIGURE 4.24

The starting state and the state as of Step 4

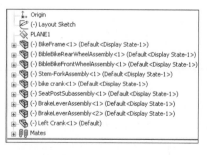

5. **Select both wheels and then select Add To New Folder from the RMB menu.** Name the new folder **Wheels**, and move it to the bottom of the tree.

6. **Expand the Mates folder, select the first four mates, and put them in a new folder (select Add To New Folder from the RMB menu).** Name the new folder **Centering Mates**.

Summary

Assemblies are more than simply parts and subassemblies put together with mate relationships; several other types of features and placeholders can also exist in the assembly FeatureManager. Organizing assembly components is fairly straightforward and can offer benefits for finding parts as well as controlling suppression and display states globally.

The assembly FeatureManager contains several options for the data to display for subassemblies, parts, configurations, and features within. Remember that all the data that you include in your SolidWorks documents can be accessed and reused later on, so it is worth the effort to name it properly. Descriptions can be very important, both at the part level and also for features and configs.

Getting More from Mates

In SolidWorks assemblies, mates are the basic units that make everything work together. When properly handled, mates enable your assembly to react predictably to changes in parts in exactly the same way that sketch relations drive changes in part features. As a result, mates and sketch relations often have the same function and even the same weaknesses to watch out for.

This chapter goes one step further with mates, by not just simply putting parts together with Coincident and Concentric mates, but also mating parts when tolerances, gaps, and symmetry become issues. You will also learn about the more advanced mate types that may be useful for special situations.

One of the assumptions made in this chapter is that assembly mates are not just used for positioning parts, but also for motion. Making motion work takes a little more than just establishing the right spatial relationship between parts; it usually also involves analyzing the open degrees of freedom.

Some users take a static approach to putting parts together into assemblies, by simply placing parts at the correct X- and Y- coordinates without assigning any relationships to the parts around them. This defeats most of the purpose of creating parametric, associative assemblies in the first place. Assembly mates are an extremely powerful tool for enabling your assemblies to react predictably to change.

Applying Mates

An average assembly of 100 parts is likely to have almost 300 individual mates. If you created these parts one at a time, taking perhaps a minute for each mate, you would spend five hours just applying mates. You should avoid applying mates whenever possible — assuming you still get the correct results — because this allows you to spend more time doing something else. In this section, you will learn efficient mating strategies, as well as speedy techniques.

As you apply mates to parts in your assembly, keep in mind that SolidWorks has high- and low-risk mating schemes (see Chapter 1). High-risk schemes generally involve mate techniques that are easier, but are also more likely to have problems later in the evolution of your model, such as lost references or conflicts with other mates. More stable mating schemes favor reference geometry such as planes and axes, and possibly sketches over model faces and edges.

Mating through the Mate PropertyManager

The Mate PropertyManager is the default method for applying mates, and you used it briefly in Chapter 4. The Mate PropertyManager interface is shown in Figure 5.1. You can create mates by pre-selecting entities before applying the Mate command or selecting them after you open the Mate PropertyManager. The three types of mates are Standard, Advanced, and Mechanical.

FIGURE 5.1

The Mate PropertyManager interface

Understanding the mate workflow

If you make a lot of mates, it is important to have an efficient rhythm when working with the interface. Assuming you have the Mate PropertyManager already active, the most efficient way to use the Mate interface is as follows:

1. Click the first entity.

2. Click the second entity.

3. Click OK on the right mouse button (RMB) cursor icon to accept the default.

   Alternatively, if the automatic default mate type is not the mate that you want to apply, select it from the popup list, shown in Figure 5.2.

FIGURE 5.2

The Mate selection popup list

4. Click the green check mark icon on the popup list.

5. Repeat Steps 1 to 4.

6. After the last mate, press Esc, the green check mark icon, or the red X icon in either the PropertyManager or the confirmation corner (located in the upper-right corner of the graphics area).

Changing the view and model position

Sometimes you will have to rotate the model to achieve the correct view in order to select faces or edges. There are also times when you will want to *pre-position* so that the model snaps into the correct position automatically. You can rotate individual parts in an assembly by clicking and dragging with the RMB. (Dragging the RMB over a part rotates that part.) You rotate the view by dragging with the middle mouse button, or MMB. You can move parts by dragging them with the left mouse button, or LMB. You can pan the view by pressing Ctrl and dragging with the MMB. When you drag a part with the LMB while the Mate PropertyManager is active, SolidWorks does not add the selected entity to the Mate Selections list.

To summarize these actions:

- To rotate an individual component in an assembly, click and drag with the RMB.

- To move an individual component in an assembly, drag with the LMB.

- To rotate an assembly view, drag with the MMB.

- To pan an assembly view, Ctrl+drag with the MMB.

Also, be aware of the view manipulation tools, available by clicking the triad in the lower-left corner:

- To rotate normal to an axis, click the triad axis in that direction.

- To rotate by 15° about an axis (you can specify the angle at Tools ⇨ Options ⇨ View), Alt+click the triad axis in that direction.

- To rotate by 90° about an axis, Shift+click the triad axis in that direction.

- To activate the mouse gesture wheel, drag the RMB in blank space (dragging the RMB over a part rotates the part).

- To zoom to fit, double-click the MMB in the graphics window (same as using the F hotkey).

Tip

If you have a Spaceball or other 3D motion controller, you can perform all these actions easily and simultaneously using one hand for view rotations and the other hand for selections. You can also use a Spaceball to move parts. ■

Applying the Select Other command

The Select Other command enables you to select items that are hidden by other items. It is often used to select faces that are hidden behind other faces without rotating the part. You can apply the Select Other command through the RMB menu. Right-click where the face would be if you could see it. A list of entities displays. You can select the entity you want from this list or from the graphics window.

Moving your mouse over an entity in the list highlights the entity in the graphics window. Pressing Tab or scrolling the mouse wheel cycles through the entities one by one. Clicking faces with the RMB hides them, which enables you to see farther down into the part or assembly. Clicking with the LMB in either the graphics window or the selection list box selects the item. Figure 5.3 shows the Select Other cursor and dialog box.

FIGURE 5.3

The Select Other cursor and dialog box

Although you can use this selection method for other purposes, it is often used for selecting faces for mating.

Using Multiple Mate mode

 Multiple Mate mode enables you to select one face in order to mate multiple parts to it. Figure 5.4 shows the interface for this mode, which you can toggle to from the Mate PropertyManager interface. The Multiple Mate mode icon looks like a paper clip with a lightning bolt running through it. This function works only with the Standard Mate types, not with any of the Advanced mates, which are discussed later in this chapter.

The Multiple Mate mode interface

You can create a special folder for all the multiple mates by selecting the Create multi-mate folder check box in the Mate Selections PropertyManager. You can also automatically link the values for distance and angle mates with link values by selecting the Link dimensions check box. When you use the Link Dimensions check box, distance or angle values for mates made in multi-mate mode will be set equal with link values.

Taking advantage of SmartMates

SmartMates are mates that you can create automatically by dragging one part onto another without invoking the Mate command. There are three different methods that you can use to apply SmartMates:

- Alt+dragging the part
- Dragging the part from one window to another
- Using Mate references

Alt+dragging a SmartMate

Probably the easiest way to create a SmartMate quickly is by Alt+dragging. One, two, or even three mates can be applied at once by holding down the Alt key while dragging a face or edge from one part onto a face or edge on another part.

When you are dragging a part while pressing the Alt key, the part is made transparent to enable you to see other part faces that you may want to mate it to. A special cursor appears when a SmartMate is about to be applied. Figure 5.5 shows the cursors that appear for adding Concentric and Coincident mates.

FIGURE 5.5

Applying a SmartMate

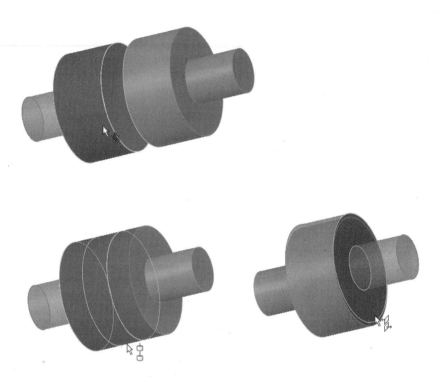

When you drop the face or edge onto the mating face or edge to complete the mate, you must use the popup Mate toolbar to accept or alter the mate. In the examples in Figure 5.6, a face is being dragged onto another face. However, you can also drag edges and vertices. Mates are limited to being either Coincident or Concentric.

The *peg-in-hole* mate is actually the combination of a Concentric mate and a Coincident mate. This is the type of mate that is created between a screw and a hole, and is the result of Alt+dragging a circular edge onto a circular edge. When the circular edges are created by the intersection of a cylindrical face and a flat face, the Concentric mate goes between the two cylindrical faces, and the Coincident mate goes between the flat faces. The peg-in-hole mate is illustrated in Figure 5.6. The top two images show the state of the parts before the SmartMate. The image in the lower left shows the SmartMate orienting the part in the wrong way so that the two parts interfere. In the image in the lower right, the part to which the SmartMate is applied has been reoriented by the Tab being pressed before the SmartMate is accepted by the part being dropped.

FIGURE 5.6

Using the SmartMate to create the peg-in-hole mate combination

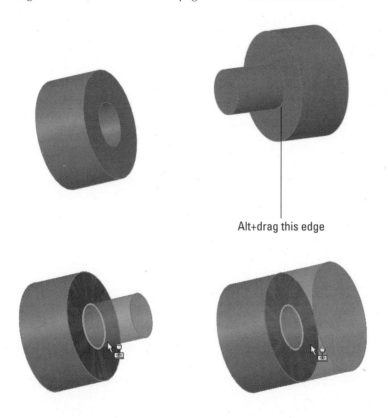

Alt+drag this edge

Tip

You can press the Tab key to flip the alignment if a SmartMate tries to put parts together in the wrong way. If you are in the process of Alt+dragging, make sure to release the Alt key before pressing Tab. The Alt+Tab combination is a Windows shortcut to show a list of open applications. ■

 You can also Alt+drag a SmartMate to mate origins and coordinate systems. When you Alt+drag one origin onto another, you get the special cursor shown to the left, and when you release the mouse button, the popup option box shown in Figure 5.7 appears. If you only want the origin points mated Coincident, turn off the Align Axes option. With the Align Axes option on, the origin points will be Coincident and the X, Y, and Z directions will be parallel to the same directions in the counterpart origin.

FIGURE 5.7

Using the Align Axes option on the popup option box for origin-to-origin SmartMates

Dragging between windows

You can simply Ctrl+drag a face of the part to the face of another part in a different SolidWorks window. It is probably most useful to tile windows before creating this kind of SmartMate.

Using Mate references

Mate references are model faces, edges, or vertices that are pre-selected and used in a SmartMate-like fashion when you drag a part in from Windows Explorer or from a library window. Mate references are discussed in Chapter 15 in the course of discussing library parts. They are a great way to automate common mates with commonly used parts, such as library parts.

Mating with macros

If not all the confirmations and extra mouse-clicks to open and close windows are for you, and you are just applying simple mates, then you may want to use macros to mate parts. Macros are not going to give you the same flexibility, but for simple and predictable mates, they greatly increase your speed. You have to have the parts ready to go when you press the macro button, or you will create the wrong mate.

You can find macros for coincident, concentric, parallel, perpendicular, and tangent mates in the DVD folder for Chapter 5. For example, to use the concentric macro, you need to pre-position the parts so that they are within 90 degrees of the proper alignment, have one of the parts mated in place such that only one part will move, select the two cylindrical faces, and then run the macro. Ideally, the macro should be connected to a hotkey, so the workflow for this process will be extraordinarily fast. You can click one face, click the other face, then press the hotkey, and the parts fly together.

Note

To connect a macro to a hotkey, first put the macro in a folder identified at Tools ⇨ Options ⇨ File Locations ⇨ Macros, and then restart SolidWorks. Then use the Keyboard dialog box (Tools ⇨ Customize ⇨ Keyboard) to assign hotkeys to the macros in the list. ■

Like SmartMates, macros work best for the simpler mate types where you do not need to select any options. The workflow with macros can be very fast, but you have to have the parts pre-positioned and be very sure of what you want.

Mating for Motion

Dynamic Assembly Motion is a powerful tool for visualizing the motion of mechanisms in SolidWorks. It works best if there is a single open *degree of freedom*. Assemblies with more open degrees of freedom can do some unexpected things when you try to move them. If there are multiple possible positions, the parts could jump between those positions. If the assembly has parts with unrelated open degrees of freedom, such as fasteners not constrained rotationally on an articulating arm, you may have some difficulty getting the motion you want.

Keep in mind that not all assemblies can function in multiple roles. For example, if you are trying to use a single assembly for an accurate BOM drawing, an exploded view, Dynamic Assembly Motion, setting up in-context references, and a rendering, you may find that even if you are using configurations (covered in Chapter 8) to divide the types, they might still interfere with one another.

For these reasons, you may want to consider separate assemblies for types of data that are most likely to interfere with other purposes, such as anything to do with moving parts around — Dynamic Assembly Motion, Animation, Rendering, or others.

Another question you need to ask yourself is whether the Dynamic Assembly Motion is actually necessary. Often people just set it up because they can, and may be paying consequences unnecessarily. For example, parts with in-context references should not have motion between the parts involved. If a referenced part moves, a hole or boss on the referencing part may also move. This sort of thing can be managed, but it requires discipline, and there is an element of risk to the integrity of your data should an untrained or forgetful employee gain access to it.

Analyzing degree of freedom

When working with motion in SolidWorks, you need to be comfortable with the concept of degrees of freedom. When inserted into an assembly, each model begins with six degrees of freedom:

- Translation in X (tX)
- Translation in Y (tY)
- Translation in Z (tZ)
- Rotation about X (rX)
- Rotation about Y (rY)
- Rotation about Z (rZ)

When applying mates, and especially when troubleshooting motion or overdefinition problems, it is important to look at how each mate translates into degrees of freedom being tied down. For example, a Coincident mate, planar face to planar face, ties down one translation degree of freedom (in the direction perpendicular to the faces) and two rotational degrees of freedom (about directions which lie in the plane of the faces). What remains are two translational degrees of freedom in the plane of the faces and one rotational degree of freedom about an axis perpendicular to the planar faces.

A point-to-point Coincident mate ties down three translational degrees of freedom, and the part can only rotate.

An edge-to-edge Coincident mate ties down two translational and two rotational degrees of freedom. As a result, a part that you mate in this way can only slide along the mated edge and rotate around the mated edge.

Tip

When using face-to-face Coincident mates, it takes three mates to define a block type part fully. When using edge-to-edge Coincident mates, it only takes two mates. ■

Something to be careful about is that a degree-of-freedom analysis frequently predicts an over-defined mate scenario when SolidWorks does not in fact display any errors or warnings. For example, if one block is mated to another with the simple case of three face-to-face Coincident mates, and each Coincident mate ties down one translational and two rotational degrees of freedom, then the mating scenario ties down nine degrees of freedom, so the part is over-constrained by three rotational degrees of freedom. However, SolidWorks has a lot of forgiveness built in, so it commonly allows situations like this, where parts are severely over-constrained. When troubleshooting any over-constrained situation, you should not take this forgiveness for granted. If SolidWorks reports an assembly as over-constrained and the reason is not intuitively obvious, try reducing some of the degrees of freedom constrained. For example, instead of making two faces coincident, consider making them simply parallel, or mate a point to a face instead of two faces.

Best Practice

This may be an overly cautious approach, but it can mean the difference between an assembly that works and one where errors are frustratingly persistent. If you are careful to approach all parts with the degree-of-freedom analysis in mind such that any newly added mate does not duplicate any of the degrees of freedom that are already tied down, you will have fewer assembly mate errors and fewer problems with assembly motion.

This means that instead of having the traditional three face-to-face Coincident mates, you would have one face-to-face Coincident mate (one translational degree of freedom, two rotational degrees of freedom), one edge-to-face Coincident mate (one translational degree of freedom, one rotational degree of freedom), and one point-to-face Coincident mate (one translational degree of freedom). This accounts for three translational and three rotational degrees of freedom without over-defining any of them.

It is true that SolidWorks internally compensates for over-defined degrees of freedom, but relying on it to do so and then tempting fate by methodically over-defining all assemblies is a risk that you do not have to take, even though it is common practice. ■

Setting up successful motion

The best bet for creating motion in a SolidWorks assembly is to leave open a single degree of freedom. This means that there is only one way the part can move, back and forth, by translation or rotation. Computers in general do not respond well to ambiguity. Dragging an item that might move in several ways is more likely to cause jerky or hesitant motion.

A good example of this kind of problem with motion can be found in one of the sample assemblies that installs with SolidWorks. This example is included on the DVD for your convenience, and is shown in Figure 5.8. The filename for the assembly is `Plunger.sldasm`.

FIGURE 5.8

An assembly displaying best bet for motion

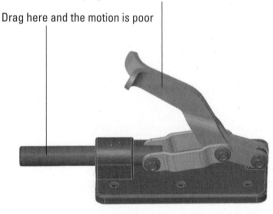

Drag here and the motion is smooth

Drag here and the motion is poor

If you drag the assembly parts from the location shown in Figure 5.8, the performance varies. This is because when you drag the handle parts, for every position of the handle, there is only one solution for the rest of the parts. However, when dragging the plunger bar, for every position of the plunger bar, there are two possible positions for both the links and the handle (one possibility is as shown, and the other would be with the handle interfering with the base of the assembly). This kind of ambiguity causes problems in SolidWorks assemblies such as assemblies that have open degrees of freedom but will not move or only move in a jerky fashion.

Another example of difficulties related to open degrees of freedom and motion is shown in Figure 5.9. The grippers at the end of the arm move when the rest of the arm moves, but the grippers cannot be independently controlled by dragging. To fix this problem, you may want to either use the Fix/Float option (available through the RMB menu) or use configurations with mates suppressed or unsuppressed. Fix the part that you want to remain stationary closest to the part you want to move. Remember to float the part when you are done. Also, be aware that fixing a part may over-define some mates. You can open this assembly from the DVD, in the filename called `Robot Assembly.sldasm`.

FIGURE 5.9

A robot arm assembly with degree-of-freedom conflicts

Working with Advanced and Mechanical Mate Types

Advanced and Mechanical mate types greatly expand the number of ways that you can put parts together into assemblies. Advanced mate types include Symmetric, Width, Path Mate, Linear/Linear Coupler, and Limit. Mechanical mate types include Cam, Hinge, Gear, Rack and

Pinion, Screw, and Universal Joint. You can access Advanced and Mechanical mates by expanding the corresponding panels on the Mate PropertyManager shown in Figure 5.1.

 If you understand sketch relations, the standard mate relations fall into place easily. One exception is the Lock mate. Lock is different from Fix, which pins a part to the background. The Lock mate locks two parts to one another, so that they always maintain the same relationship to one another, regardless of how they move with respect to other parts. This section goes into some detail of all the Advanced and Mechanical mates, with a brief example of each.

Symmetric mate

 The Symmetric mate works a lot like the Symmetry relation in sketches, except that a plane is used as the plane of symmetry instead of a construction line. Figure 5.10 shows a Symmetric mate being applied to the gripper jaws. The Symmetric mate is listed in the Advanced Mates pane of the Mate PropertyManager.

FIGURE 5.10

Applying a Symmetric mate

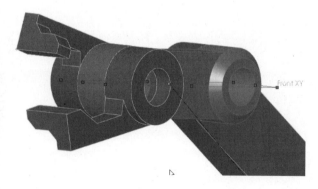

Cam mate

 The Cam mate creates a special instance of either the Coincident or Tangent mate. Four conditions exist with the Cam mate:

- **Coincident.** The vertex on the follower mated to a cam that is created from a single closed-loop face (spline, circle, and ellipse).

- **Tangent.** The cylindrical or planar face mated to a cam that is created from a single closed-loop face.

- **CamMateCoincident.** The vertex on the follower mated to a cam that is created from multiple faces. This condition enables the follower to go all the way around the cam, not stopping at the broken faces or following the extension of a single face.

- **CamMateTangent.** The cylindrical or planar face mated to a cam that is created from multiple faces. This condition enables the follower to go all the way around the cam, not stopping at the broken faces or following the extension of a single face.

Figure 5.11 shows both single-face and multi-face cams, along with the Cam Mate interface. The two assemblies are available from the DVD in the file named Cam.sldasm.

Using Cam mates

If you open the assemblies and spin the cam plate, you will notice that in both cases, the flat follower does not work very well. In fact, in the single-face cam assembly, it does not work at all.

Note

Barrel (cylindrical) cams cannot use the Cam mate to create cam motion, but they do work with the Path mate. Path mates are covered in more detail later in this section. ■

Width mate

 The Width mate is often used as a replacement for the Symmetric mate in situations where parts are modeled with some tolerance and have a gap rather than touching face to face. The Width mate requires two pairs of faces to be selected, and works particularly well when a part has to be spaced evenly between two faces and there is no mid-plane, for example, when a square key is placed in a square keyway that is somewhat larger than the key. If a mid-plane is available, the Symmetric mate may be a better option, or at least a faster one to mate, given that the Symmetric mate only requires two faces and a plane. Figure 5.12 shows a good application for a Width mate as well as the PropertyManager interface for the mate.

FIGURE 5.12

Applying a Width mate

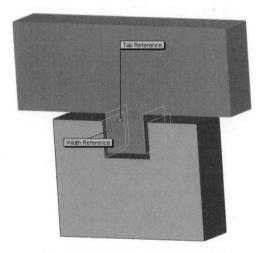

Gear mate

 The Gear mate enables you to establish gear type relations between parts without making the parts physically mesh. You can also apply gear ratios and directions without physical connections, so that you can have a shaft in and a shaft out of a black-box transmission. You can open the assembly shown in Figure 5.13 from the DVD. It is named `Gear Mate.sldasm`. To see the effect of the mate, open the assembly and rotate the parts. Then edit the mate and change the ratio and direction. The selection for the Gear mate is just two cylindrical faces.

FIGURE 5.13

Applying a Gear mate

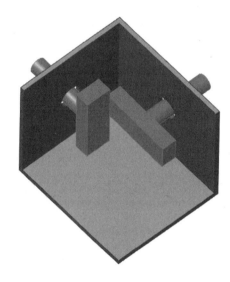

Rack and Pinion mate

 The Rack and Pinion mate takes rotational motion of one part and turns it into translational motion for a second part. Again, the parts do not need to be physically connected and can be simple representations of the actual geometry that is needed to drive the motion in the real world. Figure 5.14 shows an assembly that uses the Rack and Pinion mate. You can find this assembly on the DVD with the filename `RackPinionMate.sldasm`.

FIGURE 5.14

Applying a Rack and Pinion mate

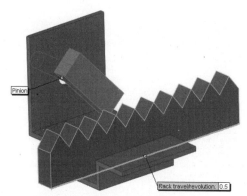

Limit mates

You can apply limits to distance and angle mates in order to allow the parts to move within a certain range of values. Figure 5.15 shows the PropertyManager interface for the Limit Angle mate. Limit mates accept zero and negative values that are not normally accepted for dimensions in SolidWorks. When used properly, Limit mates can be an extremely powerful tool for creating more realistic motion in assemblies.

FIGURE 5.15

The LimitAngle PropertyManager

On the DVD, open the assembly named `Robot Limit Mate.sldasm`. Drag the Robot Tower part. Notice that it only rotates within a limited angle. LimitAngle2 is the mate that is driving this motion.

Screw mate

The Screw mate functions just the way the name suggests. For every revolution of a part relative to another part, the part moves in a linear direction by a specified amount. This mate requires two cylindrical faces and a pitch value, as shown in Figure 5.16.

FIGURE 5.16

Setting up a Screw mate

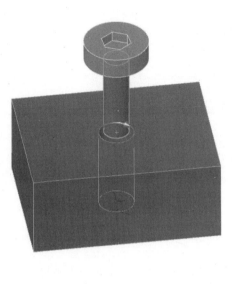

Screw mates can be handy for lead screw animations. Although they are not recommended for general modeling, for animations, they are a fantastic addition to the mate toolbox.

Path mate

The Path mate is the one that makes complex barrel cam motion possible, as well as other types of path-driven motion. Another application for this mate type beyond barrel cams is for the motion of a camera in a fly-through animation. The Path mate requires a point or vertex on one part and a curve selection on a second part. If the path selection is not just a single sketch or curve entity, it requires the use of the SelectionManager, which enables you to select multiple end-to-end entities to form closed or open paths. Figure 5.17 shows the setup for a Path mate.

FIGURE 5.17

Setting up a Path mate

Note

On the barrel cam in Figure 5.17, notice that a sketch point is being driven along the path. In reality, this does not exactly reflect the motion of the follower around the cam surface. The Path mate does not take into account the tangent contact point between the surfaces; it simply drives the point along the curve. There is a slight amount of error in this scenario, such that the leading or trailing surface of the follower will interfere with the cam on angled slopes, depending on the angle of the cam surface. Also note that the Path sketch entity has nothing to do with the Path mate; it is not required to make the Path mate work. ■

Linear Coupler mate

 The Linear Coupler mate relates the motion of one part in one direction to another part in either the same or a different direction. It also enables you to apply a ratio between the motions. The directions do not have to be parallel or anti-parallel; they can be at right angles, or at any angle. The mate only controls motion in one direction, so other directions are free to move.

You can use this mate to simulate symmetric motion or geared motion without modeling the rest of the detailed mechanism. Figure 5.18 shows the setup for this mate.

FIGURE 5.18

Setting up a Linear Coupler mate

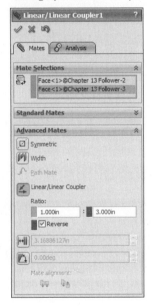

Hinge mate

 The Hinge mate is just a shortcut for making a Concentric and a Coincident mate, but it does it all in a single feature and a single interface. Figure 5.19 shows the PropertyManager interface for the Hinge mate.

FIGURE 5.19

Setting up a Hinge mate

Belt/Chain

 The Belt/Chain assembly feature is not technically a stand-alone mate type, but it uses mates to accomplish its task. You can use the Belt/Chain feature in two ways: to create relationships between sketch blocks or to create relations between parts. This feature also creates a sketch and a solid part representing the belt or chain. You can initiate the Belt/Chain function from a toolbar button on the Assembly toolbar or through the menus by choosing Insert ⇨ Assembly Feature ⇨ Belt/Chain.

Editing and Troubleshooting

You should become proficient with editing and troubleshooting assembly mates. If you are not comfortable with repairing and modifying mates, you may find assemblies frustrating to work with. However, once you master the techniques, you will be more confident and willing to experiment with assembly changes.

Editing existing mates

If you are editing just one mate, then you can simply right-click it and select Edit Feature (or if you are using Context Toolbars, left-click it and click the Edit Feature button). Remember that you can find mates in places other than the Mates folder at the bottom of the assembly FeatureManager; most notably, you can find them in folders under the parts that they are mating together.

You can also select View Mates from the RMB/LMB menu for a part in an assembly, and for multiple selections of parts. This brings up a small window that contains all the mates involving the selected parts.

You can make several types of changes to mates, including changing the selections, the mate types, and the mate alignment. These types of changes are all shown in Figure 5.20, which displays a mate being edited. The selected faces are highlighted in the graphics window.

FIGURE 5.20

Editing a mate

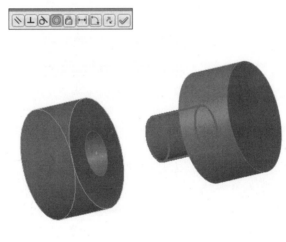

To edit multiple mates consecutively without exiting the Mate PropertyManager, it is best to pre-select the mates. Pre-selected mates are shown in the Mates panel in Figure 5.20. You can switch from editing one mate to another by simply selecting the new mate in the Mates panel. If you select only one mate before clicking Edit Feature, but realize later that you want to edit multiple mates, you can select more mates through the FeatureManager.

When mate entities are lost, the mate appears grayed out, as shown in Figure 5.21. Also shown is a mate that cannot be resolved — for example, a face coincident to two points separated in space. You can repair the missing reference problem by selecting the Invalid reference in the Mate Selections window and then selecting the correct item from the graphics window.

The yellow triangle is a warning symbol that shows that a mate is satisfied, but it is in conflict with another mate that is not satisfied.

FIGURE 5.21

Repairing mates with missing references

 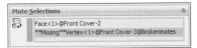

Troubleshooting assembly mates

It is best to troubleshoot an assembly mate problem as soon as it appears, and not after it has become complicated by other issues. Failed mates also cause performance problems because SolidWorks keeps trying to solve the mates that are in conflict with one another.

Assembly problems often appear to be far larger than they actually are. For example, the entire tree may light up with warnings and error symbols when one extra mate is applied. You can use several approaches to troubleshoot situations like this. For example, you can purposely over-define mates just to locate a leftover mate or a mate that is not supposed to be there.

Two types of symbols may help you distinguish the kinds of errors that are present in different mate features. The yellow triangle that contains an exclamation point is not an *error*; it is actually more of a *warning*. It tells you that this mate is in conflict with other mates (this symbol is used for a variety of warnings), but that the mate is still satisfied. One of the other mates with which it conflicts is probably not valid, and so this type of warning is usually accompanied by an actual error symbol where the mate is not satisfied.

The red circle containing the X is a failed mate. This mate is in conflict *and* is invalid. If it is also a Coincident mate, then the two Coincident entities are not coincident.

Troubleshooting warnings and errors

SolidWorks distinguishes between errors and warnings. Errors are situations where a condition is not satisfied, such as a coincident mate where the selected entities are not coincident. Errors are marked with a red symbol. Warnings are symbols that mark situations where a conflict exists, but otherwise all conditions are met. For example, both a coincident and a perpendicular mate use the same faces. One mate will have an error and the other a warning, because one can be satisfied, but not both.

You can use the following troubleshooting techniques to work with assemblies where errors or warnings exist:

- **Last in first out.** When a mate is added that causes warning and error signs to appear throughout the design tree, you can usually correct the problem by removing this last mate.

- **Single elimination.** If you are sure that the last mate added is correct, then you may want to go backward up the tree starting at the bottom, suppressing individual mates until you find one that causes the warning and error signs to disappear from the tree.

- **Single addition.** It may be easier to take the opposite approach, by suppressing all but the mates that you are sure of, and then gradually unsuppressing mates until the conflict reappears.

- **Suppress a part.** With all the mates active, try suppressing an individual part to see whether this makes a difference. If it does, then unsuppress the part and look at the mates for that part in the Mates folder under the part.

- **MateXpert.** The MateXpert is an automated routine that creates subsets of groups of conflicting mates. Each subset of mates has one mate that is not satisfied because of the conflict. This may help you to find the cause of the conflict. Figure 5.22 shows the MateXpert interface. You can access the MateXpert from the RMB menu on mates with errors.

FIGURE 5.22

The Mate Xpert interface

Examining Mate Options

The Options pane of the Mate PropertyManager is shown in Figure 5.23. Most of the options are self-explanatory, except for Use for positioning only. This option positions a part but does not apply a parametric mate. Some users select this option often for various applications where they need the part located precisely, but do not need or want a mate feature in the tree. One example of using this option is to position a part for Animator animations where the part does not move according to a mate.

FIGURE 5.23

The Options pane of the Mate PropertyManager

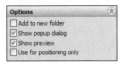

Reviewing Mate Best Practices

Sometimes best practice recommendations can contradict one another, and for each best practice recommendation that you find, there are likely several specific situations where the recommendation is invalid, or even a bad idea. As a result, you should apply the following recommendations carefully. Don't take best practices too seriously, but at the same time you should not disregard them altogether. Some companies use best practice recommendations as modeling standards. The less experience your SolidWorks team has, the more you need standards of this sort. Every situation has a different need for best practice, and probably even a need for a set of rules that are different from the ones laid out here. You can think of this set of mate best practices as a starting point for the discussion at your own company.

- Each assembly should have at least one part that is either fixed or fully mated to the standard planes of the assembly so that it cannot move relative to the assembly.

- You should use fixed parts sparingly. One part that serves as a "ground" for the assembly should be fixed. Other than that, the parts of imported assemblies are sometimes fixed to keep them from being moved accidentally.

- Do not mate to time-dependent features in the assembly tree, or to in-context features in parts. This can create circular references where the assembly must be rebuilt multiple times to fully resolve the positions of all parts and sketches.

- When possible, it is best to mate all parts to the "ground" part. Creating *daisy-chain* mates (where A mates to B, which mates to C, and so on) forces the mates to be solved in a particular order, which may take more time to solve. If all the mates relate to established assembly references, the mates may be more stable. Chapter 11 describes using a skeleton in a part to make sketch and feature relations. You can apply a similar concept in an assembly, by mating parts to an assembly sketch.

- When possible, leave part positions fully defined, especially when other geometry is dependent upon the position of parts. Some examples include in-context features, assembly features, or assembly-level reference geometry, which are dependent on part geometry.

- Constraining the rotational degree of freedom for components such as screws, washers, and nuts is usually considered excessive. At times, too many open degrees of freedom may cause problems with complex motion, such as a gripper on the end of a robotic arm. SolidWorks functions well when there is a single, well-defined path between two points, but when there are multiple options, the software may become confused.

- Do not leave errors unresolved in the tree.

- Remember to use subassemblies to break up the number of mates that are solved in the top-level assembly.

- Limit the use of flexible subassemblies.

- Do not mate to entities that may be removed later by suppressing or unsuppressing features, especially edges or faces that are created by features such as fillets. For this reason, it is usually best to wait until parts are complete before you use them to create an assembly, although this is rarely practical.

- Use a degree-of-freedom analysis to prevent mates from becoming over-defined.

Tutorial: Mating for Success

In this tutorial, you will put together a model of a robotic arm to better understand some of the mate issues discussed in this chapter. Follow these steps to mate for success:

1. **Open the part named** Chapter 5 Robot Base.sldprt **from the DVD.**

 2. **In the part document window, click the Make Assembly From Part icon, and click the cursor on the Origin of the assembly to place the part Origin at the assembly Origin.** The part is automatically fixed in place.

3. **Choose Insert ➪ Component ➪ Existing Part/Assembly.** Click the Browse button in the PropertyManager and find the part called Chapter 5 Robot Tower.sldprt. This part contains a Mate reference to help you mount it to the base. If you bring the cursor near the big circular hole in the base, you can see the preview of the tower snap into place. Click to accept this placement. Figure 5.24 shows this placement in progress. Notice that the cursor appears as a SmartMate cursor for the peg-in-hole mate. When the part is dropped, check the mate list to confirm that a Concentric and a Coincident mate have been applied by the Mate reference.

FIGURE 5.24

A Mate reference being used to SmartMate a component

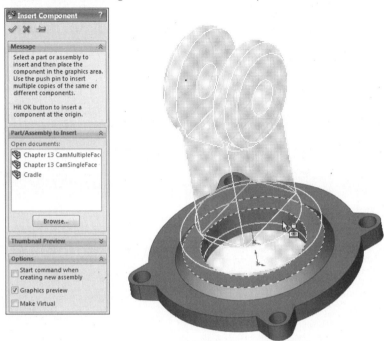

4. **Open the part with the filename** Chapter 5 Arm.sldprt, **the Default configuration, in its own window, and choose Window ⇨ Tile Vertically.** The part and the assembly should be open in adjacent windows.

5. **Click the face inside the hole without the chamfer around it in the Arm part, as shown in Figure 5.25.** Then drag it into the assembly to the cylindrical face inside the hole at the top of the Robot Tower part. The concentric SmartMate symbol should appear on the cursor.

FIGURE 5.25

Displaying a SmartMate when dragging between windows

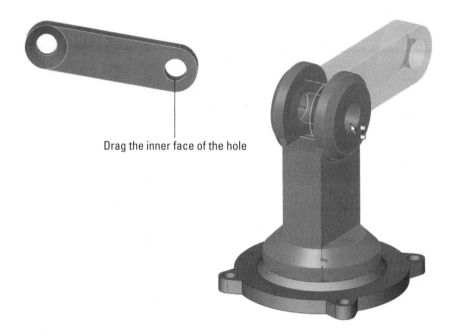

Drag the inner face of the hole

6. **Click the green check mark icon to accept the Concentric mate.** Move the part to test that the mates are correct.

7. **Click the Mate tool on the Assemblies toolbar.** Expand the Advanced Mates panel and click the Width mate.

8. **In the Width Selections box, select the two inner faces of the Robot Tower part, and in the Tab Selections box, select the outer faces of the Arm part.** The selection should look as shown in Figure 5.26.

9. **Open a Windows Explorer window, and select the following parts:** Robot Arm2 **and** Robot Gripper. Drag these parts into the SolidWorks assembly window and drop them in a blank space.

10. **Select the chamfered faces of the Arm and Arm2 parts and create a Coincident mate between them.** You can make Coincident mates between conical faces as long as the cones are the same angle. This special case acts like a combination of Concentric and Coincident mates. Figure 5.27 shows the selections and the result.

FIGURE 5.26

Creating a Width mate

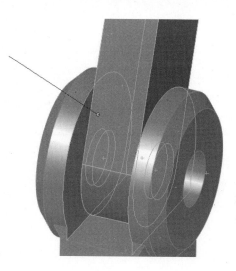

11. **Create a copy of the gripper part so that there are two instances of it in the assembly.** You can do this by Ctrl+dragging the part within the assembly window with the Mate PropertyManager closed.

12. **Mate both of the grippers to the Arm2 end using the same mating technique that you used for the previous conical face Coincident part.**

13. **Once you have applied these parts, try moving the various joints of the assembly.** Notice that it is difficult, if not impossible, to isolate the motion of just a single part. This is because there are too many open degrees of freedom, and a lot of ambiguity.

14. **Fix Arm2 to allow you to move the gripper parts as you want.** Create a Symmetric mate between the indicated faces of the grippers and the Front plane of the Arm2 part, as shown in Figure 5.28.

15. **Practice making angle mates, suppressing mates, and fixing parts to limit motion.**

16. **Save the assembly and exit the file.**

FIGURE 5.27

Making conical faces coincident

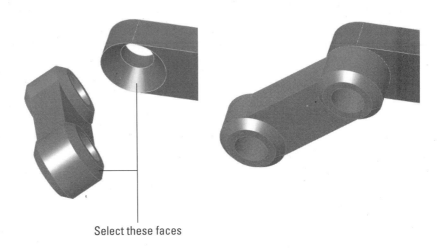

Select these faces

FIGURE 5.28

Creating a Symmetric mate

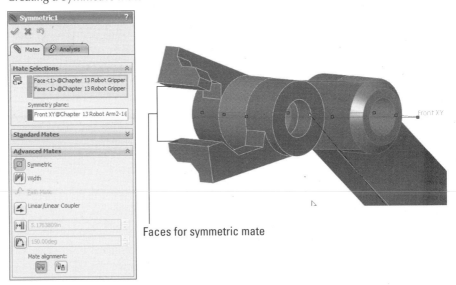

Faces for symmetric mate

Summary

A thorough understanding of mates, and editing and troubleshooting techniques in particular, makes the difference between a real assembly artist and a user who struggles through or avoids certain tasks. There is a lot about mates that is not straightforward, but with practice, you can understand and master them. You can put assemblies together quickly, with a focus on rebuild performance and Dynamic Assembly Motion.

Although best practice concepts should not dominate your designs, they are great guidelines to start from. To avoid making big mistakes, watch out for the pitfalls outlined in the section in this chapter that summarizes mate best practices to follow.

Working with Assembly Sketches and Layouts

When working on parts or assemblies, design work often begins with 2D sketches. You can follow through to 3D with data created in this phase by laying out the design as a sketch in the assembly before you start making actual 3D parts. When you use a single sketch or multiple sketches either as a visual guide or as a functional framework for a model, it is called a *layout*. Two-dimensional sketches are easy to produce, and easy to use as the first step in design or modeling work. SolidWorks provides both formal and informal techniques for achieving this sort of effect.

The topic of layout sketches involves other topics that will be covered in more detail later in this book, such as in-context modeling and master model techniques. These topics are introduced here at a conceptual level to prepare you for the detailed information later on.

In-context modeling involves the creation of relationships between parts in an assembly such that one part drives features on another part. Layout concepts apply to in-context modeling because you can use an assembly-level sketch to drive geometry within individual parts.

Master model techniques can take several forms, but usually entail making geometry in a single part that is later used to span across several parts in an assembly. Layout sketches can be used to either break up or bring back together parts created in this fashion.

Looking at the Techniques

An informal technique called assembly layout sketch has existed since early versions of SolidWorks. This technique has been included in the SolidWorks official training materials for many years, and simply allows an assembly-level sketch. You can then do one of several things with the sketch: build parts in place on it, mate parts to it, or use it to cut up a single part into multiple pieces. The assembly layout sketch technique is also often adapted for use with single highly complex parts, to use a single point of reference to change many features within a single part.

 A much newer, formal assembly feature is called the Layout. The *Layout* is an assembly-level 3D sketch that displays a specific icon and has some special properties. Although the formal feature and the informal technique have similar names, they have very different functions. SolidWorks users do not often distinguish between the two, and many do not even know there is a difference. In fact, most users are unfamiliar with the Layout feature.

In this book, you will find the word *layout* used with a lowercase "l" to refer to the informal assembly-based sketch layout method. The formal assembly-based 3D sketch with special properties will be referred to with a capital "L" as a *Layout*. The Layout icon may also accompany the formal feature.

Using the assembly layout sketch

In SolidWorks, layout sketches are a great way to simulate mechanisms, or locate the major components of an assembly. Figure 6.1 shows three examples of assemblies created with the assistance of an assembly layout sketch.

FIGURE 6.1

Assembly layout sketches can be used in a wide range of applications.

The bicycle example is used throughout this book, and the layout sketch was instrumental in establishing the geometry of the frame. Most of the components of a bicycle are purchased as off-the-shelf items that may come in different sizes but are not custom created for individual bikes. The only parts that are generally custom built for a particular size are the frame and possibly the fork. So to design the frame, you have to lay out all of the data that you are given from the individual components, such as wheels, stem, crank set, and seat. When you put everything together, there are additional pieces of information that determine the frame geometry before the detail design of the frame can be started. You need to know the following:

- The size of the wheels
- The wheelbase (distance between the wheel centers)
- The length of the pedal arm
- The necessary clearance between the bottom of the pedal and the ground
- The head angle (effective pivot angle of the front fork)
- The distance between the center of the crank and the center of the rear wheel

The workflow for using an assembly layout sketch is as follows:

1. Open a new assembly.
2. Create sketches on the standard planes, or create new reference planes (you cannot use sketch pictures in assembly sketches).
3. Mate existing parts to the sketch and reference geometry (bottom-up method).

   Alternatively, you can build parts in place using the layout sketches as reference (top-down or in-context method).

This bicycle will be used as an example to show how the frame was developed.

First, you start with the wheels. In this example, you want to design an urban utility bike based on mountain bike components, with dual suspension, but using narrow tires, and that means 26" wheels. You need a certain amount of ground clearance as the pedals rotate, and even clearance between the rider's toes and the back side of the front wheel. You will design the frame to fit a rider who is about 5' 8".

The size information is important because the distance between the wheel centers (wheelbase) creates certain characteristics for riders of different heights. A longer wheelbase generally means a more stable and comfortable ride but is less maneuverable and heavier. In this case, based on other research, you want the wheelbase to be 41".

The above information allows you to create the sketch shown in Figure 6.2.

Starting the bicycle layout sketch

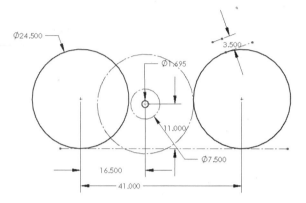

The next set of information you can put into the sketch has to do with the height of the top bar (which is important when you stand over the bike with your feet on the ground), and clearance between the frame and front wheel for the travel of the front suspension fork. This establishes most of what you need to know to design the frame, but you still have to work out the rear suspension arm.

With this information, the layout sketch looks like Figure 6.3.

Adding information to the layout sketch

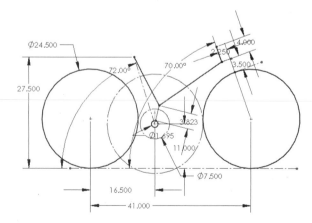

With this data, you have all of the critical point locations to design the actual frame. The first step in creating the frame is to place reference geometry (sketch planes) from which to make sketches for the extrudes or other features used to make the individual tubes of the frame. The frame will be a carbon fiber monocoque, but will still rely on tubular geometry, with smooth blends between the tubes to reduce stress concentrations. The layout with the planes and the initial tubes is shown in Figure 6.4.

FIGURE 6.4

Building the tubes for the frame

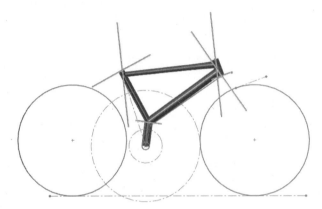

When all of the tubes are created in-place in the assembly from the assembly layout sketch, the top of the assembly FeatureManager looks like Figure 6.5.

You should notice two things right away from this FeatureManager. The first is that the BibleBikeFrame part listed in the tree displays a rebuild symbol (which resembles a traffic light), and the second is that every feature in the list has the -> symbol to the right of it. The rebuild symbol means that SolidWorks thinks there is something that needs to be recalculated in the part, although there is not. If you open the part in its own window, there are no rebuild symbols, but in the context of the assembly it seems there always are, even if you force a rebuild (Ctrl+Q). Many users who have experimented with in-context relations experience this kind of behavior with the software. This has a lot to do with why so many people have misgivings about in-context techniques — there just seem to be too many things that happen that are out of your control. Assembly layout sketches are a fantastic technique, but they are not without their quirks.

The -> symbol means that there is an external reference from the part to the assembly sketch. (External references are covered in more detail in Chapter 10.) Using the assembly layout sketch technique, an external reference is made every time a relationship is made from the part to the assembly sketch. Many users prefer to avoid external references, mainly because of the file management issues they cause, the difficulty in repairing them when broken, and rebuild speed performance issues. However, references to an assembly sketch are more stable than references between two parts in an assembly.

FIGURE 6.5

Examining the features built from the assembly layout sketch

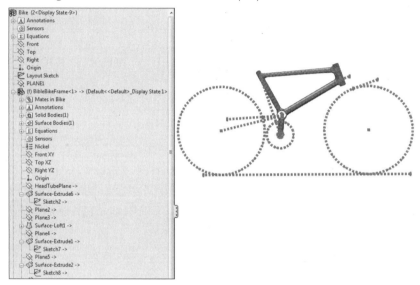

When you use an assembly layout sketch for either the in-context part building or simply part positioning, the main advantage that it offers is to give you a single driving sketch that enables you to change the size, shape, and position of the parts. You can use as many layout sketches as you want, and you can make them on different sketch planes. This enables you to control parts in all directions.

Caution

When using layout sketches, it is assumed that the relationships are created such that the sketch drives everything else. However, nothing is preventing you from using other things in the assembly to drive the sketch. You should avoid this type of conflict, called a circular reference. It can create sketches that change with every rebuild and can seriously impact rebuild times. When using any type of in-context relations, you need to be careful to establish one or more driving entities, which are not in turn driven by other entities.

To take this a step further, it is best to avoid daisy chaining, where A drives B, B drives C, and so on. It is better practice to make A drive both B and C directly. This saves on rebuild times and troubleshooting. ■

One of the drawbacks of this technique is that you give up dynamic assembly motion. By creating the parts in the context of the assembly and creating relationships between sketches or features and the assembly sketch, you cannot move the parts by just dragging them with the cursor. To move the parts, you have to move the sketch and rebuild. The part does not move until the sketch is updated. If you need to combine layout functionality with dynamic assembly motion, you can add additional instances of the in-context parts that are mated in the traditional way. However, when using this method, you have to be very careful about which instance you make your edits to, because in-context relations will be driven by the original instance.

 Another drawback of the assembly-level sketch in general is that you cannot use a sketch picture inside the sketch. Sketch pictures can contain important reference information for building a model. The lack of this capability is certainly noticeable. You can put your sketch picture in a part or even a virtual component.

Using master model

The master model technique is covered in depth in Chapter 19, but it is mentioned here because it works as an alternate method with the layout idea. The term *master model* can mean a couple of different things: It could be a single part where multiple bodies are created and that is later split up into multiple parts. Also, it is sometimes used as the name for inserting a single part with sketches and reference geometry into one or more other parts to have a single reference without creating that reference in the assembly.

This still creates an external reference, but it only creates a single external reference instead of possibly dozens, and updates of the inserted part can be locked. Performance problems with this technique are less serious. Also, if the file management fails and SolidWorks cannot find the inserted part, you can still keep working. SolidWorks keeps enough data in the child part that it does not need to constantly access the parent part.

The master model technique seems to have more advantages and fewer disadvantages than the methods using assemblies. The dynamic assembly motion problem does not exist in a master model arrangement, nor does the lack of sketch picture functionality.

An example of this kind of work is shown in the derailleur assembly in Figure 6.6.

The part shown on the left is the master model. Notice that it contains sketch, plane, and surface data. The image on the right shows some parts superimposed on the master model part.

FIGURE 6.6

Using a master model to drive the individual parts of an assembly

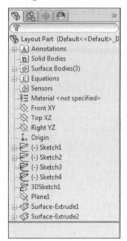
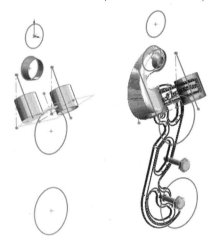

Using the Layout Feature

The Layout feature in SolidWorks is relatively new. However, due to some quirky behavior, it is not generally employed by users. Most people who have been using the layout technique described earlier in this chapter are not switching to the new method, even though it has replaced the old method in the official SolidWorks assemblies training manuals.

The Layout feature is a 3D sketch that is given special treatment within an assembly. It also works best with sketch blocks. The special properties of the Layout feature when compared to a 2D assembly sketch are as follows:

- Uses a 3D sketch
- Works best when actively sketching on a plane
- Works best when the sketch making up a part is made into a sketch block
- Enables you to extrude the first feature of a part directly from the sketch block
- Enables sketch relations between blocks to turn into mates
- Permits unlimited dynamic assembly motion — parts move with the motion of blocks in the Layout

To initiate a Layout, click the Layout button on the Layout tab of the assembly CommandManager or activate it from the Insert menu. Once you are in a Layout, SolidWorks puts you into a 3D sketch with the Front (XY) plane activated, so it displays a small grid.

For now, you treat the 3D sketch as much like a set of 2D sketches as possible. The main difference is that you can double-click a different plane to start sketching on the new plane, and you always see this small grid when a plane is active.

You may find that 3D sketches have some limitations when you are working with Layouts, such as lacking the capabilities to use sketch patterns and Sketch Pictures.

Using the Layout workflow

With most functions in software of any type, you tend to get better results when you are able to use the software in the way in which it was intended to be used. Generally, the developers have a workflow in mind when they design the function itself and the interface. Working with the software is usually also easier than working against the software.

Here is the general workflow for using the Layout feature:

1. Open a new or existing assembly.

2. Click the Layout toolbar button on the Layout tab of the CommandManager.

3. Sketch on the plane in the 3D sketch to create 2D sketches representing parts of a mechanism or other assembly.

4. Make selections of the sketch into blocks representing individual parts, as shown in Figure 6.7.

5. Insert multiple instances of the blocks to represent multiple instances of the parts.

6. Use sketch relations to put the blocks together like mating parts in an assembly.

7. Test the mechanism by dragging sketches. (Blocks function like a single sketch entity, so you can drag them within the sketch like parts in an assembly.)

8. Right-click the block (from inside or outside the Layout) and select Make Part From Block (also a button on the Layout toolbar).

Note

The Make Part From Block command uses large and small icons that are slightly different. The icon shown previously is a large icon. ■

FIGURE 6.7

Tools you encounter when using Layout

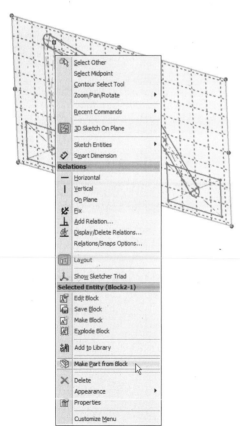

Working with virtual components

Virtual components always exist with in-context workflows, and frequently with the Layout workflow. Virtual components are parts that are saved within the assembly. You can save a virtual component externally, and you can also make an externally saved part into a virtual component. The advantages of virtual components are that you don't have to worry about saving out additional files, and that the assembly will never lose track of any virtual component.

Virtual components are primarily intended for use as quick, temporary, conceptual tools, rather than as a way to make parts that will be a permanent element in the assembly. Some SolidWorks users also use virtual components to represent non-geometric parts such as glue or paint. Any time you choose Insert ⇨ Component ⇨ New Part from the menus and select a template and a plane to put the part on, the part is placed immediately into the assembly, and you can start working without worrying about having to save the assembly and the part. This saves a lot of time initially. Later on, when you save the assembly, SolidWorks prompts you to save the parts externally as well, or you may choose to leave the parts internal to the assembly.

Virtual components are named Part1 Assem1, where Part1 and Assem1 are default names. You can easily rename the part by clicking the RMB menu and selecting Rename Part. You cannot do this for external parts. If you make an external part virtual, the name in the assembly becomes Copy of *filename* Assem1 where *filename* is the name of the external file. The name of the assembly is always included (and cannot be removed) to ensure that if you have subassemblies that also have virtual components, you will always have unique filenames for all the parts.

Virtual components can also be accessed in their own window, which makes them easier to edit for some purposes. Bills of Materials (BOMs) and numbered balloons work correctly with virtual components.

Best Practice

It is considered best practice to save any parts that will be a permanent part of the assembly as external files. Virtual components should be limited to temporary parts or possibly non-geometry, BOM-only parts such as glue or paint. ■

Balancing advantages and limitations

In theory, the Layout feature has several advantages:

- You can make parts from blocks within the Layout.
- You can move parts by moving blocks in the Layout.
- It is a great way to structure your relations within an assembly.
- A single 3D sketch does not have the history concerns that multiple 2D sketches have.
- It is useful for motion analysis studies.

In practice, this feature needs some enhancements before it is ready for use on real assemblies. Using 2D sketches as assembly layout sketches may still be a better idea than trying to avoid the following limitations of the formal Layout feature:

- The 3D sketch used for Layout has all the limitations that come with 3D sketches.

- Sketch relations are listed in the Mates folder.

- Gaining access to edit the Layout once it has been closed requires a method you don't expect from a sketch: you click the Layout button on the toolbar rather than right-click and edit an icon in the FeatureManager.

- It requires that you use blocks to access all of the functionality.

- A fully defined 3D sketch with blocks is very unstable.

- Part creation from blocks does not save time.

- You cannot paste copied sketch entities from a 2D sketch into the Layout.

- You cannot use sketch pictures in the Layout.

- You cannot use auto-dimension (or polygons or ellipses) in the Layout.

Although the formal Layout feature has serious advantages over regular layout sketches, at this time the limitations outweigh them. The rest of the discussion on layouts addresses the generic layout technique rather than the formal feature.

Tutorial: Working with a Layout

In this tutorial, you will use regular assembly sketches to lay out and build a tooling die.

1. **Open the assembly from the DVD named** Chapter 6 tutorial layout start. sldasm. Notice that three layout sketches and some of the parts have been added already. The existing parts are virtual components, saved inside the assembly.

2. **Click Add New Part on the Assembly tab of the CommandManager.** The cursor appears with a green check mark, and in the lower-left corner, the taskbar prompts you to select a plane on which to place the Front plane of the part. A sketch will automatically be opened on that plane. Click the Front plane of the assembly.

3. **Click the Corner Rectangle sketch tool from the Sketch toolbar.** Create a rectangle from the two corners indicated in Figure 6.8. It may be helpful to bring the model into a Front view before drawing these rectangles.

4. **Extrude the rectangle using the Up To Vertex end condition for both Direction 1 and Direction 2.** Select sketch endpoints in the Plane Depth Layout sketch for both directions so that the new plate matches the other existing plates.

   Be careful not to click model faces, edges, or vertices when creating these depth references. Make sure that all your references stay in the sketch.

FIGURE 6.8

Creating a new plate in the context of an assembly with layout sketches.

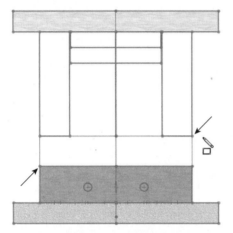

5. **Click the Exit Edit Part icon in the Confirmation Corner (the upper-right corner of the SolidWorks graphics window).** Right-click the new part in the FeatureManager and select Rename Part. Rename it **Plate4**. You can also use the Windows standard method of slowly double-clicking rename parts. The *Chapter 16 tutorial layout start* part of the name is automatically added. Assign a material from the Appearances tab for the new plate.

6. **Follow this procedure for the four remaining plates, as shown in Figure 6.9.** To summarize the steps again, you add the new part, create a sketch, and extrude the block.

Note

Be careful with the plates labeled 5, 6, 7, and 8. There is a clearance gap between the sides of the 7 and 8 plates and the vertical plates 5 and 6. ∎

FIGURE 6.9

All of the plates controlled by the layout sketches

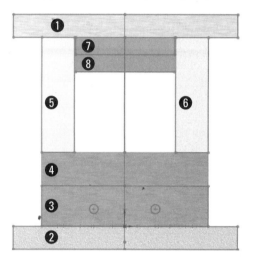

7. **Reorient the view to the Top view. Make sure you can see the Pin Layout sketch.**

8. **Select the top face of Plate 1, and click on the Hole Series toolbar.** The Hole Series may be hidden under the Assembly Features flyout on the Assembly tab of the CommandManager. The Hole Wizard no longer requires pre-selection to avoid 3D placement sketches, but the Hole Series as of 2010 has not been updated to follow the same rules as the Hole Wizard.

9. **Place two sketch points at the centers of the circles, as shown in Figure 6.10.** Make sure that the two points are both over the same plate 5 or 6. You cannot cut both plate 5 and 6 in the same Hole Series feature. Use the settings shown in Figure 6.10.

    Make sure the holes are Counterbored, ANSI Metric, Socket Head Cap Screw, M10, with a head clearance of 0.10 inch. All other conditions should follow Figure 6.9.

10. **Place two more new holes on the other side.** Make the parts transparent to see how the holes have been placed.

FIGURE 6.10

Placing screw holes through multiple parts in the die

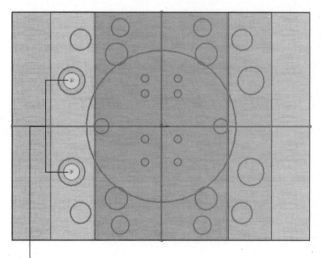

Place points for holes

11. **Initiate the Plane feature. Create a plane perpendicular to the Right plane and coincident to the line from the Plate Depth Layout shown in the Right view in Figure 6.11.** Rename the new plane Sprue Bushing Seat. (The new plane should show up right underneath the initial three layout sketches.)

 12. **Create a new part on the Sprue Bushing Seat plane.**

FIGURE 6.11

Creating a plane in the assembly driven by the layout sketch

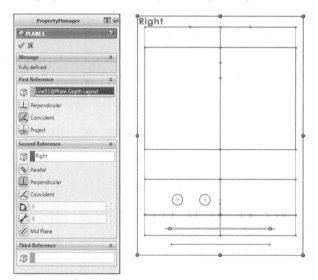

13. **Activate the Convert Entities sketch tool, select the large (approximately 4-inch diameter) circle from the Pin Layout sketch, and convert it into the sketch plane of the new part.**

14. **Draw a 1/2 inch circle in the center (at the origin).** Extrude the sketch 0.875 inch so that it protrudes from Plate 2.

15. **Exit the Edit Part mode (using the Confirmation Corner).** Rename the new part Sprue Bushing.

16. **Left-click on Plate2 and select Edit Part from the shortcut toolbar.**

17. **Open a new sketch on the Sprue Bushing Seat plane (which is part of the assembly, not part of the part).**

18. **Select the large circle used in Step 13, and use the Offset sketch tool to offset the circle 0.005 inch to the outside.** Create a Through All cut that comes out the exposed side of Plate2, clearing an area for the Sprue Bushing. You may need to switch to Wireframe display to accomplish this.

19. **Apply a chamfer to the outer edge of the new cut, 0.010 inch.**

20. **Exit Edit Part mode, and save the assembly to a new location by choosing File ➪ Save As.** Click the Save All button, and then select the Save Externally option, as shown in Figure 6.12.

Saving the internal virtual components to external parts

21. **Exit Edit Part mode using the icon in the Confirmation Corner.**

22. **Double-click the Plate Layout sketch, and change the 5.836 inch dimension to 6 inches.** Change the 7.244 inch dimension to 7 inches. Make sure the model rebuilds, and watch the individual parts update. Figure 6.13 shows these dimensions for reference.

FIGURE 6.13

Editing layout sketch dimensions to drive the size of the individual parts

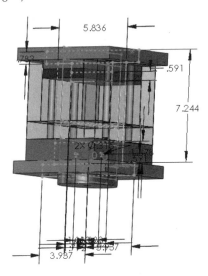

You will need to do more to finish this tooling die than is covered in this tutorial. The point is to give you some experience using the in-context features that are used with a layout sketch technique.

Summary

Laying out an assembly with reference sketches is a more disciplined way of working that can help you avoid some of the complications of external references and in-context design work. It is up to you to decide whether the informal 2D layout sketches are preferable to the formal 3D sketch-based Layout feature. Both offer tools to control positions of parts and even features of parts within an assembly.

Traditional assembly modeling methods where each part is located by mates from another part do not stand up well against changes in the parts themselves. The main goals of the layout methods are centralization of control and stability of changes. I invite you to explore some of these methods using tools you have learned in this chapter.

Using Assembly Tools

SolidWorks assemblies enable you to take advantage of several tools in addition to the standard and best-known functionality. The tools covered in this chapter didn't fit into other chapter headings easily, but deserved significant coverage.

Placing Parts without Mates

Assembly mates are great tools, but they aren't the only tools for placing parts in an assembly. Sometimes you might need to place parts without applying a mate, such as when you are setting up an animation, and the mate would prevent the animation from working correctly. You might also want to place a part and allow motion of the part it is placed relative to, while making sure the actual part remains stationary.

The use of these tools opens up best practice questions about fully defined parts in the assembly. Sometimes that gold standard is difficult to achieve. As counterintuitive as it may seem, the easiest way to deal with mates that are difficult to complete because parts keep moving around is to build the assembly without mates. This idea will not appeal to all users, but if parts do not have any relationships to one another, then moving one part cannot set off a chain reaction of parts moving around the screen.

In a perfect world, assembly mates are well controlled and easy to understand. But in reality, sometimes things happen that you cannot account for. If you build an assembly without mates (with the parts simply positioned in space using any technique that works), the parts are guaranteed not to move unless you accidentally move one.

Note

You can use the setting at Tools ⇨ Assemblies to turn off the click-and-drag method to move parts. This setting requires you to click a toolbar button to enable the cursor to move parts. If you have parts in your assembly that are simply placed with nothing holding their location, then simply clicking a part puts you in danger of moving that part.

If you have a 3D mouse device, one of the options available is for the 3D mouse to move parts in the assembly when one is selected. You cannot use the SolidWorks Undo command when you use this method to move a part. ■

On the other hand, if your design changes, and you want a set of parts to move together, they will not, and you will have to change their positions using the same technique that you used to get them to their current position.

As a final thought on an assembly of parts that have nothing holding them in place, you might consider fixing the parts in place. Parts are easy to fix or float, and it will give you peace of mind to have them locked down.

Using the Move Component options

The Move Component tool has several options for locating parts without using mates. These options are shown in Figure 7.1.

FIGURE 7.1

Selecting a positioning option with Move Component

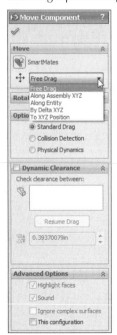

The Move Component options are different than those for the Move/Copy Bodies feature. Move/Copy Bodies is found in the part environment and is intended to help move individual solid and surface bodies by using a triad with arrows, wings, and rings, as shown in Figure 7.2. While the functionality of moving bodies within a part is very similar to moving parts within an assembly, the tools you work with in the two situations are different. Another difference between Move/Copy Bodies and Move Component is that Move/Copy Bodies creates a feature in the tree, but Move Component does not.

FIGURE 7.2

Don't confuse the Move/Copy Body triad with any of the assembly-based Move Component options.

All of the following options are described for translating (sliding) the parts, but rotation is also available for the Free Drag, By Delta XYZ, and Along Entity methods.

Also, all of the drag-enabled methods (Free Drag, Along Assembly XYZ, and Along Entity) have some available options in the Options panel of the Move Component PropertyManager shown in Figure 7.1. These options are

- Standard Drag
- Collision Detection
- Physical Dynamics

The options in this panel are activated using a toggle, so you can only activate one of the three at a time. Collision Detection and Physical Dynamics are described later in this chapter. All of the following methods for moving components assume you are using the Standard Drag option.

Using Free Drag

The Free Drag option of Move Component enables you to simply move the part around the screen by dragging with the cursor. This is the same as the default function of the cursor when in an assembly. Click a part and drag. The part follows any existing mates, and moves the part in 3D space. For a part that is completely unconstrained, it moves in a plane parallel to the screen. If you are viewing the assembly such that the screen isn't parallel to any standard plane, the part you are moving may be moving in and out of the assembly, or in some other unexpected manner. If you have some mates applied to the part, it is less likely to do something odd. You might consider using the Four View option to move parts using this method.

Free Drag is not a great method to precisely position parts, but it is okay if you are just trying to position something visually as a prop for a rendering.

Moving with Along Assembly XYZ

When you drag a part in an assembly with the Along Assembly XYZ option enabled, the part can only move along the X axis, the Y axis, or the Z axis at one time. It can't move at an angle. To use this option properly, you should use an orthogonal view so that it is easier for you to move the part in the correct direction, and to see which direction it is going in. Again, using the Four View display option is also helpful.

If you want to change directions, you have to stop dragging and then restart the drag, moving in the initial direction of the drag that you want to move the part.

Moving with Along Entity

The Along Entity option for Move Component is similar to the Along Assembly XYZ option except that you select a custom direction, and the part can only move back and forth along that direction. The custom direction has to be either linear or planar, and can be an edge, axis, face, plane, sketch line, and so forth.

Using By Delta XYZ

The By Delta XYZ method is the first one that offers direct numerical input for moving parts. The "delta" means "change," so the numbers you enter change the position of the part along the specified axis. Figure 7.3 shows the PropertyManager interface for this option.

FIGURE 7.3

Using the By Delta XYZ option to move parts

Because this is the first move option that uses an Apply button (shown in Figure 7.3), you can move a selection of parts multiple times just by entering a number in one of the boxes and clicking Apply multiple times. Each time you click Apply, it moves by the amounts listed in the three boxes, labeled ΔX, ΔY, and ΔZ.

This does not work like the Modify dialog box for dimensions, where if you change the number and click the check mark, the dimension changes from, say, 3 to 5. If you type **3** in the ΔX box, and click Apply, it moves 3 units. If you then change ΔX to **5** and click Apply again, it moves 5 units for a total of 8. If the second time you type **−5** instead of 5, then the total movement would be 2 units in the opposite direction from the original 3 units.

Also notice that the interface does not have a selection box to tell it which parts you want to move. To select a part to move, you can select a face from the graphics window, or select a part or subassembly in the FeatureManager. Clicking Apply moves all selected parts.

You can even change selections while the command is active. For example, you can move one selection of parts and then move a different selection.

Using To XYZ Position

Using the To XYZ Position option is different again from the By Delta XYZ option. You may find that this option has a few quirks. First, it is intended to move the selected point of the selected part to the x,y,z location you typed into the x, y, and z boxes shown in Figure 7.4.

Positioning a part using the To XYZ Position option

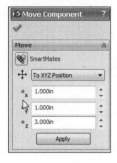

Again, this PropertyManager does not have a selection box to list parts to move or points to move to the specified XYZ location. That makes this interface slightly more limited than some of the other options.

If you do not select a point, SolidWorks assumes you want to move the origin of the part. If you have multiple parts selected, it assumes you want to move the center of gravity (CG) of the combined parts.

If in a previous move you did have a point selected on an instance of the part, and you then move a different instance, SolidWorks assumes that you want to position the same point on the second instance of the part.

The rules for which point is positioned are not spelled out, and are realistically too difficult to follow. When using this option, you should only position origins or points, and if you change between origins and points, you should cancel the command and restart it.

You can choose multiple parts by selecting them from the assembly FeatureManager, but if you do that, it does not appear to allow you to select points to position anymore.

If you select a point on a part and then want to change to a different point on the same part, there does not appear to be a way to do that. You have to first select a point on another part, and then select a different point on the original part.

In general, this option appears to be underdeveloped. What that means to you is that it may not have all the flexibility you are looking for, or it might appear to have quirks if you don't follow the perfect workflow process every time. If you need the functionality of this tool to get your job done, the tool does work, and there are few options for workarounds.

Using the For Positioning Only option

The Mate PropertyManager has an option called Use for Positioning Only, shown in Figure 7.5. This option has been available in SolidWorks for a long time, but it may not be taught in the standard SolidWorks reseller class or demonstrated in most tutorials. This option essentially allows you to go through the motions of creating a mate; however, when you are done, the part you are positioning will be in place, but there will be no mate.

The result is similar to using any of the tools described in the previous section, but you don't have to calculate a position or movement amount — the new position is driven by geometry on another part.

People tend to use this option for visualization — to help see the part in position before they really commit to a method of attaching it. Usually people who use the positioning only option do end up mating the part completely later, but may be considering multiple mate strategies that achieve the desired goal more efficiently or cleanly.

Why would you want to go through all the work of creating a mate but in the end not have a mate to show for it? Possibly to avoid deleting it later, or to avoid conflicts that it might cause later. Also, you may possibly be working in reverse — the part you are placing without the mate should be the fixed part, so you place it, fix it, and then mate other parts to it. Sometimes with animations, you want parts placed correctly without a mate to interfere with the animated motion of the part.

FIGURE 7.5

Selecting the Use for Positioning Only option

So why wouldn't you create the mate and then just suppress it? Well, configurations can be complicated enough without adding a configuration just to remove a mate. This function is available; some people use it in limited situations, and it does work.

Building parts in place

Building parts in place is a relatively easy way to place parts without mating them. This is a technique that might be called top-down, or in-context, and is dealt with in other chapters of this book.

Cross-Reference

Chapter 10 covers in-context techniques, and Chapter 19 covers master model techniques, both of which describe building parts in place and locating or placing them without mates. ■

Using Proximity Tools

In order to detect proximity between parts in an assembly, SolidWorks offers several tools:

- Interference Detection
- Clearance Verification
- Collision Detection
- Physical Dynamics
- Sensors

Using Interference Detection

 Interference detection is available through the menus at Tools ⇨ Interference Detection. You can also find it in the Evaluate tab of the CommandManager. It is a stand-alone tool that finds existing interferences in an assembly. The PropertyManager for Interference Detection is shown in Figure 7.6, after detecting interferences in an assembly.

FIGURE 7.6

Finding interferences in an assembly

You can use two different types of selections for interference detection. The first type is to simply select the top-level assembly from the assembly FeatureManager. This checks all of the parts in the assembly for interference. The second method is to select individual components (parts or subassemblies) from the assembly FeatureManager. In either case, you can click the Calculate button when you are done with the selection and ready to see the interferences.

Displaying the results

The default result display (shown in Figure 7.6) shows each interference with the pair of interfering components underneath the interference. Interferences are listed with the size (volume) of the interferences.

Remember that you cannot judge the size of a number just by looking at the left-most digit. The numbers are listed in scientific notation, so 1.05e-005in^3 means 1.05 x 10^-5 cubic inches (read 1.05 times ten to the negative 5 power), or 0.0000105 cubic inch. Interferences are not listed in any order, and you can't sort them, but as you click each interference, the interfering volume appears highlighted in red in the graphics window. You can also right-click an interference and select Zoom To Selection if the interference is very small.

Ignoring interferences

You can ignore an interference by either right-clicking the interference in the Results panel and selecting Ignore from the menu, or clicking the Ignore button in the Results panel. Once an interference is ignored, it is simply removed from the list. You can Shift+select (but not Ctrl+select) to ignore multiple interferences at once. A counter directly under the Results list keeps track of how many ignored interferences there are. Once an interference is ignored, you can display it again in the Results panel by enabling the Show Ignored Interferences option in the Options panel. Ignored interferences appear grayed out. Once the grayed-out interferences are shown, you can select them in the list and use the Un-ignore button or from the RMB menu.

Figure 7.7 shows the Results panel of the Interferences Detection PropertyManager being used to ignore interferences.

FIGURE 7.7

The Results panel with ignored interferences

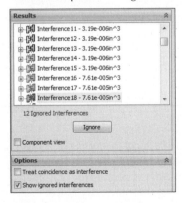

Using Component view

The Component View option at the bottom of the Results panel toggles from the default display (where components are listed under each interference) to the Component view in which all components are listed, the interference volumes are listed under the component, and then the other interfering part is listed under the interference, as shown in Figure 7.8.

Displaying interference results with the Component View option

Selecting options

The Options panel is shown in Figure 7.6. Although most of the options are self-explanatory, a couple of items should be further clarified. First, you cannot do body interference checks in multi-body parts, but you can include multi-bodies in the assembly interference detection.

Second, the Make Interfering Parts Transparent option would seem to clash with the display option in the Non-interfering Components panel. The transparent option is turned on by default.

Displaying options for non-interfering components

The final panel of the Interference Detection PropertyManager controls the display of non-interfering components. You have the option of making them wireframe, hidden, transparent, or leaving the display properties alone. You may prefer the Hidden option, because it offers the most contrast with the interfering parts to make the interferences stand out.

Working with Clearance Verification

 Clearance Verification is a tool that enables you to check that clearances between parts in an assembly or model faces exceed a minimum distance. The tool lists any clearances that are less than the clearance you specify, which means it identifies interferences as well as clearances. This applies to clearances between static parts, not moving parts. For clearances between moving parts, you can use the Dynamic Clearance option in the Move Component PropertyManager, described later in this chapter.

You can find the Clearance Verification tool in the menus at Tools ⇨ Clearance Verification, or on the Evaluate tab of the CommandManager. The Clearance Verification PropertyManager is shown in Figure 7.9.

FIGURE 7.9

Using the Clearance Verification PropertyManager

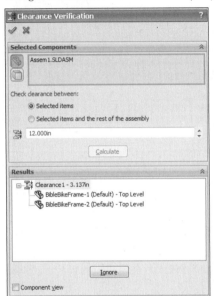
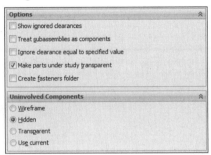

The secret to using Clearance Verification is to understand what it measures. Clearance Verification is only concerned with clearances *less* than the distance you specify. This means that parts that touch or interfere are listed as "Clearances" in the Results box.

If you are looking to find the minimum clearance between two parts in an assembly, this tool can do that, but you have to enter a value in the Minimum Acceptable Clearance box that is larger than the clearance you are looking for. Again, if you are looking for the minimum clearance between two parts, you may get a more intuitive result using the Dynamic Clearance options, which are part of the Move Component tool.

Notice that the Clearance Verification PropertyManager shown in Figure 7.9 is in many ways similar or identical to the Interference Detection PropertyManager shown in Figure 7.6. You will also find that the results can be fairly similar as well.

Using Dynamic Clearance

The Dynamic Clearance options are part of the Move Component tool. Move Component is on the Assembly toolbar, while Dynamic Clearance has a panel of its own in the middle of the Move Component PropertyManager.

To use Dynamic Clearance, activate the selection box in the upper-left corner of the panel (shown in Figure 7.10), and pick two parts that can move relative to one another. This example uses the fork assembly from the Bike model on the DVD, selecting the fork and the stem.

FIGURE 7.10

Selecting the Dynamic Clearance options in the Move Component PropertyManager

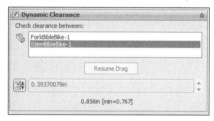

 There is an icon in the Dynamic Clearance panel that looks exactly like the Clearance Verification icon, described earlier in this chapter. Clicking the icon enables you to enter a Clearance value. This Clearance value is the minimum clearance that the tool allows when you move the parts around.

Notice the dimension in parentheses, (.856), in the right image in Figure 7.10. This is the minimum clearance between the stem and the fork, and it changes dynamically as you move one of the parts. If you specify a minimum clearance value, then SolidWorks stops the motion of the part you are dragging when the clearance between the parts reaches that distance.

Working with Collision Detection

Collision Detection is another tool in the Move Component PropertyManager, and you can use it at the same time as Dynamic Clearance. You can find the option to turn on Collision Detection in the Options panel of the Move Component PropertyManager. When you activate it, several additional options appear, as shown in Figure 7.11.

FIGURE 7.11

Choosing the Collision Detection option activates other options.

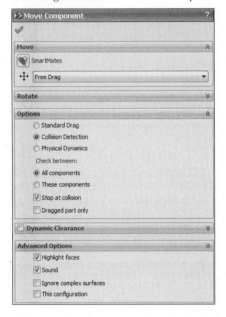

You can use Collision Detection to find collisions caused by dynamic assembly motion (dragging parts on the screen with Move Component) using all the parts in the assembly (All Components), or just selected components (These Components). Obviously, there is a performance (speed) cost to calculating collisions for all parts, and so you should limit the parts used in Collision Detection if possible, especially for larger assemblies.

You can also set an option that stops motion at collision, which helps you visualize more realistic motion of the mechanism. The Dragged Part Only option only calculates interferences for the dragged part with those around it. Activating Collision Detection also activates other options in the Advanced Options panel, as follows:

- **Highlight faces.** When faces collide, they appear highlighted.
- **Sound.** When parts collide, they set off the Windows default beep (Windows Ding.wav).
- **Ignore complex surfaces.** Faces that are created by loft, boundary, or other complex methods are more time-consuming when calculating interferences. To increase performance, you can choose to ignore these types of faces.

Using Physical Dynamics

The name Physical Dynamics may be a bit misleading. This is because it does not involve any real analytical dynamics, but involves essentially unconstrained motion and free motion and collision of parts where the parts interact to some extent. When you drag parts around the screen, Physical Dynamics allows you to visualize collisions similar to moving balls on a pool table.

You cannot use Physical Dynamics with Dynamic Clearance. The only adjustment it offers is a sensitivity control that changes the resolution of the reactions. Because it is a live tool (all the reactions happen in real time as you drag parts on the screen), calculation speed is a factor.

Using Sensors

Sensors in SolidWorks keep track of several measurable values and notify you when a value deviates from high and low limits that you can specify. You can use sensors in both parts and assemblies. The types of sensors available in assemblies are Mass, Volume, Surface area, and the following:

- **Simulation data.** Select one of a number of common simulation results to act as a trigger. (Simulation study must be available, so you cannot use this sensor type in SolidWorks Standard; you must have Simulation installed, licensed, and running for this to work.)
- **Dimension.** You can use reference dimensions or driving dimensions, including dimensions calculated by equations.
- **Interference detection.** Detect static parts in assemblies.
- **Measurement.** Any value you would normally take from the Measure tool can be tracked.
- **Proximity.** Establish a sensor location, direction, and acting distance, and the sensor returns a True value if a selected part passes through that sensor.

To add a sensor to an assembly, you must first have the Sensors folder displayed in the assembly FeatureManager. If it is not displayed, you can activate it at Tools ⇨ Options ⇨ FeatureManager, and make sure the Sensors folder is set to Show. This part of Tools ⇨ Options is shown in Figure 7.12.

FIGURE 7.12

Activating the Sensors folder in the FeatureManager

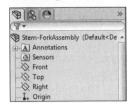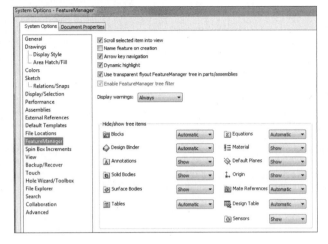

To add a sensor, right-click the Sensors folder at the top of the assembly FeatureManager and select Add Sensor. The Sensor PropertyManager is shown in Figure 7.13, with the Sensor Type drop-down list expanded.

FIGURE 7.13

Adding a sensor to an assembly

Once you have selected a type of sensor to add to the assembly, you can select the parts that are affected, set the options, and then set the alert. The alert appears as a notification balloon if the value returned by the sensor matches the expression you establish in the Alert panel of the Sensor PropertyManager.

For example, when the reference dimension shown in Figure 7.14 changes and becomes less than a certain value, say 1 inch, SolidWorks displays an alert on the Sensors folder.

FIGURE 7.14

Sensors display alerts when an established value meets established criteria.

 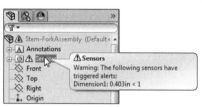

Selecting Components

In the SolidWorks Tools menu for assemblies, there is an entry called Component Selection that offers a wide range of methods, as shown in Figure 7.15. SolidWorks does not have icon-driven activations for these tools, but they are available in the Customize ⇨ Keyboard interface so you can make hotkey shortcuts to them.

FIGURE 7.15

Using the Component Selection methods in the SolidWorks Tools menu

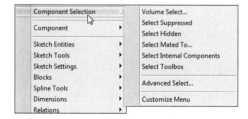

Selecting with a volume

The Volume Select option has no dialog box or PropertyManager interface. The workflow for using this option goes like this:

1. Put the assembly into a view orthogonal to a rectangular volume that you would like to create to select parts of the assembly.

2. Pre-select items to determine where the rectangular volume starts. (Pre-selecting a point makes the face of the volume go through the point; pre-selecting a plane makes the face of the volume coincident with that face.)

3. Initiate the Volume Selection command through the menus at Tools ⇨ Component Selection ⇨ Volume Select. Even though nothing appears to happen — no interface, no change to the screen, no special cursor — continue with your selection.

4. With the cursor, drag a rectangle on the screen (as you would to box-select items in a sketch). After you drag the rectangle, SolidWorks displays a temporary volume and changes to an isometric view. If you draw the original rectangle in an isometric view, the rectangular volume lines up with the screen (not the standard planes), and it rotates the view somewhat to give you access to all three dimensions of the temporary volume. SolidWorks displays arrows on the volume so you can tug and pull the faces to position it for selection of parts.

5. Use the arrows to resize the resulting volume on the screen, as shown in Figure 7.16. SolidWorks selects any part that is completely within the volume. Selection is made automatically when the volume contains the part; you don't have to do anything to activate the selection. Clicking outside of the volume dismisses the temporary display of the volume but retains the selection. While the selection is active, you can use commands from RMB menus as usual.

FIGURE 7.16

Sizing the selection volume

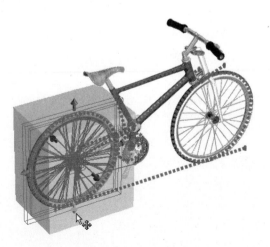

Selecting suppressed components

To select all the parts in an assembly that are currently suppressed, you can use the command available at Tools ➪ Component Selection ➪ Select Suppressed. This command does not have a toolbar button, but you can assign a hotkey to it through the Tools ➪ Customize ➪ Keyboard interface.

The only indication that parts have been selected is in the FeatureManager. Once the parts are selected, you can use RMB options with the selection.

Choosing hidden components

Selecting hidden components works just like selecting suppressed components, and again this command has no interface or toolbar icon but can be linked to a hotkey.

Selecting parts mated to another part

The Tools ➪ Component Selection ➪ Select Mated To command will, as the name suggests, select any part mated to the part you select after you execute the command. There is no interface, and no indication of what to do after you choose the Select Mated To menu option, but for whatever part you click next, SolidWorks selects all the parts that are mated to it.

Selecting internal components

The criteria for what SolidWorks means by "internal components" is not clearly defined. If you run this selection method on the Bike model, it does select a couple of parts that may not be considered strictly internal parts (parts under the seat and the small chainring on the crank). This is one of those tools you may have to experiment with to get the results you want.

Choosing Toolbox parts

The tool found at Tools ➪ Component Selection ➪ Select Toolbox selects all the Toolbox parts in an assembly, including parts at different levels in subassemblies.

Using the Advanced Select options

The Advanced Select command has been around for a very long time in the software yet is not used very often. It used to stand alone as the only advanced selection method, but now with all of these options under the Component Selection heading, it has a lot of company.

Advanced Select uses a classic dialog box interface rather than the newer PropertyManager-type interface used by the more popular tools. Figure 7.17 shows the Advanced Component Selection dialog box.

Using the Advanced Component Selection dialog box

You can use the criteria in the Advanced Component Selection dialog box to set up, save, and reuse queries (searches) based on special categories, conditions, and values. The example in Figure 7.17 sets up a search where the display is Shaded with Edges. Clicking the Apply button runs the search and selects the appropriate parts in the FeatureManager.

An example of where you would use Category 2 is if Category 1 was set to File Status; in this case, Category 2 could be Read Only, Write Access, User With Write Access, Needs Save, or Out of Date. The Condition options would be Is, Is Not, Contains, Does Not Contain, and so on.

You can use this interface to create, save, recall, and run searches based on a wide range of criteria. In most cases, a good PDM system makes these options redundant, but not everyone has a good PDM system installed and running.

Reading AssemblyXpert Results

The AssemblyXpert is a tool that provides information about assemblies. It gives statistics about parts, mates, resolved and lightweight components, subassembly depth, and other information. It may also offer suggestions for how to improve assembly performance. The AssemblyXpert presents information in three status categories, which appear on the left side of the AssemblyXpert window:

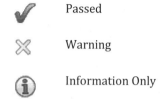 Passed

Warning

Information Only

A sample AssemblyXpert result window is shown in Figure 7.18.

FIGURE 7.18

AssemblyXpert results can help you find solutions for slow assembly performance.

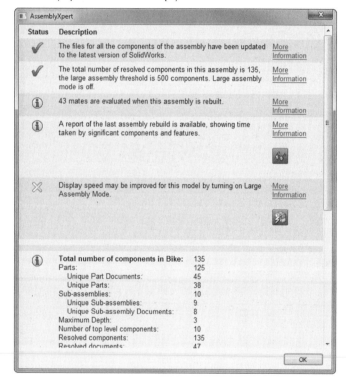

You can speed up the performance of your assemblies by combining AssemblyXpert results with your knowledge of best practice. AssemblyXpert never simply tells you what to do, but it does make suggestions. For example, it might suggest that you use Large Assembly Mode, or it may tell you 386 mates are evaluated when the assembly is rebuilt (which, along with performance problems and best practice knowledge, should tell you that you might want to minimize mates at this level of the assembly).

You should also consider using AssemblyXpert in conjunction with SolidWorks Rx, which can point out a lot of system-level issues.

Using Defeature

Defeature is a new function in SolidWorks 2011 that works in both parts and assemblies. It also works on both imported and native data. This tool allows you to share less-detailed CAD data with other CAD users. The output of this function can be internally stored simplified geometry, or simplified geometry sent to an external file or to 3D Content Central. (3DCC. com is the SolidWorks on-line sharing library for commonly used data.)

In parts, Defeature removes small features, or selected features, and leaves a folder at the top of the FeatureManager, as shown in Figure 7.19. The Defeature folder is associated with a "dumb," featureless, imported body stored in the file as a separate body. You can save these features out using the RMB menu of the Defeature folder in the FeatureManager.

FIGURE 7.19

Defeature in parts

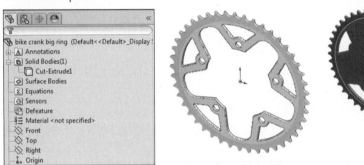

Defeature in the assembly uses a PropertyManager, as follows:

> **Components.** This step enables you to remove components, thus simplifying the defeatured assembly. You can allow SolidWorks to use an automatic method or you can make the selections yourself.

> **Motion.** This step enables you to assemble the remaining parts into groups that work like subassemblies for the purpose of motion.

> **To Keep.** This step defeatures individual parts, filling in holes, removing small features, and so on.

> **Removing Features.** You now wait for SolidWorks to make all the changes you have asked it to do. This might take some time, depending on your computer and the assembly you are defeaturing.

Figure 7.20 shows the steps for using Defeature in an assembly.

FIGURE 7.20

Stepping through Defeature in an assembly

Using the Hole Alignment Tool

 The Hole Alignment tool is found through the menus at Tools ⤳ Hole Alignment, or you can find it on the Evaluate tab of the CommandManager. Hole Alignment is a feature-based evaluation tool. It detects misalignment (defined as centerlines that are farther from one another than the distance you specify) of Hole Wizard holes, simple holes, and extruded cylindrical holes. Figure 7.21 shows the interface of the Hole Alignment tool.

This tool does have some limitations, which are mostly in the types of holes for which it can detect misalignment. The unsupported hole types are as follows:

- Multi-boundary extrudes (multiple circles in a single sketch used for an extruded cut)
- Imported geometry, or geometry created with any of the following:
  - Move Face
  - Move/Copy Body

- Split Part
- Mirror Body
- Mirror Part
- Mirror Component
- Pattern Body
- Insert Part

This list excludes a lot of potential sources for error, and doesn't leave many items of consequence. If you misalign holes using sketches or Hole Wizard holes, you have other problems.

FIGURE 7.21

Using the Hole Alignment PropertyManager

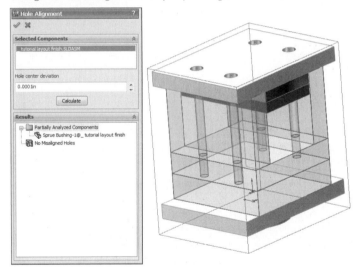

Working with Large Assemblies

Different people define large assemblies differently, but it is safe enough to say that an assembly can be considered "large" if working in it taxes your computer. You could have 10,000 parts with 3 features each, or 10 parts with 3000 features. Unless you are working with a lot of in-context relations and other assembly features, the main measure of what will slow down your computer will be mates. If you put your assembly together wisely, you can avoid some of the common pitfalls and create large assemblies that perform well.

Your approach to getting more performance out of your assemblies should encompass a combination of specialized tools and techniques discussed in this and other chapters. Most of the tools referenced in this chapter are discussed in more detail in Chapter 4, although Chapter 4 does not reference the purpose of these tools as being specifically for use with large assemblies.

Using special techniques to improve large assembly performance

SolidWorks is imperfect software. However, that doesn't mean that every time a challenge presents itself you should just throw up your arms and curse the software. For most problems that you come across in SolidWorks, there is something you can do to improve the situation. These things may not be ideal, but they give you something positive you can do, and it sure beats complaining.

So, in the spirit of making the most out of long rebuild times and waiting for the software to give you back control, here are some suggestions for techniques you can use to improve the performance of SolidWorks when working with large assemblies.

Working locally

Working locally does not help in processing time, but it does help in any save or retrieval times. This might come into play if you open an assembly in lightweight mode, and later have to resolve some parts. When SolidWorks has to reach out over the network to get data, it is always slower than getting parts off your local hard drive. Working locally is something that any PDM program is going to enforce.

Organizing data into subassemblies

When SolidWorks opens an assembly, it has to solve all the mates in the top-level assembly. It doesn't touch the mates in subassemblies unless the subassembly is set to be solved as a flexible subassembly. Therefore, obviously, minimizing the number of mates in the top-level assembly is an advantage. One great way to do that is to have no parts at the top level, only subassemblies, and then mates to locate the subassemblies. Make sure the mates go to something stable, like assembly planes or an assembly sketch.

Avoiding in-context references

In-context references have a well-documented affect on assembly performance. Chapter 10 deals with this topic directly. It can't be stressed enough how important it is to avoid this kind of modeling, especially at the top level of the assembly. For performance reasons, it might be a better idea to look into replacing in-context techniques with master model or multi-body modeling. This is not to say you should replace assemblies with multi-body part models, just that the external reference part of the modeling process can be more efficiently handled by external references between parts, without the assembly.

If you find yourself in a situation with an assembly that already has many in-context references, you may want to use the Lock References option in the List External References dialog. Do not fall into the trap of breaking references, because broken references cannot be repaired. Broken and Locked references perform at the same speed, but locked references can be reestablished later if you need to propagate some changes.

Avoid fancy display settings

Transparent parts and edges in shaded mode are probably the two display settings that cost you a far amount of time. If you use these for parts in large assemblies, just be aware that it will cost you a price in terms of performance.

Repairing errors

A huge time waster is when SolidWorks users continue working in a large assembly when there are errors. Each time SolidWorks encounters an error, it tries to resolve it. If it sees a failed mate, the software is trying to fix the issue in the background. This takes time. If you have an error or a set of errors in your assembly, one of the best things you can do for yourself is to fix the errors so SolidWorks stops trying to resolve them every time it rebuilds.

Avoiding unnecessarily complex geometry

Using things like helixes, extrude sketch text, modeled knurling, threads, large patterns of small holes, and so on can contribute to poor performance of assemblies with a lot of data to process. Even though in assemblies, you don't necessarily have to rebuild all of those part features, often the graphics load of very small features or large numbers of edges or faces contributes significantly to a speed problem. This is another reason to have a good video card.

Using special tools to improve large assembly performance

In addition to the techniques you can use to help improve SolidWorks assembly performance, there are also several tools within the software specifically designed to help you deal with the performance issue.

Using simplified configurations

Part and assembly documents can have configurations, which remove detail and rebuild intensive features. There is even an option in the Open dialog that will open an assembly and turn every part to its simplified configuration (for more information on this see Chapter 8).

The Defeature function can help you simplify parts and assemblies. Simplified configurations of parts and subassemblies can bring you noticeable results without a whole lot of effort. The most rebuild time savings will likely come from a couple of your most complex parts.

Using SpeedPak

A SpeedPak is a derived configuration that can use a subset of parts and subassemblies. The subset can include faces, bodies, and other elements to create extremely simplified configurations, Read more about SpeedPaks in Chapter 8. If you use large assemblies, and you are serious about needing more performance, you should be using SpeedPaks.

Using Display States instead of configurations

If you just use assembly configurations to turn on or off parts, or change transparency, then stop using configurations. Display states are much faster than configurations and don't add to file size. If you are not using display states and you are using large assemblies, you need to at least check them out and see what you're missing.

Using Lightweight options

Lightweight options only load minimal part data to display the assembly. If you need to do more than display and move the assembly, you may need to fully load (resolve) the part data before you can complete those actions. Lightweight saves time when opening assemblies.

Using Large Assembly Mode

Large Assembly Mode is just a combination of lightweight mode, some other settings (detailed at Tools ➪ Option ➪ Assemblies), and a limit number. Once the number of parts goes beyond the limit, the settings kick in automatically.

Using detached drawings

Detached drawings have some of the same limitations that lightweight assemblies have. You can do some things, but not others. When there is a change to the parts or assembly, you have to reload the assembly into the drawing. For more information on the advantages and limitations of detached drawings, see Chapter 16.

Suspending automatic rebuilds

You can prevent parts from rebuilding in assemblies. You can access this setting by right-clicking on the top-level assembly name in the FeatureManager, as shown in Figure 7.22. In the figure, the cursor is on the option. You can manually turn this option back off when you want rebuilds, or open individual parts and assemblies to rebuild documents independently.

FIGURE 7.22

Turn off part and assembly rebuilds

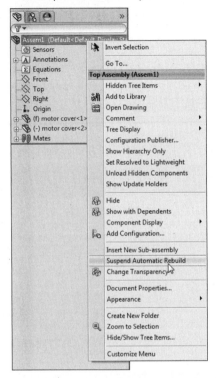

Summary

SolidWorks packs a lot of powerful and useful tools into the assemblies environment. Even if you are an experienced user, it pays to look through the list periodically, because new functions are added frequently or you may have a new use for an old tool.

Controlling Assembly Configurations and Display States

Assembly configurations enable you to control many things, including part configurations, suppression, visibility, color, and assembly feature sizes. They also enable you to control assembly layout sketch dimensions, mate values, suppression states, and several other items. In this chapter, you learn about related topics such as design tables, SpeedPak, derived configurations, and display states.

Display states are a better performance alternative than configurations for controlling visibility and displaying part styles in assemblies. Display state options are discussed at length in this chapter.

Using Display States

Display states enable you to change visual properties more quickly than configurations. Configurations save a lot of extra data if all you need to do is hide or show parts. However, they can be slow to change from one configuration to another, whereas you can change between display states almost instantaneously.

Assembly display states can also control part display states, and different instances of a part in an assembly can use different display states.

Although display states can be used in both parts and assemblies, they have the most impact on assembly work, which is why they have been included in this book instead of *SolidWorks 2011 Parts Bible* (Wiley, 2011).

Controlling display states and configurations

Display states can be either independent of configurations or linked to them, depending on your settings. To control the display, you can use the Display Pane that pops out when you click the double-arrow icon in the upper-right corner of the FeatureManager. Figure 8.1 shows the Display Pane in action, along with an assembly showing parts in different display states.

The Display Pane and an assembly with parts in different display states

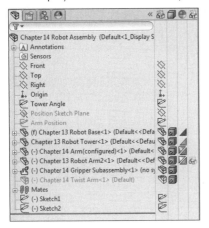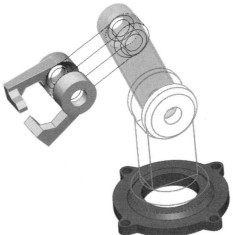

The column symbols for the Display Pane are as follows:

  Hide or show state of the part

  Display Mode options for each component:

  Appearances

  Transparency

  Default Display

  Component/Part Color

Note

The difference between a component and a part in SolidWorks assemblies is that a component is a generic way of identifying any top-level item in an assembly, and may be a single part or a subassembly. The word component always refers to a specific instance of the part within the assembly. In the case shown in Figure 8.1, the gripper jaw part is used twice; this creates two instances of the gripper jaw. One instance has its component color set to a custom color, and the other instance uses the part color. (The component color is also referred to as an override of the part color.) The part color is what you see when you open the part in its own window. The component color is only set in the assembly, and you can only see it in that particular assembly; it never affects how the part displays in any other assembly in which the part is shown.

When there is a difference between the part and component display properties (in other words, when an override exists), the component property appears as the upper-left triangle in the Appearance column of the Display Pane, and the part property appears as the lower-right triangle. You can only see these triangles in the Appearance column of the Display Pane. ■

Appearance overrides are summarized here, showing the lowest priority at the top:

- Part
- Body
- Feature
- Face
- Component
- Assembly

If you override the appearance or display mode for a component in a subassembly, and the upper-left triangle appears in the Display Pane, you can remove the override through the left mouse button (LMB) or the right mouse button (RMB) menu. Figure 8.2 shows the LMB menu from a component of a subassembly with overrides.

FIGURE 8.2

You can remove overrides in the assembly Display Pane.

When you select Clear Override, SolidWorks clears any overrides for the currently selected component. Clear All Top Level Overrides clears all overrides in all subassemblies in the entire top-level assembly. There is no intermediate option to clear all top-level overrides for a particular subassembly; if you want to distinguish between overrides at that level, you need to clear several individual overrides. The options to remove overrides do not affect top-level components.

The active display state appears in angle brackets after the configuration name and the file-name at the top of the FeatureManager, as shown in the image on the left in Figure 8.3. Display states are created and managed in a panel at the bottom of the ConfigurationManager, as shown in the image on the right in Figure 8.3. To create a new display state, simply right-click in the Display Pane and choose Add Display State.

FIGURE 8.3

Display states shown in the FeatureManager and the ConfigurationManager

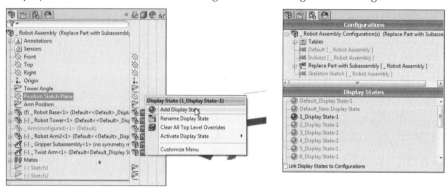

Performance

Display states offer a huge performance gain over configurations when used to control the display of parts. The reason for this is that SolidWorks saves some model information for each configuration. When a configuration is created only for the purpose of hiding or coloring a part, this takes up a lot of additional file space and CPU (central processing unit) time. Display states change much faster than configurations — almost instantaneously — and they add very little to the file size when you use them. ■

Using display states with drawings

Display states can be shown on drawings. If you only show or hide parts in display states, you can still use display states on drawings. For display states that change the display mode (wireframe, shaded, and so on) to work properly, you have to set the view to Shaded, and then select the display state from the PropertyManager for the view. The big drawback here is that you have to change the display state of the parent view; changing the display state of a projected view does nothing, even though the controls are available. Projected views cannot have a display state that is independent from the parent view.

Using part display states in parts

Parts can also have display states, including separate bodies within parts. You can control the part display state for specific instances of a part within an assembly in the Component Properties dialog box. Using part display states offers the same advantages as using assembly display states (mainly display speed), especially when compared to configurations.

Understanding Assembly Configurations

Assembly configurations are used for many different purposes, including assembly performance, simplified assemblies, variations of assemblies, assemblies in different positions or states, and many others. Like part configurations, assembly configurations also have a few best practice–type suggestions. Configuration settings for assemblies control how an assembly appears in a Bill of Materials (BOM), and what happens to parts, features, or mates that are added to other configurations, and so on. All these uses of assembly configurations are discussed in this section.

Applying configurations for performance

One of the best tools to make large assemblies easier to work with is assembly configurations. You can use several techniques to improve the speed of working with assemblies. It is important to select a method that is appropriate to the situation because each method has strengths and weaknesses.

Suppressing components and features

The most obvious use of configurations for improving assembly speed is to have a configuration or several configurations with suppressed components. Suppressed components are not loaded or displayed, so memory and video power are conserved.

Tip

Remember that you can use a folder for parts and suppress the folder. If you are just using configurations to hide parts, consider using display states, as they are more efficient for that purpose. Also, remember that a SpeedPak is a subset of configurations. A SpeedPak is a simplified representation, enabling you to select faces and bodies to represent the entire subassembly for performance reasons. ■

Schemes that you may want to use for suppressing parts need to have one of the following:

Configurations that isolate functional areas of an assembly

Configurations that remove the fasteners or purchased components

Configurations that remove complex parts

Configurations that only leave the parts used in in-context relations

Configurations that suppress patterns and assembly features

Assembly configurations that use simplified part configurations

Configurations that show the assembly in different positions

Variations of the assembly using different part configurations

If you suppress the "ground" part or any part that connects groups of parts, keep in mind that this can cause other parts to float in space unattached. Obviously, this is not a good situation, and you should avoid it if possible. One way to avoid it is to use an assembly layout sketch and mate the parts to the sketch instead of to the ground part.

Aside from components, other items can also be suppressed to improve performance, such as assembly features and component patterns. Do you really need to see all those parts patterned around the assembly to work on it in a simplified representation? You may be able to suppress the parts. If you feel you cannot suppress parts, then consider at least using display states to hide parts that are needed to complete the parametrics but do not need to display.

Performance

The biggest hindrance to assembly speed is the circular reference. You can make circular references in a couple of different ways, but they are usually the result of mixing history-based functions (mates, in-context sketch relations, feature references) with non-history-based functions (parts shown in the assembly FeatureManager). This enables you to create partial or complete loops of references, where A references B, which references A. These are a particular problem with in-context references, which are discussed in more depth in Chapter 10. ■

Configuring SpeedPaks

A SpeedPak is a configuration that uses only selected faces and bodies to represent an entire subassembly, instead of opening all the parts in the assembly. In fact, a SpeedPak stores the geometry in the assembly file so it doesn't have to open any part files at all.

SpeedPaks are mentioned here because they are a form of configuration, essentially a derived configuration, and because they are configurable. As a result, you can have top-level assembly configurations that call on subassemblies to use their SpeedPaks. That can be extremely helpful with very large assembly performance.

Using part configurations for speed

Simplified part configurations can consist of configurations with cosmetic features such as small fillets and extruded text, or other cosmetic details that are suppressed. Assembly configurations can use different part configurations, which, for example, would enable you to make an assembly configuration called "Simplified," and in it reference all the Simplified part configurations.

Tip

When opening an assembly through the Open dialog box, the Advanced option also enables you to create a new assembly configuration that uses part configurations of a given name, if available. The default part configuration name entered in the text box seems to suggest how SolidWorks intended for this function to be used. As shown in Figure 8.4, it is "Simplified." In previous versions, the Advanced button was conspicuously placed on the front of the Open dialog box, but by 2009, it was changed to a selection hidden in the list of configurations, as shown in Figure 8.4. ■

FIGURE 8.4

The Advanced option for assemblies in the Open dialog box

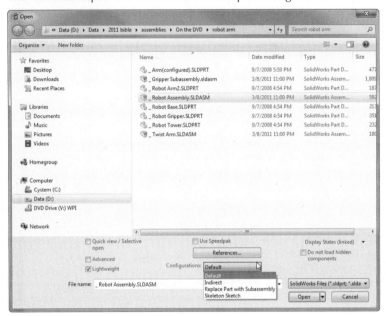

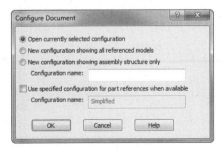

Other special operations for assembly configurations in the Open dialog box include creating a new configuration that has all the components suppressed. This enables you to see the structure of the assembly without fully resolving all the components. Another option is to open the assembly with a new configuration, where all the components are resolved. Beyond that, the Open dialog box also enables you to select a specific configuration to open to so that you do not have to wait for the last saved configuration to load and then make the change.

Getting familiar with the Advanced Component Selection

The Advanced Component Selection dialog box, shown in Figure 8.5, was formerly called Advanced Show/Hide Components. You can access this dialog box by right-clicking the configuration name in the ConfigurationManager and selecting Advance Select.

FIGURE 8.5

The Advanced Component Selection dialog box

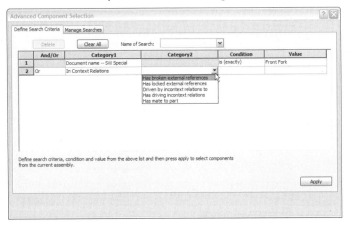

This tool enables you to establish search criteria and show or hide parts based on the criteria. Multiple criteria can be used, stored, and retrieved. This tool is generally underused, and people are often surprised to find it in the software. It has existed since about 1998 and has undergone a facelift in the last two releases. The Category 1 options enable you to search on things such as document name, in-context status, part mass, and other standard SolidWorks information. Category 2 can be either custom property information or structured options for Category 1, such as specific in-context conditions.

Taking a look at the Isolate function

Isolate works like the inverse of the Show command. If you select multiple parts and click Isolate from the RMB menu, the selected parts remain shown, and everything else becomes hidden. A little popup menu gives you the option to show the removed components in a Wireframe or Transparent display mode, or to save the current display as a new display state. This is a very useful function, as shown in Figure 8.6.

The Isolate function can create display states.

Finding features with the Simplify Assembly tool

If you have the SolidWorks Office bundle, then you can activate the Utilities add-in. You can do this by choosing Tools ➪ Add-ins, and then selecting Utilities. This displays a Utilities menu with the Simplify option. The Simplify Assembly tool is shown in Figure 8.7. (This tool appears in the Task Pane on the right side of the screen.)

FIGURE 8.7

The Simplify Assembly tool

The Simplify Assembly tool can help you find features in the parts of the assemblies that are under a certain size or that take up less than a certain percentage of the volume of the part. You can then suppress these features in special derived configurations.

Controlling display performance

Overall, SolidWorks performance is split into two categories: CPU processing and GPU (graphics processing unit) processing. Which of these functions your computer performs better depends on your hardware, drivers, and system maintenance, among other factors.

When trying to speed up the performance of an assembly, you can make the biggest impact by reducing the load on both the CPU and the GPU. You can do this by suppressing a part. When a part is suppressed, it is neither calculated nor displayed; this means the load on each processor for that part is zero.

When you hide a part, its parametric features are still calculated by the CPU; however, because the part is hidden, it does not create a load on the GPU. If you have a good main processor and a questionable video card, then you will achieve a greater benefit from removing graphics load from your display.

Using Lightweight parts settings

If you want to show a part, but not calculate any of its parametric relations, you can use Lightweight parts. You can access the Lightweight default settings by choosing Tools ⇨ Options on both the Assemblies and Performance pages. You can make parts lightweight through the RMB menu. The opposite of lightweight is resolved. *Resolved* means that the part is fully loaded, its parametrics are loaded and calculated by the CPU, and its graphics display data is calculated and shown by the GPU.

Working with SpeedPak

There is some confusion about where the SpeedPak functionality falls into this scheme of things. With a SpeedPak, the parametrics are not loaded, but the graphics are. In addition, some of the geometry is selectable, as if it were imported geometry (actual geometry but without rebuildable parametrics). However, a SpeedPak applies only to subassemblies, where the need for improvement is a lot higher.

There is a five-way relationship between the Resolved, SpeedPak, Lightweight, Hidden, and Suppressed states, as shown in Figure 8.8.

FIGURE 8.8

The relationship between the Resolved, SpeedPak, Lightweight, Hidden, and Suppressed states

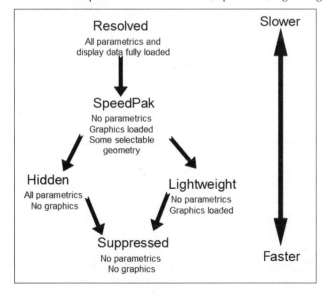

Comparing resolved to unsuppressed

The terminology becomes a little convoluted here because of the relationship between the five different states. In parts, the feature states are easy to remember because features can be either suppressed or unsuppressed. However, in assemblies, there are five states instead of two, and so *unsuppressed* could mean anything that is not suppressed, which still leaves three states. For this reason, *resolved* is used instead of *unsuppressed* when dealing with components in an assembly.

Using configurations for positions

When you use configurations to display an assembly in various positions, you can do it either by changing mates or by changing a layout sketch. Mates are configurable in two ways: mates can be suppressed and unsuppressed, and angle and distance mate values can be configured in the same way that sketch dimensions can be configured. Although creating a mate scheme that enables you to reposition the assembly using mate suppression states and values is essential to this method, it may not be the best approach. When mates are suppressed, then the components move, and if the mates are later unsuppressed, the assembly may not return to the original position. Mates can often be solved in different orientations, and may flip if turned on and off in this way.

Using a skeleton or layout sketch to mate parts may be a better approach, although this also has its drawbacks. If you mate to a layout sketch, you cannot use Dynamic Assembly Motion. If you use the mate scheme discussed previously, this generally means having a fully defined assembly, and this does not allow for Dynamic Assembly Motion.

As a compromise, a good way to handle this is by using one configuration for Dynamic Assembly Motion, with one or more open degrees of freedom. You can use other configurations to fully define the mechanism and show it in particular positions using either method. Probably the best way to demonstrate this idea is with an example using the robot arm assembly.

Positioning with mates

First, look at positioning with mates. On an assembly such as this one, the goal is to position the grippers. You can do this a couple of ways, both directly and indirectly. In the assembly used for this chapter, the grippers have been rebuilt as a subassembly, which allows different types of control. Notice that the subassembly has a configuration for the closed position and one that allows Dynamic Assembly Motion. In addition, the subassembly is being solved as Flexible. Figure 8.9 shows the assembly and the FeatureManager.

Driving the position directly

A sketch point has been added to the subassembly to identify the precise point on the gripper that is to be positioned. Sketch points have also been added to the main assembly to represent parts that need to be picked up by the robotic arm.

FIGURE 8.9

The assembly used for this example

Check the derived configurations under the default configuration. Notice that when you switch between certain configurations, the parts seem to separate. Moving one of the links causes the parts to snap back together again. This is probably because there are so many options when moving between configurations that the software has difficulty choosing a final position. This is definitely one of the potential problems when using configured mates to show an assembly in various positions.

Notice also that although the grippers are positioned correctly, the arm is still allowed to swivel around the intended target point. You can correct this by defining an orientation for the grippers for each location. If an additional pivot were added to the assembly, then fully defining the parts would become more difficult. The arm would not be able to reach any additional points, but it would not be so limited in orienting the grippers at each point.

Driving the position indirectly

You can also use mates to drive configured positions of the assembly using a series of angle mates. This makes it more difficult because to get to a particular location, you have to do some calculations, but the angle mates are more stable than simply relying on moving parts to unconstrained positions.

If you cycle through the derived configurations under the Indirect top-level configuration, you will notice that mates are not suppressed and unsuppressed; instead, the values are changed. This makes it more difficult to position the grippers precisely, but because it is specific about the positions of the individual parts, there is no ambiguity.

Positioning with sketches

Although this technique still uses mates to position the parts and to change the position, you change sketch dimensions rather than mate values. Sketches used to drive parts from an

195

assembly are sometimes called *layout sketches* or *skeletons*. They are also discussed in Chapter 10 for in-context or top-down assembly techniques. Figure 8.10 shows the same assembly that is used for the rest of this chapter.

Positioning assembly components with sketches

Position Sketch Plane

This particular assembly is driven by two sketches on different planes to govern the position of the parts. Keep in mind that this assembly has been used for all the other techniques as well; this means that all these techniques can exist together simultaneously and are controlled by configurations.

Examine the assembly to see how the parts are mated to the sketches. This is important. The first time you create a part such as this, you may be tempted to mate part planes to the sketch lines.

Caution

Beware that mating planes to sketch lines has a very serious drawback. Unlike other types of mates, which have an alignment that you can control, plane-to-sketch line mates cannot be aligned. This means that the software may not align elements correctly on any plane-to-line mate. ∎

Best Practice

A better way to mate part planes to sketch lines is to mate the Temporary Axes through the joints with the sketch endpoints. This solves the alignment problem. ∎

Applying configurations for product variations

In this case, *product variations* mean variations in size or part replacement. Some examples are a 4-foot cabinet and an 8-foot cabinet, or a two-button mouse and a three-button mouse.

As a simple example, Figure 8.11 shows the familiar robotic arm assembly, but with a variation: one of the arms has been replaced with a subassembly. The subassembly is made of the original replaced part using configurations, and there are configurations of the subassembly, which is again being used as a flexible subassembly.

A part that is replaced by a subassembly

Through the course of this chapter, the robot arm assembly has greatly increased in complexity, but it has retained the original information that was in the first version. Maintaining valid assembly data through manually managed configurations is difficult, and all it takes is a simple mistake to wipe out a lot of assembly configuration data. Appropriately, the next section discusses assembly design tables.

Using design tables for assembly configurations

This chapter augments information you need to know to use design tables effectively in assemblies. Assembly design tables can do everything that part design tables can do, except for selecting configurations of base parts and split parts, which are not valid assembly functions. Assembly design tables can also do some things that a part design table cannot, including the following:

- Suppressing the state of a part (R for Resolved or S for Suppressed)
- Assigning the component configuration for the assembly configuration
- Enabling you to activate the Never Expand in BOM option

If you have been using design tables for a while and are familiar with older versions of SolidWorks, then you may have noticed that the $show parameter, which specified whether the part was shown or hidden, has become obsolete due to the new functions of display states.

Figure 8.12 shows the design table results from auto-creation using the robot arm assembly. Some of the columns have been hidden to make it small enough to fit on the page. If you want to see the entire table, you need to open the assembly. If you edit the design table, you will probably want to use the Open in Separate Window option, which is easier to navigate and control. The *SolidWorks 2011 Parts Bible* (Wiley, 2011) has a chapter devoted to design tables in parts.

FIGURE 8.12

An automatically created design table from the robot arm assembly

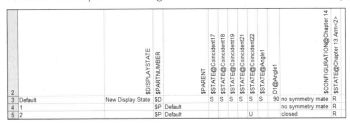

Working with Modify Configurations and the Configuration Publisher

The Modify Configuration interface is a dialog box where you can configure dimensions, features, and custom properties in parts, and that you can use in assemblies. It is sometimes used in the place of design tables when you do not need the advanced functionality of Excel.

The Configuration Publisher is used to create a PropertyManager that pops up when the part is placed into an assembly. The PropertyManager enables you to select a configuration to go into the assembly. The Configuration Publisher is also available in assemblies; this means you can use a popup PropertyManager when assemblies are placed into other assemblies as well. Library subassemblies may be less common than library parts, where the popup PropertyManager would be used to best effect.

Both tools are useful for managing assembly configurations. Design tables offer the most complete control, but also have some drawbacks associated with being tied to Microsoft Excel. Both Modify Configurations and the Configuration Publisher are internal to SolidWorks, regardless of the level of the software you have purchased, so if you use one of them, you can be sure that whomever you send data to will be able to access all the functionality.

Looking at assembly configuration dos and don'ts

Assembly configurations have some potential pitfalls that you can avoid if you pay attention to some of these dos and don'ts.

- **Avoid using Delete as an editing option when working with configurations.** Delete is forever and removes items from all configurations.

- **Avoid the use of in-context relations to size parts when you are also using configurations to size parts.** A non-configured part driven by a configured part only causes confusion.

- **Avoid using configurations to represent document control-type revisions.** When people attempt to do this, it ultimately limits the kinds of edits they can make to their parts and assemblies, and it is far too easy to make a mistake that wipes out all their work. In the end, this is not a viable technique.

- **If you are working with manually created configurations, then you should create a new configuration and activate it before making the changes.** Otherwise, you will end up trying to set the original configuration back to the way it was.

- **Remember to select the This Configuration Only option for changed dimensions instead of leaving it at the default All Configurations setting.**

Tutorial: Working with Assembly Configurations

To begin this tutorial, open the assembly named Bike.sldasm. This file contains all the aspects that you need to work with in this chapter, including subassemblies, motion, and part configurations.

To learn how to work with assembly configurations, follow these steps:

1. **Prepare to use configurations by splitting the FeatureManager window into an upper and lower pane.** Place the FeatureManager on the top and the ConfigurationManager on the bottom.

2. **Before starting to make changes to this assembly, add the top-level configurations that you will need, as follows:**

   - Small Tires

   - Motion Configuration

   - Skeleton Driven Positions

   - Mate Driven Positions

   The configurations will list alphabetically.

3. **Make sure that the Advanced options for each configuration are set to suppress new features and mates and suppress new components.**

4. **Activate the Small Tires configuration.** Figure 8.13 shows the FeatureManager up to this point.

FIGURE 8.13

The FeatureManager and ConfigurationManager up to Step 4

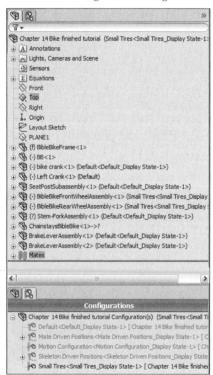

5. **Open the Front Wheel Assembly in its own window and switch to the ConfigurationManager.** Add a configuration called Small Tires, and change the tire to the configuration called Small Tires, which has already been created.

6. **Switch back to the main assembly window (Ctrl+Tab), RMB+click the Front Wheel Assembly in the FeatureManager, and select Component Properties.** Select the Small Tires configuration for the Front Wheel assembly, as shown in Figure 8.14.

FIGURE 8.14

Changing the tires in the Component Properties dialog box

7. **Repeat Steps 4 to 6 for the Rear Wheel assembly.**

8. **Double-click another configuration from the list and watch the assembly change from small to fat tires.**

9. **Change to the Motion configuration.** RMB+click the Stem-Fork assembly, select Component Properties, and set the assembly to be solved as Flexible.

10. **Exit the dialog box and check to see that the fork linkage mechanism moves by dragging the fork.** Notice that the fork works but that the front wheel does not move with it. The bike design is not yet complete, so you do not need to worry about that at this point. Putting the front wheel in the fork assembly could be used to make the wheel move with the fork.

11. **Switch to the Skeleton Driven Positions configuration.**

12. **Display the assembly layout sketch at the top of the FeatureManager.**

13. **Create two new derived configurations under the Skeleton Driven Positions configuration, one called Default Position and the other called Compressed Position.**

14. **Activate the Default Position configuration, and make a coincident mate between the Top plane of the Chainstay part and the sketch line indicated in Figure 8.15.** Again, the wheel does not move at this time.

FIGURE 8.15

Positioning the rear of the bike

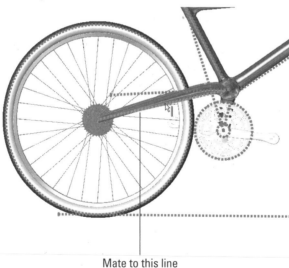

Mate to this line

15. **Activate the Compressed Position configuration and make a coincident mate between the same plane and the line that is angled up at 10 degrees.**

Note

For these configurations, you also need to set the Advanced options just as you set the top-level configurations in Step 3. If you do not do this, you may need to suppress the unwanted mates manually in the appropriate configurations. ∎

16. **Switch to the Mate Driven Position configuration.** Change the stem-fork assembly to a flexible subassembly (RMB+click and choose Component Properties ⇨ Solve as Flexible).

17. **Add new derived configurations called 1, 2, and 3.** While creating the new configurations, ensure that the Suppress new features and mates and Suppress new components options are selected. Leave the 1 configuration activated.

18. **Make an angle mate between the Bike assembly Top plane and the face of the link, as shown in Figure 8.16.**

Using angles to position the fork

19. **Once the mate is complete, double-click the angle dimension (you may have to double-click the angle mate to get it to display and then zoom out to see it), and change the value to 18 degrees.** Again, with the change, the fork may fly to an unexpected location. Pressing Ctrl+Q brings it back.

20. **Switch to the configuration 2, unsuppress the angle mate that you made in Step 18, and change the value to 25 degrees.** You may have to change the configuration 2 to Flexible, although it should inherit this property from the parent configuration.

Note

You need to set the Fork assembly to solve as Flexible for each configuration. You may also need to control the alignment for the angle mate manually for each configuration. ∎

Summary

Display states in the assembly can save you a lot of time because they change faster than configurations and offer more options for visualization, including mixed display modes. Assembly design tables can select display states and drive many other parameters in assemblies. Remember also that Modify Configurations and the Configuration Publisher work in assemblies as well as in parts. Assembly configurations are a very powerful tool for product variations and performance, especially when combined with a SpeedPak.

Patterning and Mirroring Components

In SolidWorks assemblies, the word *component* can refer to either parts or subassemblies at the top level of an assembly. Component patterns can therefore be patterns of parts, subassemblies, or combinations of parts and subassemblies.

Component patterns come in two varieties: local patterns, which include linear and circular patterns, and feature-driven patterns, which are driven by a feature pattern in a part. The local patterns are obviously somewhat limited, but because feature-driven patterns follow patterned features, they can also be driven by sketch-driven patterns. Curve-driven and fill patterns can also be used.

It is possible to focus only on the basics, making patterns that exist in the present moment. However, if you are interested in creating features that will adapt to future changes, then you will find the tools in this chapter useful.

Mirroring components in assemblies is far more complex than mirroring features in parts. SolidWorks provides options for mirrored parts, mirrored positions, left- and right-hand versions of parts, and mirroring parts and subassemblies within top-level assemblies.

Using Local Component Patterns

Local component patterns are limited to linear and circular patterns; SolidWorks assemblies do not offer the wealth of options available for patterning features in a part such as curve driven, table driven, sketch driven, and fill pattern. The linear pattern directions work just like the linear pattern feature in parts, and must reference a line, axis, edge, and so on to establish the direction. In an assembly, this means that the pattern feature uses either local reference geometry from the assembly (such as axes, planes, or assembly sketches), or model geometry from a part (such as solid or surface edges, sketches, or reference geometry). This is important to keep in mind if you are concerned about circular references. By using references belonging to the assembly rather than to parts, you avoid some common referencing pitfalls.

Best Practice

If you have a feature pattern in a part, you should take advantage of it and use a feature-driven pattern instead of a local pattern. The rebuild time may be longer, but associativity between the part and assembly helps maintain design intent. ■

Creating local pattern references

If you still need to create a local pattern, it is best to use a reference that is not dependent on part geometry. Remember that when part geometry is used as an assembly pattern reference, the parts must be solved first (sketches and features rebuilt), then the mates must be solved (to position the parts), then any in-context references must be solved (which may change the part geometry), and then any assembly features or component patterns must be solved. As a result, it is best practice to use assembly reference geometry or assembly sketches without references as pattern direction references. The assembly sketches should sit at the top of the assembly FeatureManager to ensure that they are not picking up references from the history-based features in the design tree (mated components, patterns, assembly features, and so on).

When a local pattern really requires a reference from a part, you have no alternative. However, if you can avoid this situation by using a sketch assembly skeleton to which the parts are mated and used for the pattern references, then you should do so. At all costs, you should avoid using in-context features, assembly reference geometry that is dependent on part geometry, and assembly features (other than sketches) for the local pattern reference.

Figure 9.1 shows one way that you can set up an assembly to properly control local component patterns. The three short construction lines can be created in either two 2D sketches or a single 3D sketch. The lines are dimensioned from planes, which enables them to be angled for patterns that are not square to the coordinate system of the assembly, but still lie on its main planes.

Using 3D sketch lines in each X, Y, and Z direction may be clever, but it may be a better idea to have X, Y, and Z direction axes already saved in your assembly templates for just such a purpose.

In most situations, the rebuild time penalty of using model geometry to establish pattern direction is slight. The sketch method is probably most justifiable in large, complex assemblies, or in assemblies requiring long rebuild times. Figure 9.1 also shows the PropertyManager interface for the local pattern.

FIGURE 9.1

The Assembly FeatureManager for local component pattern setup

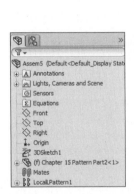

Notice where the pattern is placed in the FeatureManager. You can reorder the pattern feature in the design tree, but you cannot move it above the mates. Interestingly, you can move the sketches after the pattern, even though the pattern is dependent on one of the sketches. Obviously, SolidWorks is working with the order behind the scenes in such a way that the user cannot make mistakes.

Patterning the seed only

All the aspects of the interface should be familiar to you, such as the direction, instances, and spacing. The Pattern seed only option is used in feature patterns.

This option is designed to allow you to create a single pattern in two directions that are separated by 180 degrees, where the internal instances do not overlap one another. For example, if you take a basic two-directional pattern and change the angle between the directions so that they are anti-parallel (parallel but going in opposite directions), then all the component instances that were between the two legs of the L created by the two directions will come to overlap one another when they are laid out in a straight line.

Figure 9.2 shows how a 5-by-4 pattern with 20 instances becomes a 1-by-8 pattern (the seed is not counted twice). To be clear, the figure shows a two-direction pattern where the angle between the directions becomes increasingly shallow, until the two directions are parallel or anti-parallel. When this happens, the other 12 instances overlap the remaining ones. When you use the Pattern seed only option, you are only patterning the two legs of the L, and not the instances in between. Having parts that overlap can cause problems with Bills of Materials (BOMs) and mass properties due to having duplicate parts.

FIGURE 9.2

Use the Pattern seed only option for two-directional patterns.

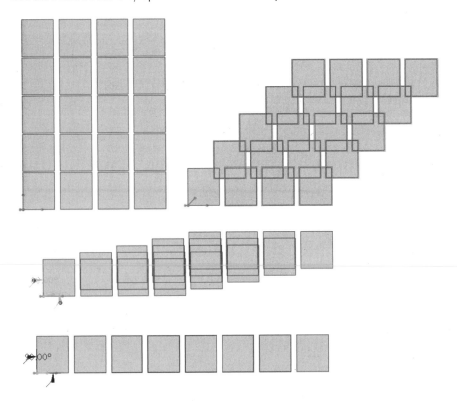

Using the Instances to Skip option

The Instances to Skip option for component patterns, shown in Figure 9.3, works just like the equivalent option for features. Click the dots in the graphics window to toggle each instance of the pattern. On the screen, the instances to keep use pink dots and the instances to skip use orange dots. The colors are almost indistinguishable at a relatively wide spacing.

FIGURE 9.3

The Instances to Skip option

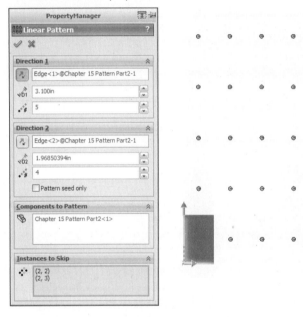

Performance

For best pattern performance, you should use subassemblies as the patterned unit as much as is practical. Multiple patterns of individual components are not as efficient as a single pattern of multiple components. A single pattern of a single component, where the single component is itself a subassembly, is the best choice, if available.

Another performance issue is the fact that component patterns require external references (for the direction or center of the pattern). These external references have the potential to increase rebuild times if you do not choose them carefully. Reference geometry internal to the assembly would be the best choice.

Although you may experience performance problems with patterns, they can also significantly decrease the number of mates in an assembly, which always improves performance. ∎

Using Mirror Components

Mirror Components leaves a feature in the assembly tree just as pattern features do. It gives you the option to align each mirrored part, and to decide which parts require opposite-handed versions and which can just use the original in a mirrored location. Figure 9.4 shows the PropertyManager for this assembly feature.

The workflow to mirror components in the assembly has three steps, as shown in Figure 9.4:

1. **Selections.** Select the parts and subassemblies that you want to mirror, along with the plane about which you want to mirror the components.

2. **Set Orientation.** Identify the components that need to have opposite-hand versions, and for the others, you can toggle through the available options for placement.

3. **Opposite Hand Versions.** For the parts that need opposite-hand versions, you can assign them to use new parts or derived configurations.

The first step should be self-explanatory. Just make selections of parts and the plane as you would in other situations. You move between the steps by clicking the arrows in blue circles in the upper-right corner of the Mirror Components PropertyManager.

Setting the orientation

The second step requires some explanation. In the PropertyManager labeled Step 2: Set Orientation (see Figure 9.4), notice that there are some mirror symbols (small bell shapes) in front of the BrakeLeverAssembly and BrakeMountBibleBike selections in the Orient Components panel. This means that these documents need to have mirrored instances. You control this option by selecting the part or assembly in the Orient Components list box, and then clicking the Create Opposite Hand Version button at the bottom of the PropertyManager.

Another part of this second step is to correctly orient those parts that do not require an opposite-hand version. To do this, select a part in the Orient Components list box, such as the GripsBibleBike part, and click through the double arrows just below the selection box. In Figure 9.4, the message, "3 of 4," is grayed out because a part that requires an opposite hand is selected. When you click the arrows, the part repositions in another possible mirrored position and orientation.

Creating opposite-hand versions

In the third step, in the Opposite Hand Versions panel of the PropertyManager, only the documents that need to be changed are listed. In this case, the brake lever assembly is made of two parts: the lever part can be used in both left- and right-hand versions, but the mount must have two different versions of the part. This means the assembly must also have two versions.

FIGURE 9.4

Mirroring components of an assembly with the Mirror Components tool

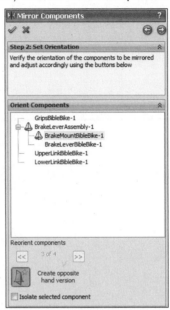

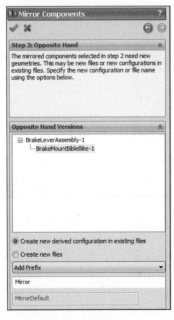

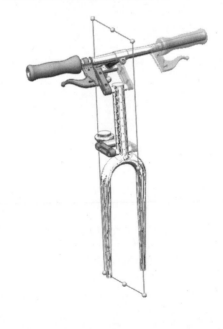

This Mirror Components functionality is fantastic, involving a well thought-out process. To make the mirrored versions, you have the option to create new files or to create a derived configuration within the existing files.

As you are setting up these options, SolidWorks displays a preview of the result in the graphics window. The preview parts are transparent and may be a pale yellow (you may want to change them to a darker orange color at Tools ⇨ Options ⇨ Colors ⇨ Temporary Graphics, Shaded). You can see how the parts are oriented and can immediately fix any problems that arise. With larger assemblies and larger sets of mirrored components, the visualization may be more difficult, but the process demonstrated here on these parts works and gives a complete set of options as you work through the process of mirroring parts and assemblies within the top-level assembly.

Completing the task

When you are done with the task, you can click the green check mark icon. In this case, SolidWorks displays a message that one of the mates in the mirrored assembly could not be duplicated, as shown in Figure 9.5. After testing the motion of the fork linkage, this missing mate does not appear to affect the assembly.

FIGURE 9.5

A mate is not created as the mirroring task is completed.

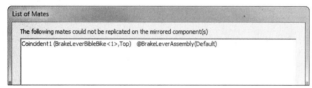

On the DVD

The files for the fork and handlebar assembly are on the DVD in the `Pattern and Mirror` folder. ∎

The Mirror Component feature leaves a marker in the assembly FeatureManager after the Mates folder. In Figure 9.6, notice that the BrakeLeverAssembly and BrakeMountBibleBike documents use a MirrorDefault configuration, as was established while mirroring the assembly and parts.

FIGURE 9.6

Examining the list of mirrored components

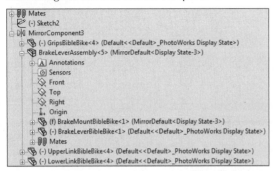

Using Feature-Driven Component Patterns

By their very nature, feature-driven component patterns defy some of the best practice suggestions in this book. This is because the pattern is driven by part geometry, and the part must first be solved (by solving features internal to the part) and then placed (by solving mates); only then can the feature-driven pattern be solved. Nevertheless, you should use feature-driven patterns over local patterns when available because of the parametric link. Parametric associativity is, after all, one of the main benefits that SolidWorks offers.

Note

For the feature-driven component patterns, the location of the initial component is important. You need to match the placement of the initial component with the position of the original feature from which the pattern was created, not one of the patterned instances. You can get around this requirement if you use the Select Seed Position option. When you do this, the feature pattern instances all appear with dots, and you can select which instance to use as the seed. Again, the selected dot is blue and unselected dots are purple, nearly indistinguishable at the size and spacing of the dots. Figure 9.7 shows the PropertyManager interface for a feature-driven component pattern. ■

You can nest feature-driven component patterns such that one component pattern is patterned by another component pattern, just as you do using feature patterns. The second pattern can be a local pattern or a feature-driven pattern.

FIGURE 9.7

The feature-driven component pattern interface

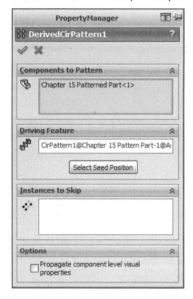 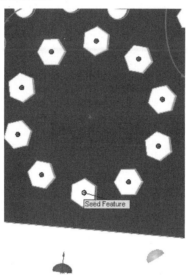

Understanding Other Pattern Options

SolidWorks provides additional options to help you work with patterns. These options can help you with component organization and visualization, which are always key elements when you are working in an assembly.

Figure 9.8 shows the RMB menu for a component pattern. The components of the RMB menu are as follows:

- **Dissolve Pattern.** The Dissolve Pattern option removes the component instances from the pattern feature and puts them in the main part of the assembly FeatureManager. The components just become normal components in the assembly without the intelligence of the pattern feature placing them. The components are left in the assembly without any mates and are simply floating in position.

- **Add to New Folder.** You can add patterns to folders. If you have a list of patterns at the end of an assembly, it may make sense to group them into related folders for the purpose of organization. This is the same as using folders for features, mates, or components.

- **Component pattern display options.** You can change the appearance of individual component pattern instances either individually or collectively as a pattern feature. Figure 9.9 shows the Display Pane where you can control these display options.

FIGURE 9.8

The component RMB menu

• **Component patterns and configurations.** Individual instances of the component pattern also enable you to control configurations. After you create the pattern, you can select individual instances and change their configurations. This can be extremely useful if you have a mechanism subassembly shown in various positions, for example, patterned around an indexing dial.

FIGURE 9.9

The Display Pane for controlling display options

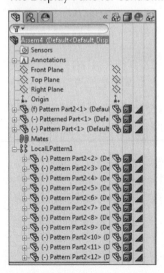

Tutorial: Creating Component Patterns

To learn how to create component patterns, follow these steps:

1. **Open a new assembly.** Create a new 3D sketch and draw three lines from the Origin out at odd angles so that they do not pick up horizontal or vertical automatic relations. Draw two of the lines; then rotate the view, press the Tab key, and draw the third line.

2. **Apply sketch relations such that each line lies on a plane: one line on the Front, one on the Top, and one on the Right.**

3. **Click Close to exit the sketch when you are done.**

4. **Open the part from the DVD named** `Pattern Part.sldprt`. This part already contains several features that you can use to practice working with feature-driven component patterns.

5. **Insert the part into the new assembly created in Step 1.** Locate the part at the assembly Origin such that the part Origin matches the assembly Origin.

6. **Open the part called** `Patterned Part.sldprt`, **and place it in the assembly.**

7. **Place the small part on the original feature of the rectangular pattern of round holes near the Origin, as shown in Figure 9.10.** All the original features are colored red. Remember that Alt+dragging the circular edge on the flat side of the part enables you to SmartMate the part to the round holes. It cannot help you with the rectangular or hex holes. For these, it may be best to show the sketch for the holes and place the part with respect to the sketch entities.

FIGURE 9.10

Placing the patterned part

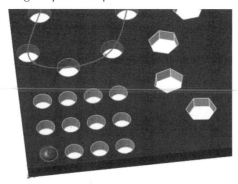

8. **Create feature-driven patterns (Insert ➪ Component Pattern ➪ Feature Driven).** Try to use each of the patterns from the pattern part. For each new pattern, make a copy of the patterned part and place it in one of the holes. Remember to use the Select Seed Position option to pick a feature pattern instance instead of the original feature.

9. **Once you have created a few feature-driven patterns and have a better understanding of how it is done, right-click the top level of the assembly FeatureManager and select Collapse Items (near the bottom of the menu).** The point of this example is simply to practice placing a part and patterning it with an existing feature pattern. The assembly will look like Figure 9.11 when you are done.

FIGURE 9.11

Several feature-driven patterns

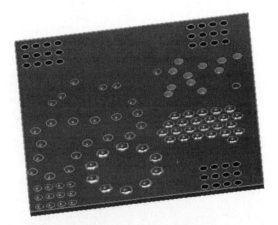

10. **Create a local pattern (Insert ➪ Component Pattern ➪ Linear Pattern).** Select one of the sketch lines drawn in Step 1 as a pattern direction.

11. **Highlight the Components to Pattern selection box.** Select the first part in the FeatureManager and then Shift+select the last pattern feature. This patterns everything in the assembly.

12. **Make the spacing 4 inches with three instances.**

13. **Create a second direction using another of the sketch lines with 6-inch spacing and four instances.**

14. **Notice how the preview shows 12 instances of the patterned assembly.** Select the option for Pattern Seed Only and see how the preview changes to seven instances. Figure 9.12 shows this difference. Click OK to accept the feature.

FIGURE 9.12

Two direction patterns, one with and one without the Pattern Seed Only option

Summary

Performance and best practice are both issues that require compromise. Patterns can cause a performance reduction because of the nature of the references. However, they can also improve performance because the need for extra mates is reduced, and it is easier to simplify the assembly by suppressing the pattern feature.

Feature-driven patterns are driven by feature patterns and transgress best practice suggestions, but they also add a parametric link, which updates the component pattern automatically. In addition, they offer many more options that are driven by the pattern options available to features in a part.

Modeling in Context

This chapter presents a balanced description of the pros and cons of in-context modeling. It provides the information you need to make informed decisions about whether or how to use this powerful tool. In-context modeling is a topic worthy of some investigation before you combine production data with external references. Almost anything you can do with in-context modeling can also be done another way, but in-context is the traditional way of using the geometry of one part to drive another.

In-context modeling extends parametric design from individual parts to top-level assemblies. With this power comes the potential for unexpected results. If you are not careful, in-context modeling can lead to difficulties with file management and loss of control over changes.

IN THIS CHAPTER

Evaluating in-context modeling pros and cons

Understanding inserted, split, and mirror parts

Understanding the Layout workflow

Working in content tutorial

Understanding In-Context Modeling

In-context modeling is also known as *top-down* or *in-place* modeling. It is a technique used to create relationships between parts in the context of an assembly in which the geometry of one of the parts is controlled by both the other part and the mates that position them relative to one another.

In-context, or top-down, modeling may be contrasted against *bottom-up* modeling. Bottom-up modeling involves making the parts in their own individual windows and mates.

assembling the finished parts into an assembly with

In its most common form, a sketch in one part in an assembly is related to an edge in another part in the assembly. The relationship is specific to that particular assembly, and is only relevant *in the context of* that assembly. For example, you may create a box and put it into an assembly. You must then create a lid that is parametrically linked to the size and shape of the box. You can create a lid part in the context of the assembly such that the lid always matches the box. Sketch relationships, dimensions, and feature end conditions from the lid can reference the box. When the box changes, the lid also changes *if the assembly is open*.

The assembly maintains a record of each in-context reference. If the box is changed with both the assembly and the top open, then the top updates, but if the box is changed without the assembly being open, then the lid will not update until the assembly is opened. The record of the reference that the assembly maintains is held in what is called an *Update Holder*. In recent versions, the Update Holder is all but forgotten, and difficult to find. One Update Holder is created for every sketch or feature that contains references to other entities within that particular assembly. To show Update Holders, right-click the top-level assembly name in the FeatureManager, and select Show Update Holders.

Cross-Reference

Chapter 4 discusses in-context reference Update Holders. These pointers in the assembly hold the reference information. These holders are hidden by default and do not enable any real functionality, but they do serve as a reminder that the assembly has in-context references and can be queried to tell you what parts the in-context relations go between. ∎

Working through a simple in-context example

Rather than discuss this topic theoretically, here is a simple set of demonstrations of in-context modeling situations. You can find the example files in the DVD folder for this chapter. You will revisit this example file throughout this chapter.

This example starts with a simple rectangular block. You have multiple options to get an in-context part into an assembly, but this example will just demonstrate one. The following steps are general, as you should already be familiar with the basics of assemblies and part modeling.

Starting a new assembly

Open a new assembly, using the template of your choice. When modeling in-context, it is especially important that the parts and the assembly use the same units. If the assembly units are different from the part units, and you edit the part in the context of the assembly, then you may be presented with one type of unit while editing the part in the assembly and another type of unit while editing the part in its own window. This difference is probably not important for library parts, but for actual design parts, it is most convenient if the units match.

The next step is to save the assembly. If you do not save the assembly before adding a new part to it, SolidWorks does not force you to save it before adding the part, but it is a good idea to save the assembly (and any file, actually) after creating it.

Inserting a new part

 To insert a new part in the new assembly, choose Insert ⇨ Component ⇨ New Part and select the toolbar icon for New Part (under the Insert Component flyout toolbar).

Note
The above icon is slightly different from what most users will see as the toolbar icon for New Part. This is because from time to time, SolidWorks allows slight differences between the appearances of large and small icons. If you didn't notice the difference, the large icon (shown in the margin) has the sparkle above and to the right, while the small icon has the sparkle to the lower left. This is a minor point, but it may be a source of confusion for some users. ∎

 After you click the New Part command, SolidWorks adds the new part to the FeatureManager of the new assembly. Note the default naming shown in Figure 10.1. Also, note the cursor with the green check mark on it. This check mark is telling you (in conjunction with the text in the message bar at the bottom of the screen) that you need to select a plane or planar face to place the Front (or first, or XY) plane on the Front plane of the assembly. Remember that every template may have the standard planes renamed to anything you choose, so the first standard plane may not be called the Front plane.

FIGURE 10.1

Inserting a new blank part into a new assembly

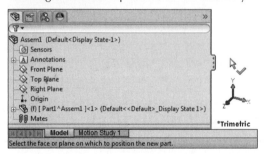

When you click the cursor with the green check mark on a plane or planar face, the Front plane of the part becomes fixed to the Front plane of the assembly, with the Origins of the two files aligned, and SolidWorks automatically opens a new sketch on the Front plane of the part. The part name also turns blue. This color means that you are editing the part in the context of the assembly. Whatever you do in this state changes the part document rather than the assembly document. A new sketch, for example, will be added to the part rather than the assembly.

Introducing virtual components

The part you have just added to the new assembly is called a *virtual component*. It is called "virtual" because the part is not saved yet; it is still just inside the assembly. This is the reason why the name appears as shown in Figure 10.1. When you save the part to an external file, it loses the part of the name that is associated with the current assembly. The "components" part of the name means that both parts and subassemblies can be virtual, or exist only within the top-level assembly. You will find more information on virtual components later in this chapter.

Creating the part geometry

Sketch a centered rectangle from the Origin, and give it dimensions of 4 inches (100mm) tall by 5 inches (125mm) wide. Extrude it 2 inches (50mm). You can find the Extrude command icon on the Assembly toolbar when editing a part in the context of the assembly.

Now exit the part. To do this, click the Edit Component icon in one of the places where it shows up on the screen. Figure 10.2 shows it in the Confirmation Corner in the upper-right corner of the graphics window. You can also find it on the Assembly toolbar.

FIGURE 10.2

Using the Confirmation Corner to exit Edit Component mode

Saving a virtual component

Next, right-click the name of the part you just added and select Save Part (in External File), as shown in Figure 10.3. Give the part the name **Box** (by slowly double-clicking the default name in the Save As dialog box that appears), and save it to your desktop (by clicking the Specify Path button in the Save As dialog box), or another place where it will be easy to find and delete later on. This part is just for practice in this chapter.

Notice that the name of the part in the assembly FeatureManager has changed, and the name is no longer surrounded by brackets or followed by the assembly name.

FIGURE 10.3

Saving the virtual components to an external file

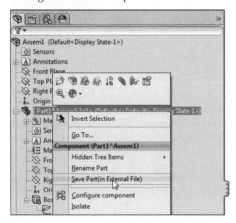

Caution

SolidWorks Help says that virtual components are particularly useful with in-context modeling. This may be true, but there is more to the story. If you create parts in-context in an assembly that has not yet been saved, you may lose all of your references when you save the assembly. To be safe, it is a best practice to avoid creating in-context relations in an unsaved assembly. ■

If you haven't done it by now, you should save the assembly file. Give it the name Box Assembly, and save it to the same location where you saved the part earlier. If you get to the end after you make the in-context relations, and then save the assembly, your in-context features will go "out of context," meaning that the parts will not know in which assembly the relations were created.

Creating an in-context part

To create another new part in the assembly, and use the first part to drive this one, you must once again click the New Part icon. When you see the cursor with the green check mark, click the 5 x 4 end face that you created using the Extrude feature.

When you do this, the first part you created turns transparent. This is to help you identify which part is being worked on (the non-transparent part is current). You can find the settings controlling this behavior at Tools ➪ Options ➪ Colors. Toward the bottom of that page is a setting called Use specified colors when editing parts in assemblies. You can find a related setting at Tools ➪ Options ➪ Display/Selection; under the heading for Assembly Transparency for In Context Edit is a drop-down list with three options: Opaque Assembly, Maintain Assembly Transparency, and Force Assembly Transparency. The default is Force Assembly Transparency. These options are shown in Figure 10.4.

FIGURE 10.4

Establishing assembly transparency while editing in-context parts

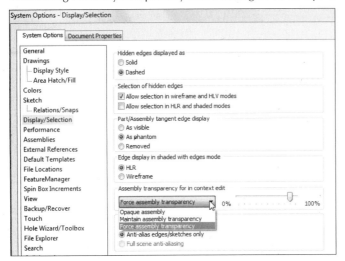

To create the sketch for the first feature of the in-context part, click the same face that you just clicked to place the second part, and use the Offset Entities to make a sketch loop offset by 0.25 inch (6mm) to the outside.

To contrast two methods of selection, after using the face selection to offset to the outside, right-click one of the edges of the face of the Box part, and choose Select Loop from the menu. Make sure that the yellow arrow shown in Figure 10.5 points as shown, not perpendicular to the sketch plane. Then use the Offset Entities to offset sketch lines from the selected loop of edges toward the inside again by 0.25 inch. Figure 10.5 shows the preview of the second offset.

With this single sketch containing a nested loop, use the Extrude feature to extrude 0.5 inch (12mm). When complete, use the Confirmation Corner again to exit the part. You should now have an assembly, which is not saved, a part that is saved with the name Box, and a second part that is just a virtual component.

After exiting Edit Component mode, you should also see that the two parts are the same color. Click a face of the newly created part, click the Appearance drop-down menu, and select the indicator for the part. Figure 10.6 shows the cursor pointing to this indicator. Change the part color using the panel that appears in the PropertyManager (don't change the entire appearance, just the color).

FIGURE 10.5

Using two methods to offset sketches in context

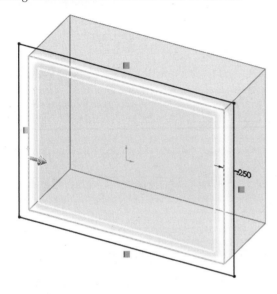

FIGURE 10.6

Changing the color of a virtual component

Editing the driving part of an in-context reference

Now comes the tricky part. You are going to change the overall shape of the Box part, and observe the effect on the virtual component. In order to do this, click the sketch under the Extrude feature in the Box part and select Edit Sketch from the popup toolbar.

Caution

In SolidWorks 2011 SP 2.0, if you have not saved the assembly yet (recall the earlier warning about losing references), the prompt to save the assembly that you get when selecting Edit Sketch on a part in an unsaved assembly does not work. If you use Edit Component, it prompts you to save the assembly for that operation too, but in that case it works. This function appears to be inconsistent, so you may need to manually save the assembly. ■

Note

Notice that there is a difference between using Save As from the menu and the Save button from the Title bar toolbar. Save As only allows you to save the assembly file, while the Save command enables you to save both the assembly and the virtual component. ■

Once this is complete, you are ready to edit the sketch of the Extrude feature in the Box part. If necessary, expand the Box part in the FeatureManager by clicking the plus symbol to the left of the name and then click the plus symbol next to the Extrude feature. Now you can click the sketch, and select Edit Sketch from the popup list.

While editing the sketch of the box, right-click one line of the rectangle and choose Select chain. With all four lines selected, click the Construction Geometry toggle in the PropertyManager. This turns all lines of the rectangle into construction lines.

Next, draw a circle concentric with the Origin, with the circumference on one corner of the rectangle. The sketch now looks like Figure 10.7.

When you have made this change, exit the sketch. The in-context references will not update until you exit the part and return to the assembly.

Just to get you prepared, what do you expect to see? Remember that one set of referenced edges was referenced by selecting a face, and the other set was referenced by selecting edges.

When you leave Edit Part mode and return to Edit Assembly mode, you will find that the outer lines have updated to the circle (because the face you selected is now circular instead of rectangular), but the edges you selected are still rectangular and display a warning symbol. This is because the edges referenced by those lines no longer exist. If you hover your mouse over one of the errors shown in Figure 10.8, it says, "Warning: Unable to offset one or more sketch entities." You can avoid this error by using the same technique to select the inner lines as the outer lines (or just using the outer lines and making a Thin Feature).

Go ahead and fix this error by editing the sketch in the Virtual Part (box lid), deleting the lines causing the problem, and remaking them by offsetting from the selected face. Offset sketch relations cannot be repaired or edited in the way you need to repair the existing relations. In general, you should avoid using Delete as an editing technique, but there is no other way in SolidWorks to repair this kind of issue.

FIGURE 10.7

Replacing a rectangle with a circle

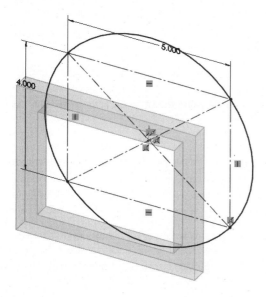

FIGURE 10.8

Responding to warnings when they occur

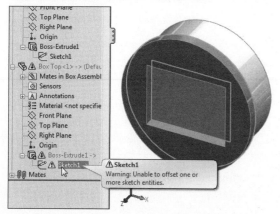

This demonstration points out some of the strengths and weaknesses of in-context modeling, but not all of them. The rest of the chapter will help you get a better idea of how to evaluate this technique for yourself.

Weighing the advantages of in-context modeling

The advantages of in-context modeling are obvious. In-context modeling is just an extension of parametric techniques to include parts in the context of an assembly. Making a change to one part and having all related parts update offers indisputable advantages. When it works correctly, all the parts of an assembly can be updated from a single change. Changes propagate all the way through to the part drawings.

Some users approach modeling haphazardly, where if it works, it's good enough. For some types of work, this is acceptable and really may be "good enough." For example, it usually works when you create something that will never be changed or if you are working on initial concept models that will not be given to other users.

On the other hand, users who need to build models that will be reused frequently, changed often, or given to other users to work on must approach the decisions they make during modeling as if they were playing chess. Each decision has consequences. You rarely know exactly how things are going to turn out, but you need to prepare for the most likely contingencies, assessing potential risks along the way.

In-context modeling presents the same types of decisions. You can do it quickly with little planning or approach decisions methodically and with much consideration beforehand. The rest of the chapter shows the many tools that are associated with more advanced in-context techniques.

Anticipating problems with in-context modeling

The overall concept of in-context modeling is a great idea; the problems occur with the practical application of the technique and the management of the results through changes. In particular, the biggest problems seem to arise when in-context techniques are combined with other techniques. You must be very careful about things such as file management, assembly motion, multiple instances of parts in assemblies, configurations, and related issues when in-context references exist in your assembly.

Major potential problems include the following:

- Lost references due to renamed parts or assemblies
- Convoluted references causing long rebuild times
- Circular references causing changes with each rebuild
- External references causing conflicts with motion

- Serious difficulties between in-context techniques and configurations

- Frustrated users who don't understand how to manage changes or references in an in-context scheme

However, you can overcome these difficulties. The remainder of this chapter shows you how to make the most of in-context modeling.

For those users who prefer to use model items in drawings, in-context techniques offer some challenges. Model items are either unavailable or limited in availability for features created in-context. This is because if you have used Convert Entities to copy edges of one part to another, no dimensions have been used, so none will show up in inserted model items. In-context model items would show up when you use offset-to-offset edges or dimension sketch elements to in-context edges. Aside from these, the only model item drawings you can create are in an assembly drawing. This is one of the many reasons why you should not use model items in drawings.

Identifying alternatives to in-context modeling

One of the most frequent problems with in-context modeling is related to file management. Inexperienced users may move or rename a file or a folder in Windows Explorer and unknowingly break links, or try to use an in-context part in some assembly other than where the in-context relation was created. As a result, they may not be able to make changes that they want to make, or changes may happen when they do not want them to.

Sometimes these problems are the result of users simply not understanding what to expect from the tool, and sometimes it is because the tool is not capable of doing what they want. Right or wrong, many users have developed an irrational fear of references that can control a part from outside of the part. In-context modeling in itself is not a bad technique, but sometimes it is not the best option, depending on the particular situation. You need to understand in-context and all related techniques first before passing judgment on any of the techniques.

It's always important to identify alternative techniques because one tool never solves all possible problems. In-context modeling is powerful, but in some situations, other techniques are more appropriate. The following sections will introduce you to a couple of techniques that share with in-context the ability to control individual parts from a centralized location, but achieve that in ways that are somewhat different: Assembly layout and Multi-body modeling. *Assembly layout modeling* enables you to control individual parts not from other parts but from an assembly-level sketch. *Multi-body modeling* enables you to control several parts from a single part without worrying about the file management issues of having another assembly as the middle agent.

Using Assembly layout modeling

Assembly layouts are powerful tools that remove much of what some people object to in in-context modeling. Relationships in this technique are controlled by top-level sketches, where a single or multiple sketches can control most of the features on all parts through relation-ships between part sketches or features and the assembly sketch. This still creates an exter-nal reference that requires the existence of an assembly to update the relationships, but it is not a direct link between different parts in the context of the assembly.

Assembly layouts do not lend themselves well to dynamic assembly motion, but they are great if you want to have a single location to drive an entire assembly. Assembly layouts come in two types: the generic layout, which is simply done using sketches in an assembly; and the formal Layout feature, which is essentially a 3D sketch in the assembly with special properties. The Layout feature is described in more detail later in this chapter. Assembly lay-out sketches are covered in more detail in Chapter 4.

Using Multi-body modeling

Multi-body modeling, like in-context modeling, is a powerful technique with strengths and weaknesses. If you model what will later turn out to be separate parts together in a single part, you can avoid in-context modeling altogether. You should not replace assemblies with multi-body modeling for a number of reasons, such as limitations of multi-body techniques for common assembly operations such as dynamic assembly motion and interference detec-tion. Used judiciously, multi-body modeling can help you save time making models that hold up well to changes. Master Model techniques are discussed at length in Chapter 19.

Dealing with the Practical Details of In-Context Modeling

Figure 10.9 shows a simple box with the sketch of a simple top for the box. Notice in the FeatureManager that two parts are listed as the top and base. The .050-inch offset is creating a sketch in the top part that is driven by the edges of the base part. This simple assembly demonstrates the in-context process in the sections that follow.

Understanding the in-context process

You can perform in-context modeling using one of two basic schemes. You can build parts from the very beginning in the context of the assembly (using the Insert ⇨ Component ⇨ New Part menu option) or you can start them using bottom-up techniques, creating the parts in a separate part window, adding them to the assembly, and then adding additional in-context features later.

Starting out in-context

 To start a new part in the context of an assembly, you will first assume that the assembly contains another part. Creating a new part in a blank assembly is not very interesting. This example uses the assembly shown in Figure 10.9. To create the new part, choose

Insert ⇨ Component ⇨ New Part. This command is also available through a toolbar button (shown to the left) that you can place on the Assembly toolbar. At this point, SolidWorks prompts you to select a face or plane on which to locate the new part. When you select the face or plane to place, SolidWorks places the Front plane of the new part on it, opens a new sketch, and adds an InPlace mate to the assembly. In-context parts start as virtual parts, saved inside the assembly; you can choose to save them as external or internal parts the next time you save the assembly. Virtual part functionality is discussed later in this chapter.

FIGURE 10.9

The top of the box being built in-context

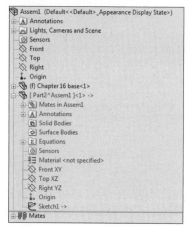

InPlace mate

The mate that SolidWorks automatically adds when a part is created in-context is called an *InPlace* mate. It works like the Fixed option, although it is actually a mate that is listed with the other mates and may be deleted but not edited.

The InPlace mate clamps the part down to any face or plane where it is applied. It is meant to prevent the in-context part from moving. You will learn later in this chapter why it is so important for in-context parts not to move.

Alternative technique

Instead of using the Insert ⇨ Component ⇨ New Part command, you can simply create a blank part in its own window and save it to the desired location. Then insert the blank part into the assembly and mate the origins coincident. You can then edit the part in-context, the same as if you had created it in-context from the beginning. The only difference between parts developed this way and parts created in-context is the InPlace mate. The InPlace mate cannot be edited and is not related to other geometry in the usual sense. Many users feel more secure with real mates to real geometry, which they can identify and change if necessary.

Valid relations

Sketches, vertices, edges, and faces from the other parts in the assembly can be referenced from the in-context part as if they were in the same part as the sketch. Most common relations are concentric for holes, and coincident for hole centers. Converted entities (On-Edge relations) make a line-on-edge relation between the parts, and Offset sketch relations are also often used.

Other types of valid in-context relations include in-context sketch planes and end conditions for extrude features such as Up to Face and Up to Body. Beyond that, you can copy surfaces from one part using the Knit Surface feature or the Offset Surface feature.

Working in-context

When you are working in-context or using in-context data, visual cues offer information about the part that you are working on. The following topics will help you understand what is going on while you are working in-context.

Text color

When you are working in-context, the FeatureManager text of the part that you are working on turns blue. This should make it immediately obvious first, that you are working in-context, and second, which part is being edited.

Part color and transparency

You can control the color and transparency behavior of parts in the assembly where a part is being edited in-context by choosing Tools ➪ Options ➪ Colors page. Figure 10.10 shows a detail of this page. The option at the bottom of the dialog box determines whether the colors specified in the list at the top are used or ignored. If they are ignored, the parts are the same colors they would be if you were not using in-context techniques.

The Tools ➪ Options ➪ Display/Selection Assembly Transparency for In Context Edit setting controls the transparency of the parts not being edited. Figure 10.11 shows this setting. Forcing the non-edited parts to become transparent helps you keep focus on the part you are editing in the assembly.

FIGURE 10.10

Part-color settings for in-context control

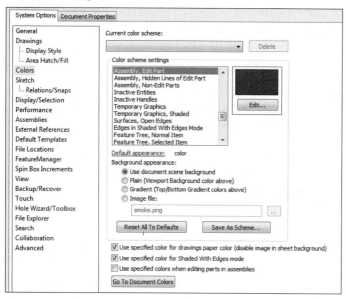

FIGURE 10.11

Part transparency for in-context control

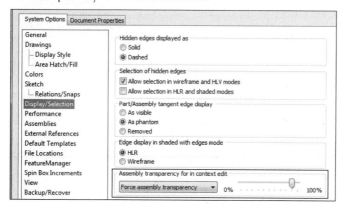

The options in the Assembly Transparency for In Context Edit drop-down list are

- **Opaque Assembly.** All parts that are not being edited when an assembly component is being edited in-context turn opaque, even if they are otherwise transparent.
- **Maintain Assembly Transparency.** This option leaves all assembly components in their default transparency state.
- **Force Assembly Transparency.** This option forces all the parts, except for the one being edited in the assembly, to become transparent.

These options reflect personal preference more than anything else does, but it is useful to have a reminder as to whether a part is being edited in the assembly or the assembly document is being edited in its own window.

Tip

The color selected in the box shown in Figure 10.2 controls both the text color and the color of the part shown in the graphics window. ■

Edit Component button

 You can use the Edit Component button in three ways. First, after you have created a part in-context, seeing the Edit Component button depressed reminds you that you are editing the part rather than editing the assembly. Along with the part color and transparency displays, this is important feedback because assembly functions such as mates, exploded views, and others are not available when you are editing the part.

Second, you can use the Edit Component button to begin or finish editing a part that is already in an assembly. When you are editing a part in the context of an assembly, the title bar of the SolidWorks window reflects the fact that you are editing a part in an assembly, the toolbar changes to a part-editing toolbar, and the lower-right corner of the taskbar displays the words *Editing Part*, as shown in Figure 10.12.

Third, a Confirmation Corner image exists in the upper-right corner of the graphics window when you are editing a part in the context of the assembly. This makes it easier to leave Edit Component mode.

Editing a component can also mean editing a subassembly in the context of the top-level assembly. You can create in-context assembly features and mates if necessary; however, you will do this far less frequently than editing parts in-context.

Note

Creating in-context relations is not the only reason to edit a part or subassembly in the context of the top-level assembly. Sometimes it is simply more convenient to do normal editing when you are in the top-level assembly; this way, you can see how the part relates to other parts after making changes in the assembly without making relations between the parts.

Editing a subassembly in the context of the upper-level assembly is often useful as well, to see how changing subassembly mates affect the top level. ■

FIGURE 10.12

Indicators that you are editing a part in-context

Probably the most common mistake you can make with in-context editing has to do with editing the part versus editing the assembly when you add a sketch. If you intend to add a sketched feature to a part in the context of an assembly, but you fail to switch to Edit Part mode before creating the sketch, then the sketch ends up in the assembly rather than the part. You can only do limited things with a sketch in an assembly. Likewise, if you intend to make an assembly layout sketch, but you do not switch out of Edit Part mode, you end up with a sketch in a part that cannot do what you want it to do.

Fortunately, SolidWorks has added a remedy for the first situation. When you make a sketch in the assembly but need to make a feature in the part, you can choose the Propagate feature to parts option in the Feature Scope area of the PropertyManager for the feature, as shown in Figure 10.13.

Notice in the image on the right that the last sketch in the part appears as derived. This means that the sketch and the feature are still driven from the assembly, but they have been propagated to the part enough to allow the feature to be edited in the part. You may not want to go this route just because you made a mistake and it's simpler to do this than to move the sketch to the part, but it is an option that is valid in some situations. Interestingly, this feature cannot be deleted from the part; you must delete it from the assembly.

External reference symbol

The external reference symbol appears as a dash followed by a greater-than sign (->). External references indicate more than just in-context features. You can also create external references by using the Split Part command as well as the Insert Part (base or derived part) or the mirrored part functions. Figure 10.6 shows the expanded FeatureManager for a part with an in-context reference in a sketch.

FIGURE 10.13

Propagating an assembly feature to the part

External references can have four states, as shown in Figure 10.14. These are In-context (->), Out-of-context (->?), Locked reference (->*), and Broken reference (->x).

FIGURE 10.14

The in-context "->" symbol on Extrude1 and Sketch1

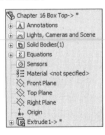
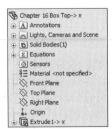

- **In-context (->).** The in-context symbol signifies that the relation created between two parts within the current assembly is fully resolved. It can find both parts involved in the relationship and the assembly where the relationship that was created is active.

- **Out-of-context (->?).** Out-of-context means that the document — usually but not necessarily an assembly — where the reference was created is not open at the time. It is indicated by an in-context symbol followed by a question mark. You can open the document where the reference was created by clicking the right mouse button (RMB) and selecting the Edit In Context option from the menu. Edit In Context opens either the parent part of an inserted part or the assembly where the reference was created for an in-context reference. When you open the referencing document, the out-of-context symbol changes to the in-context symbol.

- **Locked reference (->*).** You can lock external references so that the model does not change, even if the parent document changes. The symbol for this is ->*. Other features of the part may be changed, but any external reference within the part remains the way it is until the reference is either unlocked or removed. In the top and base example mentioned earlier, this means that if the Bottom part is changed, and the external reference on the Top is locked, then the Top will no longer fit the Bottom.

  One of the best things about locked references is that you can unlock them. They are also flexible and give you control over when updates take place to parts with locked references.

- **Broken reference (->x).** The broken reference is another source of controversy. Some users believe that if you make in-context references, the best way to respond to them is to break them immediately. However, one could argue that using the Break References function is *never* a good thing to do. You should remove the reference by editing the feature or the sketch or change it to make it useful.

  The problem with a broken reference is that it has absolutely no advantage over a locked reference. For example, while locked references can at least be unlocked, broken references cannot be repaired. The only thing that you can do with a broken reference is to use Display/Delete Relations or to edit features manually to completely remove the external reference.

Best Practice

Best practice is to avoid placing yourself in a situation where you are using broken references. Parametric relations should not change if the driving geometry does not change.

You cannot selectively lock or break external relations. For example, all the external relations in the part can be locked or broken, or none of them can be locked or broken. If you need to disable relations selectively, then you should consider suppressing features, sketch relations, end conditions, or sketch planes. ∎

List External References

You can access the locked and broken references through the List External References option on the RMB menu of any feature with an external reference symbol. Figure 10.15 shows the name and path of the assembly where the external reference was created, as well as the part names and entity types.

The External References dialog box

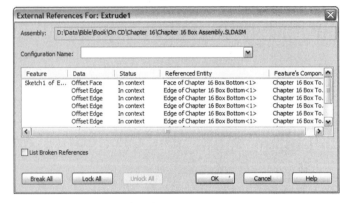

No External References

To access the No External References button on the Assembly toolbar, choose Tools ⇨ Options ⇨ External References ⇨ Do Not Create References External To The Model from the menus. As its name suggests, this setting prevents external relations from being created between parts in an assembly. When you offset in-context edges or use Convert Entities, the resulting sketch entities are created without relations of any type.

This lack of references includes the InPlace mate, which is not created when a part is created in-context. As a result, when you add the part to the assembly, if you exit and later re-enter Edit Part mode, SolidWorks reminds you that the part is not fixed in space by displaying the warning shown in Figure 10.16.

This message should remind you that in-context features should be used only on parts that are fully positioned in the assembly.

FIGURE 10.16

The dialog box that warns you about adding in-context relations to an underdefined part

External reference settings in Tools ⇨ Options

The Tools ⇨ Options ⇨ External References pane of settings controls many aspects of the behavior of external references. One of these references was discussed earlier, No External References, and the other reference, Multiple Contexts, is discussed in the next section. This pane in the Tools ⇨ Options dialog box is shown in Figure 10.17.

FIGURE 10.17

The Tools ⇨ Options ⇨ External References pane

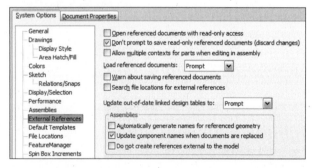

Looking at in-context best practices

This technique requires a fair amount of discipline, restraint, foresight, and judgment. The potential problems associated with overuse or misuse of in-context techniques primarily include performance problems (speed) and lost references due to file management issues. Users may also experience problems with features or sketches that change with each rebuild. The following section contains best practice suggestions that can help you avoid these situations.

Working with multiple contexts

Multiple contexts occur when a part has references that are created in multiple assemblies. By default, multiple contexts are prevented from happening. If you place a part that already has external references into a different assembly, a warning appears, as shown in Figure 10.18.

The warning message that appears about multiple contexts

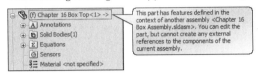

Although SolidWorks displays many warnings about multiple contexts, you may still run into situations where you need to use them. For example, you may have a subassembly where a part, such as a top plate of a stand, has in-context references to locate a set of mounting holes for legs of the stand. When you place the subassembly into the top-level assembly and mount another assembly to the top plate, another set of in-context holes is required in the top plate.

Figure 10.19, at the top, shows the first table and points out the in-context relations. At the bottom, the large bracket appears for the machine that is mounted to the tabletop using more in-context relations. The External References dialog boxes for the two different in-context features appear in Figure 10.20. Notice that the Assembly fields at the top of the External References dialog boxes are different. You can only achieve this by selecting the Allow Multiple Contexts for Parts When Editing in Assembly option shown in Figure 10.18.

Note

The Tools ⇨ Options setting for multiple contexts is a system option. This means that either this option is on or off for every document on a single machine, but when the assembly is used on another machine, the option may be off. ■

Multiple context modeling should be the exception rather than standard practice. If you do not have all the assemblies open where the in-context references were created, then you will have some out-of-context references. This can make for a troubleshooting nightmare if someone ever has to try to reconstruct how the assembly is driven.

Best Practice

The best practice is to avoid creating multiple-context references. If you need to do this, then be very careful about naming files, and remember to turn off the multiple-context option when you have finished creating the reference. ■

FIGURE 10.19

Using multiple contexts

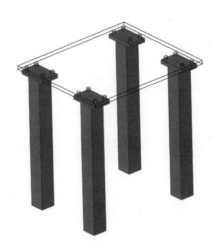

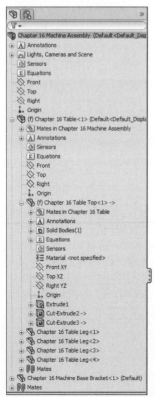

FIGURE 10.20

External References dialog boxes

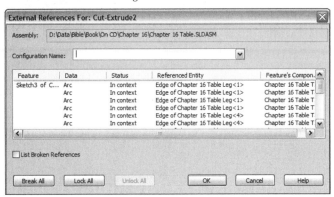

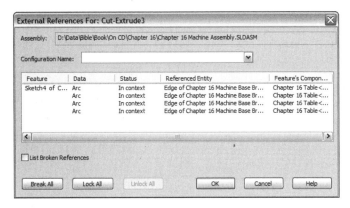

If you receive a multiple-context part from someone else, the best thing to do is to determine whether you have all the files required to make it work. Right-click the external reference symbol and select Edit In Context to determine whether SolidWorks can find the right files. Also looking for an out-of-context symbol will tell you if any of the necessary files are not currently open.

Aside from doing some programming, the only way to find out whether a part was created as a multiple-context part is to examine the External References list for each in-context feature. This can be very time-consuming. Although multiple-context parts should be very rare, it is impossible to determine ahead of time whether a part that you have received is a multiple-context part, at least without programming. The one exception to this is when some features are in-context and some are out-of-context.

Using in-context with configurations

On the surface, mixing in-context references with configurations sounds like it is combining two powerful techniques that should offer you great control over models. Although this may sometimes be true, you need to be aware of some of the effects that combining these two techniques may cause. In particular, you should be careful about part configurations, particularly configurations of the *referenced* part.

If you are using in-context relations to parts with configurations, then you may want to consider a few things. First, look at the door-hinge part shown in Figure 10.21. At the top are three configurations of one of the hinge plates. The second hinge plate is built in the context of the assembly so that it will always match the first plate. At the bottom are the results of changing the first hinge-plate part configuration in the assembly. This looks like an ideal situation because the second hinge plate always changes to match the first hinge plate. What could be wrong with this?

The problem here is that you can only show the size of the second hinge plate that corresponds to the configuration of the first plate that is active in the assembly. If you had two instances of the hinge assembly in a top-level assembly, then you would be able to show only one size for the second plate.

A second situation where combining in-context references and configurations can cause you trouble is if you have referenced the edges of a part from another part, and a configuration of the referenced part either adds or removes fillets or chamfers, thus breaking the edges. Both of these situations can cause either the in-context sketches or other features to fail. This may be a reason to reference the underlying sketches, rather than the actual model edges or faces.

In some situations, configurations work well with in-context relations. One example of this would be when an assembly has many configurations used for positioning parts. In this case, you would use one configuration for the sole purpose of creating in-context relations.

Using in-context with motion

You should make in-context references between parts where there is no relative motion. The parts themselves can move relative to the rest of the assembly, but they should remain stationary relative to one another. The parts should also be fully defined to ensure that they would not move; you should not simply assume that you would avoid dragging underdefined parts. This is because if one part drives a feature on another part, and the parts move relative to one another, the in-context feature is also likely to move within its parent part.

In some cases, such as an assembly of imported parts, it may make sense to fix parts in bulk rather than to mate them. When you are using in-context relations, you need to take extra care to ensure that the parts do not move around. When parts move around, in-context features also move.

FIGURE 10.21

Combining in-context references with configurations

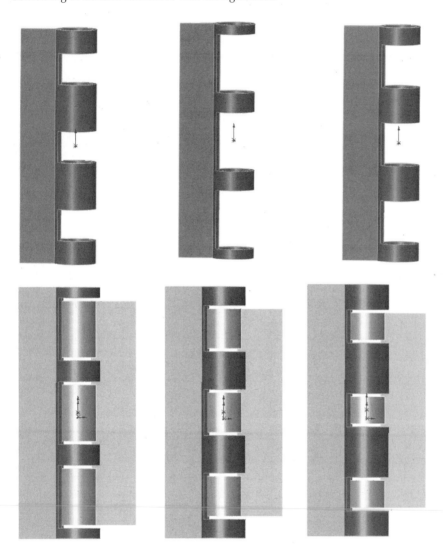

Obviously, if the motion is around a circular hole and the in-context feature is circular and is not affected by the rotation of the referenced part, then it makes less difference; however, if there is a keyway, that may change things. You need to pay attention when combining under-defined parts and in-context features.

Best Practice

For best practice, you should avoid in-context relations between parts when relative motion is allowed between these parts. ■

Working with in-context with multiple instances

Another situation that can cause problems is when multiple instances of an in-context part are being used in the assembly. In cases like this, you need to be careful and consistent, by always using the same instance to create the in-context relations. You can do this by putting parts into folders, or by giving the in-context part a special component color.

One trick is to use one instance of an in-context part for the in-context relation, and a second instance of the part to allow motion. In-context relations are tied to one specific instance of a part, regardless of how many of those parts are in the assembly. You might want to set the driving in-context part aside by putting it in a folder, changing its color, or hiding it.

Using in-context and file management

Understanding what you are doing with file management is imperative when working with parts that depend on in-context features. Because the references are stored in both the part that is doing the referencing and the assembly where the reference is created, improperly changing the name of either document or even the referenced document is bound to cause problems. For example, if you rename an in-context part using Windows Explorer, then the assembly will not recognize the part. This also means that any in-context references will not update. The part will show the out-of-context symbol.

Best Practice

For best practice, you should use either the SolidWorks Save As command or SolidWorks Explorer to rename parts and assemblies. This applies to all parts and assemblies, but even more to in-context documents. ■

Using in-context and mates

A section on in-context best practices would not be complete without issuing the warning against mating to in-context features. Mating parts to in-context features creates a parametric daisy chain, thus establishing an order in which assembly features and mates must be solved. This always creates performance problems in assemblies, especially large ones. The SolidWorks AssemblyXpert looks for this condition when examining assemblies.

Working with circular references

Circular references in assemblies are a bigger problem than most people realize. In fact, most people do not realize that circular references *are* a problem, or, for that matter, that they even exist.

A circular reference takes the form of "Part A references Part B, which references Part A." It creates a circular loop that really disrupts assembly rebuild times. Part feature design trees are not susceptible to this sort of looping because the part FeatureManager operates in a linear fashion (at least when it comes to applying relations between sketches or features).

The Assembly FeatureManager is solved in this order, or an order that is very similar:

1. Solve reference geometry and sketches that are listed before parts in order, at the top of the design tree.
2. Rebuild individual parts as necessary.
3. Solve the mates and locate the parts.
4. Solve in-context features in parts.
5. Solve reference geometry and sketches listed after the mates.
6. Solve assembly features and component patterns.
7. Loop to Step 3 to solve mates that are connected to anything that was solved after the first round on the mates.
8. Continue to loop until complete.

As you can see, even if you do not have a reference such as "Part A references Part B, which references Part A," it is still possible to get a highly convoluted, if not entirely circular, loop. Many users with smaller assemblies in the hundreds of parts complain about very poor performance.

Using skeletons and layouts

When you are making in-context references, a technique that can help you avoid circular references is to always create references to parts that are higher in the design tree. You can expand on this idea until a single entity is at the top of the design tree, to which all in-context references are made. This could take the form of a layout sketch, or a skeleton. These concepts are discussed in Chapters 6 and 11. The Layout feature, which is different from the layout sketch, is discussed later in this chapter as an additional in-context tool.

Remember that the layout sketch consists of a single or even multiple sketches that control the overall layout of the assembly, as well as all the relationships between parts. When you refer all the relations to a single entity that does not change with part configurations, or lose or gain filleted edges, the intra-part parametrics become much stronger and more stable.

When you are building a mold for plastic injection molding, a single sketch can control the size and position of the plates, pins, and so on. If all the 3D parts are mated to the 2D sketch, or use the 2D sketch by converted entities, then the parts will move with the sketch. This same technique is important and useful for any type of die or punch design, along with many other types of design.

Using in-context in libraries

Library parts should never contain in-context references, especially if the in-context references are out of context. Small library assemblies may have in-context references between the parts, but a single part should not have features created in-context. External references may be unavoidable in the form of mirrored or inserted parts, but in-context references are completely avoidable.

Removing relations

 The correct way to remove in-context sketch relations is by using the Display/Delete Relations tool. You can sort the relations by selecting the Defined in Context option, as shown in Figure 10.22.

FIGURE 10.22

Sorting sketch relations by type

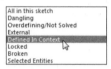

If you are considering using the Break Relations tool, then you should either reconsider and use Lock Relations instead or simply remove all the in-context relations altogether.

Other types of in-context references are not as easy to remove as sketch relations are. When you see the External Reference symbol on a sketch, it could be the sketch relations or it could be the sketch plane that was in-context. In order to remove the reference from an in-context sketch plane, you must redefine the plane locally in the part.

You should also not forget end conditions such as Up To Surface, Offset From Surface, or even From Surface. If an external reference symbol remains on a feature, you can use the Parent/Child option on the RMB menu to locate it. Remember that using an edge or vertex for a plane definition can cause an in-context relation.

Deciding whether to use mating or in-context

In-context is initially so fast and easy to use that it can be addictive, but you need to think before you use it because of the speed and file management implications these relations will have later on in your design process.

Communicating design intent

If someone else needs to use your model after you are done with it and possibly edit it, then you should leave some clues to help this person understand how the model works, and how it is best changed. For example, you can use descriptive feature and sketch names, comments that are associated with features, the Design Binder to add documentation, and the Design Journal to write notes. You can even put HTML (Hypertext Markup Language) links in notes that display in the graphics window.

In-context design intent may not always be obvious, and an impatient user may find it more expedient to delete the in-context references and replace them with either local relations or no relations at all. The more you document your intent, the more likely others will be to follow it.

Using Other Types of External References

The external reference symbol (->) indicates in-context features that have been created in the context of an assembly, but it also indicates three other types of external references: inserted parts, split parts, and mirrored parts.

Using inserted parts

In the past, inserted parts have also been called base parts and derived parts, and some users and even SolidWorks sometimes still use those names. (For more information on inserted parts, see Chapter 19.)

An inserted part is simply an entire part that has been inserted into another part. This is sometimes referred to as a *pull* operation because the data is pulled from the original part into the child part. The part may be inserted at any point in the history of the design tree, and it may create an additional body within the part or be added to the existing one. Additional features can also be added to the inserted part.

Items that can be brought along with the inserted part are solid bodies, surface bodies, planes, axes, sketches, cosmetic threads, and even features. You can also use a particular configuration of the inserted part in the child part. (For more information, see Chapter 14, which deals with configurations, and also Chapter 19, which deals with master models.)

You can use inserted parts for many modeling applications, such as cast parts and secondary operations. You first insert the original cast part into a new blank part. Then you add cut and hole features until the part resembles the finished part.

Another application for inserted parts is a single part that has been built from several models. An example might be a large, rather complicated plastic basket, where the basket is modeled as three individual parts, and then reassembled into a single part. Another application may be to insert a part as a body into a mold block to create a mold cavity. To insert a part into another part, you can choose Insert ⇨ Part.

Working with split parts

Inserted and split parts are both master model techniques, as are a few more techniques that are discussed in Chapter 19. Some people also include in-context techniques with the master model tools because this is a way of making several parts update together.

Split parts are sometimes called a *push* operation because the data is pushed from the original multi-body part to the individual child parts. The *split* function takes a single body and splits it into several bodies, optionally saving the bodies out as individual parts. This is done for various reasons, such as creating a single, smooth shape out of several different parts — for example, automobile body panels or the various covers and buttons on a computer mouse. You can use the split parts technique for other applications, as well. Sometimes a product is designed as a single solid to keep the modeling simple and because it is not known how the parts will be assembled or manufactured. When the manufacturing decisions are made, the part can be split into several models that have the engineering details added to them.

Using mirror parts

You can mirror a right-handed part to create a left-handed part. To activate the Mirror Part command, you must select a plane or planar face. Then choose Insert ⇨ Mirror Part to initiate the Mirror Part command. Mirror parts can also use configurations, and so if you have one of those "mirrored exactly except for . . ." parts, you can select the configuration of the parent from the child document.

Using the Layout Feature

When people talk about the Layout feature and layout sketches, this can lead to an unfortunate naming conflict. These two highly useful functions do nearly the same thing; one is a newly added formal feature, while the other is simply a technique that has existed for years.

For this reason, the new Layout feature is capitalized in this book, and referred to as a feature, while the layout sketch is in lowercase and is referred to as either a sketch or a technique. For more information on the Layout feature, see Chapter 6, which also describes layout sketches.

The Layout feature is simply a 3D sketch that is given special treatment within an assembly. It works best with sketch blocks. To initiate a Layout, click the Layout button on the Layout tab of the assembly CommandManager or activate it from the Insert menu. Once you are in a Layout, SolidWorks puts you into a 3D sketch with the Front (XY) plane activated, so it displays a small grid.

Cross-Reference
For more information about 3D sketches, see Chapter 20. ■

For now, you primarily treat the 3D sketch as much like a set of 2D sketches as possible. The main difference is that you can double-click a different plane to start sketching on the new plane, and you always see this small grid when a plane is active.

Three-dimensional sketches have some limitations when you are working with Layouts, such as lacking the capabilities to use sketch patterns and Sketch Pictures.

Using the Layout workflow

Here are the general steps for working with the Layout feature:

1. Open a new or existing assembly.
2. Click the Layout toolbar button on the Layout tab of the CommandManager.
3. Sketch on the plane in the 3D sketch to create 2D sketches representing parts of a mechanism or other assembly.
4. Make selections of the sketch into blocks representing individual parts.
5. Insert multiple instances of the blocks to represent multiple instances of the parts.
6. Use sketch relations to put the blocks together like mating parts in an assembly.
7. Test the mechanism by dragging sketches. (Blocks function like a single sketch entity, so you can drag them within the sketch like parts in an assembly.)
8. Right-click the block (from inside or outside the Layout) and select Make Part From Block (also a button on the Layout toolbar), as shown in Figure 10.23.

Note
The large and small icons for Make Part From Block differ slightly. All of the icons used in the left margin of this book are large icons. ■

FIGURE 10.23

Tools you encounter when using Layout

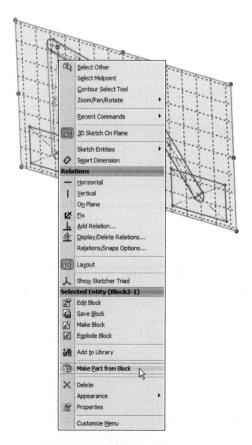

Understanding virtual components

Virtual components always exist with in-context workflows, and frequently with the Layout workflow. Virtual components are parts that are saved within the assembly. You can save a virtual component externally, and you can also make an externally saved part into a virtual component.

The advantages of virtual components are that you don't have to worry about saving out additional files, plus the assembly will never lose track of any virtual component.

Virtual components are primarily intended to be used as quick, temporary, conceptual tools, rather than as a way to make parts that will be a permanent part of the assembly. Some SolidWorks users also use virtual components to represent non-geometric parts such as glue or paint. Any time you choose Insert⇨ Component⇨ New Part from the menus and select a template and a plane to put the part on, the part is placed immediately into the assembly, and you can start working without worrying about having to save the assembly and the part. This saves a lot of time initially. Later on, when you save the assembly, SolidWorks prompts you to save the parts externally as well, or you may choose to leave the parts internal to the assembly.

Virtual components are named Part1^Assem1, where Part1 and Assem1 are default names. You can easily rename the part by clicking the RMB menu and selecting Rename Part. You cannot do this for external parts. If you make an external part virtual, the name in the assembly becomes Copy of *filename*^Assem1 where *filename* is the name of the external file. The name of the assembly is always included (and cannot be removed) to ensure that if you have subassemblies that also have virtual components, you will always have unique filenames for all the parts.

Virtual components can also be accessed in their own window, which makes them easier to edit for some purposes. Bills of Materials (BOMs) and numbered balloons work correctly with virtual components.

Best Practice

It is considered best practice to save any parts that will be a permanent part of the assembly as external files. Virtual components should be limited to temporary parts or possibly non-geometry, BOM-only parts such as glue or paint. ∎

Balancing advantages and limitations

In theory, the Layout feature has several advantages:

- You can make parts from blocks within the Layout.
- You can move parts by moving blocks in the Layout.
- It is a great way to structure your relations within an assembly.
- It is useful for motion analysis studies.

In practice, this feature needs some enhancements before it is ready for use on real assemblies. You will probably agree that using 2D sketches as assembly layout sketches is still a better idea than trying to avoid the limitations of the formal Layout feature. The limitations listed are presumably not bugs because Layout was introduced in 2009 and the tutorials in this book were created on 2010 SP 0.0. Here are some of the limitations of Layout:

- The 3D sketch used for Layout has all the limitations that come with 3D sketches.
- Sketch relations are listed in the Mates folder.
- Gaining access to edit the Layout once it has been closed requires a method you don't expect from a sketch: you click the Layout button on the toolbar rather than right-click and edit an icon in the FeatureManager.
- It requires that you use blocks to get all of the functionality.
- A fully defined 3D sketch with blocks is very unstable.
- Part creation from blocks does not offer a time savings.
- You cannot paste copied sketch entities from a 2D sketch into the Layout.
- You cannot use autodimension (or polygons or ellipses) in the Layout.

Although the formal Layout feature has serious advantages over regular layout sketches, at this time the limitations outweigh them. The rest of the discussion on layouts addresses the generic layout technique rather than the formal feature.

Tutorial: Working In-Context

Follow these steps to get a feel for working with parts in the context of an assembly:

1. **Open the assembly from the DVD named** Chapter 16 Tutorial Table. sldasm.

2. **Set the colors that are to be used during in-context editing.** Remember that two settings control this — one at Tools ➪ Options ➪ Colors, and the other at Tools ➪ Options ➪ Display/Selection — as shown in Figure 10.24.

   Set the Assembly Edit Part color to a shade of blue, and the Assembly Non-Edit Parts to a shade of gray.

   Also set the Assembly Transparency for In Context Edit setting to Force Assembly Transparency, with the slider at around 90 percent. Now you are ready to begin.

3. **Select the Table Top part, and click the Edit Component button on the Assembly toolbar.** This command is also available through both the RMB menu and the drop-down menu as Edit Part. (If you right-click a subassembly, the Edit Subassembly option becomes available.) Notice that the Table Top part and the FeatureManager text turn the same color.

FIGURE 10.24

Setting in-context colors

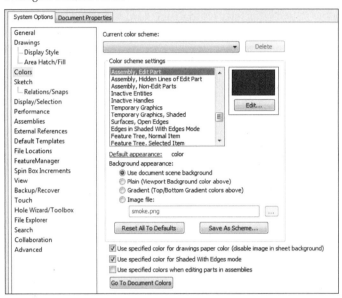

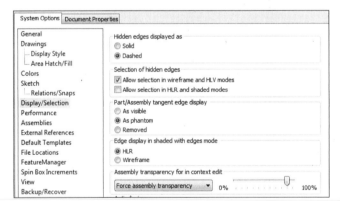

4. **Expand the Table Top part in the Assembly FeatureManager, select the Front plane, and open a new sketch on it.** Notice that you cannot select the edges of the transparent parts through the transparency, even if the Select Through Transparency option is selected (Tools ⇨ Options ⇨ Display/Selection). This setting applies only to faces, not to edges. Instead, change the display mode for the entire assembly to Wireframe.

5. **Now select the 16 hole edges on the legs.** It does not matter whether you select the top edges or the bottom, or even a combination of top and bottom. Use the Convert Entities command to project the edges into the sketch plane as circles, as shown in Figure 10.25.

Converting entities in-context

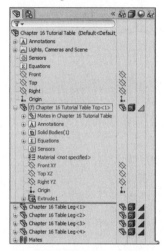
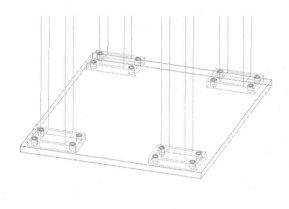

6. **Create a cut that goes Through All.** You may have to change the direction of the extrude to get it to work. Leave Edit Component mode using the Confirmation Corner and save the tutorial assembly.

7. **Now open the file named** `Tutorial Machine Assembly.sldasm`. Notice that the Table Top part in this assembly is using the Wireframe display state, which is assigned in the Display pane.

8. **Right-click the part and select Edit Part from the list, or select the part and click the Edit Component button on the toolbar.** A warning displays that the part has features that were created in the context of another assembly. You can edit the part, but you cannot add any more external references (in-context features) to it.

9. **Toggle off the Edit Component button on the Assembly toolbar to leave Edit Part mode.**

10. **Choose Tools ⇨ Options ⇨ External References and select the Allow Multiple Contexts for Parts When Editing in Assembly option.** Now try to edit the Table Top part again in the context of the assembly. This time, no warning message displays.

11. **Make sure that you are editing the Table Top part.** It does not change colors as specified in the Tools ⇨ Options ⇨ Colors settings because it is using the Wireframe display mode. Ensure that the status bar in the lower-right corner displays *Editing Part* rather than *Editing Assembly*.

12. **Open a sketch on the Front plane, and convert the four edges of the holes, as shown in Figure 10.26.**

FIGURE 10.26

Creating holes in-context

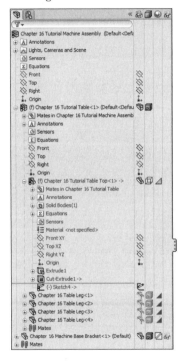
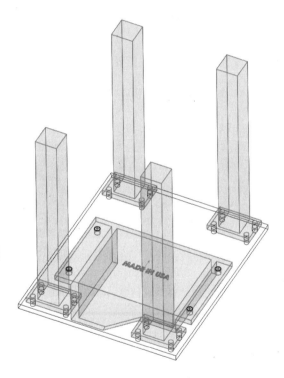

13. **Cut the holes using the Through All setting.** Again, be aware of the direction of the cuts. Toggle out of Edit Component mode and press Ctrl+S to save the assembly. Figure 10.27 shows the finished assembly.

14. **Open the Machine Base Bracket part in its own window by selecting Open Part from the RMB menu.** The part is shown in Figure 10.28.

The assembly as of Step 13

The Machine Base Bracket part, ready for mirroring

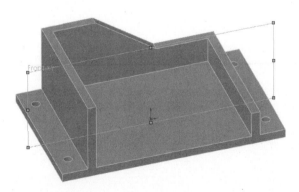

15. **Select the Front plane and choose Insert ➪ Mirror Part.** This creates a new part and opens a new PropertyManager interface, as shown in Figure 10.29.

    In this case, select Solid bodies and click the green check mark icon.

The Mirror Part PropertyManager

Note

Notice that you used the Insert ➪ Mirror Part command, but the PropertyManager says Insert Part. The Mirror Part functionality uses the Insert Part function, but adds a feature to mirror the body once it is inserted. Notice all the entity types you can transfer, and the fact that you can break the link to the original part. Also note that the template used for this part was chosen based on the settings at Tools ➪ Options ➪ Default Templates ➪ Always Use These Default Document Templates or Prompt User To Select Document Template. ■

Cross-Reference

For more information on the function of the Mirror/Insert part, see Chapter 9. ■

16. **Notice that the new part is indeed a mirrored copy of the original.** You can see that the "MADE IN USA" text on the bottom is backwards. Fortunately, a configuration exists specifically for this purpose. Change the configuration by selecting For Mirroring in the Configuration Name drop-down list in the External References dialog box (from the RMB selection, List External References), as shown in Figure 10.30. Notice that this configuration removes the extruded text from the model.

17. **Add your own "MADE IN . . ." extruded text to the bottom of the part.** Save the part.

FIGURE 10.30

Selecting a configuration

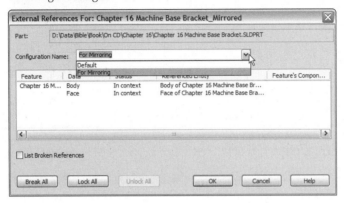

Summary

Although in-context functions are powerful and seductive, you should use them sparingly. In particular, be careful about file management issues such as renaming parts and assemblies. The best approach is to use SolidWorks Explorer or the Save As command with both the parts and assemblies open.

In-context techniques, including the Layout feature, are the pinnacle of true parametric practice and enable you to take the concepts of design intent and design for change to an entirely new level.

Creating Assembly Features

SolidWorks enables users to create features in assemblies that do not show up on individual parts. They are created in the assembly and only exist there. These tend to be features that would be manufactured after parts are assembled, and affect several parts at once, such as weld beads, or holes drilled after parts are put together. You can use standard features or the Hole Wizard to create some of these features.

You can use the following as assembly features:

- Hole features (series, wizard, simple)
- Cuts (extrude, revolve)
- Other (fillet, chamfer, weld bead)
- Patterns (patterns of existing assembly features)

Weld beads are covered to some extent in Chapter 20, which is devoted to weldments, but because weldments in SolidWorks are typically multi-body parts, weld beads are covered again here as proper assembly features.

Assembly features do not create in-context relationships between parts, but they do extend the history-based design paradigm to include the assembly. Assembly features do raise some best practice questions, however. The parts in an assembly should be fully defined with mates to the best extent possible, and this is even more important when creating features that affect multiple parts. In some situations where a shape affects multiple parts, it may be a better option to use master model techniques for sharing shapes between parts. If a feature does not cut multiple parts, it is generally best to make that feature within the actual part document, although there could be exceptions to this rule.

Which document the feature resides in may be a function of where you want the feature to be documented, such as in a part drawing or in an assembly drawing. This is probably as good a decision criterion as any other is.

This chapter explores various techniques and applications for using assembly features to model your product or process.

Creating Assembly Cuts

Several types of design require various cuts to be made after the product is assembled. For example, plates may be stacked, clamped, and then drilled to make sure that the holes line up perfectly. Cast parts may be assembled, and then given a final grinding cut to remove the cast surface finish.

 To access the cut features to make an assembly cut, you can use the Assembly Features toolbar icon on the Assembly tab of the CommandManager, or choose Insert ➪ Assembly Feature ➪ Cut ➪ Extrude.

Note

When SolidWorks users intend to make an in-context feature in a part while editing an assembly, they frequently end up adding the feature in the assembly instead of the part. To guarantee you don't do this or the opposite (putting a feature in a part when you intend to put it into the assembly), make sure the name of the assembly is in the title bar of the SolidWorks application. If the title bar says something like "Sketch1 of Part1 of Assem1.sldasm," then you are editing the part. ■

Because removing material in the assembly is the most commonly used technique, it will be discussed first. Some additive processes exist, such as welding and techniques such as adhesives and putty fillers, and they will be discussed later in this chapter.

SolidWorks allows only certain types of features to be used as assembly cuts:

- Extruded cuts
- Revolved cuts
- Hole features

For example, you cannot use a lofted cut as an assembly feature, but you can use a lofted solid in a cavity feature (which is an in-context feature, not an assembly feature). You could also do a lofted cut of a combined solid in a single part, then split the part into multiple bodies, and then into multiple parts (using master model techniques discussed in Chapter 19).

SolidWorks provides many ways to do almost anything you can imagine. Your job is to determine which methods give you the most flexibility, cost you the least time, and give the most accurate results.

When you set up an assembly cut, you do it in the same way that you would set up a cut in the part environment, but with a couple of exceptions.

First, it is best to sketch on an assembly plane rather than a part face or plane that belongs to a part. This is not a requirement; it is just a best-practice suggestion.

Second, you have to use the Feature Scope to tell SolidWorks if you want to cut through all possible components, or just selected components. Further, you can have SolidWorks automatically select parts for you. For the most stable results, it is probably best to select the parts manually you want to cut. This avoids automating mistakes and additional rebuild time that might be caused by giving the software too much control over your design.

Sometimes assembly cuts are created for documentation purposes rather than design purposes. For example, if you want to cut a model section and display it in an isometric view, or an exploded section view, you have to do that using an assembly cut, probably in conjunction with a configuration so that you can also show the assembly without the section. For example, Figure 11.1 shows an isometric cutaway view created by an assembly feature, Cut Extrude.

FIGURE 11.1

Using an assembly feature to cut away a model for illustration purposes

When you place a feature in the assembly like this, the cut only exists in the assembly. If you open up any individual part in its own window, the part is not cut. If you open the part in another assembly, the part is not cut there either. The cut only exists within the assembly in which it was made.

Figure 11.2 shows the PropertyManager of the cut. The Cut-Extrude1 feature is displayed in the FeatureManager of the assembly, after the Mate folder, local patterns, and even after an assembly sketch.

FIGURE 11.2

The assembly cut is created and then displayed in the FeatureManager of the assembly.

Using the Feature Scope

You can access the Feature Scope in the PropertyManager. In this example, all of the parts were cut because the cut went through the entire assembly. In reality, some of the parts may not have needed to be cut, but in this case, it would have taken longer to find them than it did to just cut all the parts. You can partially cut the assembly in a couple of different ways. One way is to orient the feature such that you can control the depth of the cut by the sketch, and then sketch to suit your needs. Another way is to use the blind cut depth to control the depth. Finally, of course, you can use the Feature Scope to avoid cutting certain parts.

Propagating features to parts

One of the common mistakes SolidWorks users make is sketching in the assembly when they mean to sketch in a part in order to create a feature in the part. For example, you may not be paying attention to what you are doing, and forget to click that "Edit Part" button before starting a sketch.

In addition to that common mistake, sometimes features are simply easier to draw at the assembly level, and, especially if they affect multiple parts, you may want to find an easy fix. Well, there is one. The Feature Scope panel of the assembly feature Cut-Extrude PropertyManager contains an option called Propagate Feature to Parts. You draw the sketch in the assembly, create an assembly feature, and then select the Propagate Feature to Parts option, making sure you have the correct parts selected in the Feature Scope selection box. After you click the green check mark icon, SolidWorks propagates the sketch and the feature to each one of the selected Feature Scope parts, so that the sketch and the feature reside in the FeatureManager of the individual parts.

For example, look at the assembly from Figure 11.1. First, the Feature Scope was changed to just include the plastic housing parts on the outside, so the cutaway now appears as shown in Figure 11.3.

FIGURE 11.3

The Feature Scope altered to include only plastic housing parts

Next, you select the Propagate Feature to Parts option in the Feature Scope box to enable it. When you do this, the assembly still displays the Cut-Extrude feature at the bottom of the assembly FeatureManager, but now each part included in the Feature Scope also gets an in-context Cut-Extrude feature. If you delete the assembly level feature, the feature is also deleted from each of the individual parts.

While this is a nice shortcut, it is not something you should do on a regular basis. In this particular assembly, it caused errors with about a dozen mates.

This kind of functionality also exists with the assembly fillets, chamfers, and the Hole Series functionality with Hole Wizard holes, where you specify hole locations in the assembly, and the holes show up as features in the individual parts. You can read more about the Hole Series feature later in this chapter.

Making Fillets and Chamfers in Assemblies

New in SolidWorks 2011 is the ability to make fillets and chamfers as assembly features. Once parts are assembled, the corners are sometimes filed, sanded, or machined to round them. Figure 11.4 shows a stack of plates that have been filleted and chamfered in the assembly.

FIGURE 11.4

An example showing fillets on an assembly of stacked plates

This book sometimes uses examples that don't look very realistic so that you can learn about the limitations of a feature from simplified geometry. The first thing you can learn from this particular example is that large fillets started on one part do not carry over (overflow) to other parts where you have not made a selection. First, notice the large fillets on the top corners. The fillets are larger than the thickness of the plates and are not tangent to the horizontal edges at the top.

A second thing to notice is that when you are creating these fillets, they do not automatically propagate to tangent edges of other parts, as fillets in parts do. If you want to fillet a string of edges, you have to select each edge individually.

A third thing to notice is that you can use assembly fillets to add material as well as remove material. Therefore, this goes beyond the intention that assembly fillets will be used just for filing, sanding, or machining sharp edges. This is the realm of body filler putty. Basically, it's like anything else. SolidWorks gives you capabilities here that you may not have in the real world, and what you model in the end is your own responsibility (in other words, pay attention to what you are doing).

Finally, you may notice that on the third part from the left in Figure 11.4, there is a fillet that undercuts the edge. This shows that filleting between parts does not work the same as filleting between features that are merged together into a single body. This fillet would add material instead of removing it if this were a single part.

Notice that here you also have the option to propagate the fillets to the parts.

Assembly fillets do not give you all of the capabilities that you have with individual part fillets. You can only create constant radius fillets (with and without a multiple radius option) and face fillets. You cannot create variable radius, setback, hold line, or curvature continuous fillets in this way.

Not everyone will find a use for this feature, but it does offer an alternative to the workaround options that users had to rely on in the past.

Creating Weld Beads

 Weld beads are covered in Chapter 20, but the assembly feature side of weld beads is covered here again, from a slightly different perspective. Although the SolidWorks Help refers to a Fillet Weld Bead feature, there is actually a difference between the Fillet Bead tool and the Weld Bead tool.

When comparing the functionality in the Weld Bead and Fillet Bead features, even the SolidWorks Help for the Fillet Bead recommends using the Weld Bead tool instead of Fillet Bead to insert weld beads.

The Weld Bead feature does offer some advantages over the Fillet Bead feature:

1. The same interface in parts and assemblies
2. A minimal effect on performance of even a large number of weld beads
3. A basic weld symbol is created and applied automatically
4. It works with weldable gaps
5. The Smart Weld Selection tool speeds up selection significantly
6. Weld properties serve to evaluate mass, production time, and cost
7. Weld information can be pulled onto drawings

To be clear, the Fillet Bead feature is only for weldment parts, and it creates a body with additional volume. The Weld Bead feature is for weldments and assemblies, and creates a cosmetic display body, not something that affects mass properties.

The workflow to create a weld bead is as follows:

1. Select the weld path(s). The weld path can be a set of edges (they must be between two bodies or parts) or a set of faces (they must be from adjacent parts).

   You can select multiple weld paths, and the paths don't need to touch. The weld path appears as bright pink for an active path, or orange for an existing path listed in the PropertyManager.

   The Smart Weld Selection tool creates new weld paths automatically based on your selections, and greatly simplifies face or edge selection for weld bead creation. Just roughly sketch with the pencil where you want the weld to go, and SolidWorks automatically selects the faces or edges to make that weld happen.

2. Set the size of the weld.

3. Define the weld symbol that includes all of the details about the weld for the welder on the drawing.

4. Set the length limit of the weld.

5. Establish requirements for intermittent weld from the options given.

The PropertyManager for a weld bead made in a multi-body part is shown in Figure 11.5.

Notice that the welds are organized by size and type within the Weld folder. Fillet Weld is the default weld type if you don't specify another type.

The PropertyManager looks the same for the weld bead done in a multi-body part as it does in an assembly. The results also look the same. Figure 11.6 shows the Weld folder in an assembly with a Fillet Weld feature in it, and a length of weld bead. Aside from the duplicate names, none of this has anything to do with the Fillet Bead feature that is only available in weldment parts.

To edit the weld bead, you have to right-click the Weld Bead item listed under the size of the Fillet Weld in the Weld folder. This brings you back to the original Weld Bead PropertyManager.

You can manage other weld properties by right-clicking the size of the weld and selecting the Properties option. The Weld Bead Properties dialog box appears, as shown in Figure 11.7.

If you have used previous versions of SolidWorks, then you will agree that this version offers the most successful Weld Bead feature to date.

FIGURE 11.5

Creating a weld bead

FIGURE 11.6

Results of the weld bead

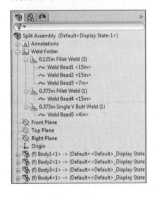

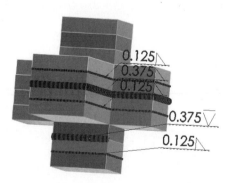

FIGURE 11.7

The Weld Bead Properties dialog box enables you to set many options

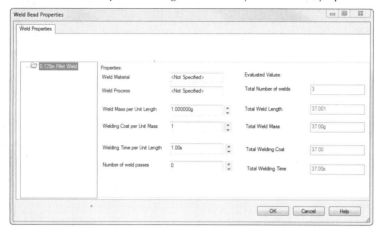

Working with Envelopes

Envelopes in SolidWorks are regular parts that are treated in a special way. Envelopes are meant to be used as selection volumes, so that you can make selections based on whether other parts are inside, outside, or crossing the envelope boundary. You can make an envelope in place in the assembly or you can make an envelope from an existing part. Envelope parts do not count toward BOM part counts or material properties.

To create an envelope, select Insert ⇨ Envelope, and then choose either New or From File, as shown in Figure 11.8.

FIGURE 11.8

Inserting a new envelope into an assembly

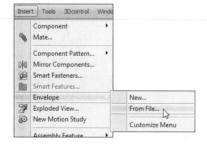

You can create envelopes on the fly with extrude or revolve features, and if you use an existing part as an envelope, you can use any part you can create in SolidWorks. Once in the assembly, the envelope displays in the graphics window as a transparent light-blue part, and in the assembly FeatureManager as an Envelope folder, as shown in Figure 11.9.

FIGURE 11.9

An envelope in the assembly

The two options that the Envelope function was meant to work with — Select Using Envelope and Show/Hide Using Envelope — are shown in Figure 11.10. You can access these options by right-clicking the Envelope folder in the ConfigurationManager window.

FIGURE 11.10

Using Envelope options

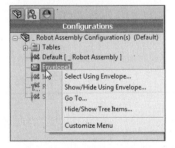

If you are familiar with the Envelope functionality from several releases ago, you will remember that it used to be part of the Advanced Show/Hide tool, which has been changed into the Advanced Component Selection dialog box, discussed in Chapter 7. Component selection also includes a Volume Select function that enables you to create a rectangular volume on the fly that works very much like an envelope.

Because of the special properties of envelopes with regard to the BOM and mass properties, users have developed many alternate uses for them. Most of these uses are now obsolete, or nearly obsolete, because you can set the mass of a part to zero and exclude it from the BOM using direct options.

Summary

Assembly features can be quirky, and are often used for specialized or niche applications. Having this functionality available just gives you another tool in your toolbox for solving design and documentation problems.

12

Using Parametric Links in Assemblies

S olidWorks enables users to create parametric links between parts in the assembly with a variety of tools, including equations, link values, global variables, and derived sketches. These options have some considerations when compared to their counterparts used in part documents, mostly around the ideas of file management and keeping the links up to date through changes to the filenames.

In addition, whenever changes in one model affect another model, you need to use extra care to make sure that you get the changes you want.

This chapter assumes that you already have an understanding of equations, link values, global variables, and derived sketches in parts. It only adds information related to assemblies, or links outside individual part files.

Using Equations in an Assembly

Assembly equations work mainly like part equations, but with some additional complications and considerations. For example, one of the additional features of assembly equations is the ability to drive the dimensions of one part from another part. The syntax is slightly different for this application, as shown in Figure 12.1. Overall, issues with equation order and using driven dimensions on the right side of the equation are the same between parts and assemblies. You can open the Equations dialog box by right-clicking the Equations folder in the assembly FeatureManager, and selecting either Add Equation or Edit Equation.

If the Equations folder does not appear in the assembly FeatureManager, then you can turn it on by selecting Tools ➪ Options ➪ FeatureManager ➪ Equations. If it is set to Automatic, you need to change the setting to Show.

FIGURE 12.1

An assembly equation driving one part from another

Tracking external references

Notice the "->" symbol after the Equations folder in the Assembly FeatureManager. This means that there is an external or in-context reference in an equation. An external reference means that an aspect of the part is dependent upon something outside of the part. This has file management implications because you must maintain the names of the files so that they always recognize the other file involved in the external relation. *In-context* means that one part has a relation to another part in positions determined by an assembly. So in this case, the in-context external reference can only be solved if the original part, the referenced part, and the assembly where the relationship was created are all open at the same time.

When one part drives another part in this way, the assembly must also be open to drive the relationship. If just the two parts are open individually, then changing the driving part does not update the driven part; because the relationship was created in the context of the assembly, the assembly must also be open to facilitate the change.

Cross-Reference
Chapter 10 offers more in-depth information on general in-context situations and external references. ■

Renaming documents referenced by equations

Equations update with new part names regardless of how the parts are renamed. Names of subassemblies also update when assembly files are renamed. This includes renaming a document using the Save As command, using SolidWorks Explorer, or using Windows Explorer. It also includes redirecting the assembly to the new part name, as well as renaming the assembly using each of these techniques. If the assembly can find the part and recognizes the part as the one that it is looking for, then the equation works.

Of the previously mentioned methods, SolidWorks Explorer is the most highly recommended. Save As methods can work properly if you use them in a disciplined way. Windows Explorer is never a recommended method for file management, at least not for name changing.

Caution

You may have unexpected results if a single dimension is controlled from more than one location. For example, if you have a part-level equation and an assembly-level equation, then one of the equations will be automatically set to Read Only and will not be used. ■

Sharing equations

In addition to the use of equations in an assembly, you can also share equations between parts or assemblies using linked text files. This is a great method for when multiple parts need to use the same equation, and the equation may change frequently. You only need to change the equations in one place, and it updates for all linked documents. This method effectively links equations between parts without using an assembly at all.

When you share equations between parts, you have to make sure you have given the dimensions, sketches, and features the same name in both parts. To start sharing equations, first build an equation in a part, and then click the Export button in the Equations dialog box, as shown in Figure 12.2.

To share an equation between two parts, you must first export the equation.

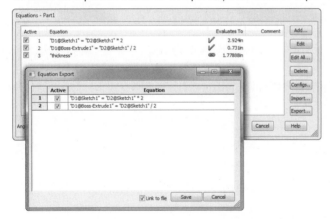

The Equation Export dialog box enables you to select which equation(s) you would like to export, by using the Active column check boxes. When you click the Save button, the equations are saved to an external text file. To link the current file to the external file, make sure the Link To File option at the bottom of the Equation Export dialog box is selected.

When a part is linked to an external equation text file, you are not able to edit the equations in the Equations dialog box. You can add more equations, and you can use the new equations either linked or unlinked. The linked equation file is listed at the bottom of the Equations dialog box, but there is no link to access the text file. You have to browse to the file and open it manually.

If you want to change the equation, you must do this in the external text file. To update the equation in the part file, just close and reopen the Equations dialog box, and the equation edits appear updated.

Note
You cannot use external equation files to share link values or global variables. ∎

To share equations saved out from another part, again open the Equations dialog box, but this time click the Import button, and browse to the location where you saved the exported text equation file. When equations are imported and linked, you cannot edit them in the Equations dialog box, only in the external text file.

Driving equations between parts

You can also use an equation in one part to drive a dimension in another part within an assembly. To do this, edit a part in an assembly, open the Equations dialog box, add an equation, and write the equation, selecting a dimension from another part. When you do this, the syntax of the equation works, as shown in Figure 12.3.

FIGURE 12.3

Local dimensions can be driven by a dimension in another part.

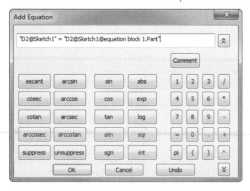

Notice that the syntax makes no mention of the assembly at all, only of the remote part (equation block 1.sldprt). This means that as long as both parts are open, the equation can work. It does not require the assembly to also be open. Shared (linked) equations do not require both parts to be open, just that the file containing the equations be accessible.

Following best practices

While assembly equations are certainly a valid way to control part sizes, you should use assembly or part configurations, possibly with design tables, to accomplish something similar. Equations and configurations do not mix well because the two methods compete to control the dimensions. Configurations with design tables are better than equations.

Using Link Values and Global Variables in Assemblies

Link values and global variables work in assembly sketches, but they do not work between parts. Local assembly sketches can use these functions, and the parts can use them as long as they do not link dimensions in different documents, but they cannot cross any document barriers (links must remain within a single document). If you need to achieve something like this, an equation can serve the same purposes.

Working with Derived Sketches in Assemblies

Derived sketches are a very powerful, but surprisingly underused, feature. They enable you to use a parametric copy of a sketch in another feature. When you edit and change the original sketch, the Derived Sketch updates immediately. The derived sketch becomes like a sketch block in that you can't change it, but you can position, orient, and even mirror it as you need, on any plane in the part without regard to the derived sketch's relationship to the original sketch's orientation.

Derived sketches enable you to create any kind of feature you can create with normal sketches, so you should not have problems using them with extrudes, lofts, sweeps, and so on. Remember that if you are just trying to copy a sketch to use the copy in the exact location of the original, you may be able to simply reuse the sketch. Some features such as curves do not allow you to reuse their parent sketches, but others such as extrudes, revolves, and lofts do.

In addition to being used within a part, derived sketches can also be used in context, in an assembly. For example, you can use a parametric copy of a sketch from Part 1 in Part 2 within a given assembly.

To create a derived sketch, select a sketch from the FeatureManager, and then Ctrl+click a plane or planar face and select Insert ⇨ Derived Sketch. This command places you in a copy of the sketch where you cannot change dimensions, relations, or add or remove sketch entities.

The best tool for moving the derived sketch is the Modify Sketch tool. You can only add relations or dimensions to the derived sketch that will locate the sketch as if it were a static sketch block. Remember that the sketch can rotate as well as translate. If one corner of a derived sketch is locked down, the rest of the sketch can rotate around that point.

When you create a derived sketch, it appears in the FeatureManager, as shown in Figure 12.4.

FIGURE 12.4

Derived sketches are identified in the FeatureManager.

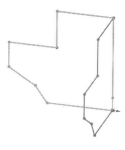

After you have created and oriented the derived sketch, if you want to break the link to the original sketch for any reason, you can easily do that. Right-click the derived sketch and select Underive from the available options. This removes all dimensions and relations from the copy of the sketch, such that it is fully underdefined.

You can also create derived sketches between parts in an assembly. The procedure is the same: edit a part in an assembly, select a sketch from another part, as well as a plane from the local part or another part, and then choose Insert ⇨ Derived Sketch. A sketch derived in this way is typically identified with the word *derived* added to the end of the sketch name, but it also has an external reference symbol (->).

Using Inserted Parts to Communicate Parametric Control

Chapter 19, which covers master model techniques, describes the Insert Part feature in more detail, but it is included here to demonstrate another technique for sharing data between parts. Inserting one part into another using the Insert Part feature enables you to transfer the following types of information from one part to another without using an assembly:

- Solid bodies

- Surface bodies

- Axes

- Planes

- Cosmetic threads

- Absorbed sketches

- Unabsorbed sketches

- Custom properties

- Coordinate systems

- Model dimensions

- Hole Wizard data

To insert one part into another, open the part into which you want to insert the other part, and select Insert ⇨ Part. Then browse for the other part, and select which types of entities you want to bring forward from the parent part to the child part. The Insert Part PropertyManager is shown in Figure 12.5.

FIGURE 12.5

Inserting data from one part into another

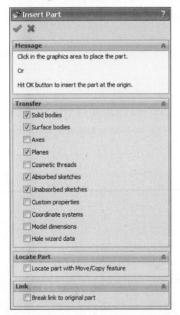

The inserted information is linked to the original file, such that if the original changes, the inserted data also changes. This sort of data sharing is very powerful and can be used for sharing many kinds of data and geometry without needing an assembly.

Summary

SolidWorks provides users with many methods for using parametric and associative links between parts within and out of assemblies. Equations and design tables are two of the most powerful ways, and derived sketches are a useful method. You can also use inserted parts to communicate parametric controls between documents.

Editing, Evaluating, and Troubleshooting Assemblies

SolidWorks assemblies give users plenty of opportunities to enhance their editing and troubleshooting skills. In fact, without evaluation and troubleshooting skills, it might be impossible to get any real work done. Most design or modeling work is not just a linear task — it is often an iterative process. If you get everything right the first time, you haven't tried very hard.

With this in mind, this chapter goes through the essential tools you need to get real-world work done, and do it in a way that shows you understand what you are doing. Editing, evaluating, and troubleshooting skills are tools that will help you deal with the reality of working with SolidWorks assemblies. These tasks can be dauntingly tedious unless you have a working knowledge of the available tools.

Working with Mates

When you think of editing in assemblies, the main task that comes to mind is editing mates, and probably editing broken mates. While there are several other kinds of editing you can do in assemblies, such as changing subassembly structure, replacing components, and managing files, mates really are the biggest item you face when you are talking about editing assemblies.

Chapters 4 and 5 introduce you to the world of creating mates between parts and other items in assemblies. This chapter is more concerned with manipulating mates that already exist.

In assemblies, you can find mates in two different locations, and display them in two different modes. The first place you find them is in the Mates folder at the bottom of the assembly FeatureManager, as shown in Figure 13.1.

FIGURE 13.1

All of the mates in an assembly are shown in the Mates folder at the bottom of the assembly FeatureManager.

Listing mates in the Mates folder

The Mates folder can contain other folders that also contain mates to help you organize them. The mates can be renamed, reordered, deleted, suppressed, and edited from this list. The mates are listed in the order in which they were created, and the name of each mate is followed by the names of the parts or assembly features between which the mate was made.

Mates can fail, or have warning markers, like other features inside parts. A red circle with an X in it means that the mate does not meet the geometric conditions. A yellow triangle with an exclamation point means that the mate is in conflict with another mate. Figure 13.2 shows examples of these errors.

FIGURE 13.2

Know the difference between a warning and an error.

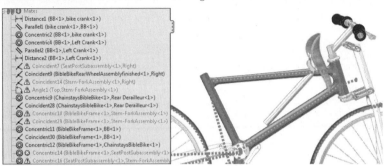

You can see from the last two mates in the list that one is an error, and the other is a warning. If you look at the assembly, you notice that the seat is not where it belongs. The mate Concentric14 is between the frame and the seat post. This is the mate that is not satisfied and is currently broken. The mate Concentric16 is shown to be in conflict with another mate, and you can see that the other mate has to be Concentric14.

Other mates are also in conflict, and this is one of the biggest difficulties when troubleshooting mates in an assembly. While several mates are in conflict, there may be only one mate that is actually causing a problem. Unfortunately, there is no automated way to determine which mate is the troublemaker, but a good rule of thumb is to troubleshoot the list of mates from the bottom to the top. This is based on the expectation that more recently added mates are the ones causing trouble.

In this case, simply deleting the Concentric16 mate fixes all of the problems in the list of mates, and the part goes back to where it belongs.

Listing mates under the component

Mates are also listed under the component in the FeatureManager. These are the same mates as are listed in the Mates folder at the bottom, but under the component, only the mates relating to that particular component are listed. Figure 13.3 shows mates listed in this way.

FIGURE 13.3

Mates are also listed in a folder under the component.

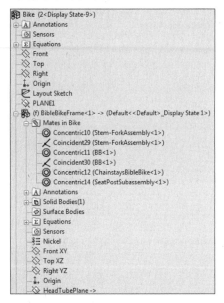

This is a very convenient way to list the mates, making them easy to find, and nicely organized. One of the drawbacks of listing them this way is that when there is a mate with an error, the error not only shows up in the Mates folder at the bottom of the FeatureManager, but an error flag also appears on each of the parts containing the bad mate.

Replacing features with mates

Another method of displaying mates under the components enables you to see the mates of more parts at once. In the previous method shown in Figure 13.3, the mates were shown along with the features of the part.

To show the mates associated with each part without the features, right-click the top-level assembly, select Tree Display, and then select View Mates and Dependencies. This option is shown in Figure 13.4.

Notice that you can still access the features if you want to. They are in a collapsed folder at the bottom of the list of mates. This is a more convenient option for looking at the mates of several parts at one time.

FIGURE 13.4

Displaying the mates without part features

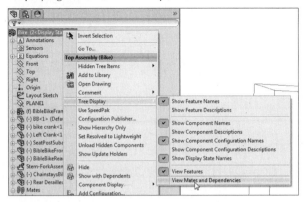

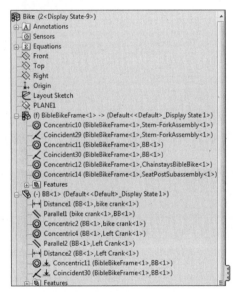

Working with the View Mates tool

 As its name implies, View Mates is a special tool just for viewing mates. You can access it from the RMB menu when you select a single assembly component (part or subassembly), or multiple assembly components. Figure 13.5 shows the View Mates window when the frame and stem-fork subassembly are selected in the bike assembly located on the DVD.

On the DVD

To view this example, open the file bike.sldasm, located in the Chapter 13 folder. ■

FIGURE 13.5

The View Mates window shows mates for selected components.

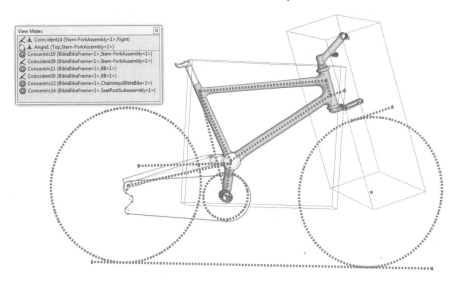

 The icon shown to the left of Coincident14 in Figure 13.5 indicates that mate is in the "path to ground," which means that it is part of the link from the part that is either fixed or mated to assembly planes to outlying parts which depend on other parts for their location. The Path to Ground parts are always listed at the top of the View Mates window. The rest of the mates in the window are all from the parts that are selected.

The parts displayed in blue in the graphics window are the parts mated together from the components selected (the entire fork subassembly is not shown, just the stem part that is actually mated to the frame). As you select mates in the View Mates window, SolidWorks highlights the faces or edges involved, as well as mate names in the graphics window.

View Mates is a useful tool for investigating mating relationships between parts, especially in assemblies that have evolved over time or assemblies that someone else built and that you must understand well enough to work with.

Using the View Mate Errors window

The View Mate Errors window looks identical to the View Mate window, but it only shows mates that have error or warning flags. It shows all of the mates with errors in the entire top-level assembly, not just for the selected component. The View Mate Errors window is only available from the RMB menu, and only on components where there are mate errors. It is only available for single selections, never for multiple components. Figure 13.6 shows this window.

Using the View Mate Errors window to troubleshoot mate problems

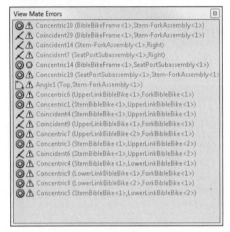

Using the MateXpert

The MateXpert tool helps you troubleshoot assembly problems. You can access the MateXpert by right-clicking a mate with an error, or from the Tools menu. Do not confuse the MateXpert with the AssemblyXpert; the MateXpert does not have an icon, and only deals with mates.

This example intentionally creates a problem in the Bike assembly so that you can see how the MateXpert deals with issues that arise. The problem created here is the same as the one from earlier in this chapter, which forced the seat post to be concentric with the stem. After clicking the Diagnose button in the MateXpert, you see the result shown in Figure 13.7.

FIGURE 13.7

Using the MateXpert to diagnose problems

The MateXpert returns three possible problems in the Analyze Problem panel of the PropertyManager. In this case, the only mate in the assembly that has the red error marker is Concentric14; the rest of the mates just display the yellow warning triangle. Notice at the bottom that SolidWorks correctly identifies the one red marker mate as a mate that is not satisfied.

This tool returns a lot of information, some of it you may find more useful than others. When troubleshooting assemblies you should use whatever set of tools you feel give you the best information for fixing the problem. If you are working through a tangle of mate errors, you may want to use other troubleshooting methods before you rely too heavily on the MateXpert. Or possibly give the MateXpert a glance to see if it points out something you had missed before you try a more robust method.

Keep in mind that users have reported in earlier versions of SolidWorks that the MateXpert was responsible for automatically flipping alignment on certain types of mates. While it is not clear if mates continue to flip, flipping of several types of entities continues to be a problem throughout the SolidWorks software, for entities such as sketches, planes, and other directional controls in certain features. If you encounter this problem, you might be able to regain some control over the automatic flipping by using the setting at Tools ➪ Options ➪ Assemblies ➪ Prompt Before Changing Mate Alignments on Edit.

Editing mates

You can edit mates using the same Mate PropertyManager that you used to create the mates. You access this PropertyManager by right-clicking a mate and selecting Edit Feature from the menu. The Mate PropertyManager for an existing mate is shown in Figure 13.8.

FIGURE 13.8

Editing a mate with the original Mate PropertyManager

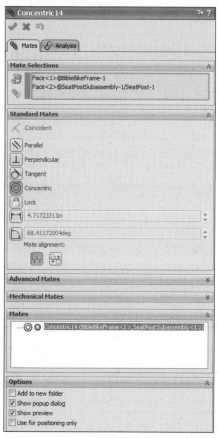

One of the advantages of using this method to edit mates is that you can change the type of mate simply by selecting it in the PropertyManager. This is different from features such as the Fillet where, once you select a fillet type and create the feature, you cannot edit it later and change the type of fillet.

If you want to replace the mated entities, you can delete the one you want to change from the Mate Selections selection box and choose a new one. You can even select an entity from a different part if you need to.

 Another feature for replacing mate entities that is more tailored to the specific task is the Replace Mate Entities tool. You can also find this in the RMB menu for a mate (as well as in the LMB menu, but you must be able to recognize it by its icon or its tooltip). Figure 13.9 shows where you would access both the Edit Feature and the Replace Mate Entities tools from the RMB menu.

FIGURE 13.9

Accessing Edit Feature and Replace Mate Entities from the RMB menu

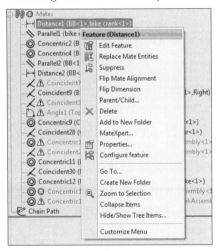

Selecting Replace Mate Entities displays a PropertyManager called Mated Entities. This interface shows which entities from which parts are used together in the mate. To replace an entity, select it from the Mate Entities selection box; it appears in the small selection box below. Then simply select the new entity.

When you open this PropertyManager, the Isolate toolbar also automatically appears. Isolate is a tool that hides parts that are not involved in the current operation. The Mated Entities PropertyManager and the Isolate toolbar are shown in Figure 13.10.

FIGURE 13.10

Changing mated entities using the Mated Entities PropertyManager and Isolate toolbar

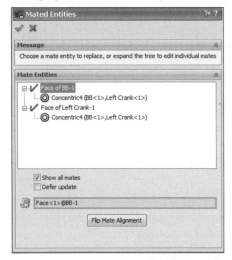

One of the nice features of the Replace Mate Entities tool is that you can select multiple mates before activating the tool from the RMB menu, and all of the mate entities appear in the PropertyManager. This makes changing several mates in one step relatively easy.

You can also select multiple mates to edit in this way using the Mate PropertyManager. The multiple-selected mates appear in the Mates panel toward the bottom of the PropertyManager (refer to Figure 13.8 where the Concentric14 mate is shown).

Note

If while manipulating mates your assembly stops to rebuild every time you make an edit, you may want to use the Suspend Automatic Rebuilds option, found at Tools ⇨ Options ⇨ Assemblies. As a reference, the Bike assembly example in this chapter has a problem like this using SolidWorks 2011 SP 3.0. The rebuild symbol keeps showing up on the frame part on the FeatureManager, even though it has just rebuilt and there are no changes. This "perpetual rebuild" problem appears to come from the in-context features of the part. ■

Editing File Management Issues

File management in SolidWorks assemblies requires a certain amount of attention. You have to be careful when changing filenames and locations, and also use the correct tools, or SolidWorks may lose track of where to find necessary data. The best tools to use for SolidWorks file management are, of course, PDM (product data management) tools such as Workgroup PDM (formerly PDMWorks) and Enterprise PDM (formerly Conisio). After that, SolidWorks and SolidWorks Explorer are good tools for users who do not have access to PDM tools.

Using Save options and Pack and Go

When making changes to the files involved in SolidWorks assemblies, understanding the Save options will serve you well. Whenever you want to change a name, change a location, or make a copy of a particular SolidWorks document, you should use some combination of the Save, Save As, and Save As Copy tools, as well as Pack and Go.

 The Save command only displays a dialog box the first time you save a document. If you are saving an assembly with virtual components, it may ask you to save the assembly with a name in addition to asking you to name and save virtual components externally. Save is typically not an option for anything other than initially placing and naming your files.

 Save As is the tool to use when you want to save the current document to a new name. When you do this, SolidWorks leaves the last saved version of the previous part behind, and going forward, the new name and location you used in Save As will be the one that remains in the assembly.

For example, if you have Assembly 1 and it is made up of Part 1 and Part 2, and these files are already saved to your local hard drive, but you want to rename Part 1 as 875003 base structure.sldprt, then you can use the Save As command to do this. First, you *must* have the assembly and parts open. Then, you can open Part 1 in its own window and use Save As from there, entering in the new part name and location in the Save As dialog box. Part 1 will continue to exist, but it will be replaced in the assembly with 875003 base structure.sldprt, and any changes moving forward will affect the base structure part. The actual assembly must also be saved once you have performed the Save As on Part 1. If you do not save the assembly, it will continue to remember the old part (Part 1.sldprt) instead of the new part (875003 base structure.sldprt).

If you make the name change using Windows Explorer, SolidWorks will not know anything about the name change, and the next time you open the assembly, it will tell you it can't find Part 1.sldprt, and will ask you to find it.

You can also use the Save As command on the entire assembly, changing the name of the assembly. Actually, this just makes a copy of the assembly, leaving the new copy open, and leaving the old copy behind on your hard drive, closed.

Using Save As on the assembly gives you the option to also change the names or folders of any or all of the components in the assembly. The dialog boxes for Save As and the Save As with References option are shown in Figure 13.11.

° FIGURE 13.11

Saving an assembly with references applies your changes to all of the documents referenced by the assembly.

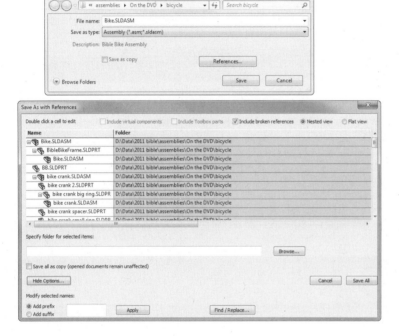

The More Options section in the Save As with References dialog box enables you to add a prefix or suffix, as well as to use a simple Find/Replace function to rename files in the list. Remember that this makes a copy of the assembly and all the parts with new names or locations.

Cross-Reference

File management issues are a great place to learn best practice rules. The SolidWorks Administration Bible has a chapter dedicated to file naming and another dedicated to file management, with best practice suggestions throughout the book. ■

SolidWorks users frequently use the Pack and Go tool to make a copy of an entire assembly in a new location, or to a Zip file used to transfer an assembly with all parts to someone who does not have access to the local network. Pack and Go has all of the functionality of Save As with References, as well as some additional options. You can also replace files, include drawings and simulation results, and get a quick summary on the number of parts, assemblies, and drawings that are being included. If you are not using a formal PDM application, Pack and Go can at least serve as a main copy, archive, and renaming utility. The Pack and Go window is shown in Figure 13.12.

Pack and Go contains most of your file management needs outside of PDM.

Replacing components

Following the philosophy that "delete is not an editing method," SolidWorks includes a tool to replace components that is an improvement over the less graceful delete-and-add technique. When you delete a component, you lose a lot of information that you could otherwise keep. Whether you delete a sketch line, a mate, or a part in an assembly, deleting more than doubles the work you have to do. You have to do a lot of repair work after you make a deletion. The deeper into a design you are, the more data you lose when you delete something from it. Each piece of information in SolidWorks has some other piece of information attached to it. That associativity is supposed to help rather than hinder you. Learning to use the tools in the way you were meant to use them is one way to improve your efficiency with the software — so that you work *with* the software rather than *against* it.

The Replace Component tool is available from the RMB menu of any component in the assembly. Figure 13.13 shows the PropertyManager for the Replace command.

Replacing a component in an assembly with another component

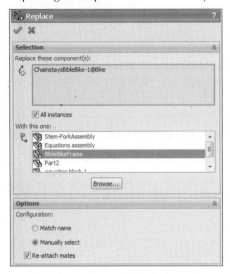

The All Instances option is an important one. Sometimes you need to only replace one instance of a particular component with some other part. The All Instances option makes it easy and convenient to replace just what you need.

Other important options have to do with configurations and mates. If the replacement part will use the same configuration name as the original part, you can use the Match Name option. If not, you can use the Manually Select option.

Reattaching mates can be tricky. If the two parts are similar in their topology (general layout of model faces), then the automatic reattachment will probably work. If the mates cannot be reattached automatically, you are presented with the interface shown in Figure 13.14. This interface shows each of the mates that cannot be reattached automatically, with a small window showing the equivalent face on the old part. It is asking you to select a face on the new part that matches the highlighted face on the old part to repair each mate.

FIGURE 13.14

Reattaching mates by selecting indicated faces on the replacement part

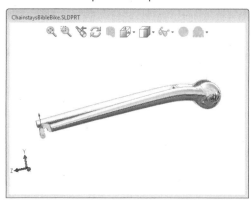

This is a fairly easy process to go through, and certainly better than deleting the original part, reinserting the part, and recreating mates.

Forming and dissolving subassemblies

When you initially create an assembly, you may not always know exactly how you want to organize it. Assemblies can serve many purposes, such as for motion, analysis, rendering, assembly instructions, inspection, or a BOM. The structure of each type of assembly with sub-assemblies might be very different. Thus, SolidWorks needs to be flexible in allowing you to change the structure on the fly, again without the wasted effort of deleting and recreating data.

To create a new subassembly within an existing top-level assembly, select a set of compo-nents through appropriate selection methods (advanced select, Ctrl+select, window select, and so on), then right-click and select Form New Subassembly Here. When the new subas-sembly is first created, SolidWorks just moves the selected components into the subassembly without any fanfare. The new subassembly is created as a virtual component, so it is just saved within the top-level assembly. If you want to immediately save the new subassembly (named in a format similar to [Assem1^Bike] where Bike is the name of the top-level assem-bly), right-click the new assembly and select Save Assembly (in External File) from the menu.

Moving parts in and out of subassemblies

If you have an existing subassembly, and you want to add to it or remove parts from it, you can drag the component name in the FeatureManager to accomplish this. To drag a part into the subassembly, drag the filename onto the name of the subassembly. You see the special cursor shown in Figure 13.15.

FIGURE 13.15

Adding the BB part to the virtual component subassembly Assem2^Bike

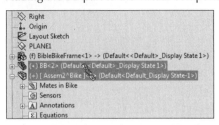

In the example shown in Figure 13.15, the Bottom Bracket part (BB) is being added to the virtual component subassembly Assem2^Bike. The virtual component has not been named yet, but it will be the top-level crankset assembly, with the left and right cranks, chain rings, and bottom bracket.

If you want to move a part out of a subassembly into an upper-level assembly, you have to drag the filename from its spot in the subassembly onto the name of the top-level assembly. If you just drag the part above the subassembly, SolidWorks may think you are trying to reorder the display of the name within the assembly FeatureManager. Remember that different symbols exist for moving parts up or down the subassembly hierarchy and reordering parts in the FeatureManager.

Moving mates from an assembly to a subassembly

Sometimes when you move a part into or out of an assembly, SolidWorks requires that you also need to move mates or destroy certain in-context relationships. If SolidWorks displays a message that it has to move mates to another level or that it will have to break some external references, you need to read the message carefully and try to determine whether you can live with the conditions mentioned in the message. You may not be able to easily undo these actions once they are complete. A typical message is shown in Figure 13.16. Losing all of the in-context relations in a particular sketch could mean a lot of repair work, so you need to consider these things carefully.

When a mate is moved from a top-level assembly to a subassembly, the mate is no longer solved in the top level, which means you may not be able to use Dynamic Assembly Motion on the parts you just moved from the top level to the subassembly level. You may need to employ a flexible subassembly, which solves the subassembly's mates in the top level. The drawback of this technique is that more mates to solve means more time to rebuild the assembly document, and thus a slower working environment.

FIGURE 13.16

Read warning boxes when they are displayed; they could be important.

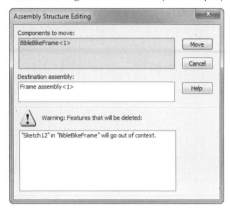

Evaluating Assemblies

Having the ability to change your assembly is not very useful unless you know what you need to change. This is where evaluation techniques come into play in SolidWorks. Evaluation tools help you to gain a better understanding of what your starting point is so that you can be more efficient with your changes.

In the sections that follow, you will learn some new ways to look at and evaluate your SolidWorks assemblies.

Using the AssemblyXpert

The SolidWorks AssemblyXpert is also described in Chapter 7 but is reviewed here as well to keep related information together. The AssemblyXpert is an informational tool that offers statistics about how many parts, subassemblies, lightweight parts, and so on are in the assembly. It also offers some advice about assembly performance and various settings. Figure 13.17 shows the AssemblyXpert window.

Notice the eyeglasses icon in the right column for one of the information entries. If you click this icon, SolidWorks displays the dialog box in Figure 13.18, which displays the Rebuild Report. This is a list of the parts that take the most time to rebuild in this assembly.

FIGURE 13.17

Using the AssemblyXpert to gain information and important statistics about your assembly

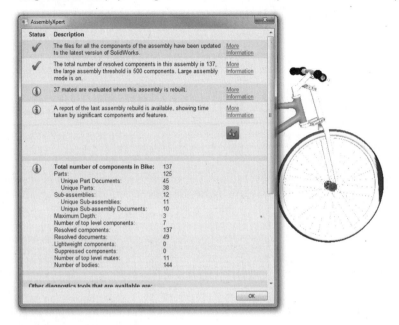

FIGURE 13.18

AssemblyXpert rebuild time analysis

Identifying FeatureManager symbols

You may be wondering what certain rarely seen symbols in the FeatureManager signify. Here is a list of some of the ones that users often ask about.

 Flexible subassembly

 Lightweight

 Out-of-date lightweight

 Path to ground is a mate that is between the part and the fully defined part

 Part made in the academic version of the software

 Toolbox part

Following are some additional symbols in the FeatureManager that are part of the text name.

(f) Indicates the part is Fixed. The opposite of Fixed is Float.

(-) Indicates the part is underdefined. There are not enough mates to lock its position.

(+) Indicates the part location is overdefined. Overdefined parts typically need to have one or more mates removed. This is a situation you should fix in any case.

-> External Reference. There is a reference to a file outside of the current document.

->? Out of Context. There is an external reference, but it is not currently loaded in memory.

->* External Reference is Locked. You can unlock locked references.

->X External Reference is Broken. You cannot repair broken external references.

Using the Isolate function

Isolate is a tool that enables you to display only selected components. If you right-click a subassembly and select Isolate, you can have it set so that all the other parts are shown as wireframe, transparent, or hidden. This is a nice method to draw attention to a couple of parts or a subassembly while still being able to see the rest of the assembly for reference.

Figure 13.19 shows the Isolate tool in use. To activate Isolate, right-click a part or a selection of parts and click Isolate in the menu.

FIGURE 13.19

Using Isolate in an assembly

When you use Isolate, the small toolbar shown in Figure 13.19 appears and gives you the option to show the rest of the parts in the assembly in one of three modes: Wireframe, Transparent, or Hidden. As long as you have the part or parts isolated, the Isolate toolbar remains on the screen.

The Save icon on the Isolate toolbar enables you to save the current display as a Display State. This enables you to get back to that particular combination of display settings for parts. To return to the previous display, click the Exit Isolate button.

Using Reload

 Reload is a command that acts as a shortcut for exiting the current document without saving, and then reopening. Reload is available for parts and assemblies but is not available for drawings. You can find Reload in the File menu, or add it to your toolbars from the Standard category in Tools ➪ Customize ➪ Commands.

Figure 13.20 shows the dialog box that appears when you invoke the Reload command. Notice that this dialog box gives you the option to load Read-only if available, and includes other file management options that you need to be aware of, especially if you are working on an assembly with other SolidWorks users.

Reload is very handy when you make a change to your part or assembly that you don't want to keep, but you cannot use the Undo command to get rid of it. Reload is useful if you are trying out a technique and don't want to save the results.

 A command that you can use in conjunction with Reload is the Check Read-only Files command. This command is only available from a toolbar icon that is not on the Standard toolbar by default but is listed in the Tools ➪ Customize ➪ Commands list.

FIGURE 13.20

Reloading an assembly to discard changes

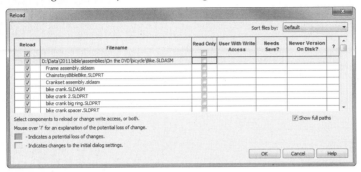

The Check Read-only Files tool checks to see if any read-only files have been changed, or if new versions exist in the folder you are working in. If new versions exist, this tool brings up the Reload tool.

Summary

You might create your work once in SolidWorks, but you are almost guaranteed to spend more time editing it than you did creating it. Because of that, you need to be even more adept at editing and evaluating your SolidWorks assembly than you are at creating it. SolidWorks has a lot of tools to help you do this.

Part III

Creating and Using Libraries

Using Toolbox

Toolbox is a hardware configurator that enables you to select from a wide range of styles and sizes to populate assemblies with standard hardware. It has many functions that allow you to automatically place and size fasteners.

Toolbox is integrated with the Hole Wizard through a database of fastener and hole sizes. The Hole Wizard is a function that applies mainly to parts but also has some relevance for assemblies. The Hole Wizard can create either holes in-context, or assembly feature holes.

Most of this book deals exclusively with SolidWorks Standard. Toolbox is part of SolidWorks Professional and so is not included in SolidWorks Standard. One way to know if you have Toolbox is to go to Tools ⇨ Add-ins, and if you see Toolbox in the list, then you have it.

Understanding Toolbox

To get the most from the automated functions in Toolbox, you need to configure it, and you may need to alter the goal of using an automated library to some extent. If you are planning to implement Toolbox, but don't already have a clear idea of what it is or does, then this chapter is a good place to start.

There are as many different ways of implementing Toolbox as there are companies who have implemented it, but they all have one thing in common: you need to have direct experience with the software or some very good help to make the right choices. The bottom line is that if you make the wrong choices (and the wrong choices are all but hard-coded into the default installation), you could put yourself in a situation where your assembly data is at risk.

If you are using Toolbox on your own and not sharing data with others, the default Toolbox settings are fine. However, if you are among a group of users, you will need a dedicated implementation effort.

This book primarily covers Toolbox from the end-user perspective. If you are looking for information from the administrative perspective, you should read *SolidWorks Administration Bible* (Wiley, 2009), which covers various schemes for implementing Toolbox.

The standard workflow for using Toolbox is as follows:

1. Turn on Toolbox and Toolbox Browser through the Tools ⇨ Add-Ins dialog box.

2. Open an assembly with parts containing holes.

3. Open the Design Library tab in the Task Pane, and browse to find the particular type of fastener you want to place in the assembly.

4. Drag the fastener to the hole where you want to place it, and select a length.

Other workflows exist for more automated functions such as using Smart Fasteners to populate a large selection of holes automatically, or using Hole Series (part of Hole Wizard) to place holes in the assembly and automatically populate the holes with fasteners immediately.

Comparing configurators and libraries

Toolbox creates fasteners and other hardware components on the fly or reuses existing parts when possible. Technically, it is not a library, but a *configurator*. Libraries store existing components, while configurators build them on the fly from a template of information and selections supplied by the user.

One advantage of using a configurator is that the parts start out very compact because there is only the default size template, and the size data is efficiently stored in a database, with each specific-size SolidWorks file being created only when needed. The downside of using a configurator is that the parts do not exist before they are created. That sounds obvious, but when you have a new Toolbox installation matched up with a long legacy of SolidWorks assemblies, it could mean the loss of all of your fastener data from existing assemblies that you thought were safe.

The advantage of a library is that it enables you to simply plug in the parts. Before most users become familiar with using configurators, all they really want is a static, straightforward library of parts that they can use anywhere, at any time. Anything more than that is only beneficial if it offers some improvement over a simple library of existing parts without introducing any risks or setbacks.

Taking a look at how Toolbox works

No one asks how a staircase works, because it does not work; it simply exists and people use it. An escalator, however, is a different issue. With an escalator, there is a complex installation, and then to use it, you have to know how to get on and get off and what to do if it stops working. The end results of using the staircase and using the escalator are the same (you start at the bottom and arrive at the top), but the complex automation of the escalator is supposed to save you some effort.

That is one way you can look at Toolbox. The end product is supposed to be the same as using a static library of parts, but there is some mechanism behind the scenes that has to be set up and maintained properly for it to work in the way you expect. Most SolidWorks books, tutorials, or training materials are going to ask you to accept what happens inside Toolbox as a "black box" and to just assume that the end results are exactly what you need and intend. This section supplies you with information about how Toolbox works, so you can decide how useful it will be for you and adjust how it works so that it meets your specific needs.

Looking at the database

Toolbox has three major components:

- Default parts of one size, with named dimensions and features
- A database containing all size information for all parts and Hole Wizard holes
- A software application with settings and an interface

These major components of Toolbox are shown in Figure 14.1.

FIGURE 14.1

A simplified representation of the components of Toolbox

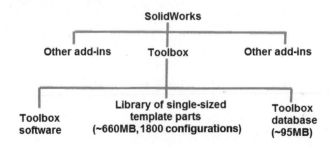

When Toolbox is installed, it starts as a set of SolidWorks parts with named features and dimensions, some suppressed features (depending on the settings), some executable programs (dlls), and a database (swbrowser.mdb). The parts have a single Default configuration, which is typically either the largest or smallest.

The database starts out at about 95MB and includes all the size information for all the parts, as well as all the standards information. If you create a *custom standard* in Toolbox, it actually replicates a section of the database. When you do this, the database file can easily double in size.

Later, you will see that a network installation of Toolbox requires the database to be on the network, and every time you create a new fastener, it has to open the database. As a result, simply placing a screw in an assembly can mean that even if your assembly is located on your local hard drive, you still have to open a very large database file across the network. The first rule about performance with SolidWorks is to work locally rather than across a network.

Note

When specifying network paths, it is best to specify a Universal Naming Convention, or UNC, path rather than a mapped address. A UNC address follows the format, \\Server\Shared Folder. The advantage of the UNC over the mapped drive is that mapped drives can vary from one computer to another, but the UNC is always the same. ■

Taking precautions when installing configurations

If you have just installed Toolbox for the first time the way that most new users do, then you have probably accepted all defaults. In this situation, the database is installed locally and Toolbox is set to use configurations for sizes. If you had a previous version of Toolbox installed when you installed the new version, you may have installed over the old version or installed a new copy. As you will see, it makes a difference which installation you have performed. If you installed over the old version, you may have made your assemblies inaccessible to older version of SolidWorks even though these assemblies have not been saved to the new version of SolidWorks.

When you put a Toolbox part into an assembly, you do not notice anything other than the part going into the assembly, although it may hesitate while the large database is opened. If you check the part configurations, you may notice that there is a Default configuration and a new configuration that represents the size that you just created. Every new size that you create makes another new configuration. Figure 14.2 shows a Toolbox part with the FeatureManager and ConfigurationManager open, displaying several configurations that Toolbox created in this particular fastener.

Next, you may receive an assembly from a client. Often, because Toolbox parts are located in an area where you would not necessarily look for parts, users send assemblies and parts, but do not send Toolbox parts. You may think that this is okay; after all, you have Toolbox on your system, and so it should pick up your Toolbox parts. The truth is that when receiving an assembly from someone else, you are better off if one of the parties does not have Toolbox on their system.

FIGURE 14.2

A Toolbox part showing the FeatureManager and ConfigurationManager

Avoiding the Huge Screws syndrome

If both you and the client who sent the assembly have Toolbox, then you should be okay, right? Well, yes and no. Yes, your client's assembly will pick up your Toolbox parts, but no, it will not work properly because you do not have all the same configurations and sizes that your client has. In cases like this, you will experience what is sometimes referred to as the Huge Screws syndrome. When SolidWorks finds the right file but cannot find the right configuration, it uses another configuration, usually the Default, which is generally the biggest size.

Part of the really bad news is that if you save your assembly with the incorrect configuration, SolidWorks has no way of knowing that the parts are not the correct size, and you can only solve the problem manually by going through the assembly and reassigning sizes to these parts.

You can work around this problem by opening an assembly that has not yet been saved with the oversized parts, using the Advanced option in the Open dialog box (you can find this in the Configurations list), and then selecting the New configuration showing assembly structure only option. With this option, all components are suppressed. You can unsuppress any non-Toolbox parts and continue working. Ask your client to send you his Toolbox parts and then unsuppress those parts in the assembly, making sure that it finds the right parts; the best way to do this is to have the correct parts already open before you open the assembly. These options are shown in Figure 14.3.

FIGURE 14.3

Opening an assembly with all parts suppressed

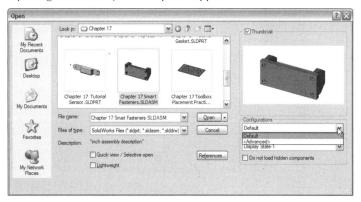

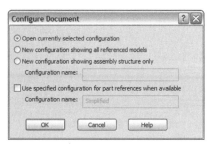

If you replace your Toolbox parts with the Toolbox parts from your client, you may experience the same problem in reverse if you had configurations that your client did not. In the end, it would be great to be able to merge the two parts to combine all the available sizes into a single file. There is a way of doing that, which you will learn later, but it is a convoluted workaround. Files that have the same names and different content are at the top of the list of things you shouldn't do in file management, and yet the SolidWorks Toolbox system frequently creates this very situation.

Using SolidWorks solutions for incorrect configurations

To be fair, SolidWorks fixed the problem with incorrect configurations in the 2007 version by coming up with a clever method for figuring out which size is missing and building it on the fly when the assembly is opened. Additional information about the Toolbox parts is now stored in the assembly, which helps identify the missing parts. Unfortunately, the fix only works for assemblies that use the parts from the 2007 or later library and assemblies that have been built in SolidWorks 2007 or later. To sum up, if you have assemblies built in an older version of SolidWorks and your Toolbox library becomes corrupted or lost, or you are sent an assembly that uses a different Toolbox library, even if you are working in a version later than SolidWorks 2007, you cannot benefit from this fix.

A new option that has been added to SolidWorks 2011 tells it to look for Toolbox parts first in your Toolbox data folder. This option is turned on by default for new installations. Figure 14.4 shows the Tools ➪ Options ➪ Hole Wizard/Toolbox location for this setting.

FIGURE 14.4

You can tell SolidWorks to look in your Toolbox data for any references to Toolbox parts.

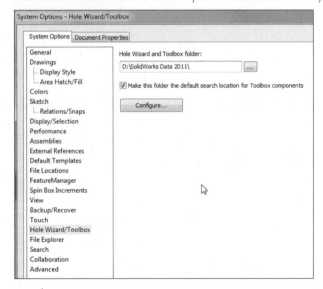

Organizing the Toolbox parts

Toolbox parts can be organized in a number of ways. The raw parts are organized as follows:

- Standard and Units. For example, ANSI Inch or ANSI Metric, most standards do not include multiple units, as they assume metric.
- Hardware Type, such as bearings, bolts, and bushings.

- Each type is organized differently, but bolts and screws are organized by drive or head type. For example, you have socket head screws, hex head, and thumb screws.
- Filenames look like `Socket Button Head Cap Screw_AI.SLDPRT`, where the `AI` represents ANSI Inch.

Figure 14.5 shows the Toolbox parts list.

FIGURE 14.5

Toolbox content organization

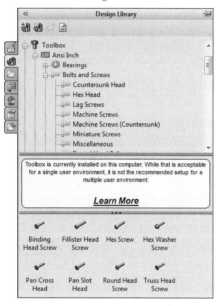

Choosing configurations or parts

By now, you may be unsure about whether to use configurations. However, keep in mind that the problem does not come from the configurations but from the practice of having files with the same names but different content.

You have two options when you create different sizes. The default option is that sizes are created as configurations within a single part. The other option is that sizes are created as individual files.

The best time to make this choice is before you install SolidWorks. Unfortunately, before you install SolidWorks, you probably do not have any idea that these issues exist. The reason for making this decision not just early, but as soon as possible before installation, is that if you start using the default setting (configurations), and make a few configurations for some parts and then switch to using the Save Parts setting, the parts that are saved out will all have the pre-existing configurations and thus different sizes.

If you find yourself in this situation, it is better to reinstall Toolbox or simply to copy over a new default set of parts with no configurations.

You can access the Create Configurations and Create Parts options by choosing Toolbox ➪ Configure ➪ Define User Settings, as shown in Figure 14.6. The other settings in this dialog box are discussed later in this chapter.

FIGURE 14.6

Toolbox settings for the Create Configurations and Create Parts options

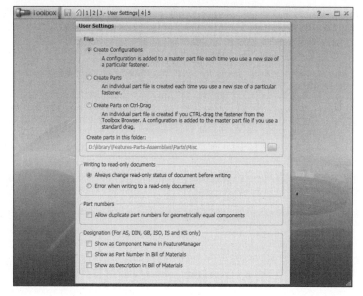

Deciding which option is better

The following list contains some of the strengths and weaknesses of each option.

Configurations are better for the following reasons:

- You can control data across several sizes. For example, a design table can drive custom properties that are added to all configurations. Doing this with many individual parts would be very messy.

- The interface to select configurations from a list is easier to work with than the interface to select a part from a list.

- File management organization is somewhat easier for configured parts.

Separate parts are better for the following reasons:

- They keep the file size small.
- You can replace all of one size part with another.
- They guarantee that you will never have a problem with incorrect configurations again.

Using Toolbox

Toolbox has two components: Toolbox and Toolbox Browser. However, in practice, the actual Toolbox component is often ignored, and the Toolbox Browser component is incorrectly referred to as Toolbox.

The Toolbox Browser is the Task Pane interface and is found on the Design Library tab, as shown in Figure 14.7. The Toolbox component is found in the Toolbox drop-down menu. It includes structural steel shapes, grooves, cams, and beam and bearing calculators.

FIGURE 14.7

Toolbox and the Toolbox Browser

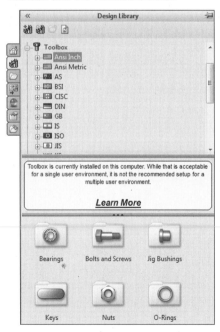

Turning on Toolbox and the Toolbox Browser

You can turn on Toolbox and the Toolbox Browser through the Tools ➪ Add-Ins dialog box. The column of check boxes on the left indicates that the add-in will be active for the current session of SolidWorks only. The column of check boxes on the right indicates that the add-in will be active every time you start up the software, as shown in Figure 14.8.

FIGURE 14.8

Turning Toolbox on in the Tools ➪ Add-Ins interface

Once the Toolbox Browser is turned on, you can use it by expanding the Task Pane at the right of the SolidWorks graphics window and clicking the Design Library icon, which looks like a stack of books. In this panel, you see the Toolbox screw symbol. Expand icons until you find the fastener or other hardware that you are looking for, and then drag the part into the assembly.

Populating holes

You can populate holes in several ways, such as by dragging-and-dropping, populating multiple holes at once, using the right mouse button (RMB) menu, and using feature-driven component patterns. Manual and patterning options are discussed here, and Smart Fasteners are discussed in the next section.

Drag-and-drop

The simplest way to bring Toolbox parts into an assembly is to drag-and-drop them. Position the part that the fastener goes into so that you can see the edge of the hole where the screw head will go. Then browse to the correct fastener and drop the fastener onto the edge, as shown in Figure 14.9.

FIGURE 14.9

Dropping a fastener onto a hole

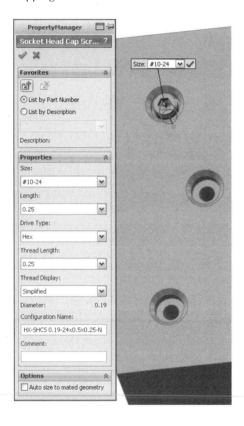

Toolbox parts even automatically size themselves based on the hole. It is best to use Hole Wizard holes if you are going to use this function of Toolbox parts, as Hole Wizard and Toolbox are meant to work together.

When you place the fastener, a PropertyManager appears that enables you to select various properties of the part (including the length) if you want to override the automatically selected size, the thread representation, and if you want the fastener to change in size when the hole changes. After placing the fastener, you can drag a handle at the end of it to change its length; the fastener snaps to predetermine lengths. You can also drag the arrow that appears at the end of the fastener to select the length graphically.

Populating multiple holes at once

Figure 14.10 shows the progression from a plate with holes in an assembly. In this example, you would Ctrl+select the edges of the holes, then select a fastener, and then choose Insert Into Assembly from the RMB menu to populate multiple holes.

FIGURE 14.10

Populating multiple holes at once in an assembly

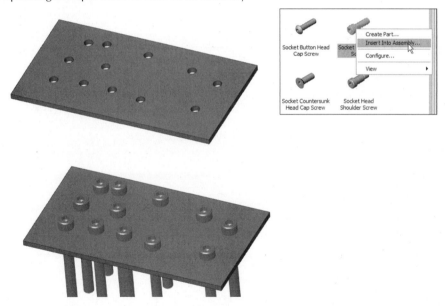

Feature Driven component patterns

With Feature Driven component patterns (also known as derived patterns), a pattern of parts in an assembly is driven by a feature pattern in a part. You can find this assembly feature by choosing Insert ➪ Component Patterns ➪ Feature Driven in the assembly menus. You can find more information on Feature Driven component patterns in Chapter 15.

Exploring Smart Fasteners

 Smart Fasteners are Toolbox parts that know what holes they go into automatically. The database that holds all the information for Toolbox part types and sizes also holds the information for the sizes of the holes. It is only natural that SolidWorks would try to combine this information and use it to its best advantage. You can use Smart Fasteners in two ways: by asking SolidWorks to automatically place fasteners in existing holes or placing Hole Series holes and fasteners simultaneously in the context of the assembly.

Using Smart Fasteners with Hole Series

One way to use Smart Fasteners is in conjunction with the Hole Wizard Hole Series. Hole Series creates the holes through multiple parts at once, producing the appropriate type of hole through each part, and then Smart Fasteners automatically place fasteners in the holes, even including nuts and washers. To do this, you can select the option on the last panel of the Hole Series PropertyManager interface, as shown in Figure 14.11. If you are planning to use Smart Fasteners, using them in conjunction with the Hole Series holes is your best bet.

FIGURE 14.11

The Place Fastener option

The Smart Fasteners with Hole Series is a function with which you should be careful. It is very effective, but it may cost you some performance (speed). The Hole Series is an assembly feature that drives several in-context features, and then parts are mated to those in-context features (fasteners).

Using Smart Fasteners Populate All

Smart Fasteners functionality has an even more automatic component. Once an assembly has parts mated into place, you can place fasteners into parts with appropriate holes by face, by part, or for the entire assembly at once.

Caution

You may not want to spend a lot of time trying to use this type of Smart Fasteners functionality. Finding documented success with Smart Fasteners is difficult. The topic is not often mentioned as a SolidWorks World, blog, or user group topic. Although in theory, it offers interesting functionality, in reality, it receives very little attention — definitely a warning sign. To get success with the tool, you have to use it in the way in which it was intended to be used. The highest-level functionality is not very flexible.

One assembly where Smart Fasteners work surprisingly well (in fact, almost perfectly) is with the sample files that install with SolidWorks. Upon closer examination, the reason this works well is because it uses assembly features for the holes, and so the holes do not appear in the individual parts. If that is the price that you have to pay just to get fasteners to populate automatically, then you may prefer to put them all in manually. ■

Understanding the limitations of Smart Fasteners

Smart Fasteners have some documented limitations where you should not expect them to work:

- Holes in single parts
- Holes created by extruding a nested loop
- A mirrored hole or cut features
- Holes in mirrored, imported, or derived parts
- Misaligned holes
- Holes with a large difference in diameter
- Holes with large gaps between them (a large gap in the axial direction)
- Holes made using different techniques (such as sketch pattern versus feature pattern)

If you would like to try out Smart Fasteners, then you can use the assembly included on the DVD called Smart Fasteners.sldasm. In this assembly, half of the holes are done correctly and the other half are not: the screws are put in either backward or headfirst. The documented method for flipping the fasteners is to expand the Smart Fastener, right-click the series, and choose Flip. In this example, your attempts may result in success about half of the time. In some cases, screws may be put in the ends of shafts without holes, on filleted edges, and in some cases you may miss most of the places that you want the screws to go.

Organizing Toolbox parts in an assembly

Assembly FeatureManagers are hard enough to manage when they become full of parts; they become even more unmanageable when they also need to include the many types of fastener parts. As a result, you should organize fasteners, as well as any other type of part that is found in large quantities in the assembly, into folders, as shown in Figure 14.12. You should also group parts of the same size or function together.

FIGURE 14.12

Organizing Toolbox parts into folders

Working recommendations

After spending almost an entire chapter saying what you *should not* do, it is finally time to describe what you *should* do. Toolbox can be problematic if you install and use it improperly; however, the following recommendations work in most situations.

Just to be clear about this, the most serious file management problems with Toolbox show up when you use configurations, which just happens to be the default option. Still, configurations are generally useful, and especially with library parts, but a Toolbox implementation with configurations is challenging. Again, this is because of the file management issue of different users having the same part names with different content (Toolbox parts with or without certain configurations created). The entire problem would be solved if SolidWorks installed Toolbox with all of the configurations created for all the parts. However, you might need an extra hard drive to store it.

Working with the simplest setup that works

If you are a single user who does not share files over a network with other users, then installing SolidWorks and Toolbox with the default settings should work for you. This appears to be the arrangement that the developers had in mind when they programmed the tool, because it is the only scenario in which it works as expected.

Be careful if you ever receive an assembly from another Toolbox user, because this is the one situation that can cause immediate trouble. If the user also sends his Toolbox parts, then you should open all these parts before you open his assembly so that the assembly is certain to access his Toolbox parts instead of yours.

If you need to include materials and mass-populate custom properties, then you should go through the exercise of building all the configurations of all the parts, and then use an auto-created design table to drive the properties. If you have more than one user, then this technique will not work for you, unless both users work independently from one another.

Using a complete setup that works

If you have multiple users that share assemblies, then you need to also share the Toolbox library. If you share assemblies only among yourselves, meaning only with other users who are also sharing Toolbox, then sharing Toolbox should be good enough. However, if you share assemblies with Toolbox users who do not share your Toolbox library, then you should probably go through the exercise of populating all your parts with all the available configurations. If you do not receive assemblies from outside of your group with Toolbox parts in the assemblies and you have network performance problems, it may be a good idea to install Toolbox locally, but to use the Create Parts setting, where the parts are on a shared network location.

If you use a Product Data Management (PDM) system, then you should definitely install Toolbox locally and use the Create Parts setting. The sharing occurs through the PDM system. Library parts should be non-revision managed parts, but you may want to have a representation of the fasteners so that you can perform where-used searches and create BOMs.

The least problematic technique is to turn Toolbox off altogether and either buy or make your own library of static parts. You can then distribute these files internally in your organization, as well as to any other people upstream or downstream from you who also share files with you. You can build this type of library by using the Toolbox configuration population tool; materials or other custom properties are then dealt with the way you want, likely using auto-created design tables.

Of course, there is also a downside to this solution, and it is that you lose all the nice automation features available with Toolbox. The best course of action if you want to keep Toolbox is to use the Copy Parts option, install locally, use a PDM system, and if you get assemblies from Toolbox users who aren't part of your network, insist that they either use your parts or send you their parts.

Considering the most popular arrangement

By far the most popular way to employ Toolbox is to use it to insert the parts, then rename the parts and save them to another location. Some users save the parts to project-specific folders, and some save them to a central library. A relatively small number of Toolbox users actually use it by the intended, orthodox method because of the heavy file management and administrative overhead associated with doing it "the right way."

The most effective way to use this method is with the Copy Parts setting. This is because having configurations within renamed parts may cause problems, as the intention is to have separate files for each size, but you will end up with multiple size configurations within each part.

For a more complete discussion of the administration issues surrounding SolidWorks Toolbox, refer to *SolidWorks Administration Bible* (Wiley, 2009).

Using the Hole Wizard

The Hole Wizard is related to Toolbox through the database that holds size information for matching fasteners and holes. The Hole Wizard is mainly used in parts but can also be used in assemblies for some situations such as Smart Fasteners in Hole Series holes.

All of this automated functionality requires that you use Toolbox following the orthodox automated method, which the better part of this chapter has warned you against. If you are very disciplined about your file management practices, and you are careful to keep your version installations properly synchronized, it is possible to make the automated Toolbox work the way it was intended to, and take advantage of advanced Hole Wizard functionality.

If you intend to try this method, you should use a test installation to make sure that you can achieve the results for which you are hoping.

 The Hole Wizard enables you to place holes for many types of screws with normal, loose, or close fits. You can create Hole Wizard holes as assembly features in an assembly or as features in individual parts that are built in the context of an assembly using the Hole Series functionality. This tool is called a *wizard* because it guides you through the process step by step. A summary of the process of creating a Hole Wizard hole is as follows:

1. Pre-select the face to put the holes on (this is optional). Starting in SolidWorks 2010, pre-selection is no longer required to avoid 3D placement sketches; the Hole Wizard now uses 2D sketches by default.

2. Select the type of hole. For example, you can choose counterbored, countersunk, drilled hole, tapped hole, pipe tap, or legacy.

3. Set the standard to be used, such as ANSI (American National Standards Institute) Inch, ANSI Metric, or ISO (International Organization for Standardization).

4. Select the type of screw. For example, a counterbored hole can accommodate a socket head cap screw or a hex head screw, among others.

5. Select the size of the screw.

6. Select the fit of the screw into the hole. Settings include normal, loose, or close.

7. Select the end condition of the hole.

8. Select options for clearance and countersinks or edge breaks.

   Alternatively, you can use or assign a favorite. A *favorite* is a hole with settings that you use frequently and want to save.

   You can use Custom Sizing when you need a hole with nonstandard dimensions.

9. Locate the center of the hole or holes. You can place multiple holes in a single Hole Wizard feature, even on different faces and curved faces.

10. Click OK to accept the type, size, and placement of the hole. Figure 14.13 shows the Hole Wizard PropertyManager interface.

FIGURE 14.13

The Hole Wizard PropertyManager interface

Exploring the Hole Series interface

 The Hole Series enables you to make a series of in-context hole features in individual parts that are connected by a Hole Series assembly-level feature. It is intended for a stack of parts where, for example, the top part has a counterbored hole, the middle part has a clearance through hole, and the final part has a blind threaded hole.

The Hole Series used to be part of the Hole Wizard but has been exported as a separate tool. It is now a five-step, wizard-based feature that ends by populating the new hole with a fastener using Smart Fasteners functionality. The Toolbox add-in is required to use Smart Fasteners. Figure 14.14 shows the interface for the various steps.

FIGURE 14.14

The Hole Series interface

When using the Hole Series feature, you must follow these basic steps:

1. Have an assembly open with two or more parts in it that need to be fastened together.

2. Initiate the Hole Series tool by choosing Insert ⇨ Assembly Features ⇨ Hole ⇨ Hole Series. It is also available as a toolbar button, but it is not on the toolbar by default.

3. If the Hole Series is to be started from an existing hole, then select it in the Hole Position panel. If not, then use sketch points, construction geometry, dimensions, and sketch relations to locate the hole centerpoints.

4. Use the tabs at the top of the PropertyManager to advance from one panel to the next.

    - The Start Hole Specification refers to the part where the series of holes starts.

    - The Middle Hole Specification is for all parts between the first part and the last part.

    - The End Hole Specification refers to the last part and is either a through clearance hole or a threaded hole.

The finished feature leaves an in-context feature in each part, with the Hole Series part in the assembly, as shown in Figure 14.15.

FIGURE 14.15

The finished Hole Series

Looking at Hole Series quirks

The Hole Series feature also has some quirks that you should know about so you don't spend too much time trying to determine why things are not working as you would expect. The first quirk is that if you start the Hole Series without pre-selection, the cursor that comes up initially is a 3D sketch cursor, but once you click the cursor to place a point on a face, the Hole Series tool creates a 2D sketch feature.

The second quirk occurs where the Hole Series drills multiple holes and the holes do not all go through the same parts. This is like the example shown in Figure 14.16, where a hole drilled down from the top of plate 1 might drill into plate 5 or plate 6. In this case, you would have to create holes that drill into different parts separately.

FIGURE 14.16

Create holes that drill into different parts separately.

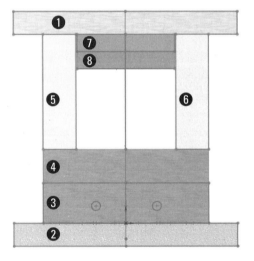

In addition, you may find that the Hole Series does not retain the information you give it for "End Part," or the depth of the tapped hole at the end of the series. Behavior like this makes the Hole Series difficult to use reliably, so make sure to double-check any data created with the Hole Series feature. It is a highly convenient feature but should be used carefully.

Tutorial: Gaining Experience with the Hole Wizard and Toolbox

Figure 14.17 shows a section view of the assembly used for this tutorial. Notice that there is a gasket under the Sensor part.

A section view of the tutorial assembly

This tutorial assumes that you have a working copy of Toolbox running on your computer. If you do not have Toolbox, then you can skip this tutorial. It also assumes that your Toolbox is using the default Create Configurations setting, although it can also work with the Create Parts setting. To get some experience using this tool, follow these steps:

1. **Open the assembly from the DVD called** Chapter 14 Tutorialstart.sldasm.

2. **Make sure that the Toolbox Browser is turned on by choosing Tools ⇨ Add-Ins ⇨ SolidWorks Toolbox and Tools ⇨ Add-Ins ⇨ ⇨ SolidWorks Toolbox Browser.**

3. **Expand the Task Pane, found on the right side of the graphics window, and display the Design Library panel, which contains the Toolbox icon.** Expand the ANSI Inch standard and the Bolts and Screws folder, and then click the Hex Head

bolt, as shown on the left in Figure 14.18. Drag-and-drop the hex bolt into any hole. It snaps into place because of the Mate Reference that is used on the Toolbox part. Toolbox automatically sizes the bolt correctly. Click the green check mark icon when you are done, and then click the red X icon to finish placing bolts.

FIGURE 14.18

Select and place a fastener.

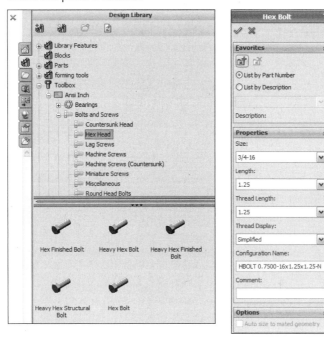

4. **Add a flat washer and nut to the bolt, as shown in Figure 14.19.** The washer is Plain Washer Type A, Preferred — Wide Flat Washer. The nut used is Hex Nut, Heavy Hex Nut.

FIGURE 14.19

Specifying the washer and nut

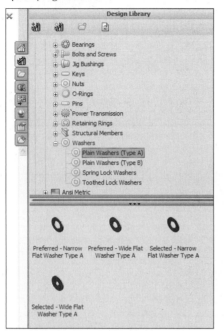

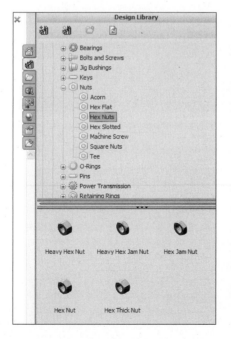

5. **Right-click the bolt, either in the graphics window or in the FeatureManager, and select Edit Toolbox Definition, toward the bottom of the menu.** Notice that the bolt is too short, as shown in Figure 14.20. Change the length of the fastener to 1.625 inches. You can make this change in the PropertyManager or by dragging the green arrow placed on the bolt in the graphics window if you are using Instant3D.

FIGURE 14.20

The bolt is too short.

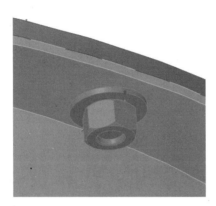

Note

If you try to apply Smart Fasteners to the hole, you will notice that the fastener is placed incorrectly, and changing fastener types is not easy. ■

6. **Create a Feature Driven component pattern (Insert ⇨ Component Pattern ⇨ Feature Driven) using the circular pattern of holes on either the Top or Base parts.** Pattern the bolt, washer, and nut all in the same component pattern.

7. **Zoom in on the sensor on the top of the assembly.** There is a gray gasket between the orange sensor and the blue top parts. Click one of the flat ends of the sensor part and then click the Hole Series toolbar button, or choose Insert ⇨ Assembly Feature ⇨ Hole ⇨ Hole Series.

8. **Make sure that you select the Place Fastener option on the final tab when you get there, as well as the Create New Hole option.** This workflow is different from previous versions. Also, be aware that Toolbox may not respond for several seconds as you initiate these features.

9. **Make three sketch points and use construction geometry and dimensions to locate the holes, as shown in Figure 14.21.** The size and types of holes are determined in a later step. (This is the reverse of the normal Hole Wizard, where you first determine the type and size of hole, and then you establish the positions.)

FIGURE 14.21

The positions of holes in Step 9

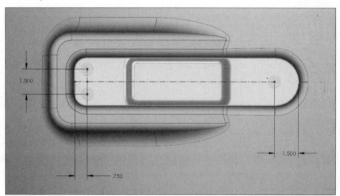

10. **Click the next PropertyManager tab to move to the First Part hole specification.** Set it to a counterbored hole, for a #10 binding head screw, with a head clearance of .025 inch, as shown in Figure 14.22 in the image to the left. Click the next tab to advance to the Middle Parts hole sizing.

11. **In the Middle Parts PropertyManager, make sure that the Auto size based on start hole option is selected, as shown in the middle image in Figure 14.22.** This creates a normal fit clearance hole for the gasket part. Click the next tab to advance to the hole definition for the Last Part.

FIGURE 14.22

Sizing the holes

12. **In the End Hole Specification panel, make sure that you select the Hole rather than the Tap option, and also select the Auto size based on start hole option.** This is shown in the image on the right in Figure 14.22.

13. **Proceed to the Smart Fasteners tab.** Make sure the Place Fastener option is selected, along with the Auto size based on start hole option, as shown in Figure 14.23.

14. **Add a washer and a nut to the bottom stack of the binding head screws.** Using the Stack Components panel of the final tab of the Hole Series/Smart Fastener interface, add a washer and a nut to the bottom stack using the Bottom Stack selection box of the PropertyManager.

15. **A dialog box appears, enabling you to add a washer and a nut, as shown in Figure 14.24.** You may want to roll the model over so that you can see the components being added to the underside of the screw. You can add other properties to the parts by clicking the Properties button. Notice that the screw has been lengthened to accommodate the added components.

FIGURE 14.23

The Smart Fasteners PropertyManager

FIGURE 14.24

Adding washers and nuts

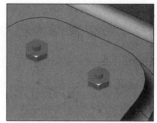

Note

If you add a washer to the top stack, the hole does not automatically become larger, and it may cause interference. Be careful about your choice of top-stack washers. ■

Note

You may have noticed that this time, Smart Fasteners worked almost flawlessly and certainly saved you some time. Although this tool is not applicable to other purposes, when used with the Hole Series, it is quite useful. ■

16. (Optional) Group the fasteners and the fasteners' mates into folders, as shown in Figure 14.25.

FIGURE 14.25

The finished Assembly FeatureManager interface

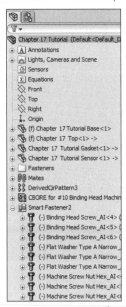

Caution

The final version of the assembly on the DVD may open up on your computer with incorrect configurations if you open it before completing the tutorial. This is because the configurations used in the assembly are from a different computer. Although you have the same parts, before doing this tutorial, you may not have the same configurations; therefore, they cannot be found and come in incorrect sizes instead. This was intentional; it is a practical reminder of this problem, and how easily it can happen to you. ■

Summary

Some people claim to have had good success with Toolbox even in a shared environment, but given that the problems with the tool are so easy to demonstrate, these people are either extremely disciplined or extremely lucky. You can also be sure that they didn't get everything right the first time they tried it. For all users except those who work alone and do not share files with other Toolbox users, Toolbox can cause a number of major problems. You can develop techniques to avoid experiencing incorrect configurations; for example, you can avoid sharing assemblies with other Toolbox users or you can pre-populate all your configurable parts with all possible configurations.

The Hole Wizard has a lot of automated functionality that requires you to be running orthodox methods in Toolbox. There is a lot to gain if you can make the automation work for you. Further, Smart Fasteners that you use in conjunction with Hole Series violate any best practice guidelines that relate to assembly performance and circular references; however, if you can accept these limitations, then it is a sophisticated technique.

Working with Libraries

One of the biggest benefits that you can take advantage of in any CAD software is reusing data that you have already created. If you are really lucky, you can use data that other people have created. Libraries are simply organized collections of data that you think you will reuse at some point. You can create libraries that include all kinds of data, including sketches, features, combinations of features, parts, and even subassemblies. This chapter focuses on libraries that you would use with assemblies. It pays special attention to items you create or customize yourself for optimal automation.

Chapter 14 covers SolidWorks Toolbox, which technically is not a library, because it doesn't store a lot of parts. Toolbox is a "configurator" because initially it only contains templates that are used to make various sizes of the parts, which you configure through an interface. This distinction is important because unless you explicitly create a specific size part in Toolbox, it does not exist. To be most reliable to multiple users, libraries should contain parts that exist.

This chapter also talks about the library automation found in Smart Components, which enables you to place several parts at once, along with the resizing and custom in-context features. This feature requires some time to set up but has the potential to save you a lot of time.

SolidWorks also considers 3D Content Central (3DCC) to be part of the library. The 3DCC component is an online repository of parts created over many years by both users and vendors. You can search and use this online content directly from the Task Pane interface, or from your Web browser, by going to www.3dcontentcentral.com. You may need to log in to take full advantage of this resource.

Setting Up a Library

SolidWorks libraries are specific folders in Windows where you store commonly used components. You can easily access these components through the Design Library interface in the Task Pane. Figure 15.1 shows the interface with some sample content.

Libraries exist in the Task Pane to the right of the graphics window.

Although the default SolidWorks installation includes some sample content for your library, it is not very extensive and not specialized for different industries. As a result, you will not be able to rely only on the sample library that SolidWorks provides. You should also move the library from its default location to a place where it will not be removed or overwritten when software is installed, updated, or uninstalled.

You may find it difficult to manually browse to the default content. It is placed by default in C:/ProgramData/SolidWorks/SolidWorks 2011/design library/. The ProgramData folder is hidden by default. Your SolidWorks installation can see the folder and the files it contains, but you cannot manually locate the folder. In order to show hidden folders, go to Control Panel ⇨ Folder Options ⇨ View ⇨ Show hidden files, folders, or drives.

Caution

File management issues are important with libraries, and may affect how you manage your libraries. If you use a library between multiple versions of SolidWorks, you need to make sure that older assemblies are not required to access newer versions of library files. ■

People who have been using the software for a long time may already have accumulated a nice library. You can also purchase libraries for specialized components. Regardless of where your library components come from, it is a good idea to put them all into a single location. This location will depend on whether you just use the library for yourself or you share it with several other users. You can locate libraries locally or across a network. You can even use remote locations if that option works best for you. Local copies are always faster, but speed is not always the most important factor to consider in a design process environment.

If you do choose to use a network location for your libraries, it is preferable to use Universal Naming Convention (UNC) names rather than mapped network drives. For example, if your server name is Jupiter, and your library data is in a folder called CAD models, then you should use a path such as `\\Jupiter\CAD Data\` rather than a mapped designator for Jupiter such as `R:\CAD Data\`. This is because mapped drives can be inconsistent from one client computer to another. For example, what is called `R:` on one user's computer might be `E:\D\ Engineering\` on another computer; however, from anywhere on the network, the path `\\Jupiter\CAD Data\` will always point to the same folder on the same machine.

Note

You may require some assistance from a system administrator to establish the correct shares between computers. Remember that shares do not always have to point to top-level drives, and shares may have associated access restrictions such as read-only access for some users. For most library users, read-only access is sufficient. ■

Figure 15.2 shows the location in Tools ⇨ Options where you set up the folders used for libraries. Note that each path entered in the list represents another top-level folder in the library.

Adding folders to the library

System Options - File Locations

| System Options | Document Properties |

General
Drawings
   Display Style
   Area Hatch/Fill
Colors
Sketch
   Relations/Snaps
Display/Selection
Performance
Assemblies
External References
Default Templates
File Locations

Show folders for:

Design Library

Folders:

C:\ProgramData\SolidWorks\SolidWorks 2010\Design Library
D:\library\Features-Parts-Assemblies
\\X\d

Add...

Delete

Move Up

Move Down

Building the Design Library

SolidWorks has two items called Design Library. The first is the tab in the Task Pane that you click to access all of the library type functionality in SolidWorks, including the Design Library, Toolbox, 3DCC, and an item called SolidWorks Content. This chapter describes each item in turn, starting with the Design Library.

You'll start with the toolbar at the top of the Design Library, right under the main title. The four icons on the toolbar are Add to Library, Add Location, Add Folder, and Refresh.

Adding to the library

 Multiple methods exist to add a part to the library. First, you'll learn how to use the Add to Library button on the Design Library toolbar. When you click the Add to Library toolbar button, the PropertyManager shown in Figure 15.3 appears.

FIGURE 15.3

Adding to the library using the Add to Library toolbar button

Even though the list box at the top of the PropertyManager has a name that implies you can add multiple items (Items to Add), and it is large enough for more than one entry, it only allows you to add one part to the library at a time.

Here is the workflow for using the Add to Library PropertyManager:

1. Click the Add to Library button on the top bar of the Design Library in the Task Pane.

2. With the Items to Add list box selected, select a single component.

3. Change the filename in the first box of the Save To panel.

4. Select the Design Library folder in the list.

5. Type a description in the Options panel.

6. Click the green check mark icon at the top of the Add to Library PropertyManager.

Add to Library is also available on the RMB menu for a part (right-click either a part in the graphics window or a component in the Feature Manager). When you choose this option, the same Add to Library PropertyManager appears as when you use the button at the top of the Design Library.

You can also save a part directly to a Design Library folder using the Save or Save As function. When you do this, you have to use the Refresh on the Design Library toolbar to display the newly added items in the preview area.

You can also drag and drop a part or assembly from its own window into the Design Library. To add a part this way, you have to drag the name of the part or assembly from the top of the FeatureManager into the preview window in the bottom half of the Design Library. If you drag from the graphics window, or drag a part from an assembly, the addition does not work.

Caution

When you copy a part to a library folder and then make changes to the copy in the library, remember that your assembly is probably still referencing a part that is not in the library. When you frequently see the message, "A part with this name is already open, would you like to use that one," this may mean that you have multiple copies of the part, which may have differences between them. Good file management practices are necessary when dealing with library components.

Be aware that if SolidWorks sees that you have multiple versions of library parts (the part in the assembly is different from the part in the library), SolidWorks does not preview the library part when you drag it onto the screen. ■

Adding a file location

 File locations create new folders in the Design Library, as shown in Figure 15.4. Notice that the paths established in Tools ⇨ Options ⇨ File Locations (from Figure 15.2) each correspond to another stack of books icon in the Design Library.

Notice that the folders in the lower Design Library panel also display in Windows Explorer below the location specified in File Locations.

Adding file locations affects the folders in the Design Library.

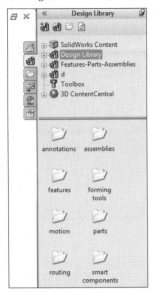

Some folders require special identification. For example, if you want to use the items in a Design Library folder as assemblies or sheet metal–forming tools, you have to identify the folders for those particular uses. To accomplish this, just right-click the folder in the upper panel of the Design Library, as shown in Figure 15.5, and select the appropriate option.

Assigning special use folders in the Design Library

Creating a new folder

You can create a new folder under a top-level folder in multiple ways. The easiest way is to use the Create New Folder toolbar button at the top of the Design Library. Another method is to use the option from the RMB, shown in Figure 15.5. A third option is to create the folder within Windows Explorer, and use the Refresh toolbar button at the top of the Design Library.

Using the Design Library

Once the folders exist and have been populated with library parts, identified in the File Locations area of Tools ⇨ Options, and added to the Design Library, you can start using them to place parts in assemblies.

Adding Mate References to library parts

Often when parts are placed into the library, they may not be specifically set up for library use. The single most effective thing you can do to improve the efficiency of library parts is to establish Mate References to help them snap into place and create multiple mates by using drag-and-drop placement.

For example, if you use a cylindrical face as a Mate Reference, when you drag that part out of the Design Library into the assembly window, SolidWorks looks for another cylindrical surface to mate the Mate Reference face to. If you select a circular edge as a Mate Reference, SolidWorks looks for a planar face for a coincident mate and a cylindrical face for a concentric mate. This is how Toolbox parts work — using circular edges for Mate References.

Mate References are easy to set up. Here is the workflow for taking an existing part in the Design Library, and assigning a Mate Reference to it.

On the DVD

If you want to follow along with these steps, copy the part called `Pulley Screw.sldprt` from the DVD folder for Chapter 15, and put it into one of the folders you have designated as a Design Library folder. ■

1. Right-click a part in the Design Library that you want to modify. Figure 15.6 shows the pulley screw part displaying an RMB menu.

2. Choose Open from the RMB menu. If the part is already open on your computer, SolidWorks asks if you want to use the same one that is open. The usual answer is yes. If you do not want to use the part that is open, you need to change the name of one of them or close the one that is already open.

3. Select Insert ⇨ Reference Geometry ⇨ Mate Reference. The PropertyManager for this feature is shown in Figure 15.7.

FIGURE 15.6

Opening a library part to add a Mate Reference

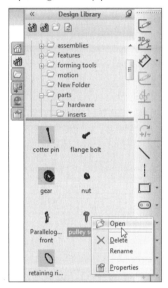

FIGURE 15.7

Adding a Mate Reference

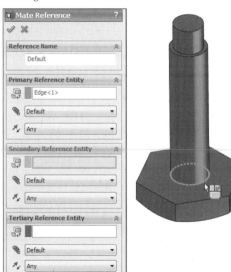

Notice that the Mate Reference enables you to select Primary, Secondary, and Tertiary references. These are in order of which will be sought first. As mentioned earlier, it simplifies things greatly if the Mate Reference is a circular edge, because it only needs to seek one other reference, but it makes two mates out of it. The circular edge snaps to another circular edge, making coincident and concentric "pin in hole" type mates.

4. Once you have selected everything you want to select for the Mate Reference, click the green check mark icon on the PropertyManager to accept it. Notice that a new Mate References folder is added to the top of the FeatureManager of that part. Figure 15.8 shows the Mate References folder and its contents.

FIGURE 15.8

Displaying the contents of the new Mate References folder

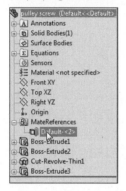

5. Save the part, and then click the Refresh toolbar button in the Design Library to make sure the next time the part is used, it uses the updated version.

Placing parts with Mate References into assemblies

When you have Mate References on parts that you use from a library, you are saving yourself a lot of time. Mating parts together can be time-consuming, and whatever you can do to accurately automate part of the process will reduce time and frustration.

Here is a workflow that is used to quickly place library parts with Mate References and size configurations into an assembly.

On the DVD

If you would like to follow along with the steps for this workflow example, use the `Pulley Screw.sldprt` file from the previous example, open the `Rear Derailleur .sldasm` assembly from the DVD material for this chapter, and hide the last two parts in the assembly (the last two Pulley Screw instances). ∎

1. Open an assembly that you want to add parts to. In this case, it is the Rear Derailleur assembly.

2. Open the Design Library, and browse to the folder with the part you want to insert. Alternately, you can use the SolidWorks Search function to find a part with a particular filename, description, or other property. Make sure that the Search Paths are set up at Tools ⇨ Options ⇨ File Locations ⇨ Search Paths. Make sure the search is set to the Files and Models option (using the drop-down arrow to the right of the search magnifying glass symbol). Figure 15.9 shows the results of the search and the two locations on the derailleur cage where it needs to be inserted.

FIGURE 15.9

Using SolidWorks Search to find library components

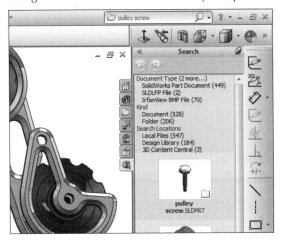

3. Drag the screw in and hover the cursor over the circular edge of the hole you want it to go into. SolidWorks previews the part and shows the preview snapping into the hole. This snapping action is due to the Mate Reference.

4. When you drop the part onto the edge, SolidWorks gives you the option to select a size, Short or Long. These are the two configurations of the part. Select Short for both instances shown. Figure 15.10 shows the popup dialog box for the configuration selection.

FIGURE 15.10

Selecting a configuration for a newly placed library component

Exploring Other Design Library Functions

The Design Library has other functions besides library features. For example, you can use it as a repository for other items that you use frequently.

Using Annotations in the library

You can store commonly used annotations in the Design Library. If you look at the Annotations folder with the default sample annotations, you see a combination of symbols and blocks. You can use symbols and notes in 3D models, but you can only use blocks in sketches or 2D drawings. Keep in mind that not all annotation types can be used in all places.

Annotations can be stored in the library as favorites or blocks. Many file extensions are used for different types of favorites, but they typically begin with `*.sld` and end with `fvt`, as in `*.sldweldfvt`. Figure 15.11 shows the default location of the Design Library and the Thumbnail view of the favorites and blocks in the Annotations folder.

FIGURE 15.11

The Annotations folder in Windows Explorer

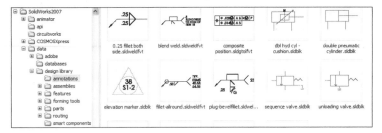

Using sheet metal–forming tools in the library

Sheet metal–forming tools are only mentioned here as a part of the library. They work much like library features, but they do so within the specialized functions of sheet metal parts in SolidWorks. Sheet metal–forming tools are discussed in the *SolidWorks 2011 Parts Bible*. Forming tools folders have special properties. If you want to use the parts in a folder as forming tools, you must right-click the folder in the Design Library and choose Forming Tool Folder. The only other library type that needs special folders is a library assembly.

Using assemblies in the library

You can use library assemblies in SolidWorks in the same ways that you use library parts because they are inserted into the top-level assembly as a subassembly. For subassemblies that require motion, such as universal joint subassemblies, you can set the subassembly to solve as flexible or simply dissolve the subassembly into the upper-level assembly, through an RMB option.

Tip

When saving assemblies to the library, it is recommended that you put the parts in a separate folder to segregate the parts of different assemblies. ■

Routing

Routing is an add-in that is included with SolidWorks Office Premium. It includes piping, tubing (rigid and flexible), and wiring. Routing makes extensive use of libraries and automation but is not part of the scope of this book. The documentation on Routing at this time is rather sparse, but SolidWorks offers a reseller training class that, at this time, is your best source for information on this add-in.

Understanding Smart Components

A Smart Component can comprise several elements:

- A single part or an assembly that may use size configurations
- A configurable library feature that usually serves as mounting holes or a viewing window for the Smart Component
- Associated hardware that may also be driven by size configurations
- A training assembly that is used to define the Smart Component

Some minor limitations exist, as you might expect:

- A Smart Component part cannot have references that are external to the Smart Component group of which it is a member.
- When placed in the assembly, the associated library feature can only affect one component.
- The associated library feature is limited to one of several feature types:
  - Extruded or revolved cuts or bosses
  - Hole Wizard holes
  - Simple hole features

The setup time for Smart Components can be significant for the first one or two that you create, especially if you use the auto-size option. The complexity of the setup depends mainly on the number of configurations and configured parts that you use. The auto-sizing function takes the most time to set up because it requires matching configurations, and the auto-size table takes a while to manage, especially for multiple parts. Still, if you end up placing a given part with associated features and other components many times manually, or you have others in your group that do it, this technique can save you and your team a lot of time.

Using Smart Components

Figure 15.12 shows a simple assembly. It took approximately 20 minutes to model all the parts, set up the Smart Component, and test it in an assembly. This example does not use auto-sizing, but it does use a library part, an in-context feature, and two instances of a single hardware piece. This is an excellent example of Smart Component functionality because it is fast to create and apply and saves you time whenever you use it.

FIGURE 15.12

A simple Smart Component

 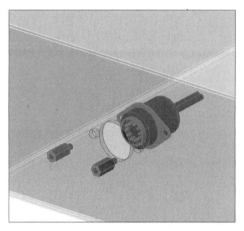

Getting started with a simple Smart Component

In this assembly, you first place the electrical connector part in the assembly, mate it in place, and then apply Smart Components. You can apply Smart Components by clicking the Smart Component icon that appears on the part in the graphics window when you select it. SolidWorks then prompts you to select the inside and outside faces of the sheet metal part (the hardware references the outside and the cut-out feature references the inside). SolidWorks then creates the cut-out as an in-context feature that it places in the sheet metal part.

When you create the Smart Component, a new folder is added to the FeatureManager of the component. This folder contains all the required information about the other elements, such as the in-context feature, any other parts that go with the Smart Component, the "training assembly" location, and the face references to locate everything. The left image in Figure 15.13 shows this folder in the connector part that is used in this example. The right image shows what is added to the assembly FeatureManager when you add a Smart Component. The only thing that existed in the design tree shown in Figure 15.13 before the Smart Component was the Test Box sheet metal part.

FIGURE 15.13

The Smart Component folder in the connector part

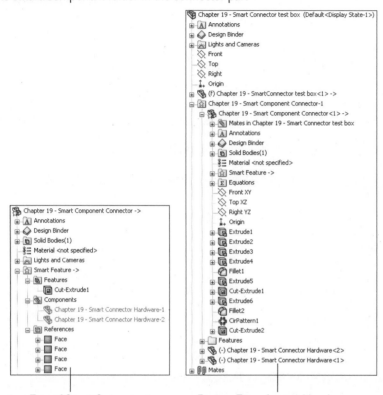

Feature Tree of Smart Component

Feature Tree of assembly where a
Smart Component has been used

A star appears on the part symbol at the top of the FeatureManager, indicating that the part is
a Smart Component. You can place this Smart Component by following these steps:

1. Create an assembly, and add the target part to it. The target part is the one that the
   Smart Component will be mated to and the one that will have the in-context cut-out
   inserted into it. In this case, the target part is a sheet metal box.

Caution

It is a good idea to save the assembly before you add the Smart Component to it. If the Smart Component is
placed before the assembly is saved, the assembly has a tendency to forget that it has not been saved, and
bumps the in-context feature to out-of-context when the name is changed from whatever the default name is
(for example, `Assem1.sldasm`) to the name that you assign to it. ∎

2. Put the Smart Component into the assembly. You can do this in the same way that you would add any normal part, including from the Design Library. If you use a part frequently enough to make it into a Smart Component, then you may want it in the Design Library for quick access. In fact, you can add a Smart Component to an assembly without using any of the Smart Component options.

3. Mate the Smart Component in the assembly. In this case, it is done with a face-to-face coincident mate and a pair of distance mates.

4. Apply Smart Components by clicking the Smart Component symbol on the part. If this symbol does not appear, then select the part in the FeatureManager. Figure 15.14 shows the Smart Component symbol on the part. If you have inserted many instances of a Smart Component, then each instance has the option to apply the Smart Component features and associated components.

FIGURE 15.14

The Smart Component symbol on a part

At this point, an interface similar to that of the Library Feature interface appears, with the small prompt window and a box for selecting references, as shown in Figure 15.15.

5. Select the references and click the green check mark icon. Then place the Smart Component, as well as the Smart Feature (in-context feature) and associated hardware components, to complete the job. You can rotate the part in the small preview window to get a better look at the part.

FIGURE 15.15

The interface for adding the Smart Feature and additional components of the Smart Component

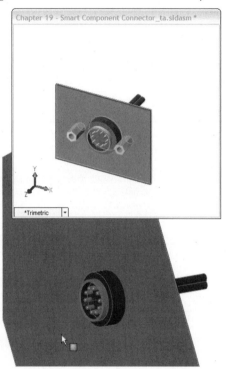

Auto-sizing Smart Components

Auto-sizing is the capability of a Smart Component to automatically select a size from a list of configurations based on the size of the geometry onto which it is being dropped. At this time, the only shape that can be auto-sized is the cylindrical shape.

Figure 15.16 shows the effects of auto-sizing. Notice the two shaft holders. These are two instances of the same part, using different size configurations. When you drag the Smart Component over the small end of the stepped shaft, the configuration corresponding to that shaft size appears. As you drag the part along the shaft and the shaft diameter increases, the next-larger Smart Component configuration appears. This is part of the functionality of Smart Components. Each configuration of the Smart Component is set up to fit onto a range of shaft diameters. If the diameter of the shaft is outside of the range or between sizes, then the Smart Component is not applied.

FIGURE 15.16

A Smart Component with auto-sizing

Sizes are governed by a configurator table, which looks similar to a design table but works somewhat differently. The configurator table relates the configurations of the Smart Component to configurations of the individual parts, which may also change size with the Smart Component. This serves as a subset of the function of a design table in an assembly, assigning part configurations to assembly configurations. Figure 15.17 shows a sample configurator table made for the assembly shown in Figure 15.16.

FIGURE 15.17

A configurator table

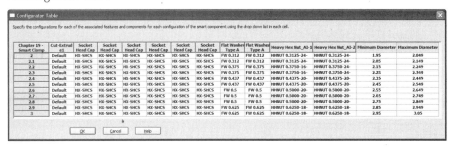

Configurator Table

Specify the configurations for each of the associated features and components for each configuration of the smart component using the drop down list in each cell.

Chapter 19 - Smart Clamp	Cut-Extrude1	Socket Head Cap	Socket Head Cap	Socket Head Cap	Socket Head Cap	Socket Head Cap	Socket Head Cap	Flat Washer Type A	Flat Washer Type A	Heavy Hex Nut_AI-1	Heavy Hex Nut_AI-2	Minimum Diameter	Maximum Diameter
2	Default	HX-SHCS	HX-SHCS	HX-SHCS	HX-SHCS	HX-SHCS	HX-SHCS	FW 0.312	FW 0.312	HHNUT 0.3125-24-	HHNUT 0.3125-24-	1.95	2.049
2.1	Default	HX-SHCS	HX-SHCS	HX-SHCS	HX-SHCS	HX-SHCS	HX-SHCS	FW 0.312	FW 0.312	HHNUT 0.3125-24-	HHNUT 0.3125-24-	2.05	2.149
2.2	Default	HX-SHCS	HX-SHCS	HX-SHCS	HX-SHCS	HX-SHCS	HX-SHCS	FW 0.375	FW 0.375	HHNUT 0.3750-16-	HHNUT 0.3750-24-	2.15	2.249
2.3	Default	HX-SHCS	HX-SHCS	HX-SHCS	HX-SHCS	HX-SHCS	HX-SHCS	FW 0.375	FW 0.375	HHNUT 0.3750-16-	HHNUT 0.3750-24-	2.25	2.349
2.4	Default	HX-SHCS	HX-SHCS	HX-SHCS	HX-SHCS	HX-SHCS	HX-SHCS	FW 0.437	FW 0.437	HHNUT 0.4375-20-	HHNUT 0.4375-20-	2.35	2.449
2.5	Default	HX-SHCS	HX-SHCS	HX-SHCS	HX-SHCS	HX-SHCS	HX-SHCS	FW 0.437	FW 0.437	HHNUT 0.4375-20-	HHNUT 0.4375-20-	2.45	2.549
2.6	Default	HX-SHCS	HX-SHCS	HX-SHCS	HX-SHCS	HX-SHCS	HX-SHCS	FW 0.5	FW 0.5	HHNUT 0.5000-20-	HHNUT 0.5000-20-	2.55	2.649
2.7	Default	HX-SHCS	HX-SHCS	HX-SHCS	HX-SHCS	HX-SHCS	HX-SHCS	FW 0.5	FW 0.5	HHNUT 0.5000-20-	HHNUT 0.5000-20-	2.65	2.749
2.8	Default	HX-SHCS	HX-SHCS	HX-SHCS	HX-SHCS	HX-SHCS	HX-SHCS	FW 0.5	FW 0.5	HHNUT 0.5000-20-	HHNUT 0.5000-20-	2.75	2.849
2.9	Default	HX-SHCS	HX-SHCS	HX-SHCS	HX-SHCS	HX-SHCS	HX-SHCS	FW 0.625	FW 0.625	HHNUT 0.6250-18-	HHNUT 0.6250-18-	2.85	2.949
3	Default	HX-SHCS	HX-SHCS	HX-SHCS	HX-SHCS	HX-SHCS	HX-SHCS	FW 0.625	FW 0.625	HHNUT 0.6250-18-	HHNUT 0.6250-18-	2.95	3.05

OK   Cancel   Help

When you look at this table, you begin to understand why creating auto-sizing Smart Components is much more involved than the first example in this chapter. The configurations of the Smart Component are listed to the left, and you can select the individual part configurations in each cell from a drop-down list of all available configurations for that part. There is no way to set configurations for multiple components at once, nor is there a copy-and-paste function. These shortcomings combine to make this format less user-friendly than an Excel-based design table.

Most notable are the Minimum and Maximum Diameter columns to the right. These columns supply the parameters that make the auto-size function work. While the range of sizes used here is too large for real-world design (+/– .050 inch), it serves to convey the idea. More important, SolidWorks understands that mating sizes are not always exactly equal, and the ability to use a range rather than exact values accommodates this limitation very nicely, although it can be tedious to set up.

Another aspect of the setup shown here is that it uses Toolbox parts. If you want to use the auto-size functionality, then you need to be using configurations for Toolbox parts. You should prebuild all the needed configurations and ensure that they are always available.

Making Smart Components

The most important point to remember about Smart Component setup is that you need to do it only once for each Smart Component. The second most important point is that the first setup is the most difficult. After that, subsequent setups become much easier to create. Adding components to the Smart Component is not so time-consuming unless the additional components are also configured and auto-sized.

Smart Components must contain at least one associated component and one in-context feature, or have the configurator table filled out and functional. If you try to create a Smart Component from a stand-alone part, then nothing happens; the Smart Component interface simply closes because there is nothing for it to do. You may combine all three elements (associated component, in-context feature, and auto-size), but you must have at least one element.

Getting started with a simple Smart Component

Because the electrical connector was already used to demonstrate the insertion of a Smart Component, it is used here to demonstrate how to create one.

All that you need to make a Smart Component with an associated Smart Feature (in this case, a cut-out and mounting holes) and mounting hardware (in this case, two stand-off screws) is the actual part. The part can even be imported (a Smart Component made from dumb geometry).

On the DVD
This example uses the file named Chapter 15 – Connector Start.sldprt from the Chapter 15 folder. The part is shown in Figure 15.18. ■

FIGURE 15.18

An electrical connector part

There is nothing special about this part. It is modeled in SolidWorks using standard features, and there are no configurations or special features. It could have been downloaded from 3D Content Central. It represents an electrical connector that may be mounted in a sheet metal electrical enclosure.

The first step in setting it up is to create a mock assembly with a dummy part representing the sheet metal box. The part does not need to be complex, or even sheet metal, for that matter; it just needs to be close to the thickness that you would expect the Smart Component to be mounted to. The assembly is called a *training* assembly, not because you are learning how to make a Smart Component but because you are training the Smart Component to be *smart*.

1. Open the part, `Chapter 15 – Connector Start.sldprt` from the DVD.

2. Make a simple rectangular part, approximately 4 inches square and about .06 inch thick. Save the part to your hard drive. Give a name to the part so that it is clear that it belongs to this training assembly.

3. Place the rectangular dummy part into a new assembly, with a name that is both unique and identifiable.

4. Put the connector into the assembly. Mate the part so that the flange is flush with the rectangular piece. Also use distance mates to locate the connector planes from the edges of the part, similar to Figure 15.19 in the image to the left.

5. Edit the dummy part in context (right-click the dummy part in the assembly and select Edit Part), and offset edges of the connector part to extrude a cut, as shown in the image to the right in Figure 15.19. Offset the two mounting holes and the area around where the connector will stick through the sheet metal by about .02 inch.

FIGURE 15.19

Placing the connector on the dummy part

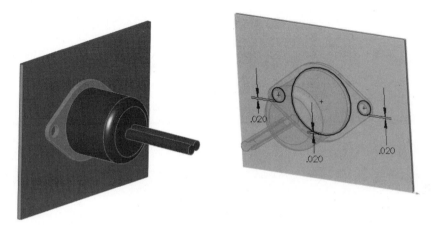

6. Exit Edit Component mode and add two instances of the part named Chapter 15 – Smart Connector Hardware.sldprt to the assembly. Mate the hardware part to the in-context hole, making sure that it goes to the outside thickness of the dummy sheet metal part.

Note

Although it is generally a best practice to avoid mating parts to in-context features, in this example you are doing exactly that. Keep in mind that best practice suggestions are more like guidelines. If you are having performance problems with an assembly, then this may not be the best technique to use. However, sometimes there is a price to pay for sophisticated functionality, and if you think that your design can afford the price and will benefit from this functionality, then you should use it. ∎

7. Now that everything is in place, click the Make Smart Component tool on the assembly toolbar. If the button is not there, you can add it to the assembly toolbar by choosing Tools ➪ Customize menu, or by choosing Tools ➪ Make Smart Component. The resulting interface is shown in Figure 15.20.

8. In the Smart Component selection box, select the connector part.

9. In the Components selection box, select the two hardware components.

10. In the Features selection box, select the in-context feature from the dummy part. You are now finished setting up the Smart Component.

11. Click the green check mark icon to accept the changes and exit out of the PropertyManager, and save the file.

FIGURE 15.20

The Smart Component PropertyManager interface

Creating an auto-sizing Smart Component

The simple Smart Component took about 20 minutes to model and set up. That is not too bad for a feature that you will probably use a lot. The benefits are somewhat modest, placing three components and a feature.

However, when it comes to the auto-sizing example that is shown next, the benefits are more extensive. A total of seven individual parts are placed (including Toolbox parts) — three of which are automatically sized, depending on the geometry into which the Smart Component is dropped — and an in-context feature is added.

To begin, open the part from the DVD named Chapter 19 - Clamp Start.sldprt. Notice that this is a multi-body part. You do not require any special knowledge about multi-body parts to complete this task. Multiple bodies are discussed in detail in Chapter 26.

1. With the Clamp Start part open, click through the configurations or examine the design table in the part; you can see that various dimensions change. Notice that several configurations already exist. The primary dimension that changes is the

diameter of the hole, and this change drives the diameter of, and distance between, the mounting holes.

Note

You can only drive auto-sizing by cylindrical geometry. ∎

Part of the Smart Component definition includes applying a Mate Reference to the part so that the big hole automatically snaps to cylindrical geometry. Another aspect is that it adds in-context holes that match the mounting holes to the plate. Figure 15.21 shows the assembly that this part is meant to go into. The clamp snaps onto the stepped shaft and adds holes to the plate.

FIGURE 15.21

The assembly where you will use the Smart Component

2. Open the file named Chapter 15 Autosize Training Assembly.sldasm. This has been prepared to help you get started with the Smart Component training.

Note

The shaft is not necessary in the training assembly. The training assembly is intended to create the in-context Smart Feature and to create the configurator table. The shaft part has been added here for visualization only. ∎

3. Insert the clamp part into the assembly and mate it concentric to the shaft and coincident to the blue plate. It does not matter where the clamp sits along the shaft, but it should be fully mated into the location so that it does not slide back and forth. A distance mate from a plane or planar face would be a good choice.

4. Edit the plate in the context of the assembly, and convert entities from the mounting holes in the clamp to create holes in the plate that align with the holes in the clamp.

5. Exit the Edit Component mode.

6. Activate Toolbox, select the four holes, as shown in Figure 15.22, and insert Socket Head Cap Screws, $^3/_8$ by 24 by $^5/_8$ inch. If you do not have Toolbox or choose not to use it, then a part with the correct name and sized configurations is provided on the DVD.

FIGURE 15.22

Inserting four screws at once using Toolbox

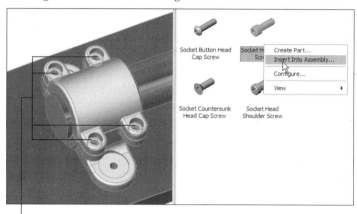

Pre-select these four edges

7. Use the same fastener to place in the mounting holes, using the correct size for the holes. You will set the length later. Use a default length of 2.25 inches for both mounting holes.

Note

Working with the length of the fasteners is not a clean operation in Smart Components. The length is dependent on the thickness of the plate, which is not controlled by the Smart Fastener, nor can the Smart Fastener account for it, except through mates. (Remember that auto-sizing is driven only by a diameter.) Later in this chapter, you will see how the washers and nuts are put in place on the underside of the plate, but the screw length cannot be automatically calculated (unless the actual screw had an in-context relation to the nut). ■

8. Place washers and nuts on the screws on the backside of the plate.

9. When the shaft diameter changes, the hole in the clamp changes to match (within the ranges that you will establish). As the clamp becomes bigger, bigger screws are needed to secure the clamp and the holes grow farther apart. Bigger screws mean additional configurations for the screw, washer, and nut parts. Remember that the configurations do not necessarily exist. You should not count on a Smart Component working if this means that Toolbox has to create new configurations.

In this example, the Toolbox parts are pre-populated with all the configurations needed for the range of sizes involved with this Smart Component. When you make your own Smart Components, you will have to do the same thing if you intend to use auto-sizing with Toolbox parts. The difficulty here is that the configurations include the diameter size of the screw as well as the length, which is unknown until you place the part.

All you have to do in this step is make sure that the configurations are available and that the screws are placed properly.

Up to this step, you have just assembled the parts as if this were the only time you were going to do it. The automation of the process comes next. Figure 15.23 shows the training assembly to this point. The shaft and plate are shown in wireframe because they are external to the Smart Component.

FIGURE 15.23

The training assembly up to Step 9

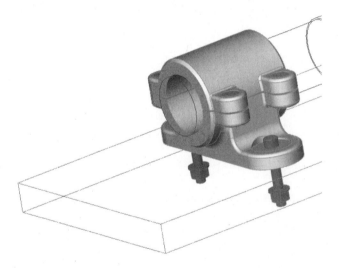

10. Click the Make Smart Component tool on the assembly toolbar. This is the point in the previous example where the Make Smart Component command was used, and it is no different here.

11. Activate the Smart Component selection box and pick the clamp part. Figure 15.24 shows the filled-in Smart Component PropertyManager.

    In the Components selection box, select the six screw instances, the two washers, and the two nuts.

    In the Features selection box, select the in-context feature or features that are associated with the Smart Component.

FIGURE 15.24

The Smart Component PropertyManager

12. The configurator table is simply a table that enables you to select which component configurations are to be used with which Smart Component configuration. It looks and works very much like an assembly design table, but it is not Excel-based, and every cell must be set explicitly rather than using techniques for mass population or assigning properties to a range of configurations, as you can do with a real design table.

Each cell has a drop-down list of all the available configurations for that component. If you have four instances of a single component, then you have to set each instance of each component. Figure 15.25 shows the configurator table for this example.

Note

If the configurator table were to ever be as easy to use as, for example, an Excel design table, then Smart Component complexity could increase significantly. The configurator table could even ideally be created from an assembly design table. Instead of a single component with its associated hardware and mounting features, think of larger-scale subassembly attachments. This sort of work is possible now, but it is difficult to apply to more than a handful of parts. ■

FIGURE 15.25

The configurator table for the Clamp Smart component

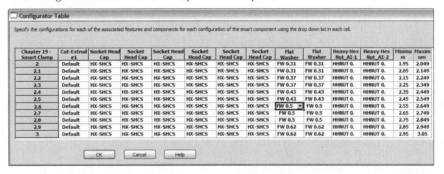

13. Click OK. You are now done creating the auto-sizing Smart Component!

Managing files with Smart Components

You may expect that with the training assembly, there is an extra burden of file management with Smart Components. This may seem counterintuitive, but in fact, the only file that you need to worry about is the actual Smart Component.

Although this is not explained very well in any of the documentation, the Help, as well as reseller demonstrations, on the topic generally recommend that you simply *delete* the training assembly once you are done with it because it is not needed any more. This implies that you should delete all the mates in an assembly or the sketch relations in a part. How do you edit the Smart Component if you delete the assembly in which it is created?

It turns out that all the information to re-create the training assembly is stored in the Smart Component. This includes the in-context feature (which is stored as a library feature) and the locations of any associated components, as well as the configurator table. Figure 15.26 shows a part of the FeatureManager of a Smart Component. As you can see, the in-context feature, the associated components, and the face references are all listed there.

Deleting the training assembly does not cause any data to be lost; you will delete an assembly in the following section.

FIGURE 15.26

Part of the FeatureManager of a Smart Component

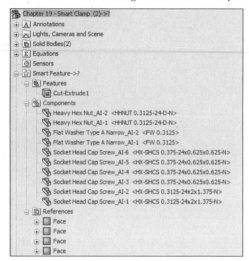

Editing Smart Components

Expanding on the discussion about whether or not to keep the training assembly file, here is a little exercise that you can try. Make a Smart Component by going through the preceding steps, using the following tutorial or creating one of your own. Just make a simple Smart Component with perhaps one associated component and an in-context feature. Then go ahead and delete the training assembly.

With the defining assembly gone, there appears to be no way to edit the setup of the Smart Component. RMB+click the Smart Feature folder in the FeatureManager of the Smart Component and select Edit in Defining Assembly, as shown in Figure 15.27. SolidWorks re-creates the defining assembly from the data that is stored in the Smart Component. This assembly is saved in a system temp folder using the name `<Smart Component name>_ta.sldasm`. If the Smart Component uses an in-context feature, it is saved to the temp directory as a library feature file using the name of the dummy part and appending `_lf` to the filename (for example, `Dummy_lf.sldlfp`).

The Edit Definition button appears in the upper-right corner of the graphics window and is shown to the right in Figure 15.27. If you click this button, the Smart Component PropertyManager interface appears again, enabling you to change the selection of associated components and in-context features, to change the auto-size setting, or edit the configurator table.

Thus, all the settings are preserved, and the training assembly exists only as a phantom in a temp directory. Although this appears to be counterintuitive, it works.

FIGURE 15.27

Selecting the Edit in Defining Assembly command

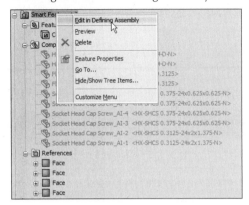

Tutorial: Working with Smart Components

This tutorial guides you through creating a Smart Component that only uses the auto-sizing feature. This enables you to manually create parts that snap to size like Toolbox parts, but without using Toolbox functionality. Follow these steps:

1. **Open the part from the DVD that has the filename** Chapter 15 – Tutorial Start.sldprt**.** This part originally came from Toolbox and already contains a few configurations.

2. **Make an assembly that contains** *only* **this part.**

3. **Make the part into a Smart Component (Tools ⇨ Make Smart Component), and turn on the option to auto-size.**

4. **Select the small diameter of the part as the concentric Mate Reference.** Figure 15.28 shows the selection.

5. **Click the Configurator Table button, and fill in the table so that it looks like Figure 15.29.** Some configurations are blank. This is because only the rows that have minimum and maximum values are used by the auto-size function. The rest are overlooked.

6. **Close the configurator table, click the green check mark icon to exit the feature, and save the assembly.**

FIGURE 15.28

Selecting the concentric Mate Reference face

7. **Exit the assembly and, in the part file, save it to a folder in your Design Library.** If you do not know where your Design Library is located, choose Tools ⇨ Options ⇨ File Locations ⇨ Design Library.

8. **Display the part in the Design Library panel of the Task pane.**

9. **Open the part from the DVD with the filename** Chapter 19 Tutorial Plate. sldprt. Place this part into a new assembly.

10. **Drag the Tutorial Start (Smart Component) from the Design Library into the assembly, and move the part over the holes in the plate.** As you drag the part up and down the row of holes, the part changes size to match each hole. Figure 15.30 shows all the holes that are populated with the matching Smart Component sizes, as driven by the configurator table. Place the part over one of the diameters.

11. **To edit the configurator table, open the Smart Component part in its own window.** Then right-click the Smart Feature folder and select Open In Defining Assembly. An assembly that was created from the data stored in the part opens.

12. **Click the Edit Definition button that appears in the upper-right corner of the graphics window.**

FIGURE 15.29

Filling in the configurator table

Chapter 19 Tutor	Minimum Diameter	Maximum Diameter
Default		
HX-SHCS 0.138-3		
HX-SHCS 0.19-32		
HX-SHCS 0.19-32		
HX-SHCS 0.19-32	0.1	0.199
HX-SHCS 0.25-20		
HX-SHCS 0.25-20		
HX-SHCS 0.25-28	0.2	0.249
HX-SHCS 0.3125-		
HX-SHCS 0.3125-		
HX-SHCS 0.3125-		
HX-SHCS 0.3125-		
HX-SHCS 0.375-2		
HX-SHCS 0.375-2		
HX-SHCS 0.375-2		
HX-SHCS 0.375-2		
HX-SHCS 0.375-2	0.25	0.449
HX-SHCS 0.4375-	0.45	0.469
HX-SHCS 0.4375-	0.47	0.479
HX-SHCS 0.4375-	0.48	0.499
HX-SHCS 0.5-20x	0.5	0.529
HX-SHCS 0.5-20x	0.53	0.549
HX-SHCS 0.5-20x	0.55	0.579
HX-SHCS 0.5-20x	0.58	0.599
HX-SHCS 0.625-1	0.6	0.629
HX-SHCS 0.625-1	0.63	0.659
HX-SHCS 0.625-1	0.66	0.699
HX-SHCS 0.75-16	0.7	0.8
HX-SHCS 0.875-1	0.801	1.109
HX-SHCS 1.25-12	1.11	2
PreviewCfg	0.801	1

FIGURE 15.30

Smart Component parts match holes in the part.

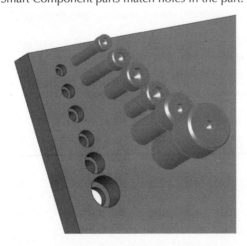

13. **Reassign the minimum and maximum diameter values for the ³⁄₁₆-inch and ¼-inch configurations to the shortest lengths.** For example, the chart shows the

$^3/_{16}$-32x.75-inch configuration to be assigned to a minimum of .1 and a maximum of .199. Move the .1 and .199 values up two cells to the $^3/_{16}$-32x$^1/_4$-inch configuration. Do something similar for the $^1/_4$-28x1-inch configuration. The edited part of the chart now looks like Figure 15.31.

FIGURE 15.31

The edited configurator table

Chapter 19 Tutor	Minimum Diameter	Maximum Diameter
Default		
HX-SHCS 0.138-32x0.5x0.5-N	0.1	.199
HX-SHCS 0.19-32x0.25x0.25-N		
HX-SHCS 0.19-32x0.4375x0.4375-N		
HX-SHCS 0.19-32x0.75x0.75-N		
HX-SHCS 0.25-20x0.625x0.625-N	.2	.249
HX-SHCS 0.25-20x1.375x1.375-N		
HX-SHCS		

Tip

You may have difficulty expanding the width of the column that contains the configuration names, thus making it difficult or impossible to read the ends of the long configuration names. However, like Excel, you can expand the height of the rows, which causes the configuration names to wrap, as shown in Figure 15.31. ∎

Summary

Smart Components can automate the placement of a main component, as well as associated mounting features and components. It can also offer automatic resizing options, depending on the geometry to which it is mated. The setup for Smart Components varies from simple to complex, with auto-sizing causing most of the complexity. Libraries, and in particular smart library parts like Smart Components, can greatly simplify repetitive tasks.

Library features are very useful in automating frequent design tasks. They are easy to create, store, apply, and automate. Setting up the features for the most flexibility often takes careful planning and attention to the detail of the references that you use. The more data you reuse, the more time you will save by automating and centralizing your libraries.

Part IV

Creating Assembly Drawings

Creating Assembly Drawings

D rawings containing assemblies often have very different uses than drawings containing parts. Assembly drawings tend to have fewer dimensions, and may be primarily for reference in assembling a product. Some assembly drawings are mainly pictorial in their purpose, particularly with exploded, section, and cutaway views.

Most of the actual tools that you might use for part drawings are the same for assembly drawings, with a few exceptions. This chapter covers these exceptions along with some special techniques that might make assembly drawings easier or clearer.

Combining Parts and Assemblies on the Same Drawing

Every company seems to do things differently when it comes to assembly drawings. Some use the drawings for BOM (Bill of Materials) illustration, some to manufacture assembly instructions, and some to dimension assembly-based features that are only applied after the individual components are assembled.

There is nothing to prevent you from putting parts and assemblies on the same drawing or even in the same sheet. Some users place an exploded view of the assembly on the first sheet, and then start detailing each part on the same sheet, using multiple sheets, so that the single drawing file documents several individual parts and the assembly. This is usually only the case for simple parts. An assembly made from several complex plastic parts could not be done this way, as a single complex plastic part will often require multiple sheets on its own.

Dimensioning assembly features

One of the more difficult questions you need to answer when dimensioning assembly features on an assembly drawing is what to use as your reference. Making cuts and measuring often takes place in some kind of fixture. Fixtures make excellent references in most situations. You might consider designing the fixture in some way that enables measurement from a fixed reference. This would require drawings that act as a qualification reference to include the fixturing reference in the drawing. This is best done as a higher-level assembly rather than adding the fixture using configurations of the product-level assembly.

Measuring to reference planes in the assembly is fine for the design, but there are no reference planes in your manufacturing floor unless they are physical faces of fixtures created for the purpose of measurement data. If your measurement spans multiple parts, then you should also keep in mind that both the individual parts and the assembly have tolerances you need to consider.

Assembly cuts are also often used to create 3D cutaway views. SolidWorks is not able to create a section view where the section cut is not perpendicular to the sheet of paper, so the workaround is to make a cut in the assembly (as a configuration) and to display the cut assembly using an isometric view.

Assigning the document driving the custom properties

When you have a drawing that has multiple parts or assemblies on it, you can control which document drives the custom properties used in the title block for that sheet. If you have multiple sheets, you can have different models driving the properties on different sheets.

To use this feature, right-click the sheet (but off of other items such as the format or views) to display the RMB menu shown in Figure 16.1. Make sure that the gray area on the RMB menu is labeled Sheet rather than View, and select Properties from the menu. The Sheet Properties dialog box appears, as shown in Figure 16.1.

Click the drop down-list in the lower-left corner, labeled Use custom property values from model shown in, and choose any view that is on the current sheet. This could be a single part or an assembly.

 Remember also that when linking to a property, you can choose to link to properties of the current document (drawing), the model specified in the sheet properties, or the component to which the annotation is attached. You can find these settings in the Link to Property dialog box, shown in Figure 16.2, by clicking the Link to Property icon in the Note PropertyManager.

FIGURE 16.1

Assigning the driving document for a sheet

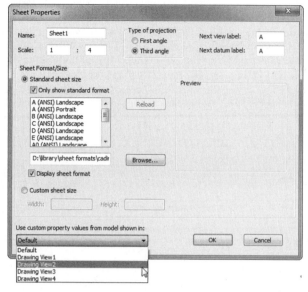

FIGURE 16.2

Linking a note to a custom property from one of various documents

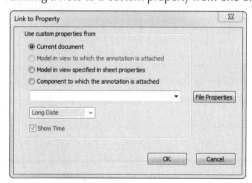

Using Multi-Page Templates

Assembly drawings often become multi-page documents. To speed up your creation of these drawings, you should have multi-page templates available to use when you need them. Most of the aspects of single page and multi-page templates are the same, such as custom property setup and formats, but adding the page gives you some options that you need to be aware of.

On the DVD

The two-sheet template and second-page format used in this chapter are in the Assembly Drawings folder, with the filenames `Bsize 2 sheet.drwdot` **(template) and** `b sheet 2.slddrt` **(format).** ■

You can use a "page two format" for any page other than page one. Generally, page two formats are just a minimal version of a page one format, removing information that might be considered redundant on every page of the drawing, and allowing more space for drawing content. Figure 16.3 shows a page one and a page two format used for a company called Dezignstuff.

FIGURE 16.3

Using a different format for the first page and subsequent pages of a drawing

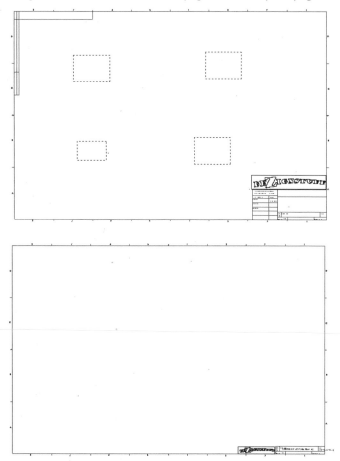

To make it easier to manage a large package of drawings, most multi-sheet drawings use the same size sheet for every drawing. However, every company has its own standards, conventions, customs, and needs.

To make a page two template from a page one template, follow these steps:

1. Open a new drawing using the sheet format that you would like to make into a page two format.

2. Right-click inside the sheet, but off of other items such as predefined views or the actual format, and select Edit Sheet Format from the menu.

3. Edit the format to suit your needs. This might include removing, moving, or adding lines to the border, removing linked notes, resizing or moving a logo or other items.

4. It is recommended to use a note linked on the drawing showing that the current page is Page X of Y. Both X (current sheet) and Y (total sheets) are available as properties you can link to the drawing from notes.

5. When you have the format the way you want it, save it to a special location in your library for drawing formats. You should avoid putting customized documents in folders in the SolidWorks installation directories or in default folders created by SolidWorks. For example, you can put your format documents on the D: drive (a physically separate drive from where the Windows operating system is installed) in a folder called D:\Library\Formats\. This ensures that installing or uninstalling SolidWorks or the operating system does not delete or overwrite your customized documents.

On the DVD
If you would like to study examples of formats, refer to the DVD material for Assembly Drawing Formats. ∎

Using Views with Special Assembly Functions

SolidWorks has some drawing view types that have special functionality when used with assemblies. The main ones that come to mind are alternate position views, exploded views (although an exploded view is not so much a function of the drawing), broken-out section views, and section views with alternating hatching.

Using the Alternate Position View

 The Alternate Position View is only available for views of an assembly and shows the assembly in two different positions (not from different viewpoints; this requires an assembly that moves). This is another view type that does not create a new view, but alters an existing view. Figure 16.4 shows the PropertyManager interface for the Alternate Position View, a sample view that it creates, and the way that it is represented in the drawing FeatureManager.

The Alternate Position View

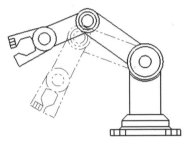

To create an Alternate Position View, ensure that you have an assembly on the active drawing that can have multiple positions, and click the Alternate Position View button on the Drawings toolbar, or choose Insert ⇨ Drawing View ⇨ Alternate Position and then select the Alternate Position View.

Next, click in the drawing view to which you want to add the alternate position. The PropertyManager shown in Figure 16.4 prompts you to select an existing configuration for the alternate position or to create a new configuration. If you choose to create a new configuration, then the model window appears, a new configuration is created, and you are required to reposition the assembly. The alternate position is shown in a different line font on the same view, from the same orientation as the original.

Tip

The best way to create this view is to either create two configurations used exclusively for the Alternate Position View or to have two configurations where you know that parts will not be moved, suppressed, or hidden. The main idea is that you need to ensure that these configurations remain in the same position or are changed intentionally, knowing that it will alter this drawing view. ■

To delete an Alternate Position View, select it in the drawing FeatureManager, and press Delete.

Creating views of an exploded assembly

Assemblies are often depicted with the parts pulled apart in a structured way to illustrate disassembly or more simply, the parts within the assembly. Exploded assemblies can be shown on assembly drawings using balloons with numbers corresponding to a BOM table.

Here is the workflow for creating an exploded view:

1. Open an assembly.

2. Click the ConfigurationManager tab at the top of the FeatureManager area.

3. Activate the configuration you want to explode, right-click the configuration, and select New Exploded View from the menu. Figure 16.5 shows the PropertyManager for the Explode command.

FIGURE 16.5

Starting to create an exploded view of an assembly

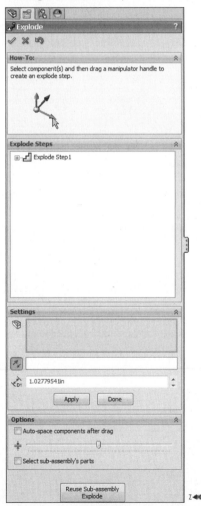

4. Select a component to explode away from the rest of the parts. Usually parts move axially if mated with a Concentric mate, and perpendicularly away from the other parts if mated with a flat to flat Coincident. Select the parts to be exploded together (in one move) in a group in the Settings selection box.

Selection in the Settings box is less fussy than selection for mates or other purposes. It doesn't matter if you select a face or an edge; SolidWorks understands you want to select the part.

5. If you need to move the parts in a direction other than the assembly X, Y, or Z, use the Explode Direction box immediately below the bigger Components To Explode selection box in the Settings panel. In Figure 16.6, the Explode Direction box contains a temporary axis.

FIGURE 16.6

Selecting rivets to explode

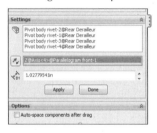 

6. With the rivets selected and the direction established, drag one of the arrows on the triad that appears in the graphics window, or type a number in the distance box in the PropertyManager. This brings up a ruler along which you can judge the explode distance.

This action produces the first Explode Step in the Explode Steps box in the PropertyManager. You can edit and delete the explode step, but you can't change its name. The expanded explode step and exploded assembly are shown in Figure 16.7.

FIGURE 16.7

Examining the explode step and exploded parts

7. To make edits, right-click an explode step and select Edit Step. This enables you to change anything you used to create the step. Immediately after releasing the drag of the component, you are no longer able to edit the component, and if you want to make changes, you have to edit the Explode Step, or you can use the small blue arrow that attaches itself directly to the part and may be hard to see. You can use this small arrow to change the explode distance. Typing in a number is better because it doesn't immediately move you out of the command, although you do have to select a direction first, using the colored triad.

Figure 16.8 shows a completed explode for the assembly.

FIGURE 16.8

The completed explode for this assembly

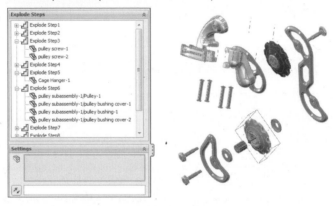

8. When you are done with the Explode command, click the green check mark icon to accept the results.

The completed results of an explode are displayed as an exploded view indented under the configuration you started the explode from, as shown in Figure 16.9. Each configuration can have only one exploded view. If you want more than one exploded view, you have to attach a second view to another configuration.

To collapse an exploded view, right-click it under the configuration and select Collapse. This allows you to toggle back and forth between a collapsed and exploded view. Another option is Animated Explode/Collapse. This option uses the order in which the explode steps appear in the ConfigurationManager and a default speed.

FIGURE 16.9

The result of the exploded view in the ConfigurationManager

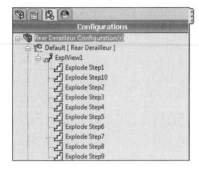

Note

After using the Animated Explode/Collapse option, make sure to turn off the Animation Controller that appears in the upper-left corner of the SolidWorks window. This controller allows you to control and save the animation, but it also blocks you from performing other actions in the assembly until you turn it off. ■

Adding explode lines

 Explode lines are 3D sketch lines that show the explode path of the parts in an exploded view of an assembly. You would think that SolidWorks would be able to create these lines automatically from the data in the exploded view, but it can't; you have to make the lines manually. The Explode Line Sketch toolbar icon is in the Assembly toolbar by default, and it activates the Explode Sketch Line toolbar, which contains only two tools: Route Line and Jog Line.

The Route Line feature is much easier to use than in previous versions. Now you simply click the features that you want to connect with an explode line, use the arrows that appear to determine which direction the sketch should connect to the part, and then click the RMB to accept the line and move on to the next. The process is shown in Figure 16.10.

In cases where you want to move a line that the Route Line feature has created, move your cursor over the line; two small arrows appear, as shown in Figure 16.11, which enable you to move that line.

FIGURE 16.10

Drawing Route Lines in an exploded view

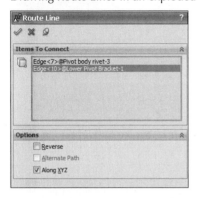

FIGURE 16.11

Moving a Route Line as it is created

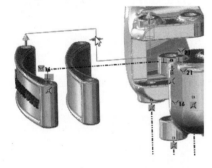

Showing exploded view

The best view orientation to use for an exploded view on a drawing is usually not one of the standard views. To create a custom view orientation, use the mouse to orient the view in the way that you want the assembly displayed on the drawing, then open the assembly and press the spacebar to open the View Orientation box. Click the New View button, and name the new view orientation.

Now you can place the new view on the drawing. To show the view in the exploded state, right-click inside the view (but off any part geometry), select Properties, and choose the Show in Exploded State option, as shown in Figure 16.12.

FIGURE 16.12

Showing the exploded state on the drawing

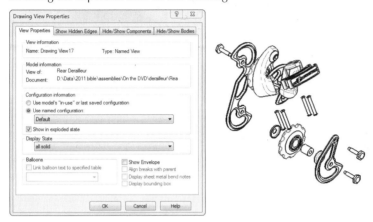

Creating section views

Section views are common enough in part drawings, but when you section an assembly, you have to consider other things, such as not cutting fasteners and shafts. You can create assembly sections with the same options that you use for part sections, partial sections, aligned sections, and broken-out sections.

Excluding parts from section views

When creating a section view, you can exclude parts from being sectioned. Figure 16.13 shows the Section Scope tab of the Section View dialog box, which enables you to do this. You can also access this dialog box when editing a section view through the Section View PropertyManager, by clicking the More Properties button at the bottom, and then choosing the Section Scope tab.

Aligning the view

In this case, the section line is slightly angled, and you would like to have the section view laid out straight. To orient a view in a particular way, select an edge that you want to be horizontal or vertical (assuming there is one; if not, then you may have to use a sketch line or axis), and through the menus, select Tools ⇨ Align Drawing View and then select either Horizontal Edge or Vertical Edge.

Remember that you can always rotate the view on the sheet with the Rotate button on the Heads Up View toolbar on the drawing. This displays a dialog box where you can type in a specific value.

FIGURE 16.13

Excluding bolts and pins from the section view of this assembly

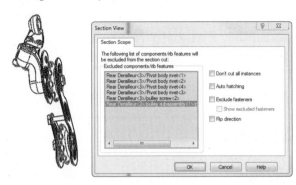

Adjusting the hatching

The default hatching may not be the right size for the parts you build. If you need to adjust the hatching — the size, the pattern, or the angle — just click the sectioned part, and the Area Hatch/Fill PropertyManager appears. Figure 16.14 shows the PropertyManager and a hatched section view.

FIGURE 16.14

Using the Area Hatch/Fill PropertyManager

 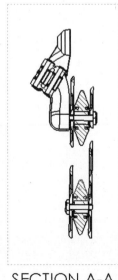

SECTION A-A

You can change hatching for each part (component), body, the entire view, or just the selected enclosed region. Be sure to make the right selection in the Apply To drop-down menu before you exit the Area Hatch PropertyManager.

Hatching is assigned with the material, found at the top of the SolidWorks FeatureManager for each part. Each material has its own crosshatch. If a material is not formally assigned to a part, the default hatching is set in Tools ➪ Options ➪ Document Properties ➪ Material Properties settings. The default is ANSI31 (Iron BrickStone). This is also where the default density is established, as shown in Figure 16.15.

FIGURE 16.15

Changing the defaults for density and crosshatch

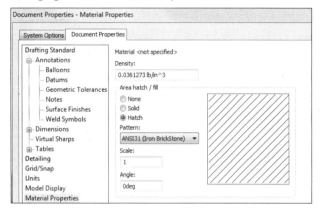

Broken-Out Section View

The Broken-Out Section View is a view type that alters an existing view rather than creating a new view. It also requires a closed loop sketch. The Broken-Out Section View is very useful in assembly views where parts are obscured by other parts, particularly when a set of parts is inside a housing and you want to show the inside parts without hiding the housing. Of course, you can also use a Broken-Out Section View on parts with internal detail.

A Broken-Out Section View acts like a cut that is created from the drawing view. Any faces created by the cut are hatched. Figure 16.16 shows a simple assembly view using a Broken-Out Section View. On the left is the view with the driving sketch (in this case, a closed loop spline), and on the right is the finished view. You cannot create a Broken-Out Section View using existing Detail, Section, or Alternate Position Views.

A Broken-Out Section View requires you to specify a depth for the break. You can use an edge selected from a different view or a distance to specify the depth. In the case of the broken-out section, the depth is into the screen, while with the regular section the depth is measured as a distance perpendicular to the section line.

FIGURE 16.16

A Broken-Out Section View

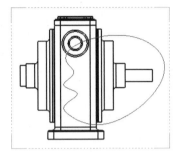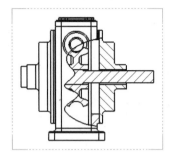

Drawing the closed loop

A Broken-Out Section View is initiated from an existing view either with or without a pre-drawn closed loop. If the loop is pre-drawn, then you must select it before clicking the Broken-Out Section toolbar button on the Drawings toolbar or accessing the command by choosing Insert ⇨ Drawing View ⇨ Broken-Out Section.

If the view does not have a pre-drawn, pre-selected loop, then initiating the function activates the spline sketch tool. It is not necessary to use a spline as the closed loop for this view type, but a Broken-Out Section View is traditionally created with a freehand sort of boundary, even when drawn manually.

If the loop is closed in an uninterrupted workflow, then after the last spline point is drawn, joining the spline back to itself, the Section Scope dialog box appears. This enables you to select any parts that are not to be sectioned. It is customary to avoid sectioning shafts, screws, or other cylindrical components.

The recommended workflow is to initiate the function from the toolbar, use the spline to create the closed loop, and not pre-draw a loop. This makes everything flow more smoothly, and you create the view surprisingly quickly. If you must use a sketch tool other than the spline, then you must pre-draw it. Even if you simply change sketch tools when the Broken-Out Section View automatically activates the spline, because the workflow has been broken, creating the closed loop does not automatically display the Section Scope interface.

Selecting the depth

After you make the Section Scope selections, the next step is to set the depth of the cut. You can do this in one of several ways. A Broken-Out Section View is usually applied to the center of a hole if available, or in other ways that show the view as cleanly as possible. If you know the depth of the cut that you want to make, then you can type it in as a distance value. Of course, that raises the question, "Distance from *what*?" The answer seems to be "from the geometry in the view that would come the farthest out of the screen toward the user." Users most often choose the distance when it does not matter *exactly* how deep the cut goes or exactly *where* it cuts, but it gives a relative position.

In situations when you want to cut to the center of a particular feature or up to an edge, it is far easier to simply select the geometry from a drawing view. For example, Figure 16.17 shows the PropertyManager interface where the depth of the cut is set. In this example, the edge of the shaft in the view to the right has been selected. This tells SolidWorks that the cut should go to the center of the shaft. Another possibility is to show the temporary axes, as shown in Figure 16.17, and to select an axis through the center of the shaft.

FIGURE 16.17

Setting the depth of the Broken-Out Section View

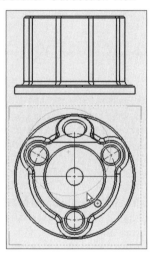
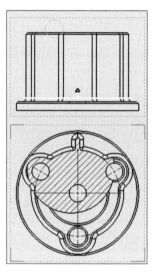

Editing the view

At this point the view is finished. Now you may choose to edit the view in some way, such as by changing the sketch, the depth, the section scope, and so on. Figure 16.18 shows how the Broken-Out Section View is positioned in the Drawing FeatureManager. It is listed as a modification to an existing drawing view. The Broken-Out Section RMB menu is also shown. Selecting Edit Definition displays the PropertyManager, shown in Figure 16.17. Selecting Edit Sketch enables you to change the section spline shape. Selecting Properties displays the dialog box shown to the right in Figure 16.18. This contains options for the underlying original view as well as the Broken-Out Section modification to the original view. Only the Section Scope tab is added by the Broken-Out Section View. The rest of the options are for normal view properties.

FIGURE 16.18

Editing the Broken-Out Section View

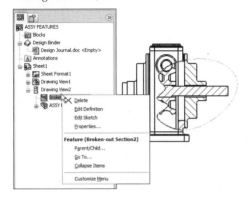

Using Color in Assembly Drawing Views

One of the newer functions in SolidWorks assembly drawings is that you can apply the same color to the wireframe display on the drawing as you have applied to the individual parts in the assembly window. Colors on drawings help distinguish one part from another, where the alternative is to look at a screenful of black lines.

On the other hand, sometimes light colors that show up well when the part is shaded on the screen do not look good when used in a wireframe line width on a white sheet. Also, with the use of part "appearances" where some people are using more realistic material displays for parts, part colors can be a range of gray to reflect surfaces such as aluminum or steel. Still, if you want to set your parts up with more abstract contrasting colors, it does help you to distinguish one part from another in the assembly model and on the drawing. Appearances, even realistic or reflective appearances, can have colors assigned to them, so you get a shiny, red steel part. The realism is far less important than the ability to tell one part from another, so the abstraction of colors that don't look realistic at all is often very helpful.

To make assembly drawings use part color, you make the first setting in the assembly document properties, shown as the setting with the cursor next to it in Figure 16.19, Tools ⇨ Options ⇨ Document Properties ⇨ Detailing ⇨ Use model color for HLR/HLV in drawings. You need to specify this document property setting in the drawing. (HLR stands for *hidden lines removed*, while HLV stands for *hidden lines visible*.)

FIGURE 16.19

The Use model color for HLR/HLV in drawings option

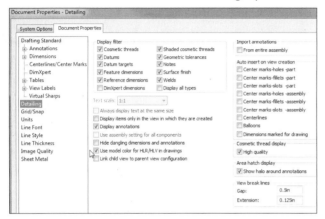

This is worth repeating: Even though this setting exists in both the assembly and the drawing, and even though there is a setting in parts that says to use the same color for shaded and wireframe, the only setting that matters in terms of getting color onto the drawing is Use model color setting in the *drawing* document properties.

Setting Up Drawings of Large Assemblies

There are several tactics you can use to try to minimize the overhead of working with large data sets in SolidWorks drawings. You have several options when working to improve the performance of large assembly drawings. Some of these options should be employed at the level of the assembly, and some you will only use in the assembly.

Using detached drawings

Detached drawings do not have the 3D document files loaded in memory; they just let you work with the geometry as-is in the drawing. They can be beneficial in two situations: first, to speed up large assembly drawings and second, when you have the drawing but don't have the part and assembly files. You must set up a detached drawing before deciding to open the drawing without the parts. On the surface, there is no difference between a regular drawing and a detached drawing, except for the icon in the FeatureManager area, and the view icons (which all display broken link symbols). So you will not be able to tell a detached drawing by looking at it in Windows Explorer or through the SolidWorks Open interface.

Note

A detached drawing is convenient when you want to send someone a SolidWorks drawing, but you don't need (or want) to give them access to the actual 3D model data. However, you first have to save it as a detached drawing. ∎

To create a detached drawing, choose File ⇨ Save As, and from the Save As Type drop-down list (shown in Figure 16.20), select Detached Drawing.

FIGURE 16.20

Saving a drawing as a detached drawing

You cannot perform some drawing operations with detached drawings. These operations include the following:

- Crop views

- Break views

- Section views

- Alternate position or relative views

- Insert model items

Detached drawings also cannot be lightweight.

Just like other operations in SolidWorks drawings, when the view needs to be updated, the view is shown as hatched.

When you need to load the model to update changes, or do one of the operations that require the part data to be present, right-click inside a view and select Load Model from the menu. When SolidWorks determines that you need to load the model, the software may prompt you to do this.

You can only add certain types of views of parts — not the assembly (aux, projected, section, broken-out section), annotations, and reference dimensions to a detached drawing. So there is a certain amount of work you can actually do with this option.

If you save a drawing as detached, load the model, and then save the drawing and close it, the next time you open it up, it will be detached. In other words, once you save a drawing as detached, it remains detached until you save it as a regular drawing. To do this, just choose File ➪ Save As, and in the File of Type drop-down list, select Drawing.

Working with lightweight drawings

Lightweight drawings have some similarities to lightweight assemblies. With lightweight drawings, SolidWorks only loads as much model data as it needs. If SolidWorks needs more data, it will load it. This helps assemblies and drawings to open more quickly, but some functions may be slower later on.

Caution
You cannot mix the benefits of lightweight drawings with the benefits of detached drawings. ■

Using lightweight settings in the drawing works just like using lightweight settings in the assembly. Right-click in a view and select Set Resolved to Lightweight, as shown in Figure 16.21. You can revert to the other setting by choosing Set Lightweight to Resolved from the drop-down list.

FIGURE 16.21

Using lightweight settings with assembly drawings

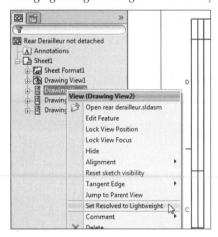

Using SpeedPak with drawings

SpeedPak is a derived configuration type that uses selected geometry to simplify the display and amount of data SolidWorks needs to load a complex assembly, with the goal of speeding up loading and work in general. If you want to use a SpeedPak in a drawing, the SpeedPak must include edges that you want to dimension to. Anything that is part of the ghost data will be shown in gray. To use an existing SpeedPak for an assembly, right-click a view, and select Properties. In the Configuration information, use the named configuration option to select the derived configuration of the SpeedPak.

Cross-Reference

Chapter 8 provides more information on SpeedPak. ∎

Using draft quality views

 Draft quality views are another way to speed up large assembly drawings. Figure 16.22 shows the difference between a draft quality view on the left and a high-quality view on the right. Each view starts as a draft quality view; however, when you change the draft to high quality, the setting is no longer available. You can find the Draft and High quality view settings in the view PropertyManager (just select a view, and the PropertyManager appears on the left), in the Display Style panel. This enables you to change from wireframe to shaded display modes. If the High and Draft quality toggles are not in the PropertyManager panel, then the view is already in high-quality mode. Once you switch a view to high quality, you cannot switch it back to draft quality.

FIGURE 16.22

Comparing high- and draft quality views

You can change the defaults for this setting in the System Options at Tools ⇨ Options ⇨ Drawings ⇨ Display Style ⇨ Display quality for new views. As you might imagine, this is not a template setting, but is only a system option. If someone with a faster computer has this option set to high quality already, and they send you drawings, then you will not be able to set them back to draft quality.

Note

With the system option set to high quality, it is still possible to create new drawings with draft quality views. This may be because I use Predefined views on my templates, where the Predefined views are set to draft quality (probably made before I changed this setting). So even though high- and draft quality views are system options, by using templates with predefined views, you can make this feature work like a document property. ■

Keep in mind that it is easy to confuse the Cosmetic Thread Display with the Display Style. They both toggle between high quality and draft quality, and when you are just looking for those features, you may settle on the first one you see with this label.

Tutorial: Creating a Simple Assembly Drawing

This tutorial guides you through creating a simply assembly drawing. Follow these steps:

1. **Create a new drawing from the New dialog box.** Select `Inch B Bible Template (no Views).drwdot`; as the filename indicates, this template document has no pre-defined views. If you select a default SolidWorks template, then you need to verify that the template uses third-angle rather than first-angle projection. An easy way to do this is to switch the drafting standard from ISO to ANSI in Tools ⇨ Options ⇨ Document Properties ⇨ Drafting Standard. If the automatic Model View interface appears in the PropertyManager, click the red X icon to cancel out of it.

2. **Expand the Task pane and activate the View Palette (the tab that looks like a drawing icon).** Click the ellipsis button (...) and browse for the assembly named `Chapter 16. SF casting assembly.sldasm`. The View Palette is shown in Figure 16.23.

3. **Drag the Back view onto the drawing.** Notice that when you use this technique, the views do not resize automatically, regardless of the setting at Tools ⇨ Options ⇨ Drawings ⇨ Automatically Scale New Drawing Views.

4. **Delete any view that you have created using this method.** Open Windows Explorer, browse to the assembly, and drag it into the drawing. The views that you create using this method are equivalent to the Standard 3 View tool. This time, the views automatically size.

5. **Select the Front view and change it to the Back view.** Notice that the rest of the views change to reflect the new parent view. You will get a warning about this change.

FIGURE 16.23

The View Palette

6. **Zoom in on the Back view.** Change the view to show Tangent Edges With Font through View ➪ Display. You can also make this change from the view RMB menu.

7. **Click the Alternate Position View toolbar button.** Type a name in the PropertyManager for a new configuration and click the green check mark icon. SolidWorks opens the assembly model window.

8. **Rotate the handle 90 degrees and click the green check mark icon.** SolidWorks returns to the drawing and shows the new position in a dashed font, as shown in Figure 16.24.

9. **Place an isometric view on the drawing.** Change the Display mode to make it a shaded view.

10. **Right-click inside the view (but away from the parts), and select Properties.** The Drawing View Properties dialog box appears, displaying the View Properties tab, as shown in Figure 16.25. Make sure that the view is set to use the Default configuration, and also select the Show in exploded state option.

FIGURE 16.24

Creating an Alternate Position View

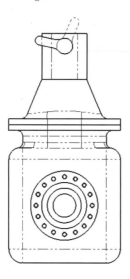

FIGURE 16.25

The Drawing View Properties dialog box

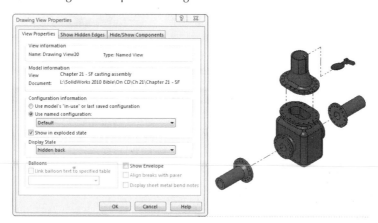

Summary

Assembly drawings require many of the same skills as regular drawings, but much less dimensioning, and much more pictorial and visualization capability. Sometimes you have to use the unique tools for assembly drawings to get the job done.

Working with Tables and Drawings

olidWorks enables you to create several types of tables on drawings, such as the Bill of Materials. Design Tables that are used in
parts and assemblies can also be shown on the drawing to create a
tabulated type drawing. Hole Tables enable you to chart the center locations and sizes of holes for easy access to manufacturing data. Revision
Tables can work with Workgroup Product Data Management (PDM) or
by themselves to help you document the revision history of a drawing.
General Tables are also available for any specialized items that are not
covered by the other table types.

Driving the Bill of Materials

The Bill of Materials (BOM) is one of the most frequently used types of
tables that are available in SolidWorks. BOMs are intended for use with
assemblies, but you can also use them with individual parts for specialized applications. The information that you can expect to see on a BOM
includes item number, filename, quantity used, description, and any
other custom property that you would like to add to it. A typical BOM is
shown in Figure 17.1.

BOMs are made in one of two ways: the default BOM is made from a
special SolidWorks table, while an Excel-based BOM is driven by Excel.
While Excel offers some advantages, many users appear to prefer the

default BOM. Excel and SolidWorks table-based BOMs are not interchangeable, so if you plan to customize the default templates, you need to decide which type of BOM (Excel or SolidWorks) you will want to use.

FIGURE 17.1

A sample BOM

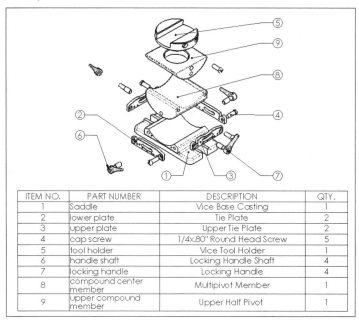

ITEM NO.	PART NUMBER	DESCRIPTION	QTY.
1	Saddle	Vice Base Casting	1
2	lower plate	Tie Plate	2
3	upper plate	Upper Tie Plate	2
4	cap screw	1/4x.80" Round Head Screw	5
5	tool holder	Vice Tool Holder	1
6	handle shaft	Locking Handle Shaft	4
7	locking handle	Locking Handle	4
8	compound center member	Multipivot Member	1
9	upper compound member	Upper Half Pivot	1

Note

You can also place BOMs directly in the assembly and even in multi-body part files. ■

Examining the SolidWorks table-based BOM

The BOM shown in Figure 17.1 is a default SolidWorks table-based BOM. The differences between the displays of the two types of BOM are mainly cosmetic; the bigger difference is in the functionality. The PropertyManager interface for the SolidWorks BOM is shown in Figure 17.2.

FIGURE 17.2

The PropertyManager for a table-driven BOM

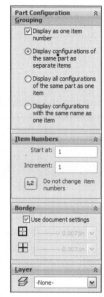

Creating table-based BOM templates

Like other types of data, the SolidWorks table-driven BOM starts from a template. The BOM in Figure 17.1 was created from the default BOM template. When a BOM is initiated, you can select the template in the Table Template panel near the top of the PropertyManager, as shown in Figure 17.2.

You create table-based BOM templates in much the same way that you create other templates:

1. Specify the settings.
2. Delete the document-specific data.
3. Save the template.
4. Access the template from a library location.

To save the template, right-click the BOM and select Save As. In the Files of Type drop-down list, select Template (*.sldbomtbt) — sldbomtbt stands for SolidWorks Bill of Materials

Table Template. Any of the settings, additional columns, links to properties, and so on are saved to the template and reused when you create a new template from it.

Best Practice

Put the BOM template in your library area outside of the SolidWorks installation folder. Then specify the path in the Tools ⇨ Options ⇨ File Locations area. ∎

Setting a table anchor

A table anchor locks a corner of the table to a selected point on the drawing sheet format. If you do not select a point in the format, then the table is placed at a corner of the sheet. To specify a point in the format to act as the anchor, you must be editing the format. Right-click the sheet and select Edit Sheet Format. Then right-click a sketch endpoint in the format, select Set As Anchor, and specify which type of table the anchor is for. You can set different anchor locations for different types of tables. Figure 17.3 shows the selection and menus for this option.

FIGURE 17.3

Setting a BOM table anchor

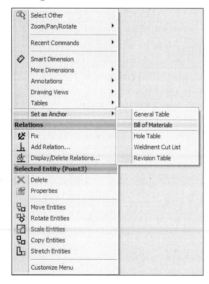

Tip

You should save the format and drawing template with these table anchors specified so that you do not need to re-specify them for each new document. If you want to check a Sheet Format to see what anchors exist, you can expand the sheet in the FeatureManager of the drawing. ∎

Using BOM types

You can use one of three BOM types in SolidWorks: Top-level only, Parts only, or Indented. As the name suggests, the Top-level only BOM only shows components on the top level. It treats subassemblies as a single entry. As a result, if the top-level assembly shown on the drawing is made up of five subassemblies and two individual parts, and you select the Top-level only option, then only seven items are shown in the BOM.

The Parts only BOM ignores subassembly structure and only displays parts in an unindented list. The Indented BOM shows the parts of subassemblies in an indented list under the name of the subassembly. This is the most complete list of SolidWorks documents used because it includes all parts and assemblies.

The Show Numbering option for indented assemblies is only activated after you have selected the Indented option and placed the table. When you use this option, it causes subassembly parts to be numbered with an X.Y number system. For example, if item number 4 is a subassembly and it has three parts, those parts are numbered 4.1, 4.2, and 4.3.

Using configurations

The Configurations panel of the BOM PropertyManager displays slightly differently for Top-level only BOMs compared to the other types. The Top-level only BOM type enables the option to show multiple assembly configurations and display the quantities for top-level components in separate columns, as shown in Figure 17.4. This figure shows that the configuration named "D" has some suppressed parts, including some parts that are now not used in the "D" configuration, and that therefore have a zero quantity. Notice the available options for dealing with zero-quantity parts.

Locating the Keep Missing Items option

When you are making changes to a model, parts are often either suppressed or deleted altogether. Some company documentation standards require that parts that are removed from a BOM remain on the bill and appear with strikethrough formatting; this may be a relic from the past, when it was more difficult to remove items from hand drawings.

Keep Missing Items and Zero Quantity Display have both been moved to Tools ⇨ Options ⇨ Document Properties ⇨ Detailing ⇨ Tables screen.

FIGURE 17.4

Configuration options with the BOM

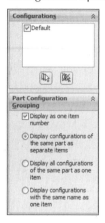

ITEM NO.	PART NUMBER	DESCRIPTION	Default/QTY.	d/QTY.
1	Saddle	Vice Base Casting	1	1
2	lower plate	Tie Plate	2	2
3	upper plate	Upper Tie Plate	2	2
4	cap screw	1/4x.80" Round Head Screw	4	4
5	Assem1	inch assembly description	1	1
6	handle shaft	Locking Handle Shaft	4	2
7	locking handle	Locking Handle	4	2
8	compound center member	Multipivot Member	1	-

Choosing Zero Quantity Display options

The Zero Quantity Display settings are only used for configurations where a component is not used. The three options that are available are

- **Quantity Of Dash.** Substitutes a dash for the quantity value.

- **Quantity Of Zero.** Uses a zero for the quantity value.

- **Blank.** Sets the quantity value to blank.

Assigning item numbers

Item numbers for components listed in the BOM can start at a specific number and be given a particular interval. The Do not change item numbers option means that even when rows are reordered, item numbers stay with their original components.

The Follow Assembly Order option, which is also available through the right mouse button (RMB) menu, means that the order of the components in the BOM follows the order of the components in the Assembly FeatureManager. If the order is changed in the assembly, it also updates in the drawing.

Displaying the BOM contents

The BOM contents can be changed on the BOM or through the RMB menu. Figure 17.5 shows a simple BOM with the RMB menu. For example, you can drag the row numbers to reorder BOM items, and right-click to hide them. Row numbers are only displayed after you select the BOM table.

FIGURE 17.5

The BOM contents interface

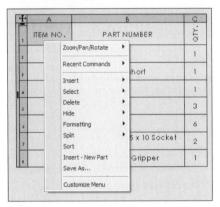

You can add columns or rows to the BOM for additional properties or manually added parts (such as items you wouldn't model, like paint or glue). To change the property displayed in a column, double-click in the column header. In previous releases, many of the settings and options now found on the RMB menu were found in a more complex Bill of Materials Properties window. The newer arrangement is more intuitive. Most SolidWorks users know to try the RMB menu if they select something and don't find the option they are looking for in the PropertyManager.

Controlling the appearance of the table-based BOM

If you are already familiar with formatting an Excel-based BOM, then you will quickly get used to formatting the SolidWorks table-based BOM. Figure 17.6 shows the table unselected on the left and selected on the right. While it's selected, you have access to a full range of appearance and organization options through the RMB menu.

FIGURE 17.6

Selecting a column, row, cell, and table

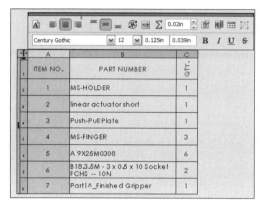

To move the table, click outside the upper-left corner and drag the table to a new location. When you select the table, a border appears around it that is not normally visible and is not printed with the drawing. You can change the properties of a row or a column by selecting just outside of the row or column to the top or the left.

You can establish spacing and width of rows or columns by dragging the border on the left side of the column with the split cursor or by accessing the column width setting through the Formatting option in the RMB menu.

While the selection is activated, you can also expand a panel to the left and another to the top by clicking the three small arrows in the selected BOM border. Figure 17.7 shows the left panel, called the Assembly Structure panel, expanded with the cursor pointing to the three small arrows. In addition to showing the assembly structure, this panel can also show which parts are ballooned on the drawing.

Notice item 7 on the BOM, which has a different symbol and no name. This is a virtual component (a component created in context but not saved to its own document file); it exists only within the assembly.

Dissolving, combining, numbering, and restructuring for indented BOMS

You can dissolve an assembly in the BOM. To do this, the BOM has to show an indented list. You can then access the Dissolve option from the RMB menu on the assembly icon. You can delete any restructuring you have done to the BOM by right-clicking the assembly icon with red arrows and selecting Restore restructured components.

If the BOM shows several parts that are identical, and you would like to combine them, again, you can access the option from the RMB menu.

FIGURE 17.7

An expanded BOM border

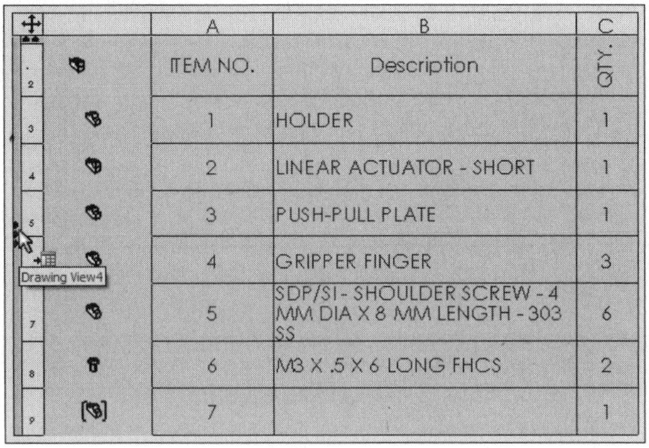
A
B
C
ITEM NO.
Description
QTY.
1
HOLDER
1
2
LINEAR ACTUATOR - SHORT
1
3
PUSH-PULL PLATE
1
4
GRIPPER FINGER
3
Drawing View4
5
SDP/SI - SHOULDER SCREW - 4 MM DIA X 8 MM LENGTH - 303 SS
6
6
M3 X .5 X 6 LONG FHCS
2
7
1

Item numbers in indented BOMs can be flat (such as 1, 2, 3), or they can be detailed (such as 1.1, 1.2, 1.3, 2, 2.1, 2.2) to reflect parts as members of subassemblies. This formatting option is available in the BOM Type panel in the BOM PropertyManager, under the Indented option.

Adding columns or rows

To add a column, right-click near where you want to add the column, and choose Insert ➪ Column Right or Column Left. Inserting rows is exactly the same. The next thing you want to do with a column is to assign what kind of data goes into it. You can use a custom property such as Part Weight or Vendor, as shown in Figure 17.8. Access this interface by double-clicking a column header and selecting Custom Property from the drop-down list.

FIGURE 17.8

Establishing the property driving the column content

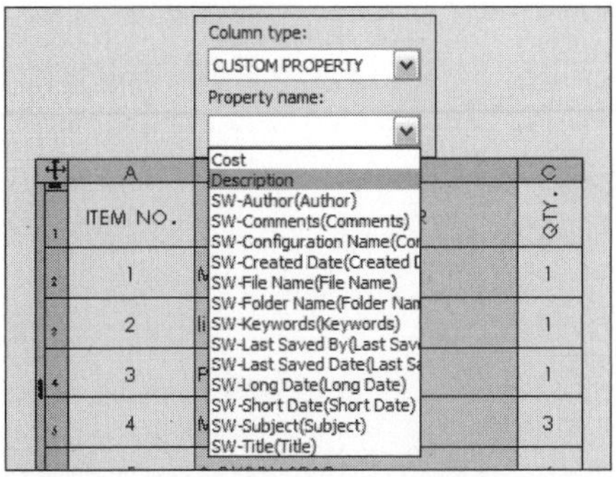
Column type:
CUSTOM PROPERTY
Property name:
Cost
Description
SW-Author(Author)
SW-Comments(Comments)
SW-File Name(File Name)
SW-Keywords(Keywords)
SW-Long Date(Long Date)
SW-Short Date(Short Date)
SW-Subject(Subject)
SW-Title(Title)
A
C
ITEM NO.
QTY.
1
2
3
4

One of the really beautiful aspects of custom property management in the BOM is that if you just type text in a column set up to be driven by a part property, SolidWorks automatically updates the part with the property. If the property didn't exist in the part previously, SolidWorks also creates the property. This is another very nice addition to the software.

Note

If you create a BOM with the columns and properties that you like, then you can save it to a template, as described earlier in this chapter. ■

Editing BOMs

When you need to manually enter text in a BOM, for example in General Tables or custom properties in BOMs, you can use the tab and arrow keys to move the cursor between cells. In fact, most of the Excel-like functionality has been added back into the SolidWorks native table format.

Here is a summary of the added Navigation functionality:

- **Enter.** Move to next cell down.
- **Tab.** Move to next cell to the right.
- **Arrow.** Move cursor in any direction.
- **Shift+Arrow.** Increase selection size.
- **Shift+Tab.** Move cursor backward.
- **Shift+Enter.** Move cursor up.
- **Home.** Move cursor to first column.
- **Ctrl+Home.** Move to upper-left corner of table.
- **End.** In combination with arrow keys, move to end indicated.
- **Ctrl+End.** Move cursor to bottom-right corner of table.

Here is a summary of the added Editing functionality:

- **F2.** Edit contents of cell.
- **Double-click.** Edit contents of cell.
- **Alt+Enter.** Add multiple rows to cell.
- **Delete.** Delete contents of cell without activating cell.
- **Backspace.** Delete contents of cell and activate cell.
- **Ctrl+Delete.** Delete one word at a time.
- **Edit.** Edit multiple row heights simultaneously.
- **Lock.** Lock row height and column width.
- **Copy.** Copy cells from Excel to SolidWorks tables.

Retiring the Excel-based BOM

 In previous releases, the Excel-based BOM was the only way to add a BOM to a drawing. This feature has been replaced in most respects by the SolidWorks native table-driven BOM, but many people still use the Excel-based BOM either out of habit or to comply with legacy standards. Figure 17.9 shows the interface for the Excel-based BOM.

FIGURE 17.9

The interface for Excel-based BOMs

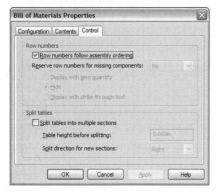

Best Practice

Unless you have a compelling reason to do otherwise, you should use the SolidWorks table-based BOM because this function will be best supported in future versions of SolidWorks software. ■

Using Design Tables

 Design Tables that are used to drive configurations of parts and assemblies can be shown on the drawing. This is often called a *tabulated* drawing and is typical of parts that have a basic shape that is common among several sizes or versions of the part. The sizes are shown by a symbol on the drawing, with a column headed by that symbol showing the available dimensions and the corresponding size (configuration) names.

You can insert a Design Table into a drawing by choosing Insert ⇨ Tables ⇨ Design Table or by clicking the Design Table button on the Tables toolbar. In either case, you must pre-select a drawing view of a part or assembly that contains a Design Table before the menu selection or toolbar button becomes activated.

Design Tables that are displayed in this way are often formatted to some extent. It is necessary to hide columns and rows unless you want the dimension or feature name syntax to display on the drawing as well as the values. Extra columns and rows are often added to make the Design Table readable. The image to the left in Figure 17.10 shows a Design Table that is formatted to be placed on a drawing. The image to the right shows the same Design Table with all the information visible. The first column and the first row are hidden to make the table more readable on the drawing, and the second column and second row use the $user_notes header to format the names.

FIGURE 17.10

A Design Table prepared to be placed on a drawing

	Pipe Thickness	Length	Flange Thickness	Inside Diameter	Flange Diameter	Bolt Circle Diameter	Hole Diameter
Size1	0.25	3	0.275	0.8	3.6	2.7	0.25
Size2	0.25	3.5	0.275	0.9	3.7	2.8	0.25
Size3	0.25	4	0.275	1	3.8	2.9	0.25
Size4	0.3	4	0.3	1.1	3.9	3	0.25
Size5	0.3	4.5	0.3	1.2	4	3.1	0.25
Size6	0.3	5	0.3	1.2	4.1	3.2	0.25
Size7	0.35	5	0.35	1.3	4.1	3.2	0.38
Size8	0.35	5.5	0.35	1.4	4.2	3.3	0.38
Size9	0.35	6	0.35	1.5	4.3	3.4	0.38

Worksheet in Chapter 24 - DT Part.SLDPRT

	A	B	C	D	E	F	G	H	I	J
1	Design Table for: Chapter 24 - DT Part									
2		$user_notes	PipeThickness@Sketch1	Length@Sketch1	FlangeThickness@Sketch1	ID@Sketch1	FlangeDia@Sketch1	BoltCircle@Sketch2	HoleDia@Sketch2	
3	$user_notes		Pipe Thickness	Length	Flange Thickness	Inside Diameter	Flange Diameter	Bolt Circle Diameter	Hole Diameter	
4	Size1	Size1	0.25	3	0.275	0.8	3.6	2.7	0.25	
5	Size2	Size2	0.25	3.5	0.275	0.9	3.7	2.8	0.25	
6	Size3	Size3	0.25	4	0.275	1	3.8	2.9	0.25	
7	Size4	Size4	0.3	4	0.3	1.1	3.9	3	0.25	
8	Size5	Size5	0.3	4.5	0.3	1.2	4	3.1	0.25	
9	Size6	Size6	0.3	5	0.3	1.2	4.1	3.2	0.25	
10	Size7	Size7	0.35	5	0.35	1.3	4.1	3.2	0.38	
11	Size8	Size8	0.35	5.5	0.35	1.4	4.2	3.3	0.38	
12	Size9	Size9	0.35	6	0.35	1.5	4.3	3.4	0.38	
13										
14										
15										
16										
17										

Figure 17.11 shows the drawing with the table inserted. To display the table properly, you have to edit the table in the window of the parent document and adjust the border of the table to be exactly how you want it to appear on the drawing. The adjusted table is shown in Figure 17.11.

A drawing with the Design Table inserted

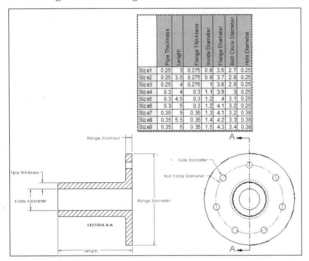

The labeled dimensions are created by simply making reference dimensions and overwriting the <DIM> value in the Dimension Text panel of the Dimension PropertyManager. If you would like to examine this data more closely, the drawing and part are included on the DVD. The drawing is named DT.slddrw.

This drawing uses a part Design Table, but you can also place assembly Design Tables onto the drawing. This is often called a *tabulated* drawing.

If you need to place something on your drawing such as a Design Table, but it does not appear that the Design Table is going to meet your needs, you can simply copy the data out of the Design Table and re-create it in a static Excel spreadsheet. The Design Table that you place on the drawing updates if it is changed in the part or assembly, just like the drawing geometry, but you must manually update an Excel spreadsheet that is created from copied data. Keep in mind that you must decide whether the automatic functions are worth the time you invest in setting them up. In many cases they are, but in other cases they require more work than they save.

Placing Hole Tables on Drawings

 You can place Hole Tables on drawings to include information such as the size, position, and number of holes or slots of a given size on a drawing. Only circular holes and through slots are recognized. You do not have to use the Hole Wizard or simple hole features to make the holes. The Hole Table does not recognize counterbored slots or even slots with a chamfer edgebreak. The position is given relative to a selected reference position, and the holes are labeled. You should not use a Hole Table for slots unless you first test to make sure that you are getting correct data.

Like other table types, Hole Tables can use templates. As with other templates, you should store Hole Table templates in a library area outside of your local SolidWorks installation folder. You can then direct SolidWorks to this location by choosing Tools ➪ Options ➪ File Locations and specifying the path settings.

Hole Tables use anchors in exactly the same way as BOMs. For more information, see the section on table anchors earlier in this chapter.

You can find the options for Hole Tables by choosing Tools ➪ Options ➪ Document Properties ➪ Drafting Standard ➪ Tables ➪ Hole.

Figure 17.12 shows the PropertyManager for a Hole Table. The left image shows the PropertyManager that appears when you create the table, and the right image shows the one that appears when you edit the table. Figure 17.13 shows the resulting Hole Table on a drawing with a part that contains holes. The table incorporates holes from multiple views, using a different zero reference for each view.

To initiate the Hole Table function, you must first select a view. You can access the Hole Table function by choosing Insert ➪ Table ➪ Hole Table.

To specify the datum, either select an edge in each direction to serve as the zero mark for the X and Y directions or select a vertex or point to serve as the Origin in both directions.

To select the holes to be included in the table, activate the selection box in the Holes panel, and either select the hole edges directly or select the faces on which the holes are located. Once you place the table, you can add holes or change the datum information. To do this, right-click the Hole Table entry in the Drawing FeatureManager, and select Edit Feature. You can resize columns and rows in the same way as for BOM tables.

FIGURE 17.12

The PropertyManager for the Hole Table

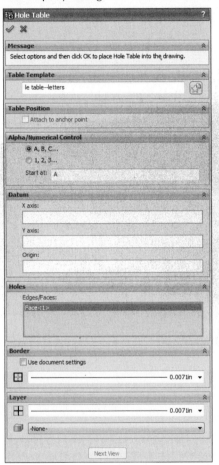

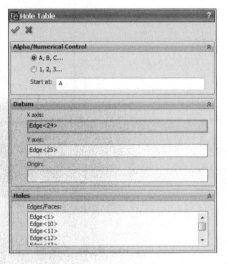

In the table in Figure 17.13, the Combine Same Sizes option is used, which causes several of the cells in the table to merge. If you use the Combine Same Tags option, then the hole locations are not displayed — only the hole callout description and the quantity appear. Figure 17.14 shows this arrangement.

FIGURE 17.13

A Hole Table combining holes in different views

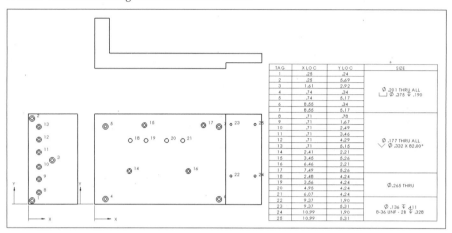

FIGURE 17.14

The Combine Same Tags option used with a Hole Table that includes a slot

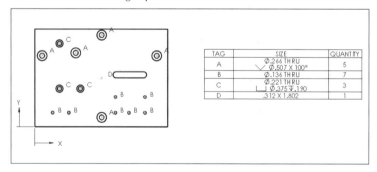

You can control the hole callout description used in Figure 17.14 by using the file named `calloutformat.txt`, which is found in the `lang\english` subdirectory of the SolidWorks installation directory. Again, if you customize this file, then you should keep it in a library external to the installation directory and list it in the Tools ⇨ Options ⇨ File Locations area. This text file enables you to define how hole callouts are specified for different types of holes.

Using Revision Tables

 You can use Revision Tables in SolidWorks in conjunction with SolidWorks Workgroup PDM, but this integration goes beyond the scope of this book. The Revision Table uses a table

anchor in exactly the same way as the BOM table. Revision Tables also use templates in the same way as the other table types, and you should move customized templates to a library location and specify the location in Tools ➪ Options ➪ File Locations.

Figure 17.15 shows the Revision Table PropertyManager interface where you can create and control the settings for the table. You can find the default settings for Revision Tables by choosing Tools ➪ Options ➪ Document Properties ➪ Drafting Standard ➪ Tables ➪ Revision.

The Revision Table PropertyManager interface

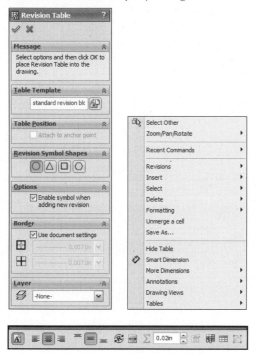

The upper-left image in Figure 17.15 is the PropertyManager interface that appears when you initially create the Revision Table. The upper-right image is the RMB menu for the Revision Table, and the bottom image shows the formatting toolbar that displays when you select the Revision Table.

You can initiate the Revision Table function through the menus or the Tables toolbar. However, this function simply creates the table; it does not populate it. You must set the table anchor in the drawing format in order for the Table Anchor to work. You can add or format additional columns to accept other data. Once you have created the columns or formatting, you can save the changes to a template, which is also available through the RMB menu.

You can add a revision to the table by right-clicking the table and choosing Revisions ⇨ Add Revision. This includes control over whether the revision uses numerical or alphabetical revision levels, but does not provide for more complex revisioning schemes.

Immediately after you have created the revision, if the option is enabled, you are prompted to place a balloon that contains the revision level to identify what has been changed. To finish placing symbols, you can press Esc. When you are finished placing the balloons, you can fill in the description of the revision by double-clicking in the Description cell where you want to add text. Figure 17.16 shows a Revision Table with balloon symbols placed on the drawing.

FIGURE 17.16

A Revision Table with balloon symbols

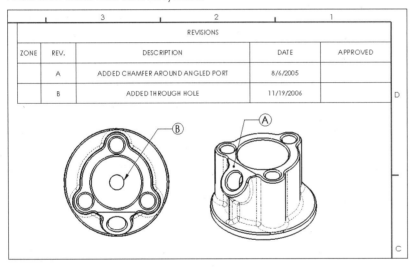

Revision Tables work by creating a Revision custom property in the drawing document, and by incrementing this revision each time a revision is added to the table. You can add more columns linked to custom properties to Revision Tables and Revision Table templates.

Cross-Reference

Gauge Tables and Bend Tables are specific to sheet metal parts and are covered in detail in Chapter 21. Weldment Cut Lists are a special type of table that closely resembles a BOM table in many ways. These are discussed in Chapter 20, which covers weldments. ■

Using General Tables

You can use General Tables for any type of tabulated data. Column headers can be filled with either text labels or custom property links. You can also use regular Excel OLE objects for the same purpose, and depending on the application, you may prefer to use them.

The General Table uses the filename extension *.sldtbt. You can create it without a template, as a simple block of four empty cells, or you can use a template that has a set of pre-created headers.

Working with Tables in Models

Proponents of solid modeling have been saying for years that 2D drawings are going to disappear. However, not everyone is convinced. Paper drawings will continue to be useful until all old manufacturing methods are abandoned, and this probably won't happen in your lifetime.

However, because some companies rely less on 2D and paper drawings, the industry is developing new ways to create 2D type documentation inside a 3D document. The ANSI Y14.41 standard deals primarily with this transition.

SolidWorks is responding to this type of requirement by adding features that enable you to document the 3D data. Placing BOMs in assembly files is one way of doing this. Placing 2D type data into 3D model documents can reduce the need for paper or even electronic 2D documentation. Figure 17.17 shows a BOM inside an assembly model document.

FIGURE 17.17

Displaying BOM data inside an assembly document

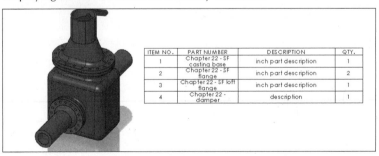

It can be difficult to match the relative scale of the table to the model. To do this, you have to adjust the zoom state of the model until it is fairly small within the screen, and then place the table. After you place the table, the assembly and the table zoom together. Most users avoid this issue by viewing the table in a separate window. Alternately you can use the BOM Scaling box in the Bill of Materials PropertyManager that enables you to scale the BOM without using the previous method, although the previous method still works.

Another type of table that you can use within a 3D model document is the Title Block table, which can be used inside parts and assemblies. You can use Title Block tables in the drawing to fill in information about the part or assembly and at the same time avoid creating a full 2D drawing.

Tutorial: Using BOMs

Rather than having tutorials for every table type, this chapter has tutorials only for the BOM, Hole Table, and Revision Table. You can transfer the skills you use with these types to the other types.

This tutorial guides you through the steps that are necessary to prepare an assembly for the drawing and BOM. Configurations and custom properties are used in this example. Remember that if a drawing view is cross-hatched and you cannot see the geometry, then you may have to press Ctrl+Q to rebuild it. Follow these steps:

1. **Begin this tutorial with SolidWorks closed and Windows Explorer open.**

2. **If you have not already done so, create a folder for a library that is not in your SolidWorks installation folder.** Call it D:\Library\ or something similar. Make a folder inside this folder called Drawing Templates. Copy the files from the DVD named inch B.drwdot and inch B (no views).drwdot to this new folder.

3. **Launch SolidWorks and choose Tools ⇨ Options ⇨ File Locations ⇨ Document Template.** Click the Add button and add the new library path to the list. Shut down SolidWorks and restart it.

4. **Open the assembly** BOM Assy.sldasm **from the DVD.**

5. **Click the Make Drawing From Part/Assembly button, and make a new drawing of the assembly from the drawing template in the folder created in Steps 2 and 3.**

6. **Delete the isometric view, and in its place make a new drawing view using the model view labeled "exploded."** If prompted to use true dimensions in an isometric view, click Accept.

7. **Edit the sheet format.** Right-click the sketch point at the location indicated in Figure 17.18. In the popup menu that appears, select Set as Anchor and then select Bill of Materials.

FIGURE 17.18

Setting the Table Anchor

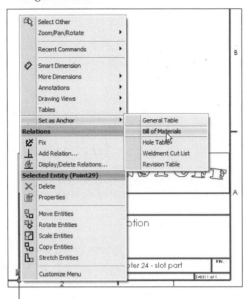

RMB on this point

8. **Exit Edit Sheet Format mode by selecting Edit Sheet from the RMB menu.**

9. **Select the new view and show it in the exploded state (right-click and select Properties ⇨ Show in Exploded State).** Then choose Insert ⇨ Table ⇨ Bill of Materials or click the Bill of Materials button in the Tables toolbar. Use the default selections, except in the panels shown in Figure 17.19.

10. **Click inside the exploded view, but not on any part geometry, and then select the Autoballoon tool from the Annotations toolbar.** Toggle through the available options to see whether any of the possible autoballoon configurations meet your needs. If not, use the standard Balloon tool to select the part and place the balloon. This gives you more control over the attachment points and placement of the balloons.

11. **Change the balloon for the short pin to be a circular split-line balloon (do this by clicking the balloon and then switching the style in the PropertyManager).** Notice that the quantity appears in the bottom of the balloon. The drawing view and the BOM should now look like Figure 17.20.

    Add a second leader to the balloon for the short pin by Ctrl+dragging the attachment point for the first leader from one pin to the other.

FIGURE 17.19

Creating the Bill of Materials

ITEM NO.	PART NUMBER	DESCRIPTION	Angle 1/QTY.	Angle 2/QTY.
1	Chapter 24 - Bracket	description	1	-
2	Chapter 24 - Pin Block	description	1	1
3	Clevis Male	description	1	1
4	Long	Long Pin	1	1
5	Clevis Female	description	1	1
6	Short	Short Pin	2	2
7	Chapter 24 - Bracket	description	-	1

FIGURE 17.20

The drawing view and the BOM after Step 11

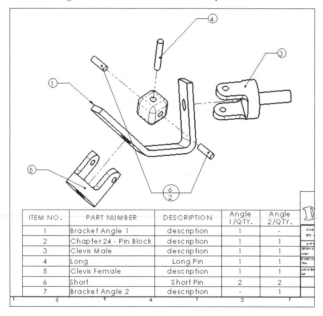

ITEM NO.	PART NUMBER	DESCRIPTION	Angle 1/QTY.	Angle 2/QTY.
1	Bracket Angle 1	description	1	-
2	Chapter 24 - Pin Block	description	1	1
3	Clevis Male	description	1	1
4	Long	Long Pin	1	1
5	Clevis Female	description	1	1
6	Short	Short Pin	2	2
7	Bracket Angle 2	description	-	1

12. **Notice that several of the parts use a default description of "description."** Edit each of these parts by right-clicking the part's row in the BOM table and selecting Open *<filename>* from the menu. Change the Description custom property in each part. Keep in mind that this may be handled differently for configured parts.

13. **The Bracket part is listed twice using the configuration name because of the way the configurations are set up for the parts.** To list the bracket only once using the filename, open the bracket, right-click one of the configuration names in the ConfigurationManager, and select Properties. In the Bill of Materials Options panel, select Document Name from the drop-down list. Do this for the other configuration, as well.

    Notice also that the Description field holds the configuration-specific custom property for Description, which is used in the BOM.

14. **Toggle back to the drawing (press Ctrl+Tab), select anywhere on the BOM table, and then select Table Properties from the PropertyManager.** Expand the Part Configuration Grouping panel, and select the Display all configurations of the same part as one item option. This changes how the bracket displays, as well as the pins.

15. **Now add a column to the BOM that calls on an existing custom property that is already in all the parts.** Place the cursor over the last column on the right and right-click it. Choose Insert ➪ Column Right. This places a new column to the right of the last one and displays a popup menu that enables you to set the column to be driven by a custom property, as shown in Figure 17.21.

16. **In the first drop-down selection box, select the Weight custom property.** Click the green check mark icon to accept the changes. If the popup menu disappears and you need to get it back, double-click the column header to re-display it.

FIGURE 17.21

Adding a column to the BOM

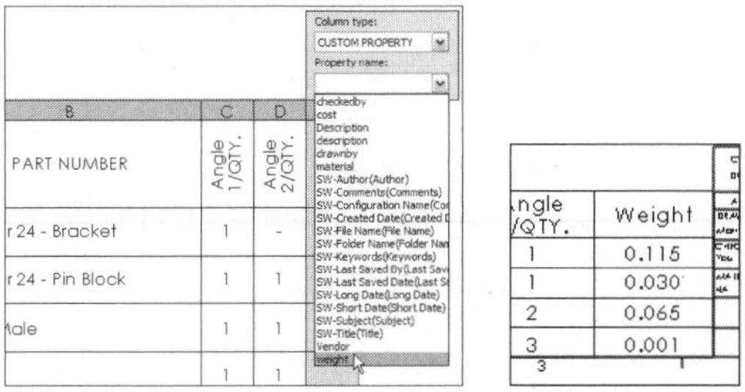

17. **You can save the BOM with the additional column as a BOM template by right-clicking anywhere in the BOM and selecting Save As.** You can then set the type to a BOM template and the directory to the library location for BOM templates.

If you would like to compare your results against those in this example, the finished drawing is called BOM Tutorial Finished.slddrw.

Tutorial: Using Hole Tables

This tutorial guides you through creating and changing settings that are common in SolidWorks Hole Tables. Follow these steps:

1. **Create a new drawing from the** inch B (no views).drwdot **template.** If you have not created the BOM tutorial, then move the drawing template named inchB.drwdot from the materials on the DVD to your library location for drawing templates. Then create the drawing from the template.

2. **Click the Model View button on the Drawings toolbar, and browse to the part named** Hole Table Part.sldprt.

3. **Place a Front view and project a Left view and an isometric view.** Then press Esc to quit the command. Finally, delete the four pre-defined views.

4. **There is not an anchor in this template for a Hole Table, and so if you would like to create one, do this now.** Follow the steps in the BOM tutorial for specifying the anchor point.

5. **Click the Hole Table button in the Tables toolbar.** Figure 17.22 shows a section of the Hole Table PropertyManager with the selections that you need to make for this Hole Table.

6. **Once you have completed the selections, click the Next View button at the bottom of the PropertyManager, and make similar selections in the Left view.** The holes for both views are added to a single Hole Table.

   The table is created using the default settings established in Tools ⇨ Options ⇨ Document Properties ⇨ Tables, but you can change them here for this specific table.

7. **Click anywhere in the table, and then select Table Properties at the bottom of the PropertyManager.** Changing from numerical to alphabetical assigns a letter to each hole type and a number to each instance of the type. Make this change and update the table. Figure 17.23 shows the table before and after the changes.

8. **Change the number of decimal places used in the Hole Table from two places to three.** You can do this in the PropertyManager.

9. **Deselect the Hide Hole Centers option in the Visibility panel.**

FIGURE 17.22

The Hole Table PropertyManager and selections

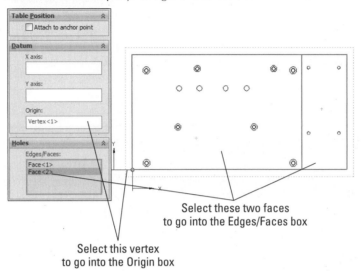

Select these two faces
to go into the Edges/Faces box

Select this vertex
to go into the Origin box

FIGURE 17.23

Using numerical and alphabetical hole tag identification

TAG	X LOC	Y LOC	SIZE
1	.25	.24	
2	.25	5.69	
3	1.61	2.92	Ø .201 THRU ALL
4	.74	.34	⌴ Ø .375 ▼ .190
5	.74	5.17	
6	8.55	.34	
7	8.55	5.17	
8	.71	.78	
9	.71	1.67	
10	.71	2.49	
11	.71	3.46	
12	.71	4.29	Ø .177 THRU ALL
13	.71	5.15	⌵ Ø .332 X 82.00°
14	2.41	2.21	
15	3.45	5.26	
16	6.46	2.21	
17	7.49	5.26	
18	2.48	4.24	
19	3.56	4.24	Ø.265 THRU
20	4.95	4.24	
21	6.07	4.24	
22	9.37	1.90	
23	9.37	5.31	Ø .136 ▼ .411
24	10.99	1.90	8-36 UNF - 2B ▼ .328
25	10.99	5.31	

TAG	X LOC	Y LOC	SIZE
A1	.25	.24	
A2	.25	5.69	
A3	1.61	2.92	Ø .201 THRU ALL
A4	.74	.34	⌴ Ø .375 ▼ .190
A5	.74	5.17	
A6	8.55	.34	
A7	8.55	5.17	
B1	.71	.78	
B2	.71	1.67	
B3	.71	2.49	
B4	.71	3.46	
B5	.71	4.29	Ø .177 THRU ALL
B6	.71	5.15	⌵ Ø .332 X 82.00°
B7	2.41	2.21	
B8	3.45	5.26	
B9	6.46	2.21	
B10	7.49	5.26	
C1	2.48	4.24	
C2	3.56	4.24	Ø.265 THRU
C3	4.95	4.24	
C4	6.07	4.24	
D1	9.37	1.90	
D2	9.37	5.31	Ø .136 ▼ .411
D3	10.99	1.90	8-36 UNF - 2B ▼ .328
D4	10.99	5.31	

10. **Select the Combine same sizes option in the PropertyManager.**

11. **Save the drawing.**

Tutorial: Using Revision Tables

In this tutorial, you create a basic Revision Table and make a template. Follow these steps:

1. **Using a drawing that you completed in one of the previous tutorials, make sure that a Revision Table Anchor has been placed in the upper-right corner of the Sheet Format.** You must edit the Sheet Format to do this, by right-clicking the point that you want to use for the anchor. Remember to select Edit Sheet from the RMB menu to exit Edit Sheet Format mode.

Note

Ideally, the anchors for all table types should be set in templates and formats, but it is set up here to give you some practice creating the anchors. ∎

2. **Click the Revision Table button on the Tables toolbar.** Select the Attach to Anchor option in the PropertyManager. Click the green check mark icon to accept the table. Figure 17.24 shows the initial stub of the Revision Table.

FIGURE 17.24

The initial stub of the Revision Table

Tip

You can save drawing templates with the Revision Table stub if it also has a format. The Revision Table is not saved with the format because it has to go on the drawing sheet. ∎

3. **To initiate a new revision level in the Revision Table, right-click the table and choose Revisions ⇨ Add Revision.**

    Depending on the default settings in Tools ⇨ Options ⇨ Document Properties ⇨ Drafting Standard ⇨ Tables ⇨ Revision, the first revision will be either A or 1. If you are using PDMWorks Workgroup, then you may have other options.

    Depending on your options settings, you may immediately be prompted to place a balloon that contains the new revision level. You can place balloons with or without leaders. The balloons are meant to indicate areas of the drawing that are affected by the revision. Press Esc when you are finished placing the balloons.

Note

Be careful when using balloons on assembly drawings or other drawings that already have balloons on them for other purposes. It may be a good idea to use a distinctively shaped balloon for Revision Tables. ∎

4. **To add text to the Description field, simply click in the field and start typing.** The text automatically wraps to fit the box.

5. **Practice by adding a couple of revisions, balloons, and descriptions.**

6. **After you have added a couple of revisions, check the custom properties by choosing File ⇨ Properties ⇨ Custom.** Notice that a revision property has been added, and the latest revision is represented by the value of the custom property.

Note

The number of revisions kept in the Revision Table is no longer an option as it was in previous releases, but in its place you can now control how Revision Tables interact with multiple sheets. ∎

7. **Add columns in the same way that you added them to the BOM.** You can merge and unmerge cells, and link properties to cells. With the cursor over the last column (Approved), right-click and choose Insert ⇨ Column Left. In the Column Properties, select Custom, and from the Properties drop-down menu, select DrawnBy. Accept the changes by clicking the green check mark icon.

8. **Save the template by right-clicking anywhere in the Revision Table and choosing Save As ⇨ Rev Table Templates.** Then save the template to the appropriate location outside the SolidWorks installation directory.

Summary

SolidWorks enables you to work with both tables that are highly specialized for particular uses, and General Tables that are available for any type of tabulated data. The most frequently used types are BOMs, Hole Tables, and Revision Tables. Design Tables that drive part and assembly configurations can also be placed on a 2D drawing, but in these cases, some formatting is usually necessary to make these tables presentable and the information on it easy to read.

Part V

Using Specialized or Advanced Techniques

Using DriveWorks Xpress

DriveWorks Xpress — DWX for short — is rules-based design automation software that is aimed at engineered-to-order businesses. The version you find in SolidWorks 2011 is free and available with all levels of SolidWorks. It enables you to drive the creation of variations of parts, assemblies, and drawings based on rules attached to a simple form that you fill out. SolidWorks 2011 contains a new version of DWX, where the interface resides mainly in the Task Pane.

The basic workflow with DWX is as follows:

1. Understand the various factors that drive the design of a product.

2. Reduce the factors and the potential values to a form with questions requiring responses selected from a list, or that are numerical.

3. Create a model parametrically driven by dimensions linked to the form.

4. Make sure that assemblies, parts, and drawings all update properly in response to data from the form.

5. Run the project, fill out the form, and watch the assembly, parts, and drawings update.

The results of using DWX are very familiar – the ability to make many versions of an assembly. When you first use DWX, it just looks like a nice interface on a design table. While these do describe some of what DWX does, they don't describe all of it. DWX does not work by using configurations. Every time you run a DWX job, it makes new copies of the original files and follows the rules you establish during setup. This method offers several advantages. Primarily, you never have to worry about separate projects being tied up together like different configurations in the same assembly do. You save them out with unique filenames, and the projects are not connected at all. Doing this with configurations would be difficult and problematic. You could certainly do it manually by copying assemblies, parts, and drawings, but with DWX it happens automatically.

Introducing DriveWorks Xpress

You access DWX from the Tools menu in SolidWorks. It is not an add-in, and it is available in all versions of SolidWorks. Figure 18.1 shows the initial Task Pane interface.

Getting started with DriveWorks Xpress

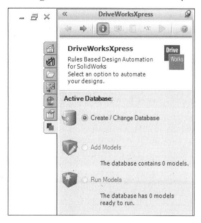

If you are new to rules-based or knowledge-based engineering tools in general, DWX offers you an easy and out-of-the-box method to automate repetitive design work. If you are already familiar with one of DWX's big brothers, DriveWorks or DriveWorks Solo, you may notice that the Xpress version lacks certain functionality of the paid versions, such as advanced file management, non-SolidWorks-based interfaces, web configurator, Product Data Management integration, administrator interface, and so on. SolidWorks users do use the Xpress version for real production work. You should try it, and if you need to use the more advanced features, you can always upgrade.

Exploring DriveWorks Xpress for your products

If your place of business produces built-to-order products and you are not using a rules-based configurator tool like DWX, then you may be missing design automation savings.

Many products can benefit from DWX. If you think of any type of product that can have unlimited variations due to size or replaceable parts, then you can probably automate the design of that product. For example, think of windows that you might buy for your home. Windows can be built to order and are made from many smaller parts that must be cut to different sizes, which change from order to order. Design automation collects information about the new design from the user, and then automatically creates the changes from a default model. Figure 18.2 shows a window that might be ordered in this way.

FIGURE 18.2

Windows can be built to order by using the process that DWX implements.

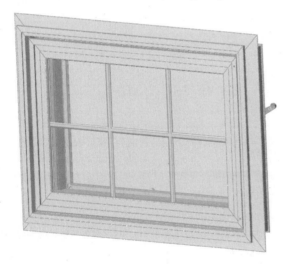

If you visit the DriveWorks Xpress website (www.driveworksxpress.com), you will find several live examples of automated assemblies that demonstrate the capabilities of DWX, including a window. This chapter will use a ceiling fan to demonstrate the capabilities of DWX.

DriveWorks Xpress is produced by DriveWorks Software, which is based in the United Kingdom. DriveWorks Software also produces and sells DriveWorks Solo and DriveWorks Pro. Because the Xpress version of their product is free, it is included with every copy of SolidWorks and is a very valuable tool. It is discussed here so that you will get the most out of your investment in SolidWorks.

How do you know if your models need DriveWorks Xpress? If a SolidWorks model and a questionnaire that has multiple-choice or numerical answers can describe your product line and you build a large number of different configurations of the same basic design, then your product is a great candidate for rules-based design automation. (The word *configurations* is used here in its generic sense, meaning an arrangement of details, rather than the specific meaning of SolidWorks configurations. Rules-based design automation software is sometimes called a *configurator.*)

Examples of products that could benefit from rules-based design are

- **Automobiles.** One model with many options.
- **Windows.** Same construction, many sizes.
- **Pre-fabricated buildings.** One layout, established options, or sizes.
- **Pneumatic or hydraulic power cylinders.** Same construction, many sizes.
- **Cranes and gantries.** Definable options, scalable engineering.
- **Storage racks.** Numbers-driven design.
- **Conveyors.** Same basic design from customer to customer, resized overall with custom components.

Aligning expectations with some estimates

What kind of output can you realistically expect from a program such as DriveWorks Xpress? It really depends on the volume of design that you can automate, and how often your models change or update. You have to do some basic business calculation and some good old-fashioned work estimation to get an idea of how much you can save by automating your design process.

The first step is to estimate how much time it will take you to automate your design. This is the initial investment of setup that you need to do. You will probably be able to start from the models that you already have. Like regular modeling in SolidWorks, modeling for DWX automation also has some "best practice" type suggestions that you should try to follow.

For example, measure how much time it currently takes you to copy a design and make a new set of models. Think of all the input that you need to accomplish that task. Can you build a form that captures that information? Can you now relate the input values to specific model dimensions, or sets of dimensions?

As an initial estimate, it may take you about four times as long to automate a model as it would to do the changes the "old" way (manually editing all the parts). Running an automated job does take time, when you include checking the results and cleaning up the drawing (dimension and annotation placement). You may also need to create some components manually — components that weren't accounted for in the automation, perhaps.

Therefore, as an example, you might find that you can run and check a DWX job in one-tenth the time it takes to do the work the "old" way. Therefore, in four jobs, you start breaking even on the investment you made in automating the design. If a single job takes a week using the "old" method, then automating it might take a month, but you can now do a month's worth of work in about two days.

Of course, these are all rough theoretical estimates, and they will certainly vary greatly with the size of the automation project, and the detail involved, but it works as an approximate estimate for you to get a feel for the size of the time that you will invest and save.

Building the Original Model

When building a model to automate with DriveWorks Xpress, users often find they must "unlearn" some of the modeling methods that they normally use for propagating changes through a regular SolidWorks assembly. For example, in regular SolidWorks modeling, you might want each part to be driven by a layout sketch or other parts when necessary. You might choose configurations to save versions of parts or drawings. However, with DWX, you drive changes to models with the form field data, after the model is built. For this reason, SolidWorks users often have to back away from the urge to drive features parametrically between parts, and instead allow DWX to drive the changes. This makes modeling much more straightforward.

You should still use the relationships between features within a part to keep the normal relationships within the part, but any option that you want to be driven by the form input fields should be left independent.

So in short, when building a model to be automated by DWX, you can design each part independently; don't use the layout methods, master model, or in-context design techniques. All of the parametrics are handled by the DWX rules.

Note
Just because it is recommended to drive changes from the form field inputs doesn't mean that you cannot use in-context and other external reference types of relations to drive changes in your models. Driving all changes from the same location is the simplest and most straightforward method, but you certainly can mix methods if you need to. For example, you might drive changes to one part through the DWX form field inputs, but then allow those changes to propagate to other parts through in-context relations. In the end, you are the one maintaining the model, so you make the decisions about how it is constructed. ∎

Automating an Example

The best way to learn what automating a design is about is to walk through an example. The example will also help you understand the overall workflow for these tools. In this example, the first step is to identify what types of variables will change between designs, and compare that against the list of things that DWX allows to be changed. Then we build a form, and finally attach the fields on the form to actual variables in the SolidWorks documents.

Now you will move on to a more concrete example where you will take an existing design of a ceiling fan and use DWX to automate the design to create hundreds of configuration possibilities. The initial fan model is shown in Figure 18.3.

FIGURE 18.3

Starting from a basic ceiling fan design

In this case, the variables in the design will be as follows:

- Number of blades, 1 to 6
- Length of blades, 30" to 36"
- Light, yes or no
- Shape of motor housing, A or B
- Flush mount or hanging

You need to match up what you have to change with what DWX enables you to change. DWX can control the following within SolidWorks parts:

- Suppress and unsuppress parts, components, and features
- Control dimensions
- Delete parts
- Rename parts
- Change configurations
- Add or change custom properties
- Create comparative rules with operators such as if, then, else, greater than, and less than

Getting Started: Automating a Design

To start automating the ceiling fan, take the list of items that will vary. Then, for each change, list the items that will be affected, and specifically what will have to change.

For example, the first item on the list is the number of blades (1 to 6). A one-bladed ceiling fan seems odd, but it does exist. Here is a list of what has to change to accommodate the changes in blades:

- For a one-bladed design, the pattern of blades, traditional blade, and blade holder are all suppressed, and replaced by the monoblade, still mounted to the blade mount ring.
- The monoblade also requires a different motor and motor housing, to accommodate the higher speed and more modern style.
- For all other blade number changes, only the number of instances of the component pattern change. The ring is pre-drilled to handle all patterns.

Activating DriveWorks Xpress

The DriveWorks Xpress interface is found in the SolidWorks Task Pane, on the right-hand side of the graphics window, but it will only show up when you activate it. DWX is not active until you load it. This makes sure that when you don't need it, it is not in your way. Once activated, all of the necessary tools become available.

Continuing with the ceiling fan example, the next step is to make these changes happen within DriveWorks Xpress. You can activate DWX by selecting it in the Tools menu. When the Task Pane interface displays, use the Push Pin feature to lock it open. Figure 18.4 shows the DWX Task Pane interface.

Initiating a new database for your DWX design automation

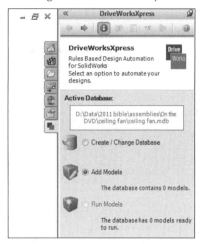

Creating a database

The secret to DWX's capabilities lies in the use of a database. The database enables DWX to access different kinds of data, which it stores in the database. The data can be directly related to dimensions or other variables from the model, or they can be derived values, such as aspect ratio, or power per pound. In short, the database is simply a place to organize all of the information about the model.

When you start to automate a new design, the Create/Change Database option is selected in the DWX Task Pane. The Active Database field may have a database listed. To select a different database, click the blue right arrow at the top of the DWX Task Pane interface, and browse for an existing file, or name a new one.

The next step is to add models to the database. Any parts or assembly that you want to be controlled by DWX need to be in the database. To add files, click the blue right arrow at the top of the interface again. Figure 18.5 shows the next interface.

In this case, you want to add the ceiling fan model that you already have open, but you could also browse for a different model. Select the method you want for which models to add, and click the blue right arrow again.

Adding models to the new database

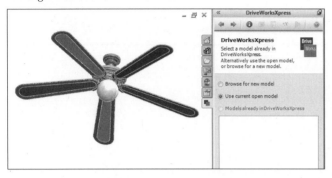

Capturing models

To get the information in the database organized properly, one of the things that DWX needs to do is to identify the various parts that are involved in the automation. These can be parts that will serve as a source for data or as a target for changing variables. Any SolidWorks document that is referenced by the assembly needs to be captured. The main reason for this is that all the parts in the assembly need to be copied and renamed. In order to do that, you have to write a rule to rename the file, and in order to do that, the file must be listed in the database. Capturing is quick and easy, and you have to do it.

The interface shows the captured model as the ceiling fan assembly. You need each of the individual parts to be captured. Therefore, click the blue Next arrow when you have the Captured Assembly Structure tab activated at the bottom of the interface, as shown in Figure 18.6. You need to click each part individually to allow it to be captured by the DWX database.

FIGURE 18.6

Capturing the models used in the database

Adding features and dimensions

The next step is to start adding features and dimensions that the automation will drive, and you do this by adding specific features and dimensions to the DWX database. DWX doesn't need to know about all of the parametrics or dimensions in the model, it only needs to know about the ones that it will use as inputs or that it will calculate as outputs. Identifying specifically what values you want to change is why you made a specific list earlier for the items that the first goal (number of blades) will change. To do this, click the Dimensions and Features button at the bottom of the interface, and in the graphics window or FeatureManager, find the feature or dimension you want to add. DWX requires that you add a custom name to the feature or dimension.

After you name the feature and click the Add button below the Dimensions and Features list, as shown in Figure 18.7, DWX records the custom name in the list.

FIGURE 18.7

Adding dimensions and features to the list of controlled items

Creating fields for the form

DWX essentially helps you distill your design down to some specific well-defined decisions. These decisions are presented to the user in a form, which you need to fill out with numerical values or with options from a list in most cases. Each decision is driven by a field on the form. The field is where you put your answer.

Once you have captured the dimensions and features that need to be controlled, it is time to create the form for filling in the information. The screen capture in Figure 18.8 shows how you start setting up the form. Begin by typing a name in the first input field, such as Number of Blades. Next, select what kind of input the first item will be, such as a drop-down list to select the number of blades. Because not all combinations are stylistically acceptable, this design does not allow all numbers of blades between 1 and 6. It does allow 1, 3, 5, and 6 blades.

FIGURE 18.8

Setting up the first field on the form

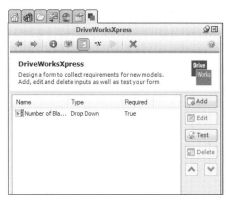

When you have added the first field to the form, DWX adds it to the list, and you can then test it, add another field, edit, or delete the field.

Building rules

Rules in DWX are conditional statements used to calculate output values based on the input values from the form. These rules resemble programming to some extent. For example, a rule for a variable called BladePattern might look like this:

```
= IF (NumberOfBlades = 1, Suppress, Unsuppress)
```

In English, this reads: If the variable NumberOfBlades is equal to 1, then suppress the feature called BladePattern. If the NumberOfBlades is not equal to 1, then unsuppress the pattern.

Click the blue right arrow to advance to the Rules interface, which is shown in Figure 18.9. Notice that it tells you that rules are missing for filenames. DWX renames the files for each job you do, according to a set of rules. You will return to this later. For now, you will work on the feature and dimension.

FIGURE 18.9

The Rules interface and editing rules

To create a new rule for the feature (BladePattern), make sure the Features row has a check mark in the far-right column, and click the blue arrow. In Figure 18.10, two rules have already been created. If the Show Missing Rules Only option is checked, you do not see existing rules, only items that do not yet have a rule assigned.

FIGURE 18.10

Building logical statements

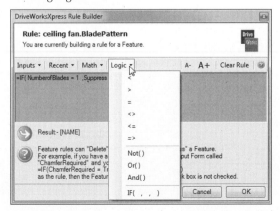

Building a rule to suppress a component pattern

To build the rule, use logic and math statements, along with the input values given. For example, in the case of the BladePattern, if the number of blades is equal to 1, then the pattern should be suppressed. For any other value, the BladePattern should be unsuppressed. Therefore, in logic, you want to build the following rule statement:

```
IF(NumberofBlades = 1, Suppress, Unsuppress)
```

The first condition (Suppress) tells DWX what to do if the equation (NumberofBlades = 1) is true, and the second condition (Unsuppress) tells it what to do if the equation is false.

The Inputs, Recent, Math, and Logic drop-down lists allow you to select the items that are available for whatever you are doing at the moment. The statements are easy to create, and can include more elaborate schemes such as nested IF loops (an IF statement executes as a true or false condition).

Note

If the rule box turns pink, it is telling you that there is a problem with the rule. If DWX sees a problem with a rule, the default value for text rules is [VALUE]. ∎

Building a rule to change filenames

For each job that you run, DWX saves out a set of files that are independent copies of the originals, with new names. A necessary part of automating a model is establishing rules for filenames. The output of the rule is a text string that will be added to the end of the existing filename. DWX cannot apply a prefix to a filename, only a suffix.

With this in mind, for this project, a field is established on the form that asks the user for a project name, and then DWX uses a rule to append the project name to the end of the filenames to ensure unique filenames for all files.

Figure 18.11 shows the rule list and the Rule Builder for building filenames. In this case, you can just copy the syntax of the rule from one part to the rest of the parts in the assembly.

Using custom properties with DWX rules

Up to now, this chapter discusses automating geometrical changes to the models, driven by selections on an electronic form. DWX also enables you to take advantage of changing custom properties with rules. Of course, you can then use custom properties to automatically fill out fields on the drawing, in tables, add properties to annotations on the drawing, and other uses.

Automating changes to the custom properties starts with capturing the properties in the DWX interface. In the Capture step, click the Custom Properties button at the bottom of the interface. DWX calls up all of the custom properties in the documents. You place a check mark next to the ones you want to capture and automate. Figure 18.12 shows this step.

FIGURE 18.11

Building rules for filenames

After the custom properties have been captured, they show up in the rules summary as missing rules. Place a check mark in the Edit column (shown in Figure 18.12) and click the blue right arrow.

This only captures the custom properties for the current document. To capture the properties of the assembly, you must have the assembly active. You must go through all the parts in the assembly to capture properties for individual parts.

FIGURE 18.12

Capturing custom properties

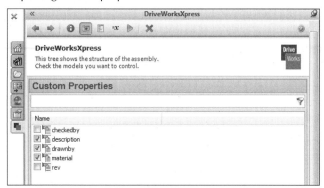

Building a rule for custom properties

The list of inputs for custom properties rules are the outputs from every field on the form. You can use these inputs to create a description of an item. For example, Figure 18.13 shows the rules and the result. You have to add quotes around text, add your own spaces to the text, and use an ampersand (&) to append words.

Running the example job

Once you have all of the pieces of design automation in place — the models, the database, and the rules — you need to run the job, in the same way that you might run a program after writing it. Running the job calculates all the values, renames all the parts, applies all the rules, and causes SolidWorks to update with all of the changes you are applying to the assembly through DWX.

FIGURE 18.13

Using rules and input values to create a description for a part

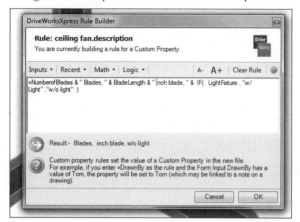

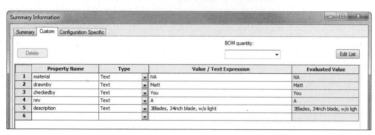

When you run a job, DWX presents you with the form to fill out, and then it updates the models and drawings. After a job is run, the results, which in most cases will be the SolidWorks parts, assemblies and drawings, are saved to a special folder with the name of the job. The green triangle in the DWX toolbar is the button that runs the job.

After creating your automation rules, DWX enables you to run the job. The DWX Summary shows numbers in red if any rules are missing (see Figure 18.12). In addition, the green, triangular Play button automatically appears in the DWX toolbar when the job can be run.

The interface does not offer a lot of control; it is not like programming interface elements with a high-level programming language. However, it is functional, and it can only be seen by the SolidWorks user — it cannot be distributed to non-SolidWorks users.

The fields in the form at this point are

- **Number of Blades.** Drop-down list to select 1, 3, 5, or 6.
- **Project Name.** Text box allowing free text entry.

- **Blade Length.** Numerical field accepting a range of manually typed numbers from 33 to 36 (it uses a tool tip to notify the user).
- **Light Fixture.** Check box (check for yes, uncheck for no).
- **Hang or Flush Mount.** Drop-down list.

Each one of these fields, except Light Fixture, has a yellow triangle with an exclamation point, indicating that it requires input from the user. Figure 18.14 shows a sample form with all of the fields set up during this example.

FIGURE 18.14

Filling out a form to run a job and generate a new set of assemblies and parts

When you fill in all the fields and start the job by clicking the Create button in the lower-right corner of the DWX Task Pane, SolidWorks opens each document and makes the changes dictated by the rules. When the job is complete, DWX displays a log of the process, including new filenames and locations, and the status of each step in the process, as shown in Figure 18.15.

This is the backbone of automating the design. To this, you need to add the rest of the features and dimensions and other file-related manipulations mentioned earlier to make the ceiling fan configurable from a form, based on your outline of what you want to automate that you have already created.

FIGURE 18.15

Confirming that the job processed the data correctly

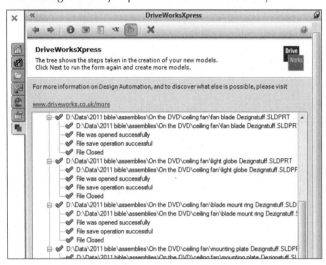

Working with drawings

Much of the time you save with DWX comes from automating the creation of the drawings. DWX does not give you a great deal of latitude for controlling the drawings, but the views updating automatically from the models and the use of custom properties on the drawing with automatic Bill of Materials (BOM) add a great deal of flexibility to the tool. Depending on the nature of the changes, you may need to move dimensions, annotations, tables, or other items manually to keep them from overlapping.

One of the best things about how DWX handles drawings is that it automatically copies them and keeps the references intact. You have to create the drawings yourself as part of the automation setup, but any time you run a job using the automation tools, DWX copies the assembly, parts, and all the drawings.

Summary

DriveWorks Xpress is free software that contains the necessary tools to automate simple designs. If your product is engineered to order and can be specified by filling out a form with multiple choice and numerical answers, then you may be able to take advantage of this time-saving tool that is provided for you in all levels of SolidWorks.

Employing Master Model Techniques

The master model topic fits into both the parts and assemblies workflows. It is included in this book because the end product of a master model technique is most frequently an assembly. The material in this chapter follows closely on multi-body topics, which you can find discussed in detail in the *SolidWorks 2011 Parts Bible*.

In this book, the term *master model* refers to a technique where an entire assembly is laid out or has its major faces constructed in a single part, and that part is then placed into other files from which the individual parts are created. Master model techniques are generally used in situations that in-context design cannot deal with, or where in-context design is cumbersome.

Master model techniques are comprised of four separate features or functions that have some similarities, and rely heavily on the knowledge of parent/child concepts, as well as multiple bodies. These four features are Split, Save Bodies, Insert Part, and Insert Into New Part.

As an example of a master model technique, consider the mouse model shown in Figure 19.1. The overall shape is modeled as a single part and is then split into several bodies using multibody methods. Then, using the four master model features, the individual bodies are used to create individual part files, where detail features are added.

IN THIS CHAPTER

Applying Pull functions

Applying Push functions

Working with master model techniques tutorial

FIGURE 19.1

A mouse master model

Understanding the concepts of *parent* and *child* documents is key to understanding how master model techniques work. A parent document is always the driving document — the one that existed first — so changes to the parent propagate down to the child. The child document is always dependent upon the parent. In these master model schemes, it is not always possible to find the child document from the parent, but you can always find the parent from the child.

The concepts of Push and Pull type functions are developed for this book, and so you may not find them in other documentation. Classifying the techniques can be helpful in understanding which tool is best for various situations. *Push* simply means that data from the parent document is pushed out to the child and the relationship is defined in the parent document. *Pull* means that the child document pulls data from the parent and the relationship is defined in the child document.

Here is a quick summary of the four master model tools that this chapter covers:

 • **Insert Part.** Enables you to pull all the solid and surface bodies, sketches, reference geometry, and even features from an existing part into the current part. This feature is available as a toolbar icon and from the Insert menu.

- **Insert Into New Part.** Enables you to insert a selection of solid and surface bodies from the current part into a brand-new part. Even though this function is initiated from the parent document, it is classified as a Pull function because it doesn't leave a feature in the parent but does leave one in the child. This function does not have an icon.

- **Split.** Enables you to split a single solid body into multiple solid bodies and save (push) each body out to a separate part file. This function is available as a toolbar icon and a menu entry in the Insert ➪ Features menu. It creates a feature in the FeatureManager of the originating (parent) part file.

- **Save Bodies.** Enables you to save (push) all the solid bodies from a part out to separate part files. This function is available only through the RMB menu on the solid bodies folder. It does not create a feature in the FeatureManager of the parent part and does not have an icon.

The one common weakness of all these tools is on the file management side, or more precisely, the body management side. It comes down to a question of what happens to the child document if you rearrange the bodies in the parent document. Body management issues can arise in a number of ways. The Insert Part feature is the one that has received the most development attention from SolidWorks when it comes to the robustness of file and body management issues, but Insert Part still does not cover all the functionality. (You cannot insert selective bodies; you must insert all solids or all surface bodies.)

Using Pull Functions

Pull functions are initiated from the child document and pull data from the master model (parent document) into the child document. These functions insert a feature into the child that points to the parent but do not insert a feature into the parent that points to the child. The features that fall into this category are Insert Part and Insert Into New Part.

Understanding the Insert Part feature

You initiate Insert Part from the child document by choosing Insert ➪ Part from the menus or clicking the Insert Part button in the Features toolbar (which may not be on your toolbar by default). As the name suggests, this feature pulls one part into another. Insert Part gives you the option to bring forward all solid and surface bodies, planes, axes, and sketches in addition to other options. You can even break the link between the inserted part and the parent data. This simply copies all the sketch and feature data into the current part. The Mirror Part feature also uses this same PropertyManager with the same options. The Insert Part PropertyManager interface is shown in Figure 19.2.

FIGURE 19.2

The Insert Part PropertyManager

Figure 19.3 shows the FeatureManager of a part where the only feature is an Insert Part feature. All the solid bodies are listed under the normal Solid Bodies folder as well as under a second Solid Bodies folder under the inserted part icon. Other inserted items, such as surface bodies, planes, sketches, and axes, are also listed in folders under the inserted part icon.

You cannot be selective about which bodies are pulled forward, but you can delete unwanted bodies once you have brought them all in (using Delete Solid/Surface). If you are trying to handle data efficiently, this may not be the best option for you. Because you have to first bring forward all the bodies and then delete those you don't want, the body data is still stored inside the part. Remember that the Delete Bodies feature does not actually delete anything; it simply makes it inaccessible after the Delete Bodies feature in the part history. If you are inserting a part with many complex bodies, you may want to use a more selective method such as Insert Into New Part or Save Bodies, each of which is described in more detail later in this chapter.

One of the advantages of using Insert Part is that you can insert the part at any point in the child part's feature history. Using configurations, you can also insert the parent part at any point along the parent's feature history. Using part history is one of the trickiest aspects of working with multiple models, whether you are working in the context of an assembly or using a master model technique.

FIGURE 19.3

The FeatureManager showing items inserted with an inserted part

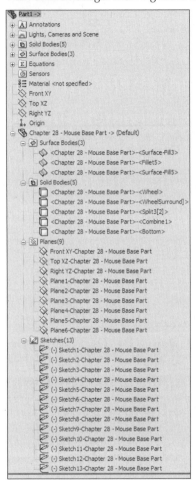

For the inserted part, you can set configurations of the parent document in the External References dialog box, which is available through the RMB menu of the feature that is inserted into the child document FeatureManager. The External References dialog box is shown in Figure 19.4. If the overhead of bringing many bodies forward only to be deleted is an issue for you, then you can use parent part configurations to delete the bodies first; then, from the child using List External References, you can select which configuration to insert.

FIGURE 19.4

The External References dialog box

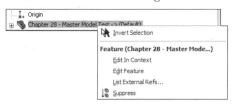
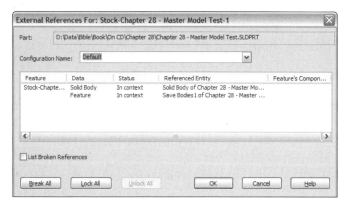

As the original inserted bodies are modified by additional features in the child document, the names change, and they are removed from the folder under the inserted part and only appear in the body folders under the top level.

File management is a real issue with all these master model functions; in fact, it may be the *biggest* problem that arises with them, although you could say the same thing about overall body management. It is safe to say that you should be careful and follow file management best practice recommendations when performing name changes for documents with external references, especially if they use any of these features.

If you would like to get a little practice with the Insert Part feature, follow this workflow:

1. Open a new part. Call this the child part.

2. Identify an existing part that you would like to make some references from. Call this the parent part. Examples of the kinds of references that you might want to make between parts in an in-context assembly include matching a size or location of a feature on the parent part. To make it most interesting for experimentation, the parent part should have multiple solid or surface bodies.

3. With the child part open, click Insert ⇨ Part.

4. In the PropertyManager that appears (shown in Figure 19.2), select the entities that you would like to bring forward from the parent to the child.

5. Experiment with making relations between new geometry and the inserted geometry. Use multi-body techniques to manage the visibility and access to the inserted bodies.

The Insert Part feature has received a lot of attention from SolidWorks developers. For this reason, Insert Part in more recent versions of SolidWorks is most resilient to changes and is the most flexible when allowing the user to make changes.

For example, if the name of the parent file changes, you can edit Insert Part to recover from that error. If the number of bodies in the parent part changes, you can edit the results in the child part to prevent more downstream errors.

Unfortunately, this feature is also inefficient for inserting parts with large numbers of bodies. You may want to choose one of the following techniques for using a single body from a part with a large number of bodies. Insert Into New Part would be a good function for this because it allows you to be more selective about which body is brought forward from the parent to the child.

Understanding the Insert Into New Part feature

Insert Into New Part qualifies as a Pull function because it does not create a feature in the FeatureManager of the parent file, even though it is actually initiated from the parent rather than from the child. This function does not have a drop-down menu location, nor does it have a toolbar button. You can only initiate it through the RMB menu from either the FeatureManager Solid or Surface Bodies folders or from the individual bodies within the folders.

This gives Insert Into New Part both advantages and disadvantages when compared to Insert Part. The advantages are that it can selectively insert either solid or surface bodies, or even selections of both types. You can Ctrl+select multiple bodies (solid and/or surface) to bring only the bodies forward that you need. However, it cannot bring forward planes or axes, or change the selection of what is brought forward after you create the feature. You also cannot use it to add a body to an existing part file; you can only use it to create new documents. This is definitely a good news/bad news situation, but with this information, you can make a more informed decision about which function to use.

When you use Insert Into New Part to place bodies into a part, the bodies are not shown in the same way that the Insert Part function shows them. Figure 19.5 shows that the Stock feature symbols are used rather than the Inserted Part symbol.

Keep in mind that if this feature loses its referenced bodies, they cannot be reattached. This means that you cannot intentionally replace a body. For most users, neither situation (lost references or the need to replace bodies) should arise often, if at all, but it may still be a roadblock when implementing this function.

FIGURE 19.5

Bodies placed in a part using Insert Into New Part

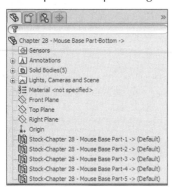

Using Push Functions

Push functions are initiated from the master model (parent document) and push data from the parent part out to a child part. A feature in the tree of the parent identifies the point at which the model is pushed out to the child, and the child file can be found from the parent. These options combine to give the push functions better overall control than the pull functions; however, there might be other factors that are more important.

The first feature in the child part is a Stock feature and contains a reference back to the parent, so that the parent can be found from the child. The features that fall into this category are Split and Save Bodies. The bidirectional identification of the source (parent) and target (child) of the feature offers a distinct advantage over the Pull functions, which do not allow you to identify the child from the parent document.

Working with the Split feature

 The Split feature has three functions, two of which are plainly visible and one that is hidden. Its main function is of course to split a body into multiple bodies. It can also save the bodies out to individual parts. The hidden function is that it can then create an assembly, and reassemble the individual parts back into a complete assembly where all the parts are placed in their original relationships to one another. The Split PropertyManager is shown in Figure 19.6.

Splitting a body

The primary function of the Split feature is to split a single solid body into multiple bodies. You do this with sketches, planes, or surface bodies. The Split feature can save both the pre-existing bodies and any bodies that result from the split as individual part files using the Stock feature as the initial feature in the part.

FIGURE 19.6

The Split PropertyManager

Assigning names automatically

The ability to save solid bodies out to part files directly from the lower half of the Split PropertyManager caused some serious file management problems in earlier versions of SolidWorks. Fortunately, recent versions of SolidWorks have removed most of the bugs from this complex feature.

When you save the bodies out to individual part files, SolidWorks automatically assigns names for the parts. These names take the form of `<Body1>.sldprt`. You can manually assign names either in the lower half of the Split PropertyManager or in callouts on the screen. You can change the names later if necessary. Features added to the parts created from the Split feature should update correctly when you rename the parts in the Split feature.

One drawback of creating parts using the Split feature is that you cannot insert the body geometry at any point in the child feature history. It only goes at the top. You cannot insert the data into an existing part; it can only be put into a new part.

Creating an assembly

After you create the Split feature and save bodies out to new parts, the RMB menu displays the Create Assembly option, which puts all the parts from the bodies in the original part back together in the correct positions. Parts within the assemblies that you create this way are fixed in space with the same relationship to the assembly origin that they originally had as bodies to the part origin. Although this arrangement does not need mates to be properly positioned, it does not easily allow motion. To allow motion, you have to mate the parts using more traditional assembly methods.

Working with the Save Bodies feature

To access the Save Bodies feature, you can either right-click the bodies folders and select it from the RMB menu or choose Insert ➪ Features ➪ Save Bodies from the menu options. Save Bodies works by displaying path and filename information in the Resulting Bodies selection box of the Split PropertyManager. However, Save Bodies enables you to create an assembly right in the PropertyManager for the feature, rather than as a hidden feature with no record of the assembly name created by the feature. The PropertyManager for Save Bodies is shown in Figure 19.7.

FIGURE 19.7

The Save Bodies PropertyManager

Save Bodies is found in the lower half of the Split feature PropertyManager. You can use it to save bodies out to parts if the bodies already exist. Save Bodies also has the Create Assembly functionality built right into the PropertyManager.

In both the Split and Save Bodies PropertyManagers, the Consume cut bodies option means that if a body is saved out to a part, it is removed from the parent part. So if you saved all the bodies out to files, the parent part would be empty after the Split or Save Bodies feature in the FeatureManager.

Tutorial: Working with Master Model Techniques

Some of the concepts presented in this chapter may not make much sense until you apply them to a specific situation. The goal of this tutorial is to demonstrate the strengths and weaknesses of the various functions, as well as to give you some practical experience with the file management issues that you will encounter. In the following tutorials, you will use each of the four tools with the mouse multi-body part to become familiar with their different functions.

To work with the Insert Part function, follow these steps:

1. **Make sure that you have access to the material from the DVD for Chapter 19.** Create a new part, and insert the part named `Mouse Base Part.sldprt`. You can access Insert Part by choosing Insert➪ Part from the menu options. After issuing the command, SolidWorks attaches the part to your cursor and prompts you to specify a location for the inserted part in the PropertyManager. Drop the part at the Origin of the child part, or simply click the green check mark icon to accept the part. There is no need to use the Move dialog box; if it appears, then deselect the option that enables it. For this part, do not transfer any of the optional items, only the solid bodies.

2. **After the feature is accepted and in the tree, right-click it and select List External Refs from the menu.** The External References dialog box appears with the list of configurations displayed, as shown in Figure 19.8.

3. **Select the Wheel configuration from the list.**

4. **Save and name the part file in such a way that it has the name of the technique used to create it (Insert Part) and the name of the body that it represents (such as Wheel).**

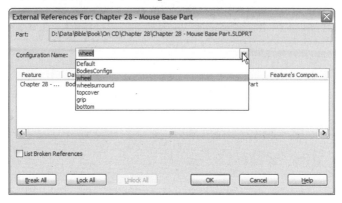

FIGURE 19.8

The External References dialog box

Note

This tutorial has been prepared to flow smoothly. If you ever choose to do modeling in this way, then you will need to know what this preparation work entails. In the mouse master model, you should make a separate configuration for each body, and in that configuration create a Delete Body feature that deletes all the bodies except one. The alternative to this approach is to bring all the bodies into each new part, and use a Delete Body feature in each child part that deletes all but the one body that is needed. The advantage to using configurations is that bringing in a single body theoretically decreases the overhead for the individual part files. ∎

5. **Repeat Steps 1 to 4 for each of the five bodies in the master model.**

6. **If the mouse master model (**`Mouse Base Part.sldprt`**) is open, then close it.** In any of the child parts, the inserted part feature shown in the tree should display the Out Of Context symbol (->?). Right-click the inserted part feature and select Edit In Context; this opens the master model.

   Notice that from the master model, you have no way of knowing where the child parts are or even *if* any child parts exist. Notice also that there is no easy way to create an assembly.

7. **Create a new assembly document.**

8. **Drop all the individually created parts into the assembly by selecting them in Windows Explorer and dragging them onto the assembly Origin.** This is probably the easiest way to create an assembly using the Insert Part feature.

Note

There is no link from the parent to the child; if you rename the child part, the parent does not lose track of it. However, there is a link from the child to the parent; if you rename the parent without the child being open at the same time, the child loses track of the parent. If you change the parent, the child does not update unless the symbol is showing In-Context (->). If it is out of context, broken, or locked, the child does not update with the parent. Both documents need to be open at the same time to make the update happen (although they do not both need to be open when the original edit happens to the parent master model). ■

9. **Save and close all the parts and assemblies.**

To work with the **Insert Into New Part** function, follow these steps:

1. **For this feature, start from the master model; open the part** `Mouse Base Part. sldprt`**.** Make sure that the part is set to the Default configuration. If it is set to a different configuration, inserting bodies will require an extra step of assigning which part configuration to use in the assembly.

2. **Expand the Solid Bodies folder in the FeatureManager.** Right-click the first body in the list (Wheel), and select Insert Into New Part from the menu.

Note

You could select multiple bodies and even combine solid and surface bodies to insert using this technique. ■

3. **When prompted, name the new part using the same convention used in the previous tutorial, which was to use the name of the technique (Insert Into New Part) and the name of the body.** In this part, leave the configuration setting in the External References dialog box to the Default configuration.

4. **Repeat Steps 1 to 3 for each of the bodies.**

5. **Right-click the Stock feature in the tree, and select Edit In Context.** SolidWorks opens the master model part.

Note

Once again, there is no way back to the child document from the master model using the Insert Into New Part feature. ■

6. **Create a new assembly document and use the same technique from the previous tutorial to put all the parts in the assembly located from the Origin.** Again, no automated assembly creation tool exists for this method.

7. **Save all documents and close them.**

To work with the **Split** function, follow these steps:

1. **This time, start from a copy of the master model part.** The Split feature makes additions to the model, and because you have already created assemblies based on the original, you should create any additional features using a copy of the part rather than the original. Copy it using the Copy and Paste feature in Windows Explorer, and rename the copy as **Split Tutorial**.

Note

It is best to copy and rename this document before continuing with the rest of the tutorial. Otherwise, you may encounter problems with the file references, from which it is difficult to recover. ■

2. **With the newly copied and renamed document open, initiate the Split feature by choosing Insert ⇨ Features ⇨ Split.**

3. **Because the bodies already exist, there is no need for the Trim tools or Cut Part functions in the Split feature, only for the resulting bodies.** To save the bodies to individual files, you must give each one a unique name. You can click the Auto-assign Names button to automatically name them with the existing names of the bodies. It might be difficult to discern where the callout flags are pointing. Once the names are all satisfactory, click OK to accept the feature.

Note

The Consume Cut Bodies option deletes any bodies involved in the Split feature. For most purposes, you should deselect this option. Deselecting the option makes sure that the bodies are still available after the Split feature. If you want to eliminate the bodies once they are saved out, then you should select the Consume Cut Bodies option. ■

4. **To automatically create an assembly with all the components located in the proper location, right-click the Split feature in the Master Model FeatureManager, and select Create Assembly.** Multiple Split features can be included in this command if bodies have been created by multiple Split features. Click the Browse button to locate and name the new assembly. Click OK when you are done. Completing this step opens the assembly that you just named and located. When you create the assembly, the parts appear but may not be displayed in the FeatureManager until you have saved and reopened the assembly file. You should still have access to the data through the RMB menu from the graphics window.

5. **Right-click one of the parts in the assembly to open it.** Notice that a Stock feature is used in the tree, so it is possible to access the parent part and change the parent part configuration used in the current part. Right-click the Stock feature and select Edit In Context.

6. **With the master model open, right-click the Split feature and select Edit Feature.** From here, it is possible to see where each of the child parts is located.

7. **If you rename any of the documents, then you should do this by using either SolidWorks Explorer or the Save As command with the other documents open as well.** If you want to rename the parent part (master model), then make sure that all the child parts are open as well. (You can easily do this by opening the assembly; although the assembly was created from the master model, there is no direct link between the Split feature and the assembly.)

8. **Save and close all the files before proceeding.**

To work with the **Save Bodies** function, follow these steps:

1. **As before, create a copy of the original master model part and rename the copy** Save Bodies Tutorial.

2. **Open the renamed copy, and right-click the Solid Bodies folder.** Select Save Bodies from the menu. (Save Bodies has its own icon, which looks like the Split icon and is used to denote the placeholder feature in the FeatureManager.)

3. **Use the Save Bodies PropertyManager to save the solid bodies out to separate files.** (This interface is nearly identical to the lower section of the Split PropertyManager.) The major addition in the Save Bodies dialog box is that the Create Assembly function is directly within the PropertyManager. The primary benefit of this addition is that it retains the name and path of the assembly in this interface so that you can look it up later if necessary.

Note

In both the Split/Create Assembly and Save Bodies features, when you create an assembly, SolidWorks may rebuild the tree of the part as many times as you have bodies to save out. This may take some time for a complex model with a lot of bodies. ∎

4. **Open the reconstructed assembly.** Right-click one of the parts and select Open Part to open it in its own window. Notice that the Stock feature has again been used to push a single body into the part.

5. **Right-click the Stock feature and select Edit In Context, which takes you back to the master model.**

6. **Save and close all of the files.**

Summary

Each of these four functions has strengths and weaknesses. The Insert Part feature is probably the most flexible of them, mainly because of the additional items you can bring forward from the parent document, and the fact that it can handle both solid and surface bodies. The Split feature also has unique strengths because of its ability to split bodies, save multiple bodies to files, and reassemble the parts as an assembly.

If you are working with surface bodies, you must use Insert Part or Insert Into New Part. The other most important strength belongs to the Save Bodies feature, which makes the child accessible from the parent and identifies the assembly in the parent.

Using Weldments

Weldments in SolidWorks are built on structural profiles along sketch entities in a multi-body part environment. Weldment members can be straight or curved, you can make them using standard or custom profiles, and you can build them from both 2D and 3D sketches. A cut list within the part keeps track of the length of each profile that is needed to fabricate the weldment.

Weldments are specialized parts that are similar in some ways to sheet metal parts: they are identified as a special kind of part by a Weldment feature in the FeatureManager, and you use a special set of tools to create and edit them. The specialized part enables specialized functionality such as cut lists, special body trimming functions, and gap creation between bodies.

You can use weldments for round or rectangular tubular structures, structures made from channels, flanged sections, standard or custom shapes, gussets, and end caps, and they can also represent weld beads in the part. You can also use weldments to create structures that are bolted together, structural aluminum extrusion frames, vinyl window frames, and wooden frames and structures, and you can put them into assemblies with other parts such as castings, sheet metal, and fabricated plates.

Weldments are part files in SolidWorks, but they are included in this book because the functionality is similar to assemblies in several ways. The cut lists are similar to BOMs, and weldment drawings have some of the same concerns as assembly drawings. Weldments can be made from individual parts, and can even be included with other parts in assemblies to create a finished product. Strictly speaking, weldments are parts,

IN THIS CHAPTER

Using 3D sketching techniques

Creating weldment-specific features

Adding non-structural components

Creating sub-weldments

Understanding cut lists

Placing the weldment cut list on a drawing

Working with weldments tutorial

but after working with them for a while you may agree that they have more in common with assemblies than parts.

Sketching in 3D

 The 3D sketch is an important tool for creating weldments (and many other features) in SolidWorks. Structural frames are a large part of the work that is typically done using weldment functionality in SolidWorks, and frames are often represented as 3D wireframes. You can represent 3D wireframes with a combination of 2D sketches on different planes, with a single 3D sketch, or with a combination of 2D and 3D sketches. If you have confidence in your ability to use 3D sketches, then that is the best way to go. Three-dimensional sketches can be challenging, but they are certainly manageable if you know what to expect from them.

Navigating in space

When drawing a line in a 3D sketch, the cursor and Origin initially look like those shown in Figure 20.1. The large red Origin is called the *space handle*, with the red legs indicating the active sketching plane. Any sketch entities that you draw lie on this plane. The cursor also indicates the plane to which the active sketching plane is parallel. The XY graphic shown in Figure 20.1 does not mean that the sketch is going to be *on* the XY plane, just parallel to it.

FIGURE 20.1

The space handle and the 3D sketch cursor

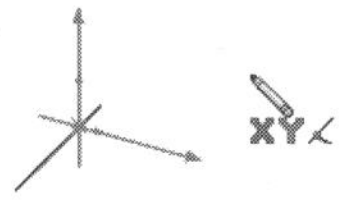

Pressing the Tab key causes the active sketching plane to toggle between XY, YZ, and ZX. The active sketching plane indication does not create any sketch relations; it just lets you know the orientation of the sketch entities that are being placed. If you want to create a skew line that is not parallel to any standard plane, you can do this by sketching to available endpoints, vertices, Origins, and so on. If there are not any entities to snap to, then you need to accept the planar placement, turn off the sketch tool, rotate the view, and move one end of the sketch entity.

An excellent tool to help you visualize what is happening in a 3D sketch is the Four Viewport view. This divides the screen into four quadrants, displaying the Front, Top, and Right views in addition to the trimetric or isometric view. You can sketch in any of the viewports, and the sketch updates live in all the viewports simultaneously. This arrangement is shown in Figure 20.2. You can easily access the divided viewport screen by clicking buttons on the Standard Views toolbar. You can also manually split the screen by using the splitter bars at the lower-left and upper-right ends of the scroll bar areas around the graphics window.

FIGURE 20.2

The Four Viewport view

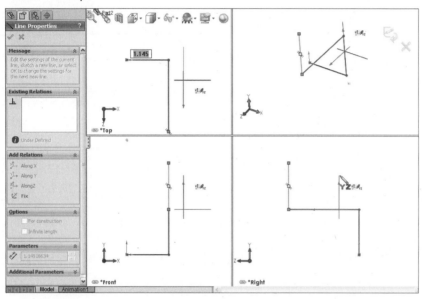

When you move unconstrained entities in a 3D sketch, they move in the plane of the screen. You can use this to your advantage to create or edit lines in 3D space, but it can also lead to unexpected results. When you view the sketch at an angle, move it, and then rotate the view, you may notice that the sketch has shot off into deep interplanetary space. This is another reason for using the Four Viewport view, which enables you to see what is going on from all points of view at once, thus avoiding any surprises.

Understanding sketch relations in 3D sketches

Sketch relations in 3D sketches are not exactly the same as in 2D sketches. Improvements have been made in the past several versions of SolidWorks, but 3D sketches still lack some important bits of functionality. Pierce is not applicable in a 3D sketch, and is replaced by Coincident, because in 3D sketches, there is no difference between Pierce and Coincident. Relations are not projected into a plane in a 3D sketch the way they are in 2D.

On the other hand, several other relations are available in 3D sketches that are not found in 2D sketches, such as AlongX, AlongY, AlongZ (which act as replacements for horizontal and vertical), and OnSurface, for which there is no 2D equivalent.

Relations in 3D sketches are not projected as they are in 2D sketches. For example, an entity in a 2D sketch can be made coincident to an entity that is out of plane. This is because to make the relation, the out-of-plane entity is projected into the sketch plane, and the relation is made to the projection. In a 3D sketch, Coincident means Coincident, with no projection.

Keep in mind that solving sketches in 3D is more difficult than it is in 2D. You will see more situations where sketch relations fail, or flip in the wrong direction. Angle dimensions are particularly notorious in 3D sketches for flipping direction if they change and go across the 180-degree mark. When possible, you should work with fully defined sketches, and also be careful (and conservative) with sketch relations.

For example, the sketch shown in Figure 20.3 cannot be fully defined without over-defining the sketch. The main difficulty is that the combination of the tangent arc and the symmetric legs of the end brace cannot be located rotationally, even using the questionable reliability of 3D planes that are discussed next. The only workable answer to this problem is to create a separate 2D sketch on a real 2D sketch plane, where the plane is defined by the elements of the 3D sketch.

FIGURE 20.3

Three-dimensional sketches may be difficult to fully define.

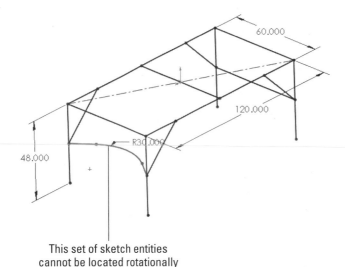

48.000

60.000

120.000

R30.000

This set of sketch entities
cannot be located rotationally
within the 3D sketch

Creating planes in space

 It is possible to create planes directly inside 3D sketches. These planes are defined by constraints and selections rather than selecting a type of method to define a plane. Sketches can be created on these planes, and move with the planes. Having planes in the sketch also enables planar sketch entities such as arcs and circles in 3D sketches.

Unfortunately, there is a lot to watch out for with 3D planes. Be aware that they do not follow their original definition like normal Reference Geometry type planes. Planes inside 3D sketches act more like sketch entities in that if they are under-defined, they can move around inside the sketch. Watching their sketch planes move in a sketch is very unsettling for most users. Figure 20.4 shows the PropertyManager interface for creating 3D planes; however, keep in mind that the plane does not maintain the original relation to these initial references. The parent-and-child relations that SolidWorks users are used to are suspended for this one function, or work in the reverse from what you normally expect.

The PropertyManager for creating 3D planes

A 3D plane cannot be fully defined unless there is some sketch geometry on the plane that is in turn related to something else. Limited types of sketch relations can be applied directly to the actual plane. Horizontal and vertical relations cannot be applied directly to the plane to orient it. Horizontal and vertical relations of entities on the plane are relative only to the plane and not to the rest of the part; therefore, making a line horizontal on the plane does not mean anything when the plane rotates (which it is free to do until it is somehow constrained to prevent this).

Beyond this, when a plane violates a sketch relation, the error is not reported, which severely limits the amount of confidence that you can place in planes that are created in this way. The biggest danger is in the plane rotating, because that is the direction in which it is most difficult to fully lock down. The best recommendation here is to create reference sketch lines with relations to something stable, preferably outside of the 3D sketch.

If you choose to use 3D planes, you can activate them for sketching by double-clicking a plane. The plane is activated when it displays a grid. You can double-click in an empty space to deactivate the plane and return to regular 3D Sketch mode. The main thing that you give up when abandoning 3D sketch planes is the ability to use the dynamic drag options when all loft or boundary sketches are made in a single 3D sketch.

Limiting path segments

Some path segments that are allowed in 3D sketches can only be used if you sketch them on a plane. These entities include circles and arcs, and can include splines, although splines are not required to be on a plane. To sketch on a 3D plane (a plane created within the 3D sketch), you can simply double-click the plane.

Some sketch entities and tools exist which you cannot create or use inside a 3D sketch, even if a sketch plane is activated. These are

- Autodimension
- Fully Define Sketch
- Modify Sketch
- Sketch Slot
- Ellipse
- Polygon
- Dynamic Mirror
- Sketch Mirror
- Offset Entities
- Split Entities
- Sketch text
- Sketch Picture

To sketch on a standard plane or reference geometry plane, you can Ctrl+click the border of the plane with the sketch entity icon active or double-click the plane. The space handle moves, indicating that newly created sketch entities will lie in the selected plane.

Using dimensions in 3D sketches

Dimensions in 2D sketches can represent the straight-line distance between two points, or they can represent the horizontal or vertical distance, depending on the position of the cursor when you place the dimension. In 3D sketches, dimensions between points are *always* the straight-line distance. If you want to get a dimension that is horizontal or vertical, you should create the dimension between a plane and a point (the dimension is always measured normal to the plane) or between a line and a point (the dimension is always measured perpendicular to the line). For this reason, reference sketch geometry is often used freely in 3D sketches, in part to support dimensioning.

This is one of the differences between 2D and 3D sketches that users find difficult to manage. If you are used to visualizing dimensions within 2D sketches, direction-controlled dimensions in 3D sketches can be difficult to visualize, and even more difficult to create.

Using the Weldment Tools

Like the Sheet Metal tools, the Weldment tools in SolidWorks are specialized to enable you to create weldment-specific features in a specialized environment. Everything starts from a sketch or set of sketches representing the wireframe of the welded Structural Members.

Using the Weldment feature

The Weldment button on the Weldment toolbar simply places a Weldment placeholder in the FeatureManager. This placeholder tells SolidWorks that this part is a special weldment part, much in the way that the Sheet Metal feature in sheet metal parts is a placeholder, and denotes a special part type. The Weldment feature moves to the top of the tree, regardless of when you create it in the part history. If you do not create a Weldment feature manually, then one is automatically created for you and placed at the top of the tree when the first Structural Member feature is created. Structural Members are discussed in the next section.

This feature offers only a few special default settings: you can set custom properties that transfer to all cut list items that are created in the current part, and the Merge Result option is deselected by default in weldment parts. The ability to set custom properties is important when multiple weldments go together to make an assembly. To access the custom properties interface, shown in Figure 20.5, select the Properties option on the Weldment feature RMB menu.

FIGURE 20.5

The Weldment Properties interface

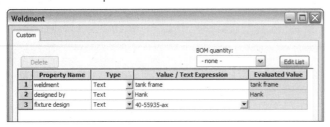

The general workflow for creating weldment parts is as follows:

1. Create a new part, and insert a weldment feature.

2. Create a structural layout of 2D sketches, 3D sketches, or use a combination of 2D and 3D sketches to represent a structure to be fabricated by cutting and welding structural shape stock.

3. Ensure that you have a library with appropriate structural shape sketches, properties, materials, and so on.

4. Make sure that you have allowed for sketch lines in the structural layout to represent a corner, centerline, or some other reference in the library structural shape sketch. This can greatly affect intersections between structural members.

5. Assign structural shapes to individual lines in the structural layout. Be sure to understand the rules on using groups.

6. Trim and miter intersections between structural members to suit your design.

7. Add plate entities such as end caps and gussets.

8. Add weld beads as needed.

9. Place the weldment into an assembly and add castings and sheet metal parts, as well as holes and fasteners to attach non-welded components.

Introducing the Structural Member feature

 A Structural Member is the basic building unit of weldments in SolidWorks. You can create a Structural Member by extruding or sweeping a profile along one or more path segments, and it may result in a single body or multiple bodies. The path segments may be in the form of 2D or 3D sketches.

Note

A single Structural Member feature may create multiple bodies, with each body corresponding to a single cut length of stock. In other words, the feature name "Structural Member" does not necessarily refer to a single piece of the weldment, although it may. ■

One limitation of using sketches in Structural Member features is that only two selected sketch entities may intersect at any one location. For example, at each corner of a cube, three path segments intersect, and so you can only select two of those elements at one time to create a Structural Member feature. Because each of the path segments requires a piece of metal, a second Structural Member feature may use the leftover path segments.

When creating the sketch for the weldment, it is important to decide what the sketch represents. For example, does it represent the centerline of the structural elements, or does it represent a corner? You can orient and position structural shape profiles relative to the frame sketch in several ways, with positioning at the shape centroid being probably the most intuitive for closed shapes and a corner being most intuitive for angle channels.

Figure 20.6 shows a single 3D sketch of a simple frame and a Structural Member feature in the process of creation. You must select the standard first, then the type, and finally the size. A limited number of profiles come with the software, and although you will probably need to create some custom profiles, they are fortunately very easy to create.

To access a large number of weldment profiles in various standards, open the Design Library and click the SolidWorks Content icon. Under that, the Weldments folder has several Zip files containing weldment profiles. Ctrl+click an icon to download the file, and then extract the contents of the Zip file to the library location you have established for your weldment profiles.

FIGURE 20.6

A 3D sketch of a frame

Grouping selected path segments

The concept of groups is simple. You can organize selected path segments within a structural member feature into two kinds of groups: parallel or contiguous. A single structural member may have multiple groups.

Parallel groups contain parallel path segments that do not touch. Parallel groups also require that you select the structural profile before you can select more than one path segment.

Contiguous groups contain path segments that touch end to end, two segments at a time. A contiguous group cannot have one path segment intersect in the middle of another, or more than two path segments intersecting at a corner.

Each group can only have a single orientation of the structural profile. For example, if each frame leg needs to have the profile rotated to a different orientation, you need to rotate the legs in four separate groups instead of all in a single group.

Given those requirements, if the frame shown in Figure 20.6 were to be created entirely from the same structural profile, say ANSI (American National Standards Institute) inch, square tube, $3 \times 3 \times .025$, then it would require a minimum of five groups, as Figure 20.7 shows, in exploded form. The file used to create this image is included on the DVD under the name `Weldment groups.sldprt`.

FIGURE 20.7

Using groups to create the welded frame

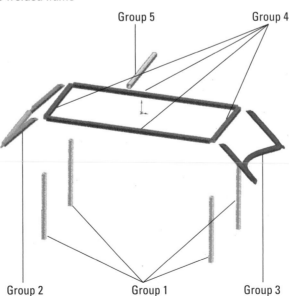

The main advantages of the groups functionality are that each member within the group is automatically trimmed to other members of the group, and that you can control gaps within or between groups. The only trimming you need to take care of separately is the trimming between members of different groups.

Locating and orienting the profile

When you apply a profile to a path segment in a Structural Member feature, the profile must have some relationship to the path segment. The default point where the path "pierces" the profile is at the sketch Origin. To change the pierce point, you can click the Locate Profile button at the bottom of the Structural Member PropertyManager, which zooms the view to present the profile sketch so that you can select another sketch point to use as the pierce point. You can select any sketch point on the profile, including endpoints, sketch points, and virtual sharp points if they are present in the sketch.

Profile sketches are generally surrounded by several sketch points, which may seem unnecessary until you consider that you can use any of the points to position the profile. The Settings panel at the bottom of the Structural Member PropertyManager is shown in Figure 20.8 and displays a profile sketch with the interface.

FIGURE 20.8

Locating the profile

In addition to locating the profile sketch, you can also rotate the profile using the Angle field in the Settings panel. This rotates all the bodies that are created by the Structural Member feature at the same time. In the example of the four-legged frame, if the legs are rectangular or circular, they can all be created in the same Structural Member feature because they are all rotated in the same way. However, if the legs are made from an asymmetrical shape such as an angle, then each leg needs to be made using a separate Structural Member feature, with each leg rotated differently.

Using disjoint sketch segments

You can select disjoint sketch segments in a single Structural Member feature if they are parallel to the first segment and use the same profile height location and orientation. For example, in Figure 20.6, notice the four angled supports in the corners attaching to the legs. Because they are parallel in pairs, all four of these supports could not be made in a single group. Later in this section, when those path segments are actually used to place Structural Members, the additional requirement of using an angle profile means that the profiles each need to be rotated differently from one another, and thus cannot be used in a single group.

Using custom profiles

Most of the custom profiles that you will need may be simply new sizes of existing profiles. You can easily create a custom profile by opening an existing profile, editing it, and saving it under a different name using the Save As command. It is important to note that when creating a weldment profile, you must select a sketch prior to initiating the Save As command. Weldment profiles are library features, and use a `*.sldlfp` filename extension. Each size must be saved as a separate library feature in order to appear in the selection list. While library features are configurable, the configurations are not selectable for weldment profiles.

Other sources for custom profiles include 3D Content Central, which has a large number of erector-set aluminum extrusion profiles and the accessory hardware for those systems. Toolbox also has a Structural Steel sketch generator, shown in Figure 20.9, which enables you to generate most standard shapes. If you have Toolbox installed on your system, then you can find this tool in the Toolbox menu.

Weldment profiles are a great candidate for storing in your special library folder, separate from the SolidWorks installation directory. To establish this library location, you can choose Tools ⇨ Options ⇨ File Locations ⇨ Weldment Profiles. Also keep in mind that if you share design duties with other users, then either the library location should be shared among users on a network or the libraries should be copied to each user's local library. You can also share library data through a Product Data Management, or PDM, program.

If you are creating completely new custom profiles, then remember that when locating the profile relative to the path segments, you can use any sketch point. As a result, you should provide ample selections for pierce points. Virtual sharps function well around filleted corners, as well as sketch points at the centroid of a shape.

In addition to sketch geometry, the library part files should also contain custom property information about the structural shape, such as part number, supplier, material, and so on. This information propagates to the cut list.

FIGURE 20.9

The Structural Steel sketch generator interface

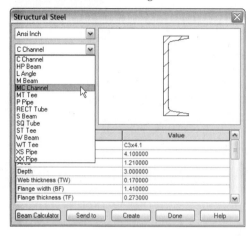

Adding corner treatments

Any intersection of sketch lines at mutual endpoints within a single group, except as noted in this section, creates a situation that requires that the corners be cut to match. Figure 20.10 shows an example of the options that are available when lines meet at right angles. Notice that within a group, you have the option to set a weld gap at the intersections.

FIGURE 20.10

Corner treatment options

To access the toolbar with the Corner Treatment options, you can click the pink dot at the intersection of the path segments. Default corner treatment settings are made in the Structural Member PropertyManager, but you may need to adjust them individually.

Two situations do not require corner treatments. The first situation is when a line intersects another line at some location *other* than an endpoint in the same Structural Member feature — for example, a support meeting the main member in the middle. In this situation, the member that ends in the middle of the other member is trimmed to a butt joint. The second situation is when an intersecting member is created by a later Structural Member feature. You deal with this situation by using the Trim/Extend function, which is described later in this chapter.

Note

You may encounter a situation where it seems like a good idea to create collinear sketch segments. In a typical extrusion, the faces created from collinear lines are simply merged together as one. However, in a weldment, this does not work when it is done in a single feature. In order to create Structural Members on collinear sketch lines, you must either extend one line to encompass the length of both lines or do the work in two separate Structural Member features. ■

Using arc segments

When arc sketch segments are part of the selection for a Structural Member, a Merge arc segment bodies option appears after the selection box in the Selections panel. This means that any *tangent* arc segment will be joined to the entities to which it is tangent, but any non-tangent entities will create separate bodies.

A tangent arc is shown in the curved leg brace shown in Figure 20.11, along with the Merge arc segment bodies option in the PropertyManager.

FIGURE 20.11

A tangent arc segment used in a Structural Member feature

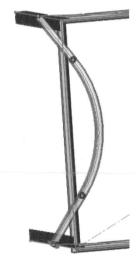

If the Merge arc segment bodies option is not selected, then a separate body is created for arc segments. The Merge arc segment bodies option applies to the whole feature, and cannot be set selectively for individual arc segments within the selected sketch entities; it is either selected for all or deselected for all. If some arc segment bodies are merged and others are not, then you should create separate Structural Member features.

It is also a curious limitation that only one arc may be selected if the selected path segments are disjointed. For example, you cannot select the two arcs for two J shapes that do not touch in the same Structural Member feature. The obvious work-around is to create two separate groups.

Patterning bodies and sketching with symmetry

Bodies created by the Structural Member feature can be patterned and mirrored. Remember that there is a difference between patterning *features* and patterning *bodies*. The Move/Copy Bodies feature is also appropriate for creating bodies to be used in the weldment, although the Structural Member feature does not create them directly.

This is mentioned here to emphasize the point that sketching with symmetry is still important, although it is more difficult with 3D sketches than with conventional 2D sketches. Symmetry in a 3D sketch can only be used when a plane is activated, and you can activate regular reference geometry planes, not just 3D sketch planes. This is also mentioned because in larger weldments (or when using slower computers), performance may be an issue, and mirroring or patterning bodies is certainly a performance enhancement over building parametric features.

Creating configurations

When you start creating a weldment, SolidWorks automatically creates a derived configuration. Both configurations are named Default, but they have different descriptions. The parent configuration description is As Machined, and the derived, or indented, configuration description is As Welded.

This arrangement holds true for any additional top-level configurations that you create in the part; they will all get the description As Machined and inherit an identically named derived configuration with the description As Welded. These configurations are meant to help you create drawings where the raw weldment is distinguished from the weldment after it has been machined, ground, and drilled.

Using the Trim/Extend feature

In situations where you must create multiple Structural Member features, thus creating intersecting bodies, you must deal with the interferences using the Trim/Extend feature. An example of this is shown in Figure 20.12. The legs and braces shown are all being trimmed by a single face on the bottom side of the rectangular section of the frame, where the small arrow appears.

FIGURE 20.12

Using the Trim/Extend feature

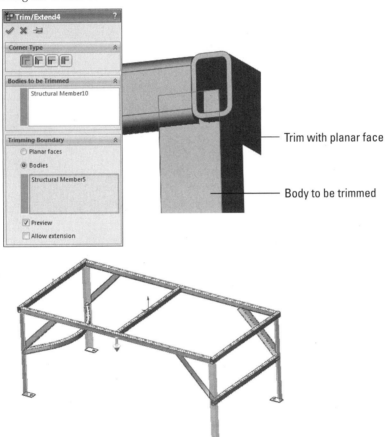

Trim with planar face

Body to be trimmed

Bodies may be trimmed by planar faces or other bodies. Bodies may also be trimmed before they are mirrored or patterned. Although trimming with faces is faster, it may not give the same geometrical results.

The Extend option enables either trimming or extending, as appropriate. If the Extend option is not selected, then trimming is the only action available.

Using the End Cap feature

 The End Cap feature closes off an open-ended Structural Member. You can add multiple end caps in a single End Cap feature. The PropertyManager and the end product are shown in Figure 20.13.

FIGURE 20.13

Using the End Cap feature

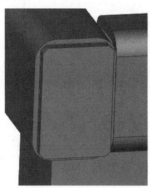

The end cap using the Outward option sits on the outside face of the member, and overlaps the thickness of the member by the inverse of the Thickness Ratio that is applied in the Offset panel. If the Use thickness ratio option is turned off, then it functions as an offset from the outer faces of the member from which it is created. When this option is turned on, the thickness ratio can range from zero to one. For a value of zero, it is flush with the outer faces of the member, and for a value of one, it is flush with the inner faces of the member. Using the Inward option, the cap fits inside the hole in the member.

Working with the Gusset feature

 The Gusset feature creates a three-, four-, or five-sided gusset in a corner between Structural Members, as shown in Figure 20.14. You can place the gusset at specific locations along the edge in the corner, or offset it by a specific dimension in a specific direction by using the settings in the Parameters panel. You can control the size and thickness of the gusset in the Profile panel. There is no sketch for this feature type; it is simply created from the parameters that you enter in the PropertyManager interface. Again, if you need to make multiple Gusset features in succession, you can use the pushpin icon to keep the interface displayed until you close it by clicking the red X icon.

FIGURE 20.14

Using the Gusset feature

Using Non-Structural Components

Non-structural components are frequently needed in weldments, and include items such as feet, plates, brackets, mounting pads, and castings. Simpler items that can be easily modeled in place can be placed directly into the weldment part. You can also insert parts into the weldment using the Insert Part feature, and move them into place by using dimensions or mates. In general, if any item is actually welded into the weldment, then you should place it in the weldment part; however, items that are bolted on should probably be placed into an assembly. Of course, this probably depends more on your company's documentation standards, part-numbering standards, and assembly processes than on software capabilities.

When adding a plate such as the footplate shown in Figure 20.15, the geometry is added using the standard Extrude feature, except that the Merge option is deselected by default. This ensures that non-structural components that are manually modeled, such as this part, are created as separate bodies, and not merged together with the existing structural items.

FIGURE 20.15

A footplate added to the weldment

Using Sub-Weldments

From a modeling point of view, sub-weldments are generally used for either organizational or performance reasons to group together elements of a weldment or to break a larger weldment into more manageable pieces. This is in much the same way that subassemblies are created for the same purposes within larger assemblies. From a fabrication point of view, sub-weldments are also used to break a large weldment into pieces that can be transported or handled.

To create a sub-weldment, you can select several bodies from the cut list, and then select Create Sub-Weldment from the RMB menu. (You can also select the bodies from the graphics window if you use the Select Bodies selection filter.) This creates a separate folder for the sub-weldment bodies. You can then right-click the sub-weldment folder and select Insert Into New Part.

Working with Cut Lists

The cut list that is maintained in the model FeatureManager is simply a replacement for the Solid Bodies folder. It has most of the same functionality as the Solid Bodies folder, as well as a few additional items. The Cut List folder symbol in the FeatureManager can appear in one of two potential states; these symbols are shown in the left margin. When the cut list requires an update, the top image is shown, and after the update has been performed, the bottom image is shown. Cut lists are updated automatically when you access a drawing that uses the cut list, but you can also update them manually through an RMB option or by the forced rebuild, Ctrl+Q.

You can access the Update command by right-clicking the Cut List folder and selecting it from the RMB menu. Figure 20.16 shows the result of the update. The weldment solid bodies are broken down further into subfolders that reflect quantities of identical bodies. Notice that the weld beads at the bottom of the list are not in a folder.

The cut list in the model FeatureManager

Note
You can assign different materials to bodies within a part in SolidWorks. SolidWorks does not account for weldability of different materials. ■

Using Cut-List Properties

In addition to the custom properties for the document, SolidWorks weldments also make use of Cut-List Properties. You can access Cut-List Properties by right-clicking a Cut List Item folder (other than the top-level Cut List folder) at the top of the FeatureManager and selecting Properties. The Cut-List Properties may not be available for a newly created weldment until you have updated the cut list (right-click the top-level Cut List icon and select Update).

Figure 20.17 shows the Cut-List Properties dialog box, which allows users to enter data such as length and material for BOMs and cut lists.

Notice the Properties Summary tab, which enables you to look at each property, and see what the values for each cut list item are. You would select a property such as Description, and then assign descriptions for each cut list item, and then go on to the next property, say Material, and assign values for that property.

FIGURE 20.17

FIGURE 20.17

Use the Cut-List Properties to enter relevant data for BOMs and cut lists.

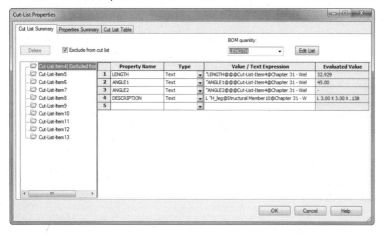

The Cut List Table tab shows you a preview of the cut list and enables you to use cut list templates that might have different default columns established. Figure 20.18 shows the Cut List Table tab of the Cut-List Properties dialog box.

FIGURE 20.18

The Cut List Table tab previews the cut list for you and gives you the opportunity to edit values in the table.

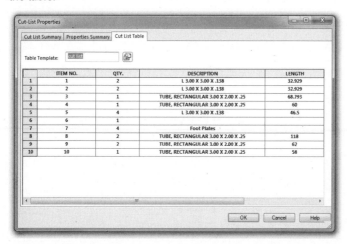

As Figure 20.18 shows, you may need to enter information for items added to the weldment such as end caps or gussets.

Excluding and reordering cut list items

To exclude a feature in the FeatureManager from the cut list, you can select Exclude from cut list from the feature's RMB menu. The next time the cut list is updated, the members that were created by that feature will be listed at the bottom of the Cut List folder with the weld beads. To include the item again in the cut list, select Include in cut list from the feature's RMB menu and update the cut list again. Figure 20.19 shows a folder that has been excluded from the cut list.

FIGURE 20.19

Excluding an item from a cut list

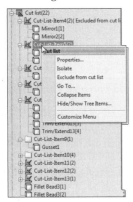

Only entire cut list item folders can be eliminated from the cut list, not individual bodies. To reorder items in the cut list, just drag and drop the folder to where you want it to be in the list.

Using weld beads and fillet beads in weldments and assemblies

In SolidWorks 2011, there is a difference between a fillet bead and a weld bead. All of the weld functionality is new in 2011, and the Fillet Bead feature is a new tool on the Weldment toolbar. Some of the tools from the Weldments CommandManager tab are shown in Figure 20.20 to help you identify the names with the icons.

FIGURE 20.20

Differentiating the Fillet Bead feature from the Weld Bead feature

The Fillet Bead feature creates actual solid geometry, which shows up in a weldment part as a feature. Figure 20.21 shows the Fillet Bead features in the FeatureManager and the actual fillet bead between a plate and a Structural Member.

FIGURE 20.21

The Fillet Bead feature in the FeatureManager and on the part

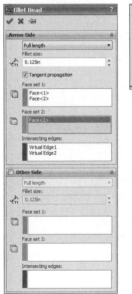

To create a weld in an assembly, you still use the Weld Bead tool, just as you did prior to SolidWorks 2011. However, the Weld Bead interface is now much different from the old dialog-driven interface. The results of the feature are also very different. In SolidWorks 2011 and later, the Weld Bead feature produces a cosmetic display of a weld and keeps track of it in a folder at the top of the Assembly FeatureManager or the weldment part FeatureManager. Weld bead parts in the assembly were always confusing and clumsy, and now they have been eliminated.

Figure 20.22 shows the Weld Bead PropertyManager and the preview it applies to a weldment part.

The Weld Bead feature shows up in the Weld folder and as a cosmetic display on the part.

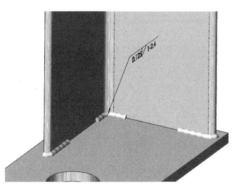

The Weld Bead feature does not show up in the part or assembly FeatureManager as a feature (even though you access the command at Insert ⇨ Assembly Feature ⇨ Weld Bead), and it doesn't create geometry that adds mass. It does produce a cosmetic weld bead on the part, and creates a new folder in the FeatureManager right below the Annotations folder. The entries in the folder show how many weld beads of what length are applied to the entire weldment. Fillet beads do not add anything to the Weld folder. As a result, the type of information you need to have in your model will help you determine if you want to use the Fillet Bead or Weld Bead feature. If you need to show welds in an assembly, you have to use the cosmetic display of weld beads.

The Weld Bead PropertyManager also gives you the option to define the ANSI weld symbol before the feature is complete. The interface for defining the weld symbol is shown in Figure

20.23. Use the Define Weld Symbol button in the Settings panel of the Weld Bead PropertyManager to access this interface.

FIGURE 20.23

Assigning a weld symbol in the Weld Bead feature

In the long run, these changes are for the best because they offer a standardized display option between parts and assemblies without adding such a burden of added parts to the assembly. The 2011 changes have also vastly improved the interface for weld beads.

Creating Weldment Drawings

Weldment drawings have a couple of special features that distinguish them from normal part drawings. The first is obviously the cut list. Like a BOM in an assembly, you can place the weldment cut list on a drawing by choosing Insert ➪ Table ➪ Weldment Cut List. Figure 20.24 shows a sample cut list on a drawing. In this case, the blank rows represent non-structural components, being the footplates and the gusset. You can manually add data for these parts either directly into the table or by adding it to the properties of the corresponding folder in the cut list in the model document.

FIGURE 20.24

A cut list on a drawing

ITEM NO.	QTY.	DESCRIPTION	LENGTH
1	2	L 3.00 X 3.00 X .138	32.929
2	2	L 3.00 X 3.00 X .138	32.929
3	1	TUBE, RECTANGULAR 3.00 X 2.00 X .25	68.793
4	1	TUBE, RECTANGULAR 3.00 X 2.00 X .25	60
5	4	L 3.00 X 3.00 X .138	46.5
6	1		
7	4		
8	2	TUBE, RECTANGULAR 3.00 X 2.00 X .25	118
9	2	TUBE, RECTANGULAR 3.00 X 2.00 X .25	62
10	1	TUBE, RECTANGULAR 3.00 X 2.00 X .25	58

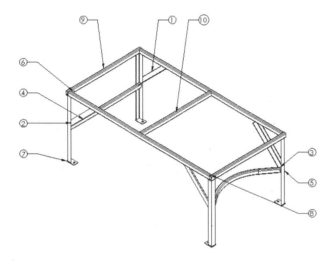

Figure 20.24 also shows an auto-ballooned isometric view of the entire weldment. This works the same way that assembly auto-ballooning works, and it also corresponds to the cut list in the same way that the assembly corresponds to the BOM.

Weldment drawings can also include views of individual bodies. You can do this by making a Relative view, selecting both faces from the same body, and then using the PropertyManager of the Relative view in the window of the solid model to control whether the view shows the entire part or just selected bodies. The Relative View PropertyManager is shown in Figure 20.25.

When you place a drawing view of a weldment, you can also link a cut list to a particular view. This might help you with putting multiple weldments on a drawing or laying out the process for fabricating a weldment, showing the weldment in various stages of completion.

FIGURE 20.25

The Relative View PropertyManager

To access the Relative View PropertyManager interface, follow these steps:

1. Click the Relative View button on the Drawings toolbar or choose Insert ⇨ Drawing View ⇨ Relative To Model.

2. Right-click a blank space on the drawing sheet and select Insert From File. Browse to the part file.

3. Identify the faces to be shown in the particular orientations, and specify whether the entire part or the selected bodies should be shown in the view.

Tutorial: Working with Weldments

This tutorial guides you through building a section of a tubular truss support. You can create many different types of weldments, from simple small-gauge frames to large architectural designs such as this one. This tutorial also helps you to navigate successfully through some 3D sketch functionality for creating fully defined sketches.

Follow these steps to learn about working with weldments:

1. **Open a new part.** If you have Toolbox, then activate it by choosing Tools ⇨ Add-Ins ⇨ SolidWorks Toolbox. If you do not have Toolbox, then simply draw two concentric

circles on the Front plane of a new part. The circles should have diameters of 10.02 inches and 10.75 inches. Alternatively, you can copy the library feature from the DVD to the location specified at the end of Step 5.

2. **If you have Toolbox, then choose Toolbox ⇨ Structural Steel.**

3. **Select ANSI Inch, P Pipe, P10.** This profile has an inside diameter of 10.02 inches and an outside diameter of 10.75 inches. Click the Create button, and then click Done.

4. **Use Custom Properties to add any properties that you would like to have automatically added to the cut list.**

5. **Remembering the techniques on library features, first close any open sketches, select the sketch from the FeatureManager, and then save the part as a Library Feature Part file to a path such as** D:\Library\Weldment Profiles\ Custom\Pipe\P-Pipe10in.sldlfp.

Note

The Custom folder (located in the first level under the Weldment Profiles) is recognized as the Standard, similar to ANSI or ISO (International Organization for Standardization). The next folder down, Pipe, is recognized as the Type, and the name of the file is recognized as the Size, in the same way as shown in Figure 20.6. ■

6. **Choose Tools ⇨ Options ⇨ File Locations ⇨ Weldment Profiles, and add your non-installation directory location to the list of folders.** Alternatively, you can remove the Program Files location from the list, and copy the files from that location to your own library location.

7. **Open another new part, and open a new 3D sketch in the part.** Double-click the Top (ZX) plane to activate it, and click the Center Rectangle sketch entity.

8. **Draw a rectangle around the Origin.** The sketch should now look like Figure 20.26. Apply an Equal relation to two adjacent sides of the rectangle, and dimension any of the lines as 120 inches.

FIGURE 20.26

A centered rectangle in a 3D sketch

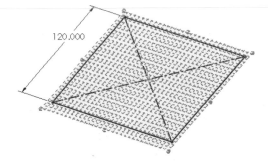

9. **Turn off the rectangle, and double-click in a blank space to deactivate sketching on the Top plane.**

10. **Activate the Line sketch tool and press Tab until the cursor indicates the XY plane.**

11. **Draw a line from one corner of the square down, trying to avoid any automatic relations such as coincident relations to other points and any AlongX, -Y, or -Z relations.** Connect the other three corners of the square with the free endpoint of the new line, as shown in Figure 20.27.

Adding lines

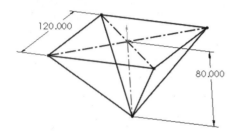

12. **Rotate the view slightly.** Notice that the first line that you drew in Step 10 and one other line are on a plane. Drag a right-to-left selection box around the point where the four lines converge, and assign an Equal relation to all the lines. This makes the shape into an upside-down pyramid.

13. **Drag the point.** Notice that it moves up and down, although it seems a little erratic. Place a dimension between the point and the part Origin. Notice that the sketch becomes over-defined and turns red and yellow. Theoretically, this combination should work. SolidWorks does not accept it.

14. **Using the Display/Delete Relations tool, delete all the Equal relations that you just added to the part (it may be faster to select Undo from the File menu or to press Ctrl+Z).**

15. **Draw a vertical construction line from the part Origin to the point where the four lines meet, and assign this line an AlongY relation.** Notice that the point drags much more smoothly. This is a good reason for using simpler relation schemes when possible. The four equal relations in this case that had to be solved simultaneously are now replaced by a single relation that is easier to solve when you drag the sketch. Apply a dimension of 80 inches to the new construction line.

16. **Draw a new line from the point where the four lines come together AlongX in the positive X direction.** Dimension this new line as 120 inches. The sketch should now look like Figure 20.28.

FIGURE 20.28

The sketch after Step 16

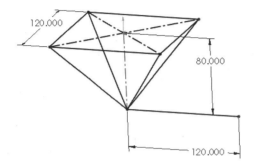

17. **Exit the sketch.** Click the Structural Member toolbar button on the Weldments toolbar. In the Standard drop-down list in the Structural Member PropertyManager, select Custom. In the Type drop-down list, select Pipe. In the Size drop-down list, select P-Pipe10in. This is the name that corresponds to the way you saved the library feature part in Step 5.

18. **In the Path Segments selection box, select the original four sides of the rectangle.** In the Settings panel, make sure that the Apply corner treatment option is selected and that the End Miter icon is selected. This is shown in Figure 20.29. Accept the command when you are done.

19. **Expand the Structural Member feature.** Notice that the four bodies are listed under it. Click the Cut List folder to expand it. The bodies should also be listed there.

20. **Open the 10-inch pipe library feature that you created at the beginning of this tutorial.** Edit the two dimensions to subtract 2 inches from each dimension, and add a custom property description called Support Leg. Choose File ⇨ Save As to save the library feature to the same location as the original, but with the filename `P-Pipe8in.sldlfp`.

21. **Initiate another Structural Member feature, this time selecting the 8-inch size of pipe from the Custom folder.** In the Path Segments selection box, select two of the angled lines that go to opposite corners. Keep the feature open for the next step.

Note

Remember that you cannot create three intersecting Structural Members with a single group. To create material on all four lines, you need two separate groups within the Structural Member feature. ∎

FIGURE 20.29

The Structural Member PropertyManager and the sketch after Step 18

22. **Make a second group with the other pair of angled lines.** Accept the feature when you are satisfied. The model should now look like Figure 20.30.

FIGURE 20.30

The model showing the features accepted in Step 22

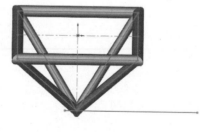

23. **Apply another Structural Member feature to the 10-foot (120-inch) section, again using the 10-inch-diameter pipe.** Notice that this member is not long enough to cut through the peak of the pyramid.

24. **Edit the 3D sketch and draw a 12-inch extension to the original line past the peak of the pyramid.** Use an additional line rather than extending the existing one. Exit the sketch.

25. **Edit the Structural Member feature to add the new line.**

Note

You have to deselect the Apply corner treatment option to get this technique to work. If this option is selected, SolidWorks tries to miter or otherwise create a corner treatment between the bodies, which fails when the parts are parallel. ■

26. **The four angled members need to be trimmed on both ends because they extend to the ends of the sketch entities rather than stopping at intersecting members.** Initiate the Trim/Extend feature. Select the four angled members in the Bodies to be Trimmed selection box. Select the four members created by the original rectangle as the Trimming Boundary, and make sure that the Bodies option is selected (as opposed to Face/Planar), as shown in Figure 20.31. Accept the feature when you are done.

FIGURE 20.31

The model after Step 26

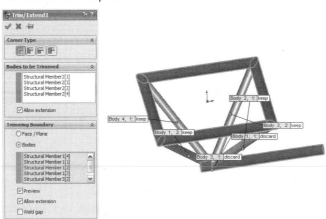

27. **Create another Trim/Extend feature.** This time, trim off the point end of the four angled members using the 10-inch horizontal pipe and the small segment as the trimming boundary. Half of the support structure has been modeled to this point.

28. **Create the rest of the support structure by mirroring the existing bodies.**
Create a Mirror feature using the free end of the 10-foot-long member as the mirror plane, and selecting all the bodies in the Bodies to Mirror selection box. Do not select the Merge solids option because you will need to merge solids manually. Click OK to accept the feature when it is set up properly. The PropertyManager for the Mirror feature is shown in Figure 20.32.

FIGURE 20.32

The PropertyManager for the Mirror feature in Step 28

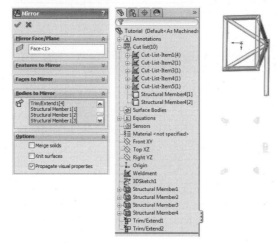

Note

An easy way to select all the bodies is to use the flyout FeatureManager, select the first body in the list, and Shift+select the last body. ∎

29. **Select the Combine feature (Insert ⇨ Feature ⇨ Combine), and set it to Add.**
Select the two 10-foot sections and the two smaller 1-foot sections to combine them into a single continuous body. Click OK to accept the feature. Also hide the 3D sketch.

30. **Right-click the Cut List folder, and select Update.** Figure 20.33 shows before and after images of the Cut List folder.

31. **Right-click the folder for the large-diameter cross member and select Properties.** Change the Description field to read Support Pod Members.

32. **Use the Create Drawing From Part/Assembly button on the Standard toolbar to make a drawing.** Place Front, Bottom, and isometric views, and then press the Esc key to quit placing views.

FIGURE 20.33

The Cut List folder in Step 30

33. **Select one of the views and then choose Insert ⇨ Table ⇨ Weldment Cut List.** When the PropertyManager displays, select the options that you want and click OK. Then place the table.

34. **Click inside the Bottom view, and from the Annotations toolbar, click Auto-Balloon.** The finished drawing looks like Figure 20.34.

FIGURE 20.34

The finished drawing

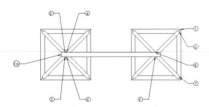

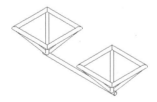

Note

Relative views are difficult to create with round pipe rather than a rectangular tube, although you can use planes as references for relative views. ∎

Summary

Weldments are based on either a single 3D frame sketch or a set of 2D sketches, usually denoting the centerlines or edges of the various structural elements. This creates a special type of part in the same way that the Sheet Metal commands create a special type of part. Structural profiles are placed on the frame sketch to propagate and create individual bodies for the separate pieces of the weldment. Custom profiles are easily created as library features; you can add custom properties to the library features, and the custom properties then propagate to the cut lists.

Using Mold Tools

Mold geometry is one of the most difficult things to visualize. To
make a mold for a plastic part, you have to be able to envision
putting air where you want plastic and putting steel where you
want air. You have to visualize your parts inside out, and in such a way
that you can get each part out of the steel. SolidWorks Mold Tools help
you with the visualization by providing a process for creating cavity and
core blocks from the model of a plastic part. The process does not guarantee that the parts are manufacturable; you still need experience in the
trade for that.

The SolidWorks Mold Tools give you a process by which you can take
plastic parts and split cavity and core blocks for them, as well as additional core pins or slides. This process is usually not 100 percent automated, and often requires manual intervention. The overall process
works, but users often find that they want to develop a hybrid system
incorporating SolidWorks tools and their own techniques.

To work with the tools in this chapter, you need to understand how surfaces work. Features such as the Boundary surface, knit, trim, and others
are covered in a basic way in the *SolidWorks 2011 Parts Bible,* (Wiley
2011) and are covered in much detail in the *SolidWorks Surfacing and
Complex Shape Modeling Bible* (Wiley, 2008).

Manual methods also exist by which you can choose your own features
to create the same cavity and core block. This chapter introduces you to
both the formal Mold Tools process and the less formal mold splitting
methods used throughout the industry.

Working with the Mold Tools Process

The goal of the Mold Tools process is to produce a single, continuous surface body (the parting surface) that splits the plastic part into two. The split is done in such a way that if the plastic part were subtracted from the center of a bigger block of material, the parting surface, if extended larger than the block, would be able to split the block through the cavity of the part. If you are new to mold design, you are not alone in having difficulty visualizing this. Figure 21.1 shows the solid block with the cavity and the parting surface, along with the individual blocks created by the split.

Visualizing the goal of the Parting Surface feature splitting a cavity/core block

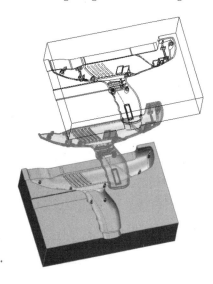

The SolidWorks Mold Tools are intended to help you create cavity and core blocks for molds. The tools and process are generic enough that you could use them to create casts, forging dies, powder metal dies, and tooling for most plastic forming processes. SolidWorks does not provide libraries or functionality for building the entire mold or mold components. Mold Tools require you to follow a semiautomatic process, with the tools appearing on the toolbar in the order in which they are intended to be used, from left to right.

Mold Tools rely heavily on surfacing, and require a fair amount of manual intervention for certain types of parts. The first half of this chapter deals with the semiautomatic process — the way it is *supposed* to work. The last half of the chapter deals with the manual side of the process — the way things really work with day-to-day models.

The general workflow for using Mold Tools to create cavity and core blocks for a mold is as follows:

1. Create split lines to add draft where needed.

2. Create draft as needed (you can use Move Face to angle faces much like the Draft feature).

3. Scale the part up to compensate for shrinkage during molding.

4. Identify the parting lines that separate cavity faces from core faces.

5. Create shut-off faces, which are surfaces that close any through holes (windows or pass-throughs) in the part and represent places where the steel from the cavity side of the mold directly touches steel from the core side of the mold. These openings in the part are capped by surface features.

6. Create parting surfaces. These are the faces outside the part where the steel from opposite sides of the mold touch.

7. Create the tooling split. The Tooling Split feature uses the faces of the shut-offs and parting surfaces and the faces of either the cavity or the core side to split a block into two sides.

8. Create any core features. In SolidWorks, the word *core* refers to the material used to make core pins, side action, slide, lifter, or pull in a mold.

With the formal SolidWorks process, you start in the part file with just the final plastic part in it, and then build both the cavity and core blocks around the plastic part. You also build any side actions or core pins within the part file.

Figure 21.2 shows the part of the Mold Tools toolbar that identifies the process. This toolbar also includes many surfacing and plastics analysis tools, but only the tools directly related to the Mold Tools process are shown in Figure 21.2.

FIGURE 21.2

The Mold Tools

Mold Tools are really meant for tooling engineers, but part designers often use the first part of the process to apply draft to parts. Tooling engineers often need to add or correct draft to plastic parts they receive from part designers when these parts are without draft or are not designed with any process in mind.

If you were to create a mold with manual modeling functions, you might go through roughly the same steps in the same order. The SolidWorks process often runs into problems in the automated surface modeling areas, such as shut-offs and parting surfaces. You may need to intervene in the process manually for these steps. Fortunately, the SolidWorks process is flexible enough to allow for manual modeling as needed.

Each one of these process steps may have several steps of its own. Cavity and core creation is far from a push-button operation, but when you understand the overall process, the detailed steps become clearer.

Preparing the plastic part for Mold Tools

The Mold Tools process formally starts with identifying edges as parting lines. Before you get to that point, there are some things you have to do to the plastic part model, such as shelling the part, creating draft, and accounting for shrinkage.

For this example, you will use a part from the DVD (see Figure 21.3). This part uses a master model technique to create multiple parts from a single surface model, and then is inserted into a new part for the Mold Tools process, so three levels exist for the part. The one you are concerned with in this example is called `Mold Tools medical device.sldprt`, which contains a single feature, an inserted part called medical device frame.

FIGURE 21.3

The plastic part for the example in this chapter

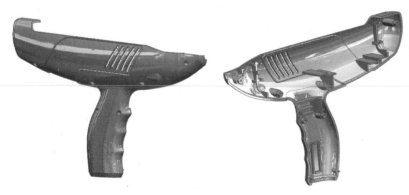

Shelling the part and applying draft

Shelling and applying draft to a plastic part isn't something you can cover in a couple of paragraphs. Shell and draft features, including the evaluation techniques to determine the wall thickness, direction, and amount of the draft that was applied, are covered in detail in the *SolidWorks 2011 Parts Bible* (Wiley 2011).

Adding the plastic part to a blank part

The Mold Tools process works in multi-body mode rather than in assembly mode. This makes sense as long as you don't start by putting all of the Mold Tools features into the same file that contains all of the plastic part features. This would make a single part with many features that exist for different purposes.

The best practice to follow when preparing a part for Mold Tools is to insert the part into a new part using the Insert Part feature at the top of an empty new part. This does a couple of things. First, it gives you more control over the rebuild times for the Mold Tools from the rebuild times for the plastic part. In addition, if you are just working on the plastic part, you don't want to have to worry about the Mold Tools features. Second, it separates the features of the Mold Tools so you don't have to be working with the live plastic part data when all you need is the final geometry.

This step is just a recommended part of the process that has been added; it is not part of the process that SolidWorks has established for the tools, but you will probably find that it is useful.

Using the Scale feature

The Scale feature is used to make the plastic part slightly larger to compensate for plastic shrinkage during molding. Scale is driven by a multiplier value, so a part that is twice as big gets a scale factor of 2, and one that is half as big gets a scale factor of .5. Plastic materials have a shrink rate that is usually measured in thousandths of an inch per inch of part. Five thousands inch per inch is equal to a 0.005 scale factor. If the part is 4 inches long, the mold cavity to produce it must be 4.020 inches with that material.

Some materials have *anisotropic* shrink rates, meaning they shrink different amounts in different directions, with the primary direction being considered the direction of the molten plastic through the mold cavity. SolidWorks has a means to compensate for this, although it may not always be practical. Usually the shrink directions are identified as "in the direction of flow" and "across the direction of flow," and the direction of flow of molten plastic inside a mold cavity is not always a straight line. Any anisotropic shrink applied to a part in SolidWorks is an approximation at best. If you deselect the Uniform scaling option in the Scale feature, SolidWorks enables you to set different scale factors for X, Y, and Z directions. The Scale PropertyManager is shown in Figure 21.4, in both its Uniform Scaling and non-Uniform Scaling configurations.

FIGURE 21.4

The Scale PropertyManager

Where you should put the Scale feature is debatable. Some people argue that it should be placed in the plastic part file, so that it is ready to create the mold geometry. Others believe it should be placed in the part file that the mold tools are created in, because you might design a mold for polypropylene differently from a mold for 20 percent glass-filled nylon — so the mold is at least in some ways specific to the material.

This is where the story begins for the medical device example. If you are following along:

1. Add a Scale feature to the Mold Tools medical device part, using uniform scale, and a scale factor of 1.05.

2. Scale the part about the origin. Figure 21.5 shows the FeatureManager and PropertyManager for the new feature.

FIGURE 21.5

Adding a Scale feature to start the Mold Tools process

Inserting Mold folders

 The first step in the process of using SolidWorks Mold Tools is to insert Mold folders. Mold folders are folders in the FeatureManager that the Mold Tools add underneath the Surface

Bodies folders. You can add these folders manually using the Insert Mold Folders button on the Mold Tools toolbar. They are used to organize the different groups of faces used in separating the cavity and core solid bodies. The folders that are added are shown in Figure 21.6.

FIGURE 21.6

Adding the Mold Tools folders to the Surface Bodies folder

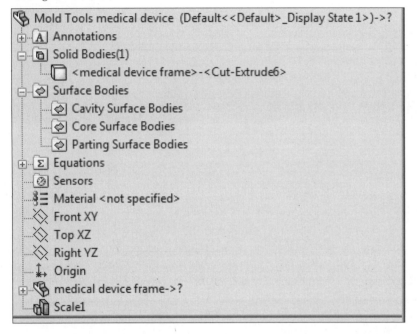

Parting lines

The Parting Lines feature identifies (semi-automatically or manually) the edges that separate the cavity faces from the core faces. If you are following along and want to perform this part of the process while reading, follow these steps:

1. Click the Parting Lines toolbar icon in the Mold Tools toolbar.

2. With the first selection box in the Mold Parameters panel active, select the Right (YZ) plane; and make sure the arrow is pointing in the direction of pull for the inside of the part, as shown in Figure 21.7.

3. Set the draft angle to 1 degree, which is the minimum angle allowed for this mold. In practice, the minimum draft applied to this mold is 1 degree, so you could use .5 degree here.

Setting the mold parameters for the parting lines

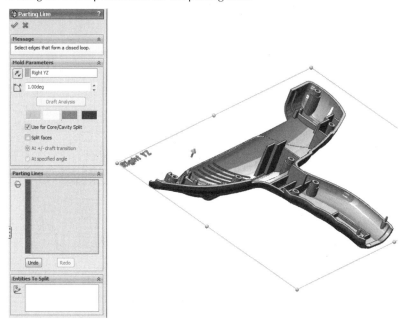

You should have done the draft analysis already before getting to this point so that you are not depending on this analysis to make sure everything is okay. For example, this draft analysis inside the Parting Line PropertyManager cannot tell you how many faces need draft.

4. Select an edge that is between a green and red face. The wavy edge along the finger grip area is a good one. SolidWorks cannot identify the parting line as the set of all edges that share green and red faces, so you will perform this step semi-automatically.

    The easiest way to do this is to click the wavy edge, and then click the Propagate tag that appears as shown in Figure 21.8.

    This propagating selection should select all of the parting line edges automatically, and it does, but in the example shown in Figure 21.9, it also selects some redundant edges. SolidWorks labels the redundant edges on the screen to help you see which ones need to be deselected. Notice that the message box at the top of the Parting Line PropertyManager tells you that the feature is not yet ready.

FIGURE 21.8

Propagating the parting line edge selection

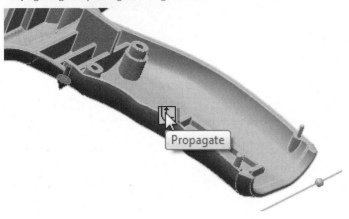

FIGURE 21.9

Correcting redundant selections

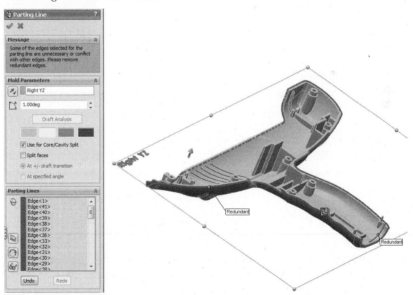

After deselecting the redundant edges, the message box in the PropertyManager turns yellow, because the Parting Line feature does not to split the mold. In this case, the part has screw holes that go through the part, so you need to create shut-off surfaces to close them. However, you are now done with the Parting Line feature.

5. Click the green check mark icon to accept the feature.

There should be 48 edges selected in the Parting Lines selection box.

Note

The parting line color is blue, and cavity and core colors are red and green. As a result, it is a good idea at this point to change the model to a neutral color, such as gray. You can do this by clicking the Appearances icon in the Heads Up View toolbar, and then clicking the Remove Appearances button. If the button does not become grayed out, it is renamed Remove All Appearances, and you can click this button again to remove overrides such as face, feature, or body appearance assignments. ∎

Initiating the shut-off surfaces

The mold industry is full of terminology that other design or manufacturing people might not be familiar with. *Shut-offs*, in mold lingo, are just locations inside the mold where the two sides of the mold dies touch one another. Shut-offs in the mold usually create holes within a plastic part. The shut-off surface – where the steel from one side of the mold touches the steel from the other side of the mold - is usually flat. Shut-off faces touch each other with significant pressure, so they are usually flat and perpendicular to the clamp force so they don't induce sliding. However, angled shut-offs can exist, and passing shut-offs are highly angled – as much as 80 degrees or so.

 The screw holes that go through the plastic part require shut-off faces in order to create the mold cavity and core. You can't just seal off any end of the holes; you have to pay attention to which end of the hole is where the drafts in opposite directions meet. In this case, the counterbored holes from the outside have to be drafted from the outside, so they must be sealed or shut off from the inside.

When you initiate the Shut-off Surfaces feature, SolidWorks identifies some of the necessary shut-offs for you, as shown in Figure 21.10.

To use the Shut-off Surfaces feature, follow these steps:

1. Click the Shut-Off Surfaces toolbar icon on the Mold Tools toolbar. SolidWorks should automatically select the inside edges of the seven screw holes. If not, then select these edges manually.

2. Locate the slanted ventilation slots in the plastic part, right-click the edge of one of them, and choose Select Tangency from the RMB menu. Four edges are added to the list box for each slot, and there are five slots.

When all 27 edges are selected, the message box at the top of the Shut-Off Surface PropertyManager turns green, as shown in Figure 21.11.

FIGURE 21.10

Creating shut-offs

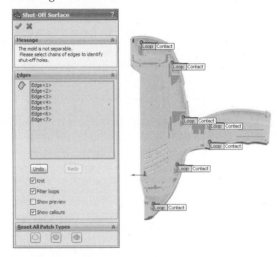

FIGURE 21.11

Sealing the shut-offs with surfaces

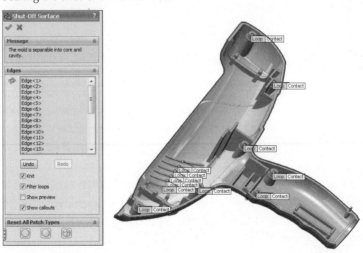

3. Ensure that the center option (All Contact) is selected in the Reset All Patch Types section before you finish.

4. When you are satisfied with the results, make sure the settings match those in Figure 21.11, and click the green check mark icon to accept the feature.

Note

If the feature does not work, and displays an error message stating that it cannot knit, then deselect the Knit option. While this isn't ideal, you will be able to troubleshoot later, as the automated Shut-Off feature does not allow you to troubleshoot in the middle of the command.

If you have to disable the Knit option, and the feature works, you may notice that some of the shut-off surfaces turn red and some turn green. This is just because SolidWorks actually creates one red and one green shut-off surface for each location. The red surfaces are knit together into the Cavity Surface body and the green surfaces are knit together into the Core Surface body. ■

When all appropriate edges around all the holes and slots are selected, the Shut-off Surfaces PropertyManager message window turns green and displays the message, "The mold is separable into core and cavity."

The tags on the loops in the graphics window display the text "No Fill," "Contact," or "Tangent." The No Fill condition means that you do not want SolidWorks to create the shut-off surfaces. You will do these manually. Sometimes shut-off surfaces require complex or multi-feature shut-offs, which you have to do manually. The Contact condition means that the shut-off surface just needs to touch the edges, usually at a right angle. The Tangent option creates a surface that is tangent to the surrounding faces all the way around.

Sometimes you need a combination of conditions in a single shut-off, in which case you need to finish the feature manually. When the parting line and shut-off surfaces are complete, SolidWorks automatically knits together all the surfaces in each Cavity and Core folder into a single surface body.

Parting surface

 The Parting Surface feature in SolidWorks Mold Tools works best on planar parting lines that are convex all the way around. On the sample medical device part used in this chapter, Figure 21.12 shows what SolidWorks makes of the parting surface.

Therefore, SolidWorks is not going to create the entire parting surface for this part automatically. The goal for the Parting Surface tool is to create a surface that looks rectangular from the direction of pull. Most molding dies are rectangular (although some inserts are circular), and you have to be able to describe the surface between the halves of the mold.

The default-parting surface on the medical device part

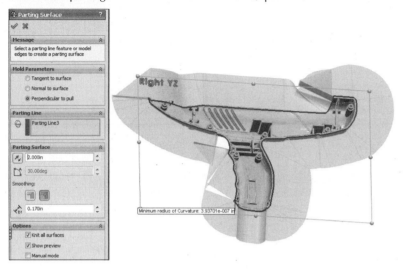

Working example

In the following example, a very simple part is created and the Mold Tools process is applied. When the process works as it should, and even when you have to create surfaces manually, you end up with one complete surface body in each of the Mold Tools folders — cavity, core, and parting surfaces. From this, you can see that the parting surface and cavity surface define the top side of the cavity block. Likewise, the parting surface and the core surface define the top side of the core block.

In Figure 21.13, the parting surface is transparent so you can see both the cavity and core surface bodies. The figure may not show this distinctly, but if you open the part from the DVD, it will be very clear.

Using the manual options

SolidWorks 2011 has added some manual intervention options with the Parting Surface tool, specifically because there were very few cases in which the automatic method worked. In this case, it turned out that the manual intervention options worked with less intervention than the default options.

FIGURE 21.13

A completed parting surface

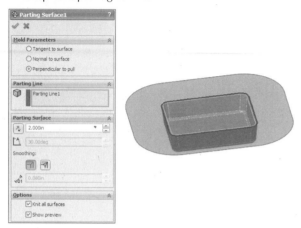

From the disappointing result shown in Figure 21.12, you can just change to manual mode, and change the parting surface distance to 10 inches. The result is shown in Figure 21.14.

There are still some things to change here, and every mold designer might do this differently. One solution is to use the black rectangle as the useful boundary of the surface, and to trim off anything outside of the rectangle. The one thing that definitely has to be changed is the upper-left corner, where the parting line is changing levels and sweeps around the corner at the same time. You will fix this shortly.

Note

If there is a weakness in using manual mode, it is in the connector-like dots shown in Figure 21.15. To get this to work, you have to arrange the pink dots around the perimeter such that none of the black lines overlap one another or the part to be molded. In the area where the inset face curls around the bottom of the part, this becomes difficult, and causes SolidWorks to create bad faces. If you are doing this exercise on your own, try to arrange the pink dots as shown in Figure 21.15. If you see a gap in the surface along the edge, or a place where it appears to overlap itself, this will cause an error in the finished surface. This is not an ideal method for creating tooling surfaces, but it does work. ■

Although the Parting Surface feature is very slow (this example may take about 30 seconds to process), it is a definite improvement over the default method for any but the simplest mold splits.

FIGURE 21.14

Using manual mode

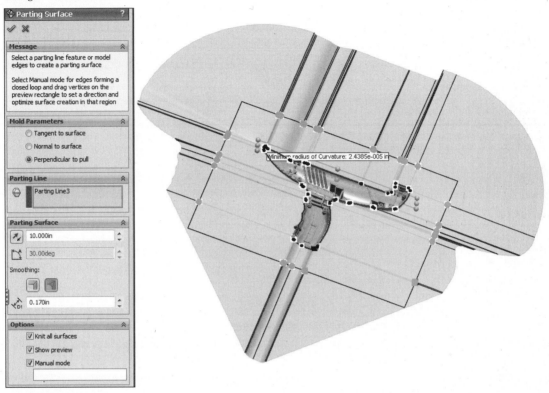

FIGURE 21.15

Aligning the dots to eliminate overlaps

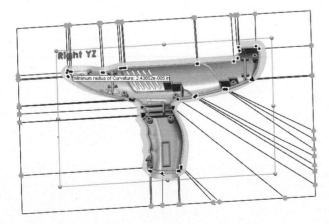

Repairing the manual mode parting surface

To repair the surface made in the last step:

1. Use Delete Face (with the Delete option) to delete the upper-left corner face. Delete Face can be found on the Surfaces toolbar or through the menus at Insert ⇨ Face ⇨ Delete.

2. When you delete the face, right-click the Parting Line feature in the FeatureManager and hide it.

3. Start the Boundary surface from the Surfaces toolbar, right-click in the Direction 1 selection box, and start the SelectionManager.

4. With the SelectionManager open, activate the Select Group option, and select the exposed edge of the mode and the surface edge parallel to the Y direction (no need to hold down Ctrl); then click the green check mark icon on the SelectionManager.

Next, in the Boundary Surface PropertyManager, switch to the Direction 2 selection box, pick the open edge parallel to the Z-axis (no need for the SelectionManager), and click the green check mark icon on the Boundary PropertyManager, as shown in Figure 21.16. You should now have a surface as shown in Figure 21.17.

The final steps for the parting surface are to knit it together into the core surface and the cavity surface. Follow these steps to accomplish this:

1. **Use Knit to knit together the Boundary surface and the Parting Surface body resulting from the manual mode process.**

2. **Make sure this knit surface goes into the Parting Surface Bodies folder, as shown in Figure 21.18.**

FIGURE 21.16

Setting up the Boundary surface

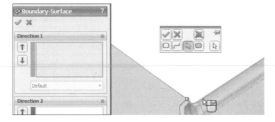

The parting surface is larger than you need it to be, and it is not a pretty shape, but neither of those issues matters.

FIGURE 21.17

The completed Boundary surface

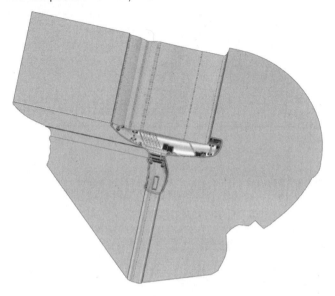

FIGURE 21.18

The completed Parting Surface and Feature tree

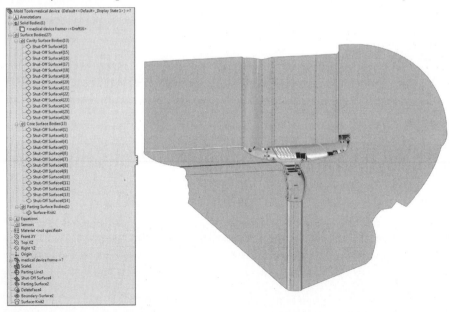

Tooling split

 Assuming either you have completed the parting surface manually or through the SolidWorks Mold Tools, the next step is the tooling split. If you complete the parting surface manually, make sure it is knit together as a single surface body, and then in the Surface Bodies folder, drag the knit surface into the Parting Surface folder. The Tooling Split feature does not work unless all the surface bodies are in their correct folders.

Figure 21.19 shows the PropertyManager for the Tooling Split feature, along with a preview of the feature. The feature will produce two solid bodies, representing the cavity and core blocks of the mold. This model is included on the DVD with the material for this chapter.

FIGURE 21.19

The Tooling Split PropertyManager and the finished product

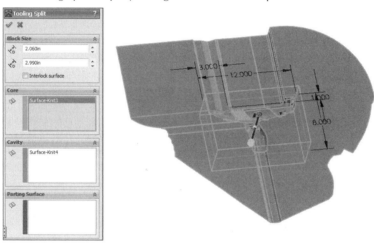

A tooling engineer would probably change a few things about the layout of this split, but for learning how the tools work, this is sufficient. The parting line of the front part of the device should probably face forward instead of up to reduce the amount of vertical steel in the mold. To send the cavity and core blocks to a shop for mold building, you will probably want to separate the multi-body part into individual part files.

Note
To check the cavity and core blocks to ensure that they make the desired shape, make a new block that is larger than the original part, ensuring that the Merge Result option is deselected. Then use the Combine tool to subtract the mold parts from the new block. Finally, use the inverse scale to shrink it back down to the finished part size (½ the original scale factor). ∎

Using the Core feature

The following example uses the Core feature to create a set of core pins. All the standing steel that creates the counterbores for the screw bosses is made from separate replaceable pins. You can use many techniques to locate pins rotationally. This is not a lesson in mold design, but only in mold modeling techniques.

You can either pre-create a sketch or just make a sketch when the Core feature asks you for it. The Core feature is looking for a sketch that will cut out the block of mold material from which you want to make a core. Again, you can use this for side cores or core pins. In this case, you will make several core pins.

To start, activate the Core feature; then sketch circles centered on each of the screw boss cores in the cavity body. When you exit the sketch using the Confirmation Corner, SolidWorks prompts you for an extrusion depth for the sketch to create the feature. The Core PropertyManager and the feature preview are shown in Figure 21.20.

FIGURE 21.20

The Core feature

Again, you can save out these core pins as individual part files. You can use similar techniques to create side cores, lifters, or other types of side actions.

Intervening Manually with Mold Tools

You can conduct the entire mold modeling process manually, without using any of the semi-automated tools from Mold Tools. You may even come across situations where you do not need to use surface modeling at all. These situations will often involve parts with a planar parting line, with no shut-offs or cores.

Experienced mold designers tend to use different techniques, from cutting away chunks with solids to using all manual surfacing methods to using about 80 percent Mold Tools techniques and the rest manual surfacing. It probably makes most sense to use the Mold Tools for the techniques you are good at, because they do speed up some tasks, such as planar shut-offs and separating out the cavity and core faces.

You will now run through two examples of manually intervening in the Mold Tools process. In the first, you will learn how to create a passing shut-off (a shut-off with a stepped parting line), and in the second, you will learn how to create the parting surface.

Passing shut-offs

Snap features are often achieved in molds by using passing shut-offs rather than some sort of lifter or horn pin slide. Eliminating actions from a mold can be economical, as long as the passing shut-off does not introduce wear or alignment problems. When creating parts that require this sort of feature in the mold, it is a good idea to consult your mold builder.

Passing shut-offs can be difficult to visualize, even for seasoned professionals. It might be a good idea to open up the part and study the geometry.

On the DVD

The file `passing shut off start.sldprt` from the material for this chapter on the DVD is a clip that holds a CD in place in a plastic case. The draft analysis colors have been left on it to help you see which faces belong to which side of the mold. There are no undercuts on this part, as shown in Figure 21.21. ■

Two pair of passing shut-offs are modeled in this part.

Using the rollback bar is probably the best way to see what is going on with this part. The surfacing involved here may be confusing to you if you are not well versed with surfacing, but looking at the part and understanding the steps will help you learn. The basic steps to create the surface body called Shut-off 1 are as follows:

1. Create a ruled surface for the planar edges.
2. Loft surfaces between the parting line edges and the ruled surface.
3. Extrude a flat shut-off face at the parting line of the Snap feature.

4. Use the cavity or core knitted body to trim the extruded surface.

5. Use the extruded surface to trim the ruled and lofted surfaces.

6. Knit the surface bodies together.

FIGURE 21.21

A part that requires passing shut-offs

The hardest part of creating this passing shut-off is visualizing what the interface between the steel from opposite sides is going to look like. It is best to keep it as simple as possible. Tool builders request a wide range of angles for the passing shut-off (mold steel touching at steeply angled faces). The minimum draft they can possibly stand ranges from 5 to 15 degrees of draft. You should try to give at least 8 degrees and more if you can. The tool builder will also look for a minimum land (flat steel making contact from either side) on the top of the shut-off boss, generally not less than 1mm, or approx 0.050 inch, to work with round numbers.

Don't be discouraged if you don't completely understand this the first time around. The concept itself is difficult, and visualizing the geometry is even more difficult.

Creating non-planar parting surfaces

The method SolidWorks uses to create the parting surface is adequate for simple tasks, such as molding a range of Frisbees or dinner plates, but it will not work well for more complex projects such as handheld medical devices. Figure 21.22 shows the part on the DVD named frame parting surface.sldprt. The result is entirely unacceptable for several reasons, including big gaps in the parting surface, and unnecessarily complex parting surface.

FIGURE 21.22

An automatically created parting surface for the handheld medical device

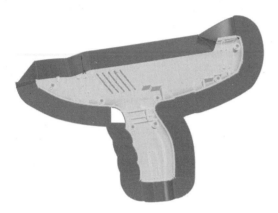

From this, you can learn that the SolidWorks Mold Tools are not reliable for concave parting lines or non-planar parting lines. Flat parting line disks and boxes work well. Beyond that, you should expect to do some manual surface modeling.

Note

If you want software that will create automatic parting surfaces for you, consider MoldWorks and SplitWorks from R&B Mold and Die Design Solutions (www.RnBUSA.com). This software also includes highly automated mold libraries and aids to help you model and document every aspect of mold hardware. ■

To manually create the parting surfaces for this part, you will tackle the difficult step first, which turns out to be easy once you know a couple of tricks. The first step is to create a sketch and use it to lay out directions that you can pull off the non-planar sections of the parting line. Figure 21.23 shows three lines that identify the non-planar top, base of grip, and trigger areas. The sketch lines lead in directions where those edges can be projected without running into other geometry.

Then the edges of each non-planar portion of the parting line can be converted into sketch entities in a 3D sketch and extruded as a surface along each of these three directions. From there, it is simple to create planar surfaces between the non-planar sections. This technique may not work for all non-planar parting lines, but it does work for this one.

FIGURE 21.23

Projecting non-planar sections

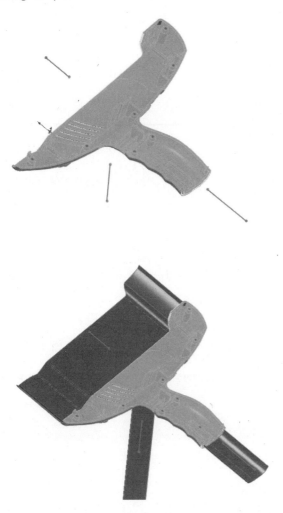

Summary

SolidWorks 2011 has added some functionality to its Mold Tools that is worth looking at if you have ignored these tools in the past. The tools are semi-automated and usually require some sort of manual intervention, although the tools greatly speed up some tasks.

Working with Large Scale Design

L arge Scale Design is the first step that SolidWorks has made into the world of architectural design and documentation. It is intended to be the first of several architecture, engineering, and construction (AEC) type tools aimed at the design of large, welded structures. According to SolidWorks marketing materials, "Large Scale Design brings together the tools you need to effectively design machinery, heavy equipment, plants, small ships, and other large objects."

Dassault Systèmes, the parent company to SolidWorks, is also working on a product called SolidWorks Live Buildings, which is a Catia V6-based full AEC design tool. This is only mentioned here to make clear the distinction between the more basic objectives of SolidWorks Large Scale Design, aimed at large welded or bolted-together structures, and the more polished architectural work for finished buildings.

Large Scale Design encompasses three topics that are covered in this chapter: walk-through animation, GridSystem, and IFC export. Look for Large Scale Design to increase in scope in future releases of SolidWorks. While Large Scale Design also uses standard SolidWorks functionality such as sketching, part modeling, assembly modeling, weldments, and drawings, these other features do not presently have capabilities that are specific to Large Scale Design.

IN THIS CHAPTER

Creating an animation simulating a walk-through

Creating a grid structure

Exporting to IFC

Creating a Walk-Through

 Walk-through is a method for creating an animation simulating what a person would see as they walk through a Large Scale Design. It was developed primarily for the new architectural tools that are being added to SolidWorks, but it may also be appropriate for certain types of equipment, facility, or site design.

This chapter looks at the case of the very large dump truck, because this is a good example of equipment design where a walk-through would be useful. Figure 22.1 shows the Walk-through area of the DisplayManager along with the model used for this example. You can create walk-throughs using an interface to direct an avatar, or you can drive the camera along a sketched path. The sketched path method has some overlap with MotionManager animation, which is covered in Chapter 23 of this book.

You can find the Walk-through command through the menu at View ⇨ Lights and Cameras ⇨ Add Walk-through, or the DisplayManager ⇨ Scenes, Lights, and Cameras ⇨ Walk-through.

FIGURE 22.1

Using the DisplayManager to manage a walk-through

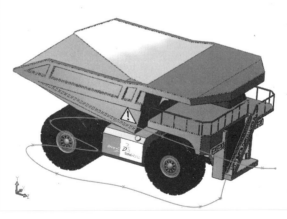

The interface for the walk-through consists of two elements, the Walk-through PropertyManager and the Walk-through toolbar. The initial setup is controlled by the Walk-through PropertyManager, shown in Figure 22.2.

In the PropertyManager, you select a base plane, which acts as a floor. You then establish a camera height to simulate the height of your eyes off the floor. If you intend to drive the walk-through using a sketch, you can select the sketch elements in the Motion Constraints selection box. For the most fluid motion, it is recommended that you use splines. You can use 2D or 3D sketches.

FIGURE 22.2

Using the Walk-through PropertyManager for initial setup

When you begin to capture the walk-through, a Map View window appears. When this window is active, it significantly slows down the performance of the walk-through. Capturing the walk-through requires an interface (shown in Figure 22.3) that is significantly different from other SolidWorks tools. While the interface and documentation refer to an "avatar," you will not see any sort of virtual manikin walking through the model, except in SolidWorks sales demonstrations.

FIGURE 22.3

Using the special Walk-through interface

Once you are in this mode, the scroll wheel on your mouse works backwards from standard SolidWorks functionality for zooming, (in SolidWorks with default settings, when you scroll the top of the wheel away from you, the screen zooms out, so in Walk-through, when you scroll the top of the wheel away from you, the screen zooms closer to you).

Walk-through is in its initial stages and is usable for simple animations. The workflow to create a walk-through goes like this:

1. Select a suitable model, preferably one with an interior that you want to virtually wander around inside. This works best with models on the scale of buildings.

2. Click the DisplayManager tab in the FeatureManager area.

3. Click the Scene, Lights, and Cameras button.

4. Right-click the Walk-through entry in the list, and select Add Walk-through.

5. Establish a floor or vertical direction and literally tell it which end is up (by selecting a plane or axis). Also, establish the height of your eyes above the floor.

6. If you are using a sketch path, select the sketch segments in the Motion Constraints selection box.

7. Begin Capture of Walk-through by clicking the Capture Walk-through button in the Walk0through PropertyManager. If you are using sketches to drive the motion, just click the Forward button on the interface, and the camera walks along the path. If you are not using sketches, use the arrows on the interface to make the camera (called an avatar in this interface) move.

8. Generate and save the video. Use the red dot to record, and the green arrows to move.

On the DVD

The Dump Truck files used for this example are on the DVD as `Dump Truck.sldasm`. **This is a good model for practice.**

Creating a GridSystem

In SolidWorks, a *GridSystem* is a 3D sketch that repeats a 2D sketch on every level of a structure. It is intended to speed construction of multi-level 3D reference geometry to help plan your machine, system, weldment, or structure. The grid can range from very large (industrial facilities) to very small (desktop tubing kits).

Intended applications include providing paths for weldment member or piping placement, and mating for large equipment to the grid for placement. Grids are typically rectangular but can also be circular. In circular grids, labeling of the grid is not supported, nor are radial lines in the circular grid.

You start by creating a 2D sketch where lines represent structural members for that level. SolidWorks uses derived sketches on planes. The actual 3D sketch only contains columns. For example, the structure could be bolted together from fabricated I-beams, a welded tubing structure, or an assembled scaffolding.

As a component of the Large Scale Design initiative, the Grid System is still in its early phases, so it may have some limitations. The GridSystem can help you identify interior and exterior walls, structural columns, and beams. Figure 22.4 shows a complete GridSystem.

FIGURE 22.4

Building a GridSystem in SolidWorks

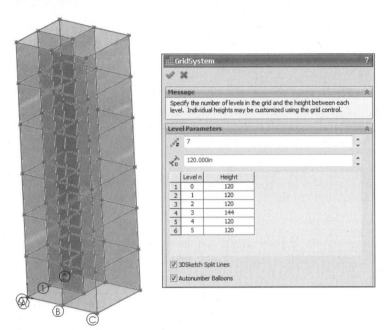

Here is the basic workflow for creating a GridSystem:

1. Click the GridSystem button on the Feature toolbar or in the Insert ⇨ Reference Geometry menu selection.

2. Draw a sketch that represents the outer shape of the structure, as well as inner structural members.

3. Use the GridSystem PropertyManager to establish the number of levels (floors), the default height for the levels, and the specific height for each level.

4. Click OK in the PropertyManager and watch SolidWorks build the GridSystem.

The following sections include the details for each of the above steps.

Starting the GridSystem feature

The GridSystem toolbar icon is listed as part of the Feature toolbar, although it does not appear there by default. If you want to add the GridSystem icon to any toolbar, choose Tools ⇨ Customize ⇨ Commands, and select it from the end of the list of icons for the Feature toolbar.

You can access the GridSystem feature through the menus by default, but it is in a different location. Through the menus, choose Insert ⇨ Reference Geometry ⇨ GridSystem.

Creating the sketch

When you start the GridSystem feature, SolidWorks puts you into a 2D sketch on the Top (XZ) plane. The software is waiting for you to create a sketch with some specific properties. This sketch essentially represents the layout of the structural members forming one level of the structure. Figure 22.5 shows a sample sketch. The sketch is dimensioned in inches, but you can also use other units, such as feet.

FIGURE 22.5

Sketching a sample structural layout

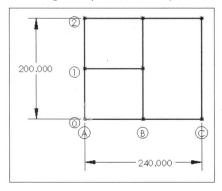

Notice also that annotations label the intersections of the lines with letters for the X direction and numbers for the Z direction. This is the method structural engineers use to identify the columns in the structure. The column in the center of the sketch shown in Figure 22.5 would be called 1B. SolidWorks automatically generates these column line labels when you select the Autonumber Balloons option at the bottom of the GridSystem PropertyManager.

There appear to be several rules for the sketch that are not obvious. First, all of the lines are planar, and either horizontal or vertical within the sketch. Presently, SolidWorks does not allow you to make a circular structure, or use the sketch to lay out something like a power-line tower. This is not to say you could not add diagonal members later, but you cannot use them as part of the initial layout for the GridSystem.

Using the GridSystem PropertyManager

When you are done, exit the sketch by clicking the sketch icon in the Confirmation Corner (in the upper-right corner of the graphics window). The GridSystem PropertyManager appears, as shown in Figure 22.6.

FIGURE 22.6

Setting up the grid in the PropertyManager

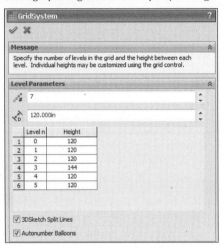

The features in the GridSystem PropertyManager are straightforward. The default level height of 118.11023622 inches is a conversion of the default 3-meter height that SolidWorks uses. Notice that you can customize the height of each level; for example, if Level 3 has some specialized equipment that needs more room than the standard level height, you can easily specify this as part of the design.

The 3DSketch Split Lines option controls whether the columns that extend through all levels of the grid will be continuous from top to bottom or will be split at each level. Which option you select depends mainly on what you plan to do with the GridSystem. If you plan to use it to create a weldment, you may want to split the lines. If you plan to simply extrude shapes the entire height of the structure, you may prefer to not split them.

Understanding the GridSystem output

The GridSystem creates a single feature in the FeatureManager with a number of derived sketches and planes, as shown in Figure 22.7. All of the additional features are listed as parents of the GridSystem and indented underneath it in the FeatureManager.

You have already looked at the derived sketches and planes, one for each level, created at the appropriate heights. A derived sketch is simply a parametric copy of the original sketch, placed on a different plane. If the original sketch changes, the derived copies are also updated. You can move or rotate derived sketches, but you cannot edit them; all changes must be performed at the parent sketch.

The 3D sketch in the FeatureManager contains lines forming the columns (Y direction lines between the levels). This sketch is hidden by default.

FIGURE 22.7

Listing the GridSystem output

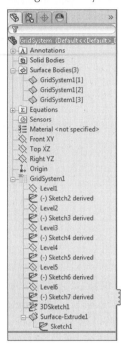
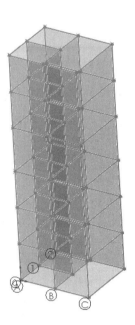

You may also notice that the GridSystem uses transparent surfaces to represent interior and exterior walls. These are hidden by default. Depending on your structure, you may or may not need information about walls, or you might only care about the exterior walls. SolidWorks Corp. has indicated that the surfaces are intended to support functionality, which has not yet been added to the software.

If you are not familiar with surfaces, in this case your interaction with them is limited to showing and hiding them. You can use either the Display Pane or RMB menus to do this. You can also refer to the *SolidWorks 2011 Parts Bible*, which contains detailed descriptions of working with and visualizing surfaces in the chapters on visualization, surfaces, and multibody modeling.

Viewing the Grid Components

If you right-click the GridSystem feature in the FeatureManager, a selection appears named View Grid Components. This is useful if you create a weldment from the grid and want to see a list of only the features that comprise the actual grid, rather than all of the weldment features. The View Grid Components dialog box is shown in Figure 22.8.

FIGURE 22.8

Isolating the grid components in the View Grid Components dialog box

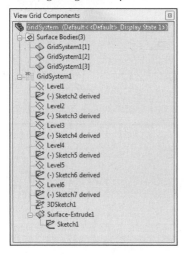

Transferring Data with the IFC File Type

IFC stands for Industry Foundation Classes and was developed by the International Alliance for Interoperability (IAI) as an open data exchange format. It is meant to transfer data on building models between building information model (BIM) software packages. ArchiCAD and Revit are two examples of BIM modelers that might use this type of information.

The IFC file type includes geometry, but it also includes non-geometrical information about the function and occupant of spaces within the building. You could think of this as the ability to transfer SolidWorks custom property information along with a STEP (Standard for the Exchange of Product model data) file transfer.

While SolidWorks is a relative newcomer to the AEC fields, it is firmly established in equipment design, which is closely related to the design of plants and industrial steel-framed structures.

To save a GridSystem as an *.IFC file, choose File ➪ Save As, and in the Save as type drop-down list, select the *.IFC file type. You can also click the Options button to set the units and OmniClass™, as shown in Figure 22.9.

The OmniClass™ classifications give you a detailed structure for classifying the data prior to importing it into a building model. Software such as SolidWorks can be used for small components in buildings rather than for the actual building, but the equipment produced in SolidWorks can still be used in the BIM model. Air conditioning equipment, windows, plumbing, and other component hardware are commonly created in SolidWorks.

If you would like to learn more about the IFC standard, you can go to the website at www.aecbytes.com/feature/2004/IFCmodel.html, which has a detailed description of the structure, purpose, and history of the file type.

FIGURE 22.9

Saving data as an *.IFC file

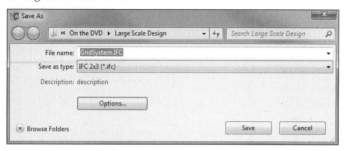

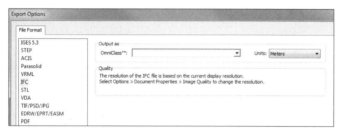

Summary

SolidWorks has long been used for the design of equipment and components that go into buildings. Recently, with Large Scale Design, the software is starting to move into the design of small plants and gridded structures. The Walk-through feature gives Large Scale Design users some animation capabilities, and the *.IFC export options allow users to share SolidWorks Large Scale Designs with other BIM software users.

Large Scale Design is an early phase in the evolution toward SolidWorks being used for AEC applications. Large Scale Design may at some point be combined with SolidWorks Live Buildings, another nascent BIM modeler intended for more traditional architectural design.

Animating with the MotionManager

The MotionManager is an interface that enables you to create movies showing motion of parts and assemblies based on a timeline. These movies can range from a simple rotating part to complex moving machinery, involving motion constrained by assembly mates or motion driven by motors, springs, gravity, and contact. You can render the movies using PhotoView 360 or show them in a SolidWorks display mode, including RealView.

Collectively, the results of any of the motion capabilities in SolidWorks are called Motion Studies. Some of the capabilities are more focused on analysis while others involve simple animation for presenting a movie, but all are able to create movie output.

SolidWorks 2011 has three primary methods and two ancillary methods of creating motion in assemblies. The primary methods are

- **Animation.** This creates simple motion driven by the Animation Wizard, key frames, mates, and motors.
- **Basic Motion.** This includes motors, springs, friction, and standard mates.
- **SolidWorks Motion (analysis).** This includes basic motion as well as forces and dampers, and will calculate loads, velocities, and accelerations. This is not part of SolidWorks Standard, but you will take a brief look at it anyway, just to get a well-rounded view of the entire topic of animation and motion in SolidWorks. SolidWorks Motion is an add-in that you must activate in the Tools ⇨ Add-ins menu, and is only available with SolidWorks Premium or SolidWorks Simulation Professional.

The two ancillary methods of capturing movies are

- **Walk-through.** This is a summary of preexisting tools paired with a simplified interface for architectural-type walk-through animations.
- **Record Screen.** This records simple view rotation and dynamic assembly model motion.

Familiarizing Yourself with the MotionManager

If it has been a couple of years since you used SolidWorks Animator to make movies, you may be a little overwhelmed by all of the new terminology. The names do not necessarily reflect the capabilities of the new tools, and you will need to know where the capabilities of one tool end and those of the next one begin.

In addition to the terminology, you need to be comfortable with the limits of the technology that SolidWorks provides in these tools. Your success with the tools depends heavily on having realistic expectations of what you can accomplish with the available tools.

Understanding the terminology

If you go to reseller or user-led events, you may hear these tools referred to by various names. For example, the Animation feature may be called Animator, Basic Animation, or MotionManager. This is the most basic tool available, but even within the SolidWorks documentation and among SolidWorks employees, the naming is inconsistent.

Basic Motion may also simply be called Motion, or COSMOSMotion, or it may even be mistakenly identified as one of the other tools. This tool offers more precise, more analytical motion than the Animation feature and includes some physics-based options.

SolidWorks Motion is an actual motion analysis tool, rather than a simple animation program. Many users may not understand the differences between motion and animation tools, or that different names even exist.

Here's an overview of the terminology used in conjunction with motion in SolidWorks:

- **MotionManager.** The MotionManager is the interface that gives you access to the Animation, Basic Motion, and SolidWorks Motion tools. This single interface controls all of the tools, which may be the source of the confusion about how different tools are named.
- **SolidWorks Motion.** COSMOSMotion is now called SolidWorks Motion. It is the most analytical of the three options. If you need detailed input and output including graphed functions, SolidWorks Motion is the best choice.

- **Basic Motion.** Physical Simulation is now called Basic Motion. Basic Motion uses motors, springs, gravity, and so on; it does not use key frames. It includes the Physical Dynamics feature, which deals with the calculation of motion due to collisions.

- **Animation.** Assembly Motion is now called Animation. Animation uses the *key frame* method, where the software interpolates between positions established by mates, free-hand drag, or positioning via triad or XYZ values. You should not confuse Animation with *dynamic assembly motion*, which is simply dragging parts in an assembly with the cursor to create motion.

If you need a function that is only allowed in another type of motion study, you need to change the motion study type in the drop-down selection box in the upper-left corner of the MotionManager. The default option is Animation, and the other two available options are Basic Motion and Motion Analysis. You can see the Study Type box in the interface shown in Figure 23.1.

Remember also that PhotoView 360 has replaced PhotoWorks as the SolidWorks photo-realistic renderer. The interface and functionality of PhotoView 360 is significantly different from that of PhotoWorks. Neither tool is covered in this book, but SolidWorks does produce a step-by-step book, called *Creating Animations with SolidWorks Step-by-Step*, that users can buy directly without taking a training class. You can get the book from SolidWorks directly or from SolidWorks resellers.

 Another method that you can use to capture screen motion to a movie file is by using the Record Video tool (View ⇨ Screen Capture ⇨ Record Video). The Record Video tool also appears as a toolbar button on the Screen Capture toolbar. You can use Record Video to record whatever happens in the graphics window, from using the Rollback bar to running Basic Motion studies.

Driving an animation

You can animate the following:

- Distance mates
- Angle mates
- Part appearance (including display modes — shaded, wireframe, and so on)
- Part transparency
- Part visibility
- Part position
- View/zoom state
- Camera position and properties

When you animate colors and appearances, simple colors can fade from one to another, but any appearance with a texture does not fade; it simply snaps to the next texture at the appropriate time. For example, you can fade red to blue, but you cannot fade marble to fabric. This is also true with fading transparency in an animation that is rendered using PhotoView 360.

You cannot animate the following:

- Changing part dimensions
- Changing PhotoView 360 materials
- Configurations

While you can't animate the changing of part dimensions directly, with some creativity, you can animate in-context changes driven by changing mates. You will see an example of creating a part that is flexible later in this chapter.

The items you can use to drive an animation are

- Key points (Animation)
- Mates (Animation, Basic Motion, SolidWorks Motion)
- Motors (Animation, Basic Motion, SolidWorks Motion)
- Gravity (Basic Motion, SolidWorks Motion)
- Springs (Basic Motion, SolidWorks Motion)
- Contact (Basic Motion, SolidWorks Motion)
- Friction (Basic Motion, SolidWorks Motion)
- Force (SolidWorks Motion)
- Dampers (SolidWorks Motion)

The types of motion that are available are

- Kinematic (mates and motors — Animation, Basic Motion, SolidWorks Motion)
- Dynamic (physics based — Basic Motion, SolidWorks Motion)
- Free motion (motion based only on key points — Animation)

When you think of "physics" in SolidWorks, you may need to adjust some of your expectations; some of the tools do not follow real physics concepts very rigorously. For example, a motor applied to a part in an assembly creates a constant velocity instantly, without regard for inertia. Friction only has a single component rather than the static and kinetic, which exist in real engineering problems. You can simulate static friction with a force and an equation, but it is not available as a function of friction.

Planning an animation

It is often useful to plan an animation that is more involved than just a few moves on the screen. You can do this in a couple of different ways. The easiest way is to write out a list of moves or positions you want to display, with the approximate time of each action or position.

Another way is to use the storyboard technique employed by professional video houses. In this method, you create a series of images to represent the state of the animation at specific points in time. You can use static screen captures from SolidWorks or hand sketches to do this, depending on the complexity of the geometry and animation.

In general, even for simple animations, the better you plan, the better the final product will be. The animation tools in SolidWorks tend to perform much better when you follow a clean workflow, without a lot of major editing. This is something you could probably say about almost any process, but the animation tools seem to be particularly sensitive to this kind of editing flow.

Identifying elements of the MotionManager

The parts of the interface that you will use the most are the key points, the design tree, and the timebar. The filters help you select or view limited sets of items, and the tabs at the bottom enable you to set up alternative studies. Playback speed enables you to change the rate of playback to either view a long animation more quickly or see motion in one area in more detail. The timeline zoom tools enable you to rescale the time interval on the timeline. Figure 23.1 identifies the major elements of the MotionManager.

FIGURE 23.1

The major elements of the MotionManager

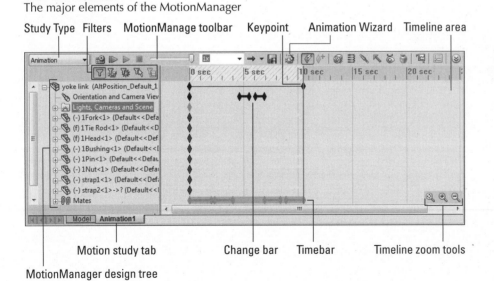

Using display options

When recording an animation to a movie file or a series of still images, you can choose from several types of display output. The first and easiest type is the default SolidWorks display, without RealView. This is most appropriate for fast, technical presentations. You might want to use this to demonstrate the function of a particular mechanism or to simply rotate around a model to demonstrate the model in 3D rather than as a flat image or an eDrawing.

You can also turn on RealView and record the animation. If you do this, you should have appropriate appearances in use for individual parts. RealView appearances enable you to use reflective or textured materials on your parts.

The highest-quality images come through the PhotoView 360 renderer. Using PhotoView 360 takes much more time than the other options because each individual frame must be rendered just like a normal PhotoView 360 rendering. PhotoView 360 is beyond the scope of this book.

Using the MotionManager interface

You can access the MotionManager interface in the lower-left corner of the graphics window. The Model and Animation1 tabs enable you to toggle the interface on and off. The Model tab shows the normal SolidWorks interface. You can add tabs to create multiple motion studies. Figure 23.2 shows the lower-left corner of the SolidWorks window with each of the buttons activated. If you cannot see this interface, you may need to turn on the MotionManager. To do this, right-click a toolbar and select MotionManager from the list of toolbars.

FIGURE 23.2

Accessing the MotionManager interface

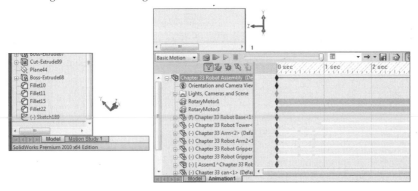

Formatting output

The MotionManager enables you to create animations within SolidWorks and output movies as * .avi files or a series of * .bmp or * .tga still images. You can use it with the default

(OpenGL) SolidWorks display, RealView display, or in conjunction with PhotoView 360 to create more realistic rendered animations.

Note
PhotoView 360 replaces PhotoWorks in SolidWorks 2011, and should have all of the animation capabilities that PhotoWorks had previously. ■

You can control the pixel size and frame rate of the recorded animation to help control finished file size, movie quality, and the amount of time it takes to record the animation. You can rotate or fly through single parts or assemblies. You can also make assembly mechanisms move through animating mates, driving them with motors or manually positioning the parts in space.

One of the beautiful things about SolidWorks animations is that you can save them to an eDrawings file. You can send eDrawings to non-SolidWorks users for review, and because the file format is small, you can easily send animations over the Internet.

Using the Animation Wizard

You can use the Animation Wizard to create simple animations. The Animation Wizard accommodates two types: the first is where a part or assembly is simply rotated on the screen, and the second uses an existing exploded view from an assembly. You can combine, reorder, reverse, copy, or move both types of animation sequences within a larger animation.

Creating a rotating animation

To create a rotating animation, first click the Animation1 tab at the bottom-left corner of the graphics window. This opens the MotionManager interface. Remember that you can turn the MotionManager on or off in the list of toolbars. (Choose Tools ⇨ Customize or View ⇨ Toolbars, or right-click any toolbar to access the setting for the MotionManager.)

 Click the Animation Wizard icon in the toolbar on top of the MotionManager. Figure 23.3 shows the dialog box that appears, where you can choose options that include Rotate model, Explode, Collapse, Import motion from Basic Motion, and Import motion from Motion Analysis. In this example, all options are grayed out except for Rotate model. The model that is loaded does not have an exploded view, or Basic Motion or SolidWorks Motion data.

After you select the appropriate type of animation and click Next, you select an axis of rotation, the number of rotations, and the direction. An important thing to note here is that the X-, Y-, and Z-axes do not refer to axes of the part; they refer to axes on the screen. Rotating about the X-axis is like holding down the right-arrow key on the keyboard. The sample animation that appears in the upper-left corner of the Animation Wizard, shown in Figure 23.4, shows what you can expect. It changes direction if you change the option.

FIGURE 23.3

The first page of the Animation Wizard: Select an Animation Type.

FIGURE 23.4

The second page of the Animation Wizard: Select an Axis of Rotation.

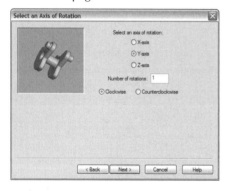

The final step in creating the rotating animation is to determine how long the animation will last, and at what point in the overall animation it should start. Figure 23.5 shows the Animation Wizard page where you can set these options.

Note

Looping is only controlled during playback. The actual animation has a beginning and an end, and so if you want to play the finished movie with smooth looping, you should make sure that the start point and the end point of the animation are the same. ■

After you click Finish, the MotionManager populates the timeline with key points for the Orientation and Camera Views. Instead of rotating the part, the software rotates the view. It seems like a semantic difference, but when you start working with moving parts in assemblies while changing the view, the difference becomes important. Notice the heavy black line with diamonds in the row for the Orientation and Camera Views in Figure 23.6. Each diamond is a key point that represents a view angle, and the line between the diamonds indicates that MotionManager will interpolate the view between the key points, making the view transition smoothly. You will learn how to create key points later in this chapter.

The third page of the Animation Wizard: Animation Control Options

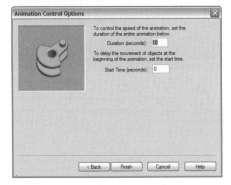

Change bars in the MotionManager

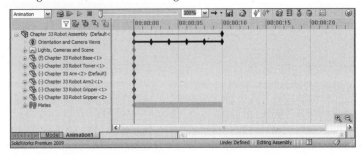

 To play the animation, click the Play From Start button or the Play button in the MotionManager toolbar. Note also that you can run the Animation Wizard multiple times to create various sequences within a single animation. You can control the start time and duration, which are added to the timeline. You can also edit the key points and even mirror the path.

Creating an exploded view animation

The sample assembly on the DVD in the Animations folder is named `Robot Assembly.sldasm`, and is saved with an exploded view. You can use this assembly or create your own. If you use this file, you must first create a new animation for practicing. To use the Animation Wizard to create an animated explode and collapse, first start with an assembly that has an exploded view and activate the Animation Wizard. Figure 23.3 shows the first page of the Animation Wizard where you select the animation type. Select the Explode option and click Next. Figure 23.7 shows the second page. (Explode animations skip the second step, which is used by Rotate animations.)

FIGURE 23.7

The second page of the Explode Animation Wizard

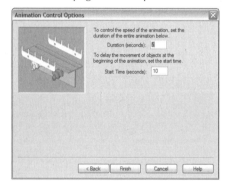

If you add the explode animation at the end of the rotate animation, the resulting animation does both: rotates then explodes, each in sequence. Later you will learn how to copy and reverse the key points for the explode to make it collapse, and how to adjust key points to make parts move faster, slower, or simultaneously.

You can also edit the animation created by the explode or collapse in the same way you would edit the rotate animation created by the wizard. If you have multiple parts moving at different times, you can edit the sequence so that certain parts move at the same time by marquee selecting (or Ctrl+selecting) a group of key points and moving them along the timeline.

Animating an assembly

Here is an example of using the Animation Wizard to first rotate a model, then explode and collapse it, along with some simple editing. If you want to follow along with this example, open the `Yoke Link.sldasm` assembly from the Animations folder on the DVD. Note that this assembly already has a complete animation, so you will need to create a second motion study when the time comes for that.

Creating an explode

The first step in creating this animation is to have an explode in place before starting the animation. To do this, start by switching to the ConfigurationManager, and create a new configuration. In this example, the new configuration is called Example (right-click the name of the part in the ConfigurationManager and select Add Configuration). Figure 23.8 shows a configuration being added.

Adding a new configuration to the assembly

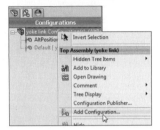

To add the new explode, right-click the new configuration name and select New Exploded View, as shown in Figure 23.9.

Adding a new explode

Adding the explode brings up the PropertyManager shown in Figure 23.10. In this PropertyManager, you can create the individual explode steps.

FIGURE 23.10

Detailing the explode steps for this example

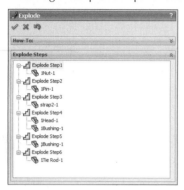

Without reviewing the material for explodes in Chapter 16 in detail, the general workflow for creating the individual explode steps is as follows:

1. Select a part.

2. Use the triad to move the part. You may have to set the explode direction for parts not aligned with the assembly axes.

3. Repeat Steps 1 and 2 for each explode you want to add.

This example uses six explode steps:

1. Explode the nut to the side (you must establish a direction — you can use the cylindrical face of the pin to do this).

2. Explode the pin in the other direction (you must establish a direction).

3. Explode the strap straight up.

4. Explode the Head and the Bushing straight down together.

5. Explode the Bushing to one side (you must establish a direction).

6. Explode the Tie Rod down half the distance of the Head and Bushing explode.

Now that the explode is complete, make sure the assembly is in its collapsed state (right-click ExplView1 under the configuration name).

Before displaying the MotionManager interface, change the assembly view to the proper orientation. Press the spacebar to display the View Orientation dialog box, and select the animation 1 view. Then close the View Orientation dialog box.

Next, right-click the Animation1 tab at the bottom-left corner of the SolidWorks window, to display the MotionManager interface, and select Create New Motion Study. This gives you a fresh start with a new animation timeline. Figure 23.11 shows how to create the new motion study.

FIGURE 23.11

Creating a new motion study

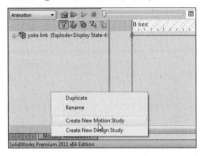

 Next, click the Animation Wizard icon in the MotionManager toolbar. The Select an Animation Type window appears, as shown in Figure 23.3. Select the Rotate model option, and click Next. In the next window, select the Y-axis option and click Next. Remember, in this case "Y-axis" means the Y-axis of the screen, not of the model. If it were the Y-axis of the model, the assembly would simply spin in place.

Putting the rotate into an animation timeline

In the Animation Control Options window, set the rotation to last 3 seconds and the start time to zero. You will change these settings later to get some practice making edits to timelines and key points. When you click Finish, you should get the result shown in Figure 23.12.

When making an animation, it is nice to have a gap between the start of the movie and the motion of the parts, to give the viewer some time to adjust to what they are seeing on the screen. Of course, if you are making a movie that you want to use as a continuous loop, the gap might interrupt the motion. You could also insert a gap between the end of the motion and the end of the movie, which might make the gap seem more natural.

In any case, you want to add a gap of a second or one-half second at the beginning of this animation. To do this, drag a marquee window around the heavy black line and black key points in the Orientation and Camera View row, and then drag them to the right by slightly less than 1 second.

FIGURE 23.12

Using the Animation Wizard to add key points to the animation timeline

Adding the explode to the animation

You can now add the explode to the animation. To do this, follow these steps:

1. Start the Animation Wizard again, but this time select the Explode option and click Next.

2. In the Animation Control Options window, set the duration again to 3 seconds, with the start time at 6.25 seconds, and click Finish. The result is shown in Figure 23.13.

Making a part look flexible

Click the Calculate button on the MotionManager toolbar. Notice that when the strap moves up, the part actually shortens. The part will also twist later in the animation when you change the angle of one of the parts. In general, SolidWorks cannot animate flexible parts, but you can use some tricks to make parts appear flexible. You do this by using in-context relations, and driving mating parts by changing distance or angle mates. Therefore, the appearance of flexibility only comes through animating parts with in-context relations.

FIGURE 23.13

Bringing the explode steps into the MotionManager timeline

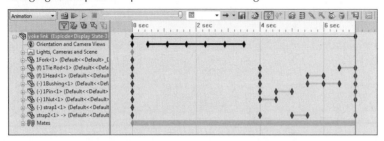

Collapsing the exploded assembly

Now you will add the collapse, but this time without running the wizard. To accomplish this, follow these steps:

1. Drag a marquee rectangle around all of the key points created by the explode.

2. Ctrl+drag them so the first copied step lands at about 7.5 seconds on the timeline.

3. With the block of key points still selected, right-click one of the copied key points and select Reverse Path. The copied explode now becomes a collapse.

4. Change the order of the explode by dragging key points or pairs of key points. For example, the Bushing has three key points in its path. You can delete the middle key point and shorten its motion to match the Head.

Animating a zoom

The next step is to zoom in to the looped area of the strap. To do this, you have to first make sure that the view is the same as the last change made to the Orientation. Do this by dragging the timebar back to the last key point of the revolve, which is about 3.75 seconds, then move the timebar forward to the end of the collapse, which should be just short of 10 seconds.

Next, copy the last key point from the rotate motion (Ctrl+drag) to the same time that the collapse finishes (about 9.75 seconds). Then move the timebar forward to 10.25 seconds, zoom in so you can see the fork and the looped section of the strap, right-click the timebar in the row for Orientation, and then select Place Key, as shown in Figure 23.14.

There are other ways to place this view orientation key, such as by enabling the Orientation and Camera Views item. If you enable the Orientation, the MotionManager records every view change you make, so it is cleaner and safer if you just use the RMB ⇨ Place Key method instead of enabling the Orientation.

Zooming in to the flexible area of the strap

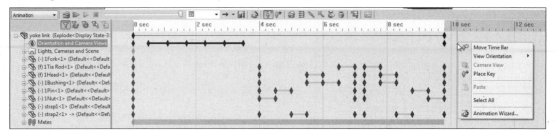

Animating a changing mate

The next item that this movie will animate is the Angle1 mate. If you expand the Mates folder in the FeatureManager, you will find that it has two folders. One folder is for model mates, and the other is for mates that drive the animation. There is only one mate in the Animation Mates folder, and that is Angle1.

Start by copying the initial key point for Angle1 from 0 seconds to 10.25 seconds. Next, move the timebar to 11 seconds (you can do this precisely by right-clicking the timebar, selecting Move Time Bar, and then typing in the time you want to move it to). Then double-click the Angle1 mate and change its value from 45 to 180.

Make the angle mate change from 45 to 180, back to 45, then 0 then 45 again, with about one-half second for each change. Remember, you can use copied key points to make the multiple 45-degree values. Finish the animation by returning to the original view. To do this, copy the first key point of the Orientation, and then the last key point (at about 10.25 seconds). Figure 23.15 shows the final result.

The finished timeline for this animation

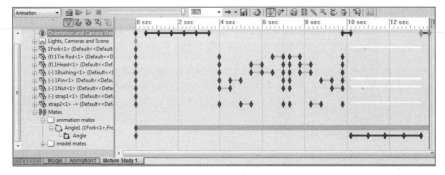

This example serves as a demonstration of the overall workflow, while the rest of this chapter offers a detailed discussion of the functions that are available.

On the DVD

The sample file, `Yoke Link.sldasm`**, is available on the DVD in the Animation folder, along with a finished AVI file saved out from the assembly.** ■

Animating the View

This section will reintroduce some of the view animation items that you have already seen earlier in this chapter — that is, tools involved in changing the point of view from which the animation is recorded. The first part of the chapter mostly offered a practical overview of the animation workflow. This section will give you a more thorough knowledge of individual tools for changing and controlling the view. You already understand how the tools combine to make an animation; now you just need to know what tools are available and how they work.

View animation is an important and even reusable function. For example, you can save an animation where the only thing that is animated is the view changes in an assembly, and then put any part or other assembly that you want to into this pre-created animation. If you also have your PhotoView 360 settings established (except materials and appearances for the individual parts), you can even create a rendered animation very quickly.

A great example is when you want to show an assembly spinning on its axis (instead of on the axis of the screen as shown in the Animation Wizard); in this case, you can record a camera following a path focused on a particular point. This is a great animation to set up as a template, so that you can reuse it for quick and easy boilerplate animations. (Thanks to Devon Sowell of `http://3-ddesignsolutions.com` for this tip.) This technique will be covered later in this chapter.

You can animate view changes in the MotionManager in the following ways:

- Orientation and Camera Views (must enabled)
- Using key points (move timebar, rotate model)
- Orientation and Camera Views disabled
- Using key points (move timebar, rotate model, right-click and select Place Key)
- Using the Animation Wizard to rotate a model
- Using any of the above techniques with a camera
- Attaching a camera to a part that moves
- Attaching a camera to a path (use an animation or a walk-through)
- Using a screen capture to record the screen

Driving the view with key points

A key point is a point on the timeline where you tell SolidWorks what state something will be in. For example, at 9 seconds, the view will be a Front view; this is represented by a diamond along the timeline. You can use key points to animate assembly motion, the view, or even properties such as color, transparency, or mate values. Figure 23.16 shows a MotionManager timeline displaying several key points with various meanings.

FIGURE 23.16

Key points locate and organize changes in position or properties.

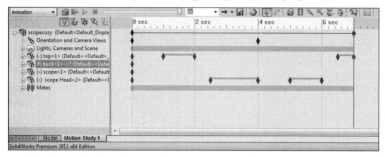

Using the Orientation and Camera Views feature

 An important fact about using view and camera key points is that the Orientation and Camera Views feature in the MotionManager is locked by default. This means that you cannot change the view in an animation by accident. To unlock it, right-click the Orientation and Camera Views entry, and deselect the Disable View Key Creation option. The icon changes from a black diamond with a red circle and line to a blue telescope.

If you don't understand why this setting is turned off by default, try working with it turned on for a while as you are learning the software. You may find that, unless you are extraordinarily well organized, you will make many unwanted changes to the view, because you are unconsciously rotating the view to see it better, and forgetting that the change is being recorded. This is a very common mistake among users when creating an animation.

Best Practice

The best way to handle the Orientation and Camera Views feature is to select the Disable View Key Creation option (allow view changes) only when you want to establish the view key points, and then deselect it when you are done. ■

To start this animation of the view, you need to deselect the Disable View Key Creation option, so that the blue telescope icon appears to the left of the entity in the design tree.

Disabling playback of view keys

This option will become important later when you start making the actual assembly move, but it is mentioned here just for the sake of being complete. You can play back the assembly and disable the view changes. To do this, right-click the Orientation and Camera Views item in the MotionManager, and select Disable Playback of View Keys from the menu. Very often when dealing with assembly motion, it helps to see the assembly from a particular point of view. You can't do that if your animation is always changing the view. Remember to deselect this setting before recording the animation to a file.

Introducing the timebar

The timebar is the vertical gray line in the timeline area that denotes the current time that you are editing in the animation. Refer to Figure 23.1, which identifies the major parts of the MotionManager interface. When you make a change to any element that can be animated, that change is applied at the time denoted by the timebar. To make a key point–driven animation, the workflow usually involves moving the timebar, making a set of changes, moving the timebar, making another set of changes, and so on.

To try this out on an assembly, open the Robot Assembly in the `Robot Arm` folder on the DVD. You can follow along with the existing motion study or create a new one and experiment on your own. Start by making sure the timebar is set to zero (all the way to the left), and then position the view to start the animation. In this case, display the View Orientation dialog box (press the spacebar) and double-click the view named 1.

Because the Orientation and Camera Views item is disabled, this view change is not recorded. In order to record it, right-click the key point to the right of Orientation and Camera Views, and select Replace Key, as shown in Figure 23.17. This replaces the existing key with the new view orientation.

FIGURE 23.17

Selecting Replace Key to change the view at a view orientation key point

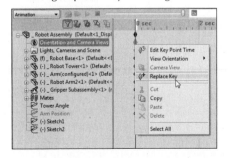

The view should remain static for a couple of seconds when the animation starts; it might be too confusing to start the animation immediately with the view changing. To create this pause, copy the first key point from the 0-second mark to the 2-second mark. It is as easy as it sounds.

Click the key point in the same row as the Orientation and Camera Views, and then Ctrl+drag it to the right to the 2-second mark. This causes the first 2 seconds of the view to be static.

Creating key points

Next, move the timebar to the 5-second mark, display the View Orientation dialog box again, activate view 2; then right-click where the Orientation row intersects the 5-second column, and select Place Key to make a new key point for the view orientation. The black bar between the 2-second key point and the 5-second key point indicates that the MotionManager will interpolate the view orientation between the two defined points. The MotionManager now looks like Figure 23.18.

FIGURE 23.18

The timeline at the 5-second mark

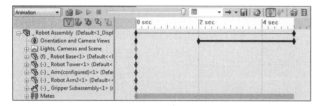

Remember that the View Orientation dialog box stores both orientation and zoom factor, so when you use view 2, it may be zoomed at a different state; thus, when the view changes from 1 to 2, it may rotate and zoom in or out slightly. If you want to measure rotation more precisely, it may be a good idea to use the arrow keys rather than something like a 3D mouse.

Zooming and free view manipulation

The next step is to zoom in to the grippers and simultaneously turn the view slightly to give a better view. Before changing the view, though, it would be nice to have another pause to give the viewer the chance to see what is there. To create the pause, click the last key point in the Orientation and Camera Views row, and then Ctrl+drag it to the 7-second mark. Then move the timebar to the 10-second mark. Remember that the workflow for copying a particular key is to select and then Ctrl+drag, not just Ctrl+drag. If you Ctrl+drag without making the initial selection, you may be copying other key points that were also selected at the time. The select operation serves two functions: first, to deselect anything else, and second, to select only the key point you are interested in.

Note

When creating an animation, you have to be very careful about making changes to anything because those changes may be incorporated into the animation. If you just want to rotate the model to look at something, switch back to the Model tab near the lower-left corner of the SolidWorks window. The first tab always hides the MotionManager, and you don't have to worry about changes to the views or positions of parts being recorded. ■

Once you have the timebar moved to the 10-second mark, use the View Orientation (press the spacebar) to move to view 3. After doing this, zoom in on the grippers using whatever method you use to zoom: Shift+Z, middle mouse button (MMB) scroll, Zoom to Area, Zoom to Selection, Zoom In/Out, or a 3D mouse. After you have made both changes, add the key point to the Orientation change bar in the same way you have done it previously. The rotate and zoom will happen at the same time. The idea is to get a good partial side view of the grippers, such as that shown in Figure 23.19. Play the animation to see what you have created.

FIGURE 23.19

The timeline at the 10-second mark

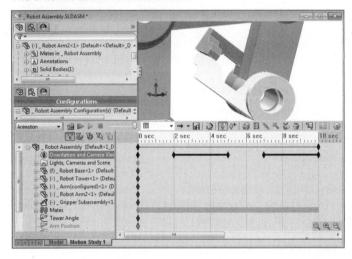

Using Interpolation modes

When you play the animation, it may appear somewhat jerky. When the MotionManager interpolates between key points, for changing either views or part positions, the default interpolation mode is linear. This means that it changes between points at a constant speed. This creates the jerkiness because the motion starts and stops abruptly.

To remedy this, the MotionManager offers several interpolation modes. Right-click one of the key points that you have created, and select Interpolation mode at the bottom of the list that appears. Another menu flies out, as shown in Figure 23.20.

The icons for the modes signify how the motion increases or decreases between key points. In any case, curves make smoother motion than lines. Ease in/Ease out creates the smoothest motion; Ease in works best at the beginning of a change, and Ease out works best at the end of a change. Snap causes an abrupt change in position from one place the part will move immediately to another location at the next key point. The Linear option causes the part to move at a constant velocity from one point to another.

Selecting Interpolation mode

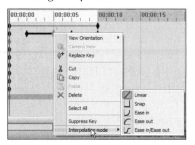

The default mode is linear, so if you want to change all four of the key points, you have to go through this selection four times, right? No, there is an easier way. You can marquee-select all four key points, then right-click any of the selected key points, and change them all to the Ease in/Ease out mode. Now play the animation again. Notice how much smoother the view changes are.

Correcting mistakes

When you start to use the MotionManager, you will probably make mistakes. Don't feel bad; this happens to even seasoned veterans. The difference between you and an experienced user is that they know how to deal with mistakes and do not panic. The MotionManager does you the favor of recording all your mistakes in the form of adding key points to the change line for either the part position or view orientation. One way to troubleshoot these types of mistakes is to drag the timeline through the key points, and identify which key points need to be removed. To remove a key point, just click it and press Delete.

If you are making an animation that covers a long period of time, say, more than 30 seconds, the key points may be close together and difficult to distinguish from one another. You can use the zoom tools in the lower-right corner of the timeline area to zoom the timeline in or out. Zooming in makes the key points appear farther away from one another, enabling you to select one that might be right on top of another.

Using paths to control cameras

Cameras are discussed in detail in the *SolidWorks 2011 Parts Bible*, so the general details won't be covered again here. You might want to refer to that book to familiarize yourself with some of the controls. The main controls you need for animations are Target by selection, Position by selection, and Set roll by selection, in addition to the Field of View settings.

Recalling the Walk-through feature

You may want to review Chapter 3, where the Walk-through functionality is covered. Walk-through is now a stand-alone feature, but its functionality is borrowed from the MotionManager for animating a camera along a path. The Walk-through feature is somewhat simplified and intended for large structures where you can go in and around the object. Remember that Chapter 3 used a very large dump truck with a staircase and an observation platform.

Rotating the model using a path

The main weakness of the Rotate Animation Wizard is that it rotates about the screen axis, which appears to make it wobble on the screen, and this is typically not what users have in mind when they ask to rotate the model. Most users envision the "turntable" sort of rotation, where the model rotates about its own axis. Changing the rotation to rotate about the part axis isn't as easy as it probably ought to be, but once you understand the process, you can simplify it. This example involves making the camera revolve around the axis of a part, regardless of the orientation of the part, to show you how to drive a camera along a path. This exercise will start simple and gradually become more complex.

The best way to spin the view around the part axis is to make a path on a plane perpendicular to the axis. The plane should in most cases be slightly elevated from the base of the model, and should probably be circular or at least a smooth, closed-loop spline.

Starting with the robot assembly from the Animation folder on the DVD (`Robot Assembly.sldasm`), move to a top view, and open a 3D sketch. When doing prep work like this, it is better to work using the Model tab, instead of the MotionManager. This prevents you from creating any unnecessary key points for animatable items.

In the 3D sketch, from the Top view, draw a four-point closed-loop spline, as shown in Figure 23.21. This is in a 3D sketch so that you can change the path to non-planar if you want to.

FIGURE 23.21

Creating a camera path

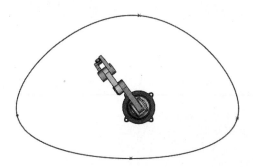

The path doesn't have to be perfectly circular; in fact, it might be better if it gets closer to the assembly on one side, making it rather kidney-shaped.

Next, press Shift+down arrow to rotate the view 90 degrees, and drag the entire spline up a little bit. Finally, tweak a couple of spline points so the spline goes higher and lower. This will give you a more interesting result than just a straight turntable rotation animation.

Note

To greatly simplify this task, you can create an offset plane and sketch an ellipse or circle on the plane rather than using the 3D spline. The 3D spline is intended to give you the most control and flexibility. ∎

The camera will be attached to this spline. You might also want to have a target point for the camera to follow as it goes around the path. You could place a sketch point inside the joint between the Tower and Arm parts. If the assembly or even a part origin is in a convenient location, you can also use this as a place to point the camera.

Once the path exists, exit the sketch and insert a new camera. You can insert a camera by switching to the DisplayManager, the multicolored ball next to the FeatureManager and ConfigurationManager tabs. Then switch to the third icon under the top tabs, which is for lights and cameras. Now right-click the Cameras folder and select Add Camera. Figure 23.22 shows the PropertyManager for the camera.

Notice that when you insert the camera, the SolidWorks graphics window splits into two viewports. The left viewport is your view of the camera, the model, and their surroundings. The right viewport is the view through the camera.

Use the Target Point selection box to aim the camera at a point on the Robot Tower part. If you aim the camera at a moving part, the motion of the camera will seem unnatural, unless the part is moving smoothly. For this assembly, you might consider using a dummy part in the assembly to aim the camera at so that it is moving in a jerky fashion, following a jaw, for example. You can use a part just floating in space, but generally moving left, right, up, or down as needed without being rigidly connected to any single part of the assembly.

Attach the camera to the spline by selecting the spline in the first Camera Position selection box. If you are at T=0 (the first time key point), make sure that the percent position is set to zero.

To get the camera to move around the spline, move the timebar to a position such as 0.4 second, edit the Camera item in the MotionManager (right-click it inside the Lights, Cameras and Scene folder found only in the MotionManager, not in the assembly FeatureManager), and select the Properties option. Then move the Percent slider under Camera Position to about 25 percent. Do this as many times as you need to go all the way around.

If parts of the model go out of the field of view, or you feel that the camera is too far away or too close to the model, you can move the camera or change the lens. To move the camera, exit the camera PropertyManager and edit the 3D sketch.

FIGURE 23.22

The Camera PropertyManager

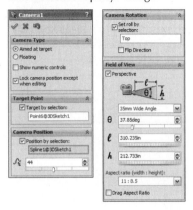

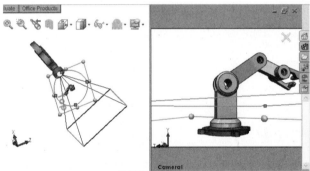

Note

Remember that when editing unconstrained 3D sketches, it is best to do it from orthogonal views. Any points that you drag move in the plane of the screen. The best way to edit the size of the spline is to view it from the Top view, and drag out individual spline points. ■

Going beyond 100 percent or 360 degrees

If you take the animation around more than 360 degrees, you will need to use a workaround to get it to work correctly. For example, if you use the Percent slider, and go 0-25-50-75-100 and then 25 percent, the animation will reverse direction between 100 and 25. The way to make this happen so that the animation maintains continuity is to place keys at both 100 and 0 close enough to one another that the time difference is less than the frame rate of the animation. The frame rate is set in the Motion Study Properties, the icon on the far-right side of the MotionManager toolbar. For a finished animation, the frame rate could be in the neighborhood of 30 frames per second (fps), which means the time for one frame would be

1/30 second, or about 0.03 second. Therefore, if 100 percent happens at 2 seconds, you could put 0 percent at 2.01 seconds and the transition would never be seen. This workaround is used widely by people who know the software well.

The same sort of tactic works if you have to go beyond 360 degrees. You have to use the zoom tools in the lower-right corner of the MotionManager to be able to see what is going on. Figure 23.23 shows two camera key points very close together in this way. To change the percent position, double-click the key point and the Camera PropertyManager becomes available.

FIGURE 23.23

Working around the 100 percent or 360-degree animation limitation

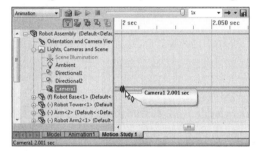

Animating with Key Points

This chapter has already briefly discussed key points to introduce the idea, but here you will learn about how to use them in more detail. You can think of key points as snapshots at particular moments in time. If you say, "At the 4-second mark, the wheel needs to be 3 inches from the wall," this statement describes a key point. To create a key point, drag the timebar to a new time, and make a change. Any of the animatable items listed earlier in the chapter can create a key point.

Getting started

Consider this easy and useful example: a customer wants you to make a little animation of a holder for a stethoscope that he will show to a potential client in PowerPoint. The holder opens, the stethoscope slides out, and then the animation reverses.

On the DVD

The assembly with the animation saved in it is in the Animation folder labeled scopecozy.sldasm. ∎

The assembly and the completed animation timeline are shown in Figure 23.24. This animation uses RealView display, which the customer has said is good enough for his purposes. This reduces the time significantly compared to using PhotoView 360 to render the animation.

FIGURE 23.24

The stethoscope animation setup

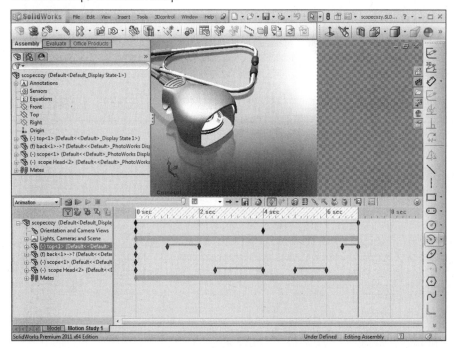

Your first task is to set up the camera. You could do this without a camera, but cameras are a convenient way to store a particular view, along with settings such as lens angle, perspective, camera position, and target. In addition, if you decide to use PhotoView 360 later, cameras are the only way to get depth of field for additional realism. Another advantage of the camera is that you are able to control the area in view more closely. If you don't use a camera, the area of view is just whatever is available in the view port. With the camera, you can specify a size and aspect ratio, and the available area is cropped appropriately.

Because the stethoscope model is cut into pieces to enable different parts of it to be positioned, you need to position the parts and the camera such that the break between the head and earpieces is not visible. Leave enough open area so that when the stethoscope comes out, it will not run out of the area of view.

Note

When adjusting the position of the camera, it is often easier to adjust the actual view than to manipulate the camera. In the Camera PropertyManager, deselecting the Lock Camera Position Except When Editing option enables you to manipulate the view directly. This setting is selected by default and will display the camera with a red X icon if you try to rotate the view when the camera view is on. Switch to camera view and deselect Disable View Key Creation. ■

Using the timebar with key points

It's a good idea to start animations with some stillness; if you start an animation with motion, your viewer may not have time to adjust. A second is usually enough. Expand the Top part file, click the key point for the Move row at the zero (0) time mark, and Ctrl+drag it to the 1-second mark. This means that the top will not move between 0 and 1 second. Now move the timebar to 2 seconds and open the top by just dragging it up slightly. It should only open about one-half inch.

Now move the timebar to the 5-second mark. You will now purposely create a mistake so you can learn how to correct it. At the 5-second mark, move the stethoscope out of the holder 3 or 4 inches. Try to make sure you do not go far enough that the rubber tube runs into the plastic parts.

Notice that this creates a change bar that shows the position of the scope head part moving continually from time 00.00.00 to time 00.00.05. The motion is supposed to start at the 3-second mark. You can see how to fix this mistake in Figure 23.25.

FIGURE 23.25

Fixing a timeline problem

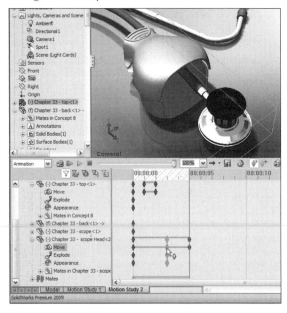

Click the key point for the motion of the scope head part. Then Ctrl+drag it from the 0-second mark to the 3-second mark.

If you run the animation at this point, you may see that the scope head makes some unexpected movement, and a yellow line appears to the left of the change bar for the part. To fix this, click the Calculate button next to the Play button.

Copying and mirroring motion

The animation is essentially done at this point, except that now the stethoscope needs to go back into the holder and it has to close. You don't have to manually create all the steps to close the device, although you could if you wanted to. It is more efficient to simply copy and reverse the paths that you have already made.

To copy both sets of motion — the top opening and the head sliding out — drag a marquee window around the key points to select them all, and then Ctrl+drag them to the 6-second mark. Notice that this creates the situation shown in Figure 23.26. If you play the animation at this point, it is not at all what you want. It simply stacks the same motion on top of the original motion; you want it to be reversed.

FIGURE 23.26

Copying motion of parts

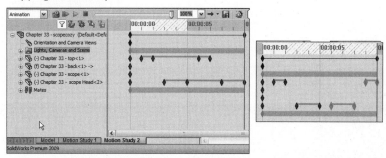

With the newly copied key points still selected, right-click one of them and select Reverse Path. Notice that this now shows symmetrical key points.

Adjusting the speed of actions

The animation is almost complete, but now you notice that it would be better if the second half of the animation went by faster than the first half. To do this, move the key points on the right side of a change bar toward the left. You might want to move both key points for the top part closing so that it starts closer to the time when the scope head is back inside the holder. You could even make some of the motion overlap, so the top starts closing before the scope head is fully inside.

Again, if you see a strange effect such as the scope head not going all the way back to where it belongs, trying clicking the Calculate button again. Calculate essentially rebuilds the animation after changes.

To make the motion a little smoother, right-click in an empty space inside the timeline area, and choose Select All; then right-click one of the key points and select Interpolation Mode. Click the Ease in/Ease out option. Click Calculate again to watch the smoother animation.

If you want variable speed, say, for the scope head coming out of the holder (for example, it starts coming out slowly and then speeds up), you need to add at least one more key point. To do this, position the timebar to the left of the middle of the first scope head change bar, and click Place Key. This adds a key point in the existing change bar. This is shown in Figure 23.27. Then move the key point to the right. Make sure the new key point uses the Ease in/ Ease out interpolation mode. Recalculate, and run the animation again.

FIGURE 23.27

Adding and moving a key point in an existing change bar

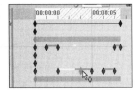

If you decide that the entire animation is too fast or too slow, you can also adjust this easily. Drag the right-most key point on the top row with the Alt key depressed. This scales the entire animation up or down.

Outputting the animation

Once you are happy with the animation, click the Save Animation toolbar button. This brings up the Save Animation to File dialog box, shown in Figure 23.28. The options for output formats are `*.avi`, or a `*.bmp` or `*.tga` series of still images. You could combine the still images to make an animated GIF to use on a website. Other types of output, such as Flash or QuickTime, are not available directly from the SolidWorks software. Movie format converters are available on the web for this purpose.

The options for the renderer are simply the SolidWorks screen or PhotoView 360. This example uses RealView and the SolidWorks screen renderer, which provides sufficient quality for your purposes. The main advantages of PhotoView 360 over RealView are that it offers a better choice of backgrounds, anti-aliasing, and more shadow control.

FIGURE 23.28

Saving output data for your animation

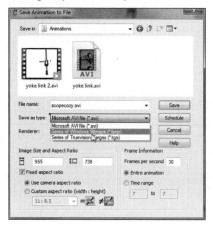

Looking at other options

Image Size and Aspect Ratio options are available only when you do not use a camera. Without the camera, you are at the mercy of the size and shape of the SolidWorks graphics window until you save the animation to a file.

The Schedule button enables you to schedule the output for a more convenient time. You would normally use this option when using PhotoView 360, because rendered animations can take many hours to complete, depending on render settings, length of animation, and the number of frames per second.

Frame Information enables you to set the quality of the finished rendering. Low frame rates result in choppy motion. High frame rates are much smoother, but the files may become unmanageably large. High-quality animations generally fall into the 25 to 30 frames fps range.

Running test animations

Depending on the length of the animation and the other settings, test animations might run in the 10 fps range. You might also consider using a specific range of time to test just a part of the animation.

Unfortunately, many of the decisions that you make regarding animation quality settings directly relate to the time you have to produce the final movie file. The biggest time-saver is to avoid PhotoView 360. If RealView suits your needs, you are well ahead on time.

Selecting a compressor

When you save the animation, the software prompts you to select a video compressor (codec). Typical options are the Microsoft Video and Cinepak compressors. Sometimes when you record or play back a movie with a particular compressor, you end up with a lot of video noise in the movie. If this happens, try another compressor. For example, if you use Microsoft Video for an animation, and it has a lot of video noise, you can switch to Cinepak to see if the results are better.

Animating with Basic Motion

Basic Motion is the functionality formerly known as Physical Simulation. It involves setting motors to turn parts, gravity to move parts and springs, and collisions to create animations that cannot be driven by mates or free motion. It uses a different solver than the rest of the animations in this chapter.

Basic Motion does not take into account effects such as momentum, bounce, resistance/friction, viscosity, and reaction forces. To analyze for these effects, you need to use Motion Analysis (formerly COSMOSMotion).

The study type selection box appears in the upper-left corner of the MotionManager. You need to use Basic Motion (refer to Figure 23.2) for this example.

Using gravity and contact

Figure 23.29 shows an assembly that demonstrates the gravity and contact functions of Basic Motion. The problem is easy to set up. The part that is to move (the ball) is under-defined, using only one mate to keep it in plane as it moves. The zigzag part uses a Fixed constraint.

On the DVD

The assembly used in this example is labeled `zig zag.sldasm`. ∎

When you have added the physical simulation items, the MotionManager design tree looks like Figure 23.30. Editing items such as contact and gravity does not use the interface options that have been available in the rest of the SolidWorks software. Left-click (select) does not bring up a context toolbar; you have to right-click and access the full RMB menu.

Because this example goes by so quickly, you may want to use the Playback Speed drop-down menu to get a better look at it. You can also set playback looping options with the drop-down menu to the right of the Playback Speed.

FIGURE 23.29

Setting up contact and gravity

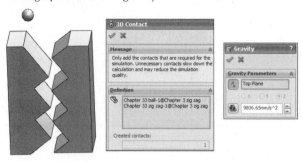

FIGURE 23.30

The MotionManager design tree with added items

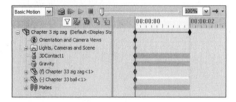

Using motors and springs

The use of motors does not necessarily require Basic Motion, but if you include springs, or contact or gravity problems, it does. Torsion springs require Motion Analysis, but linear springs only require Basic Motion. This example (on the DVD in the Animation folder as `ratchet.SLDASM`) shows a motor driving a gear with a ratchet held to the gear teeth by a spring, as shown in Figure 23.31. A swinging ball on a spring is added to show this isn't simple 2D functionality.

FIGURE 23.31

A motor, gear, and ratchet assembly driven by Basic Motion

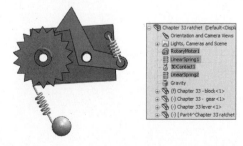

To set up this example, apply a counterclockwise motor to the inside circular edge of the gear, and select the block as the reference part. In this example, start the motor with a slow rpm (revolutions per minute), move the timebar out a few seconds, and assign a faster speed, so the motor speeds up over time.

The linear spring is easy to apply. Select the locations of both ends. This example has circular bosses on the block and the ratchet to hold the spring.

Animating a chain and a spring using motors

Two of the most common requests from people learning how to make animations in SolidWorks are animating chains and springs. This is a simple animation, but it uses a couple of tools that you should know about. Earlier in this chapter, the Yoke Link assembly was used to demonstrate how to flex a strap by using in-context relations and a loft. This chain-gear-spring example uses motors to drive a chain, which drives gears and flexes a spring. The spring is a modeled element, not part of Basic Motion. The driving element is a motor. Figure 23.32 shows the assembly ready for animation.

FIGURE 23.32

One simple assembly can demonstrate several animation ideas.

Open the `chain assembly.sldasm` from the Animation folder on the DVD. The assembly consists of the following components:

- 2 assembly sketches
- 1 assembly plane
- 1 assembly axis

30 parts making up the chain

2 gears

1 spring (modeled in-context, connecting the end of the chain to Plane1)

This is achieved with 98 mates and 1 in-context relation. The animation is driven by a single linear motor.

The model is created by first drawing Sketch1, which represents the path of the chain. This consists of lines and tangent arcs. Next, in order for the path to be a single smooth, continuous entity, a second sketch is created and Fit Spline is used to lay a spline over the lines and arcs. A very small tolerance value is used so that the curvature comb for the spline looks as close to a line-arc combination as possible.

 Several copies of the two chain pieces are then placed into the assembly. The Multi-mate mode is used to mate the Front plane of every link to the Front plane of the assembly. Next, each link is given a line that goes between the centers of each pivot. This makes it easy to connect each link to the other (with endpoint-to-endpoint coincident relations).

The final chain mate is to use Multi-mate mode again, and mate the endpoints of the pivots to the spline. This works best if you pre-position the chain links before mating them so that the chain doesn't double up or kink in any spot.

With these mates in place, the chain slides smoothly back and forth on the spline, through the S-shaped curve. Even if your computer is not particularly powerful, it should still handle even dynamic assembly motion just fine with a 15-link chain.

The gears are positioned at the centers of the arcs from Sketch1. The tricky part of the gears involves using the rack-and-pinion mate to match the linear motion of the end chain link to rotary motion of the gear. Because this is just for an animation, and not a real analysis, idealizing the assembly in this way does not have any adverse effects.

The construction of the spring is to simply use a straight line as an in-context connector between the last link of the chain and Plane1 of the assembly. This line is then used as the path of a sweep with twist enabled, which is a reasonable approximation of a spring for an animation. It doesn't flex for dynamic assembly motion, but for an animation, it does.

All that remains is the motor. Figure 23.33 shows how the motor is driven. It is a linear motor, with the Oscillating motion. The Displacement vs. Time chart shows how much the chain moves during the 6-second animation. You can also see the chart as showing how much the spring extends or retracts.

While this assembly and animation are simple, they demonstrate many of the techniques that you need to know to make animations that are more complex. Motors with controllable output are a big part of animating automatic machinery, and making parts appear flexible adds greatly to the realism of an animation.

Charting the motion of the assembly

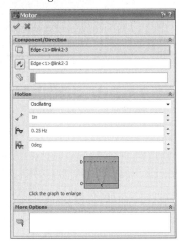

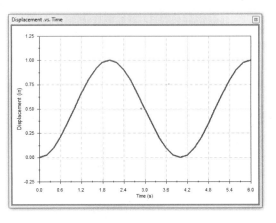

Summary

If you keep your animation relatively simple, the MotionManager tools in SolidWorks Standard should give adequate results in some situations. If you are using mates to drive motion, be sure to follow best practice recommendations for mates. If you are manually positioning parts, remember to place key points closer together if the motion curvature changes.

If you are making larger animations and the end product is just an AVI file, it is acceptable to break the animation into smaller bits. This makes each part of the animation much simpler to do, and work can even be delegated to other users or other machines for parallel processing. It may also be beneficial to use post-processing to add captions and narration to your movies; a few words of explanation might be valuable to viewers. Movie editing software is available as part of the Windows OS (Windows DVD/Movie Maker), which should be adequate for simple edits and captioning, or you can buy more advanced video-editing software, which may also require more skill or at least some practice for more complex editing and effects.

Part VI

Appendixes

Finding Help

SolidWorks software has been around for more than 15 years now. In that time, the resources available to users seeking help have increased dramatically. These resources take many forms, from personal websites with information from individual experience to commercial online magazines or forums with advanced interfaces. In this appendix, I have assembled some of the more worthy sources of quality information.

It is not the goal of this book to endorse any commercial sites or services, but some of the listed resources are commercial in nature and may feature advertisements, logins, or paid subscriptions.

SolidWorks Help

The SolidWorks Help file contains some information you need to research how functions work. There are topics for which searchability is poor, or that do not appear under expected names, but this is the exception rather than the norm. It is more common to find that some features are poorly documented or not documented at all.

However, some functions, such as sheet metal bend allowances and the referenced documents search routine, are extraordinarily well documented. Isolated topics are surprisingly thorough and extremely helpful.

SolidWorks Help is available in traditional Help files on the computer, as well as web-based help. SolidWorks Web Help was created because it is easier for SolidWorks to keep it up to date. You can access the Web Help by turning on the Use SolidWorks Web Help option in the Help menu in SolidWorks or at `http://help.solidworks.com`.

SolidWorks Web Help

The SolidWorks Web Help was new in SolidWorks 2010. Web Help was introduced to help SolidWorks keep the Help files updated without having to send out help updates in the service packs. It also enables the use of other search tools and links to online data sources to make finding help that much easier.

You can access SolidWorks Web Help through the Help ⇨ SolidWorks Help menu selection as usual, but you need to make sure that the Use SolidWorks Web Help option also in the Help menu is activated. The following three sections only pertain to the traditional (non-web) Help.

Contents

SolidWorks terminology has been a sticking point at times in the writing of this book because terms are either unclear or overlap. Still, it is difficult for two people to talk about the software if they are not using the same terminology. The Glossary, found at the bottom of the Help Contents list, is one of the most useful and yet most underused portions of the Help files. Often when a new user asks me a question, it can be impossible to discern what the user is talking about because he is not familiar with the SolidWorks terminology, is substituting AutoCAD or Inventor terminology, or is assuming all modeling terminology is universal. As dull as it may be, this Glossary should be required reading for all new users. Simply understanding the language being used by the training materials, Help files, and other users can give you a big head start when it comes to learning the software. Look through it. I promise you'll learn something useful.

Index

Starting in SolidWorks 2010, SolidWorks removed the Index from the regular Help, and of course, it does not exist in the Web Help either. An index is difficult to create, and this difficulty was the reason SolidWorks gave for not including it in the new version.

Search

The Search function is for when you are not exactly sure of what you are looking for. For example, you know there is a feature that has a funny name that uses stripes to analyze curvature across edges, but you cannot remember its name. Begin your search with the words *stripes* and *curvature*. If you use curvature, the Search function returns about 60 possibilities. The term you are looking for is Zebra Stripes, but you may not find it by scanning such a long list. If you search using the word stripe, Zebra Stripes appears at the top of the list. Therefore, a good search strategy might be to try multiple terms.

The biggest complaint you may have about the Search function in Help is that it will sometimes return too many options, and the connection between the word you searched on and the topic title shown in the list is not immediately clear. Still, too much information is better than not enough.

Many users overlook the three options at the bottom of the Search window: Search Previous Results, Match Similar Words, and Search Titles Only. All three are useful in narrowing your search. With the new Web Help, Search is improved, and includes a section that allows you to further narrow the search results that works like guided search. Guided search provides a list of results, but also provides an index-like set of topics (in the upper right-hand corner) that you can use to narrow the search further.

Additionally, most of the Help linked to from the search results has a link to search the Knowledge Base on a related phrase. This search of the Knowledge Base (KB) may or may not include any results. I have seen several links from the Help to the KB that were empty.

SolidWorks Website

Most of the valuable information on the SolidWorks website (`www.solidworks.com`) is behind the subscription login, but some free information is also available. It may be worthwhile to explore the SolidWorks site a bit, because it includes a large amount of information ranging from graphics cards evaluations to training files.

Graphics Cards Links

The link to this area of the SolidWorks website is `www.solidworks.com/sw/videocardtesting.html`, and appears on the SolidWorks website main page behind the Support ⇨ System Requirements link. SolidWorks has tested the range of most popular graphics cards and drivers for compatibility with various versions of SolidWorks and has rated them at various levels based on the following criteria:

Passed all tests

Passed with limitations

Card has significant stability or repaint problems

Uses the graphics card display settings for SolidWorks

Multi-head hardware accelerated

Supports RealView

Provides 64-bit native support

Supports 3D-Stereo effects

Customer Portal

The SolidWorks Customer Portal is full of useful information. It requires a login, and you can find it at `https://customercenter.solidworks.com`. Portions of the portal, such as the Forums, are available to anyone with or without subscription. Other areas, such as the service pack downloads, are only available to subscription customers.

SolidWorks Forums

The SolidWorks Forums have areas of wide interest for most users. These include about 40 different topic areas, each with a constant flow of information. SolidWorks employees sometimes answer questions, and knowledgeable users often give good answers and invaluable perspectives on not just modeling and CAD admin topics but also general mechanical engineering or materials sourcing.

You can read the forums without an account but need an account to post messages. Accounts can be granted to anyone, even if you are not on maintenance. You can find the forums at `http://forum.solidworks.com`.

Make sure to read the Terms of Use available at the bottom of every Forum page. The moderators do not usually apply the rules strictly, but I have seen posts removed that should have been allowed and posts allowed that should have been removed. Generally if you ask, answer, or comment in good faith, you will not have any problems.

Knowledge Base

If you think you have used the Knowledge Base before and found it less than satisfying, you owe it to yourself to try it again. The KB is constantly updated with new information, which comes from several sources, including general technical support results and the Help documentation. Searches actually turn up a lot of useful information. Results may include tech support responses to customer issues, SPRs (software performance reports — also known as bug reports), white papers, articles, and so on. In addition, you can look up SPR numbers you have received from tech support to check the reports' statuses. I have consulted the Knowledge Base several times while writing this book. It has been built from vast amounts of internal SolidWorks corporate support documentation, as well as the support database. I give it very high usability marks!

Software downloads

Manually downloading and installing software and upgrades for SolidWorks is becoming outdated, although you can still do it. The SolidWorks Installation Manager works much like Microsoft Automatic Update. It downloads and even installs updates for you automatically. There is also a new Background Downloader that will download service packs while your Internet connection is otherwise idle, to be available to you when you want to use it. You can also work with automated administrative image installations. I particularly like that it can download service packs before the links on the SolidWorks website are active. Of course, if you need or simply want to download them manually, this option is also available.

If you are still relying on DVDs to install software, you might consider using the SolidWorks Installation Manager (SWIM) to download not only service packs but also entire installation files for the software. You need adequate network bandwidth, as the downloads may take up several gigabytes. Still, this option is useful and convenient, and most importantly, it works much more reliably than it has in the past.

Release Notes

All the Release Notes for all the service packs of the current version are also available from the main Customer Portal window. This is essential information for CAD administrators. Technical Alerts, changes to the System Requirements (`www.solidworks.com/sw/support/SystemRequirements.html`), and new installation details are listed here.

Even if you think you do not need to know any of this information, it still makes for interesting (and at times alarming) reading. The Technical Alerts typically warn of severe bugs or other problems and how to work around or fix them.

What's New

What's New is a great document to refer to when you are learning a new version of SolidWorks. For the SolidWorks 2010 version, the What's New document comes in HTML and PDF formats. I find the PDF to be easier to access and read, but possibly less up to date than the HTML version. What's New is an important document to read before considering installing a new version, or if you have skipped versions. If you are looking for a What's New document from a version that you do not have installed, you can find all of the What's New documents on Ricky Jordan's blog (`www.rickyjordan.com/whats-new-guides`).

Installation and administration guides

Installation and administration guides are available for SolidWorks, eDrawings, and SolidWorks Simulation. They contain the basics about the topics and are not as detailed as other sources of information. For a complete installation and administration guide, please refer to the *SolidWorks Administration Bible* (Wiley, 2009).

PDMWorks Workgroup Vault Debug Guide

When the vault gives you an error code, you don't have to call tech support to find out what is going on. It is all listed in the PDMWorks Workgroup Vault Debug Guide. All the error codes appear with the name of the error. This is a must-have document for the PDMWorks administrator.

FLEXlm End Users Guide

The FLEXlm End Users Guide is required reading for a network license administrator. While the network license is easy to install, set up, and maintain, this guide explains many of the details and options that are available.

User Groups

The main SolidWorks site for user groups is `www.swugn.org`. There are too many individual user groups to keep track of or list here, but you can find a user group in your area on the SolidWorks User Group Network (SWUGN) site. You can also find user group information on the SolidWorks Forums.

Online Forums

There are many types of online forums for SolidWorks. I have already discussed the forum on the SolidWorks website. Other forums are not directly sponsored by SolidWorks Corporation, and they may vary in quality.

Blogs

Blogs for SolidWorks and related topics cover everything from opinion-based essays to speculation about future products, tips, and tricks or CAD industry news. Most are written by SolidWorks users rather than journalists, so you'll get specifics about a tool that you actually use.

I write a blog, which you can find at `http://dezignstuff.com/blog`. It covers advanced SolidWorks subjects such as surfacing, as well as consumer advocate type of articles, including information on enhancement request drives and subscription options. I also provide links to many other SolidWorks-related blogs, forums, and websites.

My blog has updates to books, notices of new books, lists of errors found in books, and a lot of other content. I deal with philosophical and ethical questions related to product design and CAD in general. I post advanced tips, and sometimes excerpts from books. I also post questions for readers and polls where readers can express their opinions; and I'm always looking for opinions as long as you can back up what you have to say.

Some SolidWorks blogs to check out include:

Matt Lombard at `www.dezignstuff.com/blog`

Ricky Jordan at `www.rickyjordan.com`

Rob Rodriguez — Rendering in SolidWorks at `www.robrodriguezblog.com`

Gabi Jack — Learning SolidWorks from the point of view of a student
`http://gabijack.com/`

Jeff Cope — API at `http://extensiblecad.com/words/`

Lenny Kikstra — API at `http://designsmarter.typepad.com/lennyworks/`

Josh Mings at `www.solidsmack.com`

Matt Lorono at `www.fcsuper.com/swblog/`

Many other blogs exist, including very good general CAD or other non-SolidWorks topics, and you should be able to find most of them from the links on my blog and the others listed here. These blogs do not all fit the same mold. Some are highly optimistic; others focus on tech gadgets, social networking, tech tips, or CAD news; some simply parrot press releases; and so on. For the best list of other CAD, design, 3D, rendering, and engineering blogs, view the blog roll in the right column of my blog.

Forums

Some forums are commercial, which means they are likely to contain advertising. These forums include:

- `https://forums.solidworks.com`. This is SolidWorks' site with official forums. The forums are very active in a wide range of topics and lightly moderated. This requires a login but does not require current SolidWorks subscription.

- `www.productdesignhub.com`. This site is aimed at both industrial and product designers. It has an active forum for sharing ideas as well as a lot of great articles, videos, and other useful content.

- `www.core77.com`. This is probably the premier industrial design website available.

- `www.mcadforums.com`. This site has a lot of traffic and content, but also uses Flash advertisements.

- `www.eng-tips.com`. This forum receives plenty of traffic, has a sign-in popup, and is highly censored.

- `www.3dcadtips.com`. This site is run by the owners of the *Design World* magazine and has a lot of information on general engineering topics as well as CAD.

Non-Commercial Websites

The sites listed here are run by individuals, lack advertising, and contain information created by the owner of the site. They are my favorite types of places to find information. Even though most of these folks are not professional HTML coders, the information is useful and presented well.

- **Rob Rodriguez** (`www.robrodriguez.com`) features rendering topics. Rob used to host the PhotoWorks rendering contest, but that has moved to `http://rendercontest.com/`.

- **Paul Salvador** (`www.zxys.com`) has some nice models and images.

- **Edgar Gidoni** (`www.ragde3d.com`) is a prolific creator of beautiful SolidWorks models, and he writes nice step-by-step tutorials, many of which are free.

- **Stefan Berlitz** (`http://solidworks.cad.de`) is the unofficial German SolidWorks site. If you read German, this site is loaded with great information. Although it does contain some advertisements, I still consider it a non-commercial site.

- **Scott Baugh** (`www.scottjbaugh.com`) has several sample models and a section on tips.

- **Mike Wilson** (`www.mikejwilson.com`) has some amazing things posted to his site that he has done with SolidWorks. They are great models from which to learn. The site has not been updated for some time, but the models and techniques shown are fascinating.

What's on the DVD

Extract the contents of the file to your hard drive in a location that is easy to access. The DVD contains example and tutorial parts, assemblies, and drawings, as well as templates, macros, and tables as appropriate for each chapter. The files are organized within folders for each chapter and are named for the chapter and the function they demonstrate. Some of the files are starting points for tutorials, and some are finished models meant to be examined.

If you make changes to files, I recommend that you use the Save As command (File ⇨ Save As) to keep the original file intact. You also can retrieve originals from the DVD again if needed.

The DVD also includes several video tutorials on various topics related to material in the book. The videos are narrated and offer another learning option to the print-only tutorials found in the book. The videos do not duplicate the print-only tutorials. The main goal of the video tutorials is to demonstrate the workflow or visual options for SolidWorks tools.

Caution

I do not recommend that you open files directly from the DVD or from the Zip file, because SolidWorks will respond with messages about read-only files. ■

Cross-Reference

The files on the DVD are also available on the publisher's website at www.wiley.com/go/solidworks 2011assemblies. Click the Downloads link. ■

IN THIS APPENDIX

Reviewing the system
requirements

Troubleshooting during the
install of the DVD

System Requirements

Make sure that your computer meets the minimum system requirements listed in this section. If your computer doesn't match up to these requirements, you may have a problem using the contents of the DVD:

Note

These requirements apply to Windows XP Professional, Windows Vista, and Windows 7:

- Intel and AMD processors, single, dual, or quad cores
- 1GB RAM minimum (2GB recommended)
- Virtual memory twice the amount of RAM (recommended)
- A certified OpenGL workstation graphics card and driver (Check the SolidWorks website for details: www.solidworks.com.)
- A mouse or other pointing device
- Microsoft Internet Explorer 6 minimum (IE 7 recommended)
- A DVD drive minimum

For more details about the system requirements for SolidWorks 2011 and a list of certified graphics cards and drivers, visit www.solidworks.com.

Using the DVD with Microsoft Windows

You can copy certain items from the DVD to your hard drive. Follow these steps:

1. Insert the DVD into your computer's DVD drive.
2. The DVD interface will appear. The interface provides a simple point-and-click way to explore the contents of the DVD. Click one of the buttons to continue.

If the DVD interface does not appear, follow these steps to access the DVD:

1. Click the Start button on the left end of the task bar.
2. Choose Run from the menu that pops up. (In Windows Vista and Windows 7, skip this step.)
3. In the dialog box that appears, type **d:\setup.exe**. (If your DVD drive is not drive d, use the appropriate letter in place of d.) This opens up the DVD interface described in the preceding set of steps. (In Windows Vista or Windows 7, type **d:\start.exe** in the Start ⇨ Search Programs and Files text box.)

Windows versions

Some older systems that run Windows XP Professional may not be compatible with Vista. Any hardware that runs Vista and most hardware that runs Windows XP should be able to work with Windows 7. For the latest information on system compatibility with Microsoft operating systems, visit www.microsoft.com. At this time, SolidWorks does not run on any non-Windows operating systems such as Mac OS X, Linux, or Google Chrome OS.

Realistically, you will never be satisfied with minimum requirements. If you are using PhotoWorks, PhotoView 360, or any simulation (Finite Element Analysis, or FEA) software, multiple processors or multiple cores are advantageous. Multi-body modeling makes use of multiple cores but also takes advantage of higher processor clock speeds. Maximum clock speeds are usually higher for a lower number of cores, so higher speeds take precedence over number of cores for general solid modeling. You may get better performance per dollar with dual-core processors than with quad-core processors for functionality other than rendering and FEA.

You can only take advantage of more RAM up to the limit needed by your data sets. You can check your Windows Task Manager to see how much memory your largest or most complex models consume. For example, if your largest models use 3GB of RAM, you should have at least 4GB of RAM but will probably not see a benefit from 16GB. You should use a 64-bit operating system if you intend to use more than 3GB of RAM.

All hardware produced in the last several years is 64-bit compatible, but in order to take advantage of it, you have to have a 64-bit operating system installed. XP, Vista, and Windows 7 all have 64-bit versions, but you need to have installed the 64-bit version to benefit from the huge memory advantages of a 64-bit operating system. A 32-bit operating system can handle a little over 3GB of RAM. To handle more than that, you need a 64-bit operating system.

Some software applications have 32- and 64-bit versions, and some do not. SolidWorks has both versions, and you need to make sure you have disks or downloaded data for the correct installation type. Data files are interchangeable between 32- and 64-bit versions, so the files on the DVD will work with either one.

SolidWorks versions

Files created in SolidWorks 2011 are not compatible with older versions of SolidWorks. So, if you have a version of SolidWorks older than 2011, you will have difficulty reading most of the files on the accompanying DVD. You may find some files that came from older versions on the DVD, but this only happens where the files have not been updated for new versions.

As a matter of policy, SolidWorks software does not open up future version files. So if you have SolidWorks 2009 installed, you cannot read files saved in SolidWorks 2011. If you have a question about this policy of the Dassault Corporation, you should contact your SolidWorks reseller. The author of this book does not have the ability to save 2011 files to previous versions.

This book was written using the SolidWorks 2011 version software, and while some of it may be applicable to previous versions, some of it may not due to annual changes that happen in the course of software development. Earlier versions of the book do exist (2010, 2009, and 2007) and are still available, which may benefit you if you have SolidWorks software in one of those versions.

What's on the DVD

The following sections provide a summary of materials that you'll find on the DVD.

Using the author files folder

I have gathered tutorials, assemblies, and drawings into folders per chapter. Some of the files are starting points for tutorials and some are finished models meant to be examined.

Using the video tutorials folder

I have created a few video tutorials to help you visualize some of the concepts. I hope that these videos will help you learn some of SolidWork's features more quickly.

Using the TechSmith Screen Capture Codec

I have included the TechSmith video codec for AVI (tscc.exe). This software will provide you with lossless image quality, compressed (small) file sizes, and exceptional video quality and speed at all color depths.

Accessing additional author videos

For additional SolidWorks Assemblies videos, check out my website at www.dezignstuff.com.

Troubleshooting

If you have difficulty installing or using any of the material on the companion DVD, try the following solutions:

- **Turn off any antivirus software that you may have running.** Installers sometimes mimic virus activity and can make your computer incorrectly believe that it is being infected by a virus. (Be sure to turn the antivirus software back on later.)

- **Close all running programs.** The more programs you're running, the less memory is available to other programs. Installers also typically update files and programs; if you keep other programs running, installation may not work properly.

- **Contact the author.** For problems with the content of the DVD, visit my website (www.dezignstuff.com) or blog (www.dezignstuff.com/blog), or send me an e-mail (matt@dezignstuff.com).

- **See the ReadMe file.** Refer to the ReadMe file located at the root of the DVD for the latest product information at the time of publication.

Customer Care

If you have trouble with the DVD, please call the Wiley Product Technical Support telephone number at (800) 762-2974. Outside the United States, call 1 (317) 572-3994. You can also contact Wiley Product Technical Support at http://support.wiley.com. John Wiley & Sons will provide technical support only for installation and other general quality control items. For technical support on the applications themselves, consult the program's vendor or author.

To place orders or to request information about other Wiley products, you can call (800) 762-2974.

Index

Index

Index

Index

Index

Index

Index

S

Index

Index

Index

Index

Wiley Publishing, Inc.
End-User License Agreement

READ THIS. You should carefully read these terms and conditions before opening the software packet(s) included with this book "Book". This is a license agreement "Agreement" between you and Wiley Publishing, Inc. "WPI". By opening the accompanying software packet(s), you acknowledge that you have read and accept the following terms and conditions. If you do not agree and do not want to be bound by such terms and conditions, promptly return the Book and the unopened software packet(s) to the place you obtained them for a full refund.

1. **License Grant.** WPI grants to you (either an individual or entity) a nonexclusive license to use one copy of the enclosed software program(s) (collectively, the "Software") solely for your own personal or business purposes on a single computer (whether a standard computer or a workstation component of a multi-user network). The Software is in use on a computer when it is loaded into temporary memory (RAM) or installed into permanent memory (hard disk, CD-ROM, or other storage device). WPI reserves all rights not expressly granted herein.

2. **Ownership.** WPI is the owner of all right, title, and interest, including copyright, in and to the compilation of the Software recorded on the physical packet included with this Book "Software Media". Copyright to the individual programs recorded on the Software Media is owned by the author or other authorized copyright owner of each program. Ownership of the Software and all proprietary rights relating thereto remain with WPI and its licensers.

3. **Restrictions on Use and Transfer.**

   (a) You may only (i) make one copy of the Software for backup or archival purposes, or (ii) transfer the Software to a single hard disk, provided that you keep the original for backup or archival purposes. You may not (i) rent or lease the Software, (ii) copy or reproduce the Software through a LAN or other network system or through any computer subscriber system or bulletin-board system, or (iii) modify, adapt, or create derivative works based on the Software.

   (b) You may not reverse engineer, decompile, or disassemble the Software. You may transfer the Software and user documentation on a permanent basis, provided that the transferee agrees to accept the terms and conditions of this Agreement and you retain no copies. If the Software is an update or has been updated, any transfer must include the most recent update and all prior versions.

4. **Restrictions on Use of Individual Programs.** You must follow the individual requirements and restrictions detailed for each individual program in the "What's on the DVD" appendix of this Book or on the Software Media. These limitations are also contained in the individual license agreements recorded on the Software Media. These limitations may include a requirement that after using the program for a specified period of time, the user must pay a registration fee or discontinue use. By opening the Software packet(s), you agree to abide by the licenses and restrictions for these individual programs that are detailed in the "What's on the DVD" appendix and/or on the Software Media. None of the material on this Software Media or listed in this Book may ever be redistributed, in original or modified form, for commercial purposes.

5. **Limited Warranty.**

   (a) WPI warrants that the Software and Software Media are free from defects in materials and workmanship under normal use for a period of sixty (60) days from the date of purchase of this Book. If WPI receives notification within the warranty period of defects in materials or workmanship, WPI will replace the defective Software Media.

   (b) WPI AND THE AUTHOR(S) OF THE BOOK DISCLAIM ALL OTHER WARRANTIES, EXPRESS OR IMPLIED, INCLUDING WITHOUT LIMITATION IMPLIED WARRANTIES OF MERCHANTABILITY AND FITNESS FOR A PARTICULAR PURPOSE, WITH RESPECT TO THE SOFTWARE, THE PROGRAMS, THE SOURCE CODE CONTAINED THEREIN, AND/OR THE TECHNIQUES DESCRIBED IN THIS BOOK. WPI DOES NOT WARRANT THAT THE FUNCTIONS CONTAINED IN THE SOFTWARE WILL MEET YOUR REQUIREMENTS OR THAT THE OPERATION OF THE SOFTWARE WILL BE ERROR FREE.

   (c) This limited warranty gives you specific legal rights, and you may have other rights that vary from jurisdiction to jurisdiction.

6. **Remedies.**

   (a) WPI's entire liability and your exclusive remedy for defects in materials and workmanship shall be limited to replacement of the Software Media, which may be returned to WPI with a copy of your receipt at the following address: Software Media Fulfillment Department, Attn.: *SolidWorks 2011 Assemblies Bible,* Wiley Publishing, Inc., 10475 Crosspoint Blvd., Indianapolis, IN 46256, or call 1-800-762-2974. Please allow four to six weeks for delivery. This Limited Warranty is void if failure of the Software Media has resulted from accident, abuse, or misapplication. Any replacement Software Media will be warranted for the remainder of the original warranty period or thirty (30) days, whichever is longer.

   (b) In no event shall WPI or the author be liable for any damages whatsoever (including without limitation damages for loss of business profits, business interruption, loss of business information, or any other pecuniary loss) arising from the use of or inability to use the Book or the Software, even if WPI has been advised of the possibility of such damages.

   (c) Because some jurisdictions do not allow the exclusion or limitation of liability for consequential or incidental damages, the above limitation or exclusion may not apply to you.

7. **U.S. Government Restricted Rights.** Use, duplication, or disclosure of the Software for or on behalf of the United States of America, its agencies and/or instrumentalities "U.S. Government" is subject to restrictions as stated in paragraph (c)(1)(ii) of the Rights in Technical Data and Computer Software clause of DFARS 252.227-7013, or subparagraphs (c) (1) and (2) of the Commercial Computer Software - Restricted Rights clause at FAR 52.227-19, and in similar clauses in the NASA FAR supplement, as applicable.

8. **General.** This Agreement constitutes the entire understanding of the parties and revokes and supersedes all prior agreements, oral or written, between them and may not be modified or amended except in a writing signed by both parties hereto that specifically refers to this Agreement. This Agreement shall take precedence over any other documents that may be in conflict herewith. If any one or more provisions contained in this Agreement are held by any court or tribunal to be invalid, illegal, or otherwise unenforceable, each and every other provision shall remain in full force and effect.